Preston King has taught politics and govern-
ment at the universities of Sheffield and
Nairobi, and is now Professor of Political
Science at University of New South Wales.

THE STUDY OF POLITICS

THE STUDY OF POLITICS

A Collection of Inaugural Lectures

Edited by
PRESTON KING

FRANK CASS

037620

First published 1977 in Great Britain by
FRANK CASS AND COMPANY LIMITED
Gainsborough House, Gainsborough Road,
London E11 1RS, England

and in the United States of America by
FRANK CASS AND COMPANY LIMITED
c/o Biblio Distribution Center,
81 Adams Drive, Totowa, New Jersey 07512

ISBN 0 7146 3084 5

Printed in Great Britain by
Billing & Sons Ltd, Guildford, London and Worcester

CONTENTS

ACKNOWLEDGMENTS

The following permissions are gratefully acknowledged:

Mrs Laski and London School of Economics for H. J. Laski's *On the Study of Politics*, an Inaugural Lecture delivered before the London School of Economics in 1926 and published by Humphrey Milford, London, 1926.

Cambridge University Press for Sir Ernest Barker's *The Study of Political Science*, delivered before the University of Cambridge in 1928, published in Barker, *The Study of Political Science in its Relation to Cognate Studies*, and republished under the present abbreviated title by Methuen in Barker, *Church, State and Study. Essays.* Also for Sir Denis Brogan's *The Study of Politics*, delivered before the University of Cambridge on 28 November 1945, and published in 1946.

The Clarendon Press for G. D. H. Cole's *Scope and Method in Social and Political Theory*, delivered before the University of Oxford on 9 November 1945; K. C. Wheare's *The Machinery of Government*, delivered before the University of Oxford on 16 November 1945; and Max Beloff's *The Tasks of Government*, delivered before the University of Oxford on 20 February 1958.

Associated Book Publishers Ltd. for Michael Oakeshott's *Political Education*, delivered before the London School of Economics on 6 March 1951, first published by Bowes & Bowes (1951) and republished by Methuen in Oakeshott, *Rationalism in Politics* (1962).

Oxford University Press for Sir Isaiah Berlin's *Two Concepts of Liberty*, delivered before the University of Oxford on 31 October 1958 and published in Berlin, *Four Essays on liberty* (1958).

The authors for reproduction of the inaugural lectures by J. C. Rees (*Interpreting the Constitution*, delivered at the University College of Swansea on 1 December 1955, and published by the University); Howard Warrender (*The Study of Politics*, delivered before the Queen's University of Belfast on 8 March 1961, and published by the University); W. H. Greenleaf (*The World of Politics*, delivered at the University College of Swansea on 5 March 1968, and published by the University); M. M. Goldsmith (*Allegiance*, delivered in the University of Exeter on 12 November 1970, and published by the University); A. H. Birch (*The Nature and Functions of Representation*, delivered in the University of Exeter on 7 May 1971, and published by the University); Maurice Cranston (*Politics and Ethics*, delivered at the London School of Economics on 26 October 1971, and published by Weidenfeld & Nicolson in Cranston, *The Mask of Politics and Other Essays*).

University College, London for J. H. Burns's *The Fabric of Felicity: the Legislator and the Human Condition*, delivered at University College on 2 March 1967.

Allen Lane, and Basic Books, Inc., for Bernard Crick's *Freedom as Politics*, delivered at the University of Sheffield in 1966. The lecture was originally published by Sheffield University, but follows here the slightly different version as it appeared in Crick, *Political Theory and Practice* (Allen Lane. 1972, and Basic Books, Inc., New York, 1973).

INTRODUCTION

The study of politics is as old as the most ancient of universities. We need only refer to the work of Plato and Aristotle to make the point clear. But in earlier times, no distinction was made between the study of politics and the study of philosophy, or between the study of political theory and the study of ethics. There was no distinction made either between the study of politics and the study of history, law, sociology and economics. At the least, society was regarded as a single unit of study.

If we take classical writers like Bodin, Hobbes, Locke, Montesquieu, Kant, Hegel, Bentham and Mill, what we detect is an interpenetration of 'disciplines': all of these figures are as much concerned with law as with politics, as also with philosophy, and at least three-quarters of them are equally concerned with 'economics'. They were disposed to treat society, and social problems, as a single unit of study, and this is a tradition which it is very difficult today for us to continue.

In the twentieth century, history and philosophy, the omnibus sciences, have rather definitively blown up, and their different parts describe an outward movement from a formerly common core: law, economics, politics, sociology, psychology, business studies and so on. Chairs in history, philosophy and law are of course historically commonplace. But chairs in other subjects are basically new to this century. The university study of politics is not at all new, but the separation of political studies from legal, economic, historical, sociological and psychological studies most certainly is.

The inaugural lectures republished here are, not unnaturally, restricted to the United Kingdom. This restriction imparts to them a certain coherence, and also makes it easier to reproduce more of them—although not all. All of the chairs in politics in England were established in this century. They were established initially in three universities (the first of these being Oxford), upon which other universities have subsequently drawn.

The first chair in politics in an English university was the Gladstone Professorship of Political Theory and Institutions established at Oxford in 1912. It was endowed by the General Committee of the National Memorial to Mr. Gladstone out of a surplus left from the fulfilment of the Committee's original purposes. The first incumbent was W. G. S. Adams (1874-1966), who held the chair until 1933. He was the founder and editor of *Political Quarterly* and was intimately involved in governmental affairs. It would be difficult to maintain that he made a lasting contribution to the subject and his name is almost entirely unfamiliar to contemporary students of politics. The successor to Professor Adams was Sir Arthur Salter (1881-1975), who was even more involved in public affairs than was Adams. He held his first position of public trust in the Transport Department of the Admiralty in 1904 and his last was that of Minister of Materials during 1952-53. He was certainly an extremely active man, publishing his memoirs in 1961 and a further book in 1967. But, as he himself states in his memoirs, he was far less of an academic than an administrator. Officially, he held his Oxford professorship until 1944. But in fact he rejoined the world of governmental affairs in 1940 and Sir Robert Ensor served Oxford in his stead for the remainder of Sir Arthur's tenure.

The duties attached to the Gladstone Professorship of Political Theory and Institutions were officially divided between two chairs in 1940, although no new appointments were made until 1944. One of the new chairs was labelled the Gladstone Professorship of Social Administration, the other being called the Chichele Professorship of Social and Political Theory. Professor K. C. Wheare (b. Australia, 1907) was appointed to the chair in administration and Professor G. D. H. Cole (1889-1959) was appointed to the chair in Theory. Professor Wheare was very active in Oxford life, having been Pro-Vice-Chancellor during 1958-64. His professorial tenure lasted from 1944 through 1957 and his inaugural lecture is the first in the Oxford series reproduced in this volume. Professor Cole was an extremely prolific writer. He lived much longer than Laski and his output was even greater (although pure output is of course no measure of quality). Cole was a University Reader in Economics at Oxford during 1925-44 and then a fellow of All Souls during 1944-57. He produced a considerable amount of fiction as well as numerous volumes on economics, politics, and the history of ideas. Like Wheare, Cole's professorial tenure lasted from 1944 through 1957. His inaugural, too, is reproduced in this collection.

In 1957 two new professorial appointments in politics were made at Oxford. Professor Max Beloff (b. 1913), who had previously lectured at Manchester and Oxford during 1939-56, was made the new Gladstone Professor of Government and Public Administration, while Professor (now Sir) Isaiah Berlin (b. 1909) was appointed Chichele Professor of Social and Political Theory. Berlin was a fellow of New College during 1938-50 and of All Souls during 1950-66. He served the British embassies in Washington and Moscow during and after World War II. His professorial tenure lasted from 1957 through 1967. He relinquished the post following his assumption of the Presidency of Wolfson College, Oxford in 1966. Berlin retired in 1976. The inaugural lectures of Beloff and Berlin are reproduced below. Beloff was succeeded as Gladstone Professor at Oxford by S. E. Finer (b. 1915), while Berlin was succeeded as Chichele Professor by John Plamenatz (1912-75). Plamenatz was generally regarded as far less exotic and interesting than Berlin, having spent virtually the whole of his academic life within the confines of Oxford as a fellow of All Souls during 1936-51 and subsequently as a University lecturer from 1950 to 1967. Charles Taylor (b. 1931) was appointed Chichele Professor in Oxford in 1976.

Every professor of politics at Oxford, past and present, has been an Oxford man. Virtually every other English university has subsequently inherited either Oxford men or Oxford influences in the teaching of politics. Cambridge, with the aid of a Rockefeller grant, first established a chair of Political Science in 1928. Up to now, three appointments have been made to that chair and each appointment was of an Oxford man.

Ernest Barker (1874-1960) was the first to be appointed to the new Professorship of Political Science at Cambridge and he held the chair during 1928-39. There can be no question but that this was a splendid appointment. Barker was vitally interested in the history and analysis of political ideas and we shall remain indebted to him for a considerable time to come for his work on the early, classical period of political theory. Barker was succeeded in 1939 by Professor (later Sir) Denis Brogan (1900-74), whose tenure lasted until 1967. Brogan was educated at Glasgow and Harvard, as well as at Oxford. He lectured at University College, London and at L.S.E., before becoming a Fellow and Tutor at Corpus Christi College, Oxford. Unlike Barker, he was much more concerned with institutions than with theory, and particularly with comparative political institutions in America, France and England. We reprint the Barker and Brogan inaugurals below. Brogan's successor (and the present incumbent) at Cambridge is Professor W. B. Gallie (b. 1912). Whereas Barker's interests were centred in the history of political ideas and Brogan's in the development of political institutions, Gallie's interests are far more exclusively philosophical. He was educated at Balliol College, Oxford, served the University College of Swansea during 1935-50, was transferred and promoted to Professor of Philosophy at Keele (1950-1954) and moved yet again—this time to Belfast—as Professor of Philosophy and remained there from 1954-1967.

When I said earlier that there were three universities in England where chairs were initially established in politics, I had in mind of course Oxford, Cambridge and London. But this was not the chronological sequence of establishment—which ran, rather, Oxford (1912), London (1914), and Cambridge (1928). The key Professorship in Political Science in the University of London is of course centred on the London School of Economics and Political Science. Graham Wallas (1858-1932) was the first Professor of Political Science in London and held this post for nine years (1914-23). Professor Harold Laski (1893-1950) succeeded him in this chair at the London School of Economics and Political Science in 1926 and held it until his death in 1950. Both Wallas and Laski were educated at Oxford. Laski is the better known: for being more prolific, for holding the chair over twice as long as his predecessor, and of course for being extremely active politically—especially and directly in the affairs of the Labour Party. Laski was succeeded at L.S.E. in 1951 by Professor Michael Oakeshott (b. 1901) whose tenure expired in 1969. Oakeshott, unlike his predecessors, was from Cambridge, but—like them—he was not from London. The contrast between Oakeshott and Laski could not be more dramatic—the calm and almost introverted style of the former as over against the extrovert and dynamic prolixity of the latter. The present holder of the chair of Political Science at L.S.E. is Professor Maurice Cranston (b. 1920). Cranston is possibly symbolic of the moving away of London and other English universities from the completeness of their early dependence upon Oxford—in the sense that he was initially an undergraduate in London and only later did further work at Oxford. The inaugural lectures by Cranston, Oakeshott and Laski are reprinted below.

I have provided a reasonably detailed account of the establishment and tenure of the key chairs in Politics at Oxford, Cambridge and London. We shall not deal with other universities in Britain according to the same formula. Departments and chairs in politics have so proliferated that this would take up more space than is available. There are approximately 42 universities in Great Britain and almost all of them have at least one chair in politics, many of them (like Sheffield, Essex and Exeter) have two and a few (like London) have even more. All of these chairs have been established in this century and most of them only since the war. A lot of thought, therefore, has gone into the problem of determining the boundaries of the professional study of politics, whether ambitiously labelled 'political science' or more modestly denominated 'political studies'. These inaugural lectures provide the reader with an opportunity to review directly what the major practitioners (at that crucial inaugural point in their careers) focus upon as significant and important (for them) in the study of politics.

What we shall find, in the earlier lectures, is a pronounced tendency to state what the nature of politics is. Laski, Barker, Brogan and Cole, for example, are much concerned to deliver themselves of pronouncements about the character of politics in general. This concern will of course surface in every period, but it is most visible in the period ending with the conclusion of the last great war. The problem became a problem, no doubt, because the study of politics in the universities was then regarded as a new development and it was thought to be necessary, accordingly, to fence it in so as to exclude confusion with neighbouring disciplines. Intellectually, however, this fencing off process, essentially a classificatory exercise, has little intrinsic importance and one witnesses the gradual eclipse of interest in it.

All of our lectures recognize the extreme degree of interdependence between political and other studies. But as the subject comes increasingly to be taken for granted, we note less of a concern with marking out boundaries around it and more of a concern with treating specific problems which interest the lecturer. This departure, I believe, is most notable in the 1951 lecture on *Political Education* delivered by Michael Oakeshott. In this case we are confronted with a very abrupt shift of interest from defining politics, to puzzling over particular problems internal to politics—such as the role of Tradition in directing the affairs of society. Oakeshott is of course more normative than he is himself disposed to admit. But the important thing is that he deals with a specific problem, however successfully or unsuccessfully, and not with the classificatory business of drawing a line between political and other studies. Rees, Berlin, Crick. Goldsmith, Birch, Cranston, even Greenleaf—despite the deceptiveness of the latter's title—follow Oakeshott in this. I imagine this is a tendency which we cannot expect to be reversed. Thus the inaugural lecture in politics—if it survives, and it may not—will probably be used in future as a significant occasion to deal with some limited, but important problem, and less as an excuse for reviewing the whole subject which the speaker has been appointed to profess.

What we shall find, too, in these lectures is a very large concern, direct or indirect, with the methodology of the social sciences. Further lectures will probably reflect no more nor less of a concern with this matter than have previous ones. This is only to be expected, and it is perfectly legitimate. This broad interest in methodology easily ramifies into the analysis of a great variety of concrete problems of more restricted interest to students of politics alone. Virtually all of the lectures which touch upon the problem of methodology reveal a certain scepticism about the prospect of ascertaining the true and the good in politics. Laski believes that the study of politics must be concerned with both ends and means, but also that it can only be imprecise and non-axiomatic. Barker begins by expressing his unease vis-à-vis that part of his chair which refers to political *science*. Brogan speaks of Burke as the greatest English-speaking political thinker and heartily objects, in Burke's language, to 'abstracts and universals'. Cole, while believing in the certainty of his moral intuitions, does not seem disposed to put them any higher than intuitions, and so holds that such things are at the heart of political theory, but are not really arguable. This uncertainty, which also overwhelms Oakeshott, inspires the latter to proceed *à tâtons*. Greenleaf, too, is modest in terms of what he expects from politics—but he is firm in insisting that its study is nothing apart from a study of the thought implicit in political activity. And so on.

For the student interested in the study of politics in terms of how the discipline views itself and of how these views have changed and evolved, there could be no better introduction than such a volume of introductory essays as those assembled here.

Preston T. King

1977

1

Professor H. J. Laski

ON THE STUDY OF POLITICS

The chair to which I have had the honour to be called is but the second of its kind in this country; for it is only within recent years that the right of political science to be studied as an independent intellectual discipline has been conceded. Oxford, seventeen years ago, was the first university to establish a chair in the subject.[1] London has now followed her example; and signs are not wanting that Cambridge, and some of the modern universities, will shortly follow in the path. I add that it is not unfitting that Oxford should have led the way. Her School of Modern History, to which my own debt is immense, has always been, in some sort, a philosophy teaching by example. In Green and Bosanquet she gave to English political science the makers of a tradition which, even if we dissent from it, must yet be recognized as of primary importance. For not only has that tradition influenced the character of modern legislation; its own inheritance has constantly refreshed our thought with memory of, and inspiration from, our founders in ancient Greece. We need to be reminded of what we may still learn from Aristotle and Plato.

Let us honour Oxford for that primacy. Yet let us also remember that the University of London is the special child of another great tradition in English political science. Our founders were the Philosophic Radicals; and we can claim, with abundant pride, that they changed, and changed for the better, the whole nature of the English state. I like to think that the spirit of this university is set out in that sentence which expressed from Bentham's early youth his faith and practice. 'Has a man talents?' he asked, 'he owes them to his country in every way in which they can be serviceable.' I would remark here that my own task as the occupant of this chair has been especially difficult because my predecessor has, in his own life and teaching, so finely achieved what Bentham meant by those words. Graham Wallas has followed the prescription of Spinoza in 'sedulously disciplining his mind not to ridicule, nor to lament, nor to

1

detest the actions of men, but to understand them'; that has enabled him to make teaching an exercise in the art of friendship. Whatever our differences from Graham Wallas, either as to method or results, we are all of us in part his pupils. And I, at least, am glad to proclaim my veneration for the spirit by which his work has been informed.

Political science concerns itself with the life of men in relation to organized states. We cannot omit from the field of relevant interest whatever may affect that life. We have kinship with the studies of the economist, since the pursuit of wealth is a form of behaviour that deeply affects our problems. We are connected with the lawyer; for law, on its formal side, is the body of rules behind which is the authority of government. We are concerned with the official, because the institutions he administers are those through which the purpose of the state primarily seeks its realization. Nor is this all. The results of ethics, of psychology, and of sociology, must obviously affect the conclusions at which we arrive; for whatever may influence, or be practically useful in influencing, the habits of civilized man, is clearly germane to our problems. We need not deny the vastness of our enterprise. It is not a field in which the labour of one man or one generation of men is likely to reap a harvest. We have, indeed, to define our aims, realizing that there is a vital sense in which these aims are liable to change both in time and place; liberty in seventeenth-century England, for example, does not mean what it implies to an American in the twentieth century. We have not only to define aims. We have to discover both the institutions through which those aims are likely to be realized, and the methods by which they are to work. Do we need, for instance, a parliamentary system? Does the latter require, if it is to realize its best results, a highly trained and non-elected civil service behind it to supply the *expertise* in which the general competence of an elected person is almost certain to be deficient? We have, to generalize, two sets of problems before us, those, in the convenient German terminology, of *Staatslehre* and those of *Politik*. We cannot separate them with any precision, for the simple reason that any *Staatslehre,* however independent it may seem, is, in fact, a generalization from the environment and experience of those who make it. Political science has not the axiomatic quality of mathematics. In its equations the variables are human beings whose uniqueness prevents their reduction to law in the scientific sense of that much-abused word. We deal with tendencies; we can predict upon the basis of experience. But our predictions are limited by the necessity of recognizing that the facts are not within our control. We can influence and attempt and hope; the certainty and precision of the chemist, or even the physiologist, can never be ours.

So much in preface to the basic thesis I am anxious here to lay down. If this is the context and scope of politics, how is it to be fruitfully studied in order that conclusions of value may be reached? I stand here to plead for the study of politics in the terms of history. To know how our traditions and institutions have been moulded, to grasp the evolution of the forces by which their destiny has been shaped—that, I am anxious to persuade you, is above all the key to their understanding.

I am aware that there are alternative methods, and I hope that I have a proper respect for them. There are those to whom political science is simply a branch of applied psychology. 'Let us know', they argue, 'the facts of human nature, and the necessary pattern of institutions can be deduced therefrom.' But all history is the record of those facts, and if we remain ignorant of it, we do not know our essential materials. A list of impulses and emotions does not explain them. It is only when we have them in their formidable complexity, when we see them at work, and attempt to value their results, that they begin to have political meaning. An *a priori* politics of any kind is bound to break down simply because we never start with a clean slate. A psychological theory of politics which seeks for an original human nature as the test of institutions fails us for a simple reason. Upon the foundations of inherited impulse, there is that vast superstructure the social heritage, which largely determines its working. Therein is the whole of its colour and connotation; and it is merely mysterious until we know the nature of its development. What it is and why it is, it is by reason of its history. Its becoming is the clue to its being, and it is from that becoming that we must wrest its secret.

My plea, therefore, is that, to have value, the study of politics must be an effort to codify the results of experience in the history of states. Our conclusions must remain uncertain save as they are built upon historical analysis. The reason is a simple one. We are the consequences of traditions and institutions we did not make and can only partially alter. The foundations and possibilities of our conduct are determined for us by our past. We are, so to say, terms in an infinite series, each one of which is a partial clue to the point we seek to understand. The thinkers of Greece and Rome, for instance, represented a way of life the incidence of which upon ourselves is the more profound the more we study its results. The medieval world, again, will seem less remote from us as we begin to catch the purport of its meaning; certainly our own day has special cause to insist upon a Europe which was in some sort a single commonwealth united by one of strongest ties that bind men together. The Reformation represents the consequence of the failure of the *Respublica Christiana;* and the energy it released was so gigantic that its

principles have ever since influenced every other department of
human life. The French Revolution, for example, is, in an important
sense, one chapter in its history; and the tradition emphasized in 1789
became, as it met new material conditions, the communism of Marx
and Lenin. The present is the child of the past, and we are the parents
of the future. It is not inevitable or predictable. But it is determined in
the sense that the limitations of effort, and the avenues of profitable
action, are set by our willingness to understand our own day in terms
of events by which it has been most largely made.

Obviously, I am simplifying to excess. I shall be satisfied if I can
convince you that nothing in our field of investigation is capable of
being rightly understood save as it is illustrated by the process of its
development. To know what is permanent in our own ideals and
desires we must know what they have meant in the experience of men.
Man, if I may invert the famous aphorism of Rousseau, is born
everywhere in chains, and he becomes free only upon the grim
condition of self-knowledge. A true politics, in other words, is above
all a philosophy of history. And I would ask you to observe that all
great thinkers who have seriously influenced the actions of men, have
done so because their work was precisely an effort to this end. Hobbes
sought from history the specific against disorder; Locke the facts
which justify the right of rebellion; Rousseau inquired how humble
men might be free who felt grievously the burden of social bondage.
Bentham seems to have rejected history; yet his philosophy is, above
all things, a system made by repudiating with energy the abuses of his
time. Marx challenged the institutions of capitalist society in terms of
an ideal wrought from a brilliant, if partial, scrutiny of its processes.
It is, in fact, the habit of political philosophers to transform their
reading of history into universal dogma. Much of it, naturally, is
narrow and incomplete, and unworthy to survive the special
circumstances from which it takes its origin. Yet something, if the
reading be sufficiently profound, survives to become part of a
common stock of ideas which men use, if only half-consciously, as
their chart in sailing over a but partially known sea to a harbour
which ever recedes as they advance.

My own main interest is in the history of political ideas, the attempt
to gather, in what detail one may, what men have thought about the
state. If I have one ambition above others it is to make this School a
great centre for the study of this aspect of political science. For the
study of ideas in their historical context is a source of political
illumination as valuable as any that lies to our hand. Not only does it
serve to correct, more truly than any other discipline, the tendency to
over-estimate the originality and significance of our own ideas. It
prevents, as no other study can, that vicious habit of making the

immediate need the eternal good, which is the source of some of the worst evils in contemporary politics; for we seek, wherever possible, to confound the principles we adopt with the necessary foundations of society. And by the study of ideas it becomes, I think possible to separate from the facts of history the abstract truth that interpenetrates them. It is, rightly used, the supreme source of general ideas of a character capable of compelling right action. For to understand why men have held particular political opinions is to compel the scrutiny of one's own faith with an inescapable knowledge that its value is limited. That knowledge, I believe, confers a habit of tolerance. We learn to distinguish between principle and party; we come to see that the more we immerse ourselves in the habits of party, the less our principles are true to the ends they seek to serve.

In all this, of course, there is implied a method of studying the history of political ideas about which I shall have something to say in a moment. But I should like to insist upon the moral value of this discipline by reference to that habit of tolerance upon which I have just laid emphasis. From the history of political ideas one learns nothing so definitely as the great fact that, as Leslie Stephen once put it, 'the spread of an error is part of a world-wide process by which we stumble into mere approximations into truth'. More than this. One learns also that any error of wide circulation may possibly contain some great element of truth, and will certainly contain an important index to the aspirations of men. Now in the construction of any adequate political philosophy, it is elementary that the aspirations of men are important. To satisfy demand on the largest scale is the statesman's business; and he will only know what demand he has to satisfy according as he discovers what those aspirations are. The lesson we at least are taught is to be charitable to ideas we do not share, to understand and not to suppress them. For we learn, first of all, that in the history of ideas suppression has been rarely successful, and, secondly, that the price we pay for that suppression is always moral and intellectual loss. Anyone who studies the history of toleration in religion can verify these conclusions for himself. I emphasize them here because it seems not unlikely that the modern state is seeking the terms of an orthodoxy not less rigid than that sought by the Churches at the period when they controlled by force the minds of men. And unless we are as vigilant here about the importance of receptivity even of opinions we believe to be grievously wrong, we shall be guilty of the same mistakes, even of the same crimes, as those who persecuted in the name of truths which the better judgement of mankind has declared to be without foundation.

There is implied here, I have said, a method for studying the history of ideas. It is the simple one of studying the opinion and those who expressed it in the light of their social environment. Nothing is more useless, because nothing is less revealing, than to separate the political philosophy of any thinker from the circumstances in which it was born. Rousseau is only intelligible, to take a supreme example, in the context of eighteenth-century France. The unity of his ideas is to be found in a system of personal experience set by the habits and institutions of the *ancien régime*. Every great thinker is in part the autobiography of his age. His influence springs from the fact that he expressed, in a peculiarly magistral way, some significant portion of its hopes and fears. That is the unstated major premiss we have always to discover in his philosophy if we would seek to explain it. We must avoid, that is, the fatal habit of making out a list of principles, bare and objective, as the thinker's contribution and omitting all that made his principles alive and influential. To say, to take Rousseau again, that Rousseau based the state upon contract is true and yet useless; but to say that Rousseau based the state upon contract that he might emphasize the importance of humble men in an age which treated them as unimportant is a very different matter. The little minor of circumstances, as Burke used to say, plays a great part in the actual battle.

I would draw your attention, also, to another aspect of this argument. Political philosophy is never separable from the general body of ideas in a generation. The rediscovery of ancient Greece had enormous influence on the political systems of the sixteenth century; the history of classical scholarship is a chapter in the history of political philosophy. So, too, in the seventeenth century the form of political speculation is quite largely determined by attraction to, and repulsion from, Cartesianism in its widest sense; and the method of the French *philosophes* was set, to a degree we have insufficiently examined, by the achievement of Newton in physics. And if, in another aspect of the eighteenth century, we are a little inclined to smile at the noble savage of Rousseau and his contemporaries, an examination of some such collection of voyages as those of Tavernier or Thévenot will throw much light on what might otherwise seem unprofitable apriorism.[3] The influence of Darwin on nineteenth-century political thought both for good and evil, is, of course, obvious; and I would hazard the judgement that our own day is likely to be equally affected by the amazing achievements of modern physics. We need, in a word, so to write the history of political ideas that they fall naturally into their place as the expression of one aspect of a process of thought that is not neatly divisible into two separate categories. We must seek to project our narrative on to a plane where the relation of a whole to the parts is capable of being seized in its full significance.

Let us remember, also, not to neglect the lesson of the literature of a period. It is easy for us, the contemporaries of Mr. Shaw and Mr. Wells, to see that the novel and the play are essays in politics; and a great social satirist like Mr. Siegfried Sassoon reminds us that it is not only in the age of Juvenal that we must go to the poets for information about social philosophy. Yet in the most widely-read history of political ideas I find no reference to Dickens or Disraeli, to Byron or Shelley. The great men of our subject, of course, knew better; and Leslie Stephen's *English Utilitarians* is a superb example of the way in which the whole nature of an epoch can be set out in terms of its thinkers. Nor must we neglect the historians. The thing that they do is always, even if indirectly, an index to what the age is wanting. The difference between the way in which history was written in the eighteenth century, and the way in which it is written by our own age is not merely a difference of equipment and technique; it is also a difference of social outlook. The production of books like those of Mr. and Mrs. Hammond and Mr. Tawney, the criticism to which they have been subjected, is a fact of precious import to us. But I do not need to labour this point to any who know Acton's famous essay on German historians or the extremely suggestive prelude to Vinogradoff's *Villainage in England*.

I would, however emphasize one point in the study, from our angle, of historiography. The past is never dead, because it is capable of re-creation at each moment of time. And the way in which the re-creation takes place can hardly be studied too closely by the historian of ideas. For, if I interpret it aright, historical writing in the future will be wider in character than in the past. 'It will elevate itself', to quote a German historian,[4] 'to freer movement and contact with the great forces of political life and culture, without renouncing the precious traditions of its method, and must plunge into philosophy and politics . . . thus alone can it develop its intimate essence and be both universal and national.' The new history, if I am not mistaken, is more likely to be based upon a conscious scheme of social values than the old. And this is likely to mean an increased sense of what may be termed the immortality of history. The past is being re-made to serve the needs of a new time. The historian interprets afresh the meaning he can discover in the record, that its lessons for ourselves may be made evident. The spirit, as Croce says, carries with it all of its history that coincides with itself. Wilamowitz, Zimmern, Gilbert Murray, give us a new Greece, Max Weber and Tröltsch give us a new Reformation Christianity; a history, in each case, that is pragmatic in the sense of seeking to satisfy new demands never before made, and never capable of being made, upon the documentary material. Compare the treatment of Byzantium in Gibbon with its treatment by such masters as Diehl and Baynes. One has a sense, not merely of a new body of evidence, but of a new spirit informing that evidence. And that re-creation of the past is the effort of our time to find the significance of its problems in the epochs out of which they have arisen. The past therein is made the present; and to know the historiography of a period is to know with some certainty its meaning and desires.

I do not want to leave upon you the impression that politics should be studied historically merely for the sake of the history thereby revealed. Our end is to know the causes of things, to attain a perspective whereby the philosophies we adopt may be the richer and truer in substance. I say advisedly the philosophies; the plural noun means that we do not ask in this university the acceptance of any particular creed. My object as the occupant of this chair is not to create a body of disciples who shall go forth to preach the particular and peculiar doctrines I happen to hold. It is rather that the student shall learn the method of testing his own faith against the only solid criterion we know—the experience of mankind. That does not, of course, mean that in the exposition of political philosophy it is one's business to pretend to impartiality. In any case that is impossible; for in the merest selection of material to be considered there is already implied a judgement which reflects, however unconsciously, the inevitable bias that each of us will bring. The teacher's function, as I conceive it, is less to avoid his bias than consciously to assert its presence and to warn his hearers against it; above all, to be open-minded about the difficulties it involves and honest in his attempt to meet them. For the greatest thing he can, after all, teach is the lesson of conscious sincerity. More truth is discovered along the road than can be found on any other.

May I illustrate what I mean by an example drawn from my own particular studies? To me, the central problem of politics is the problem of authority and freedom. I believe that the social conscience of the citizen is the surest guide to the conduct he should display in the face of events. That means, of course, the contingency of disobedience, the possibility that the individual should refuse submission to the powers that be where he is sincerely convinced that he can do no other. The moral obligation to resist, in other words, seems to me the root of social well-being. Now this is, frankly, at once a denial of the sovereignty of the state, and an insistence that power is only valid by winning from those subject to it their free consent to the authority it seeks to exercise. My business, as I conceive it, is not to avoid the expression of this conviction, but frankly to explain why it seems to me a more valid outlook than alternative philosophies, why, also, the difficulties it involves, grave as they are, do not seem to me at any point insuperable. As a doctrine, of course, it involves momentous consequences. Had I the time, I should like to show how it makes the state not the creator of rights so much as their creature, and judges its activities by the degree to which it protects the rights from which it derives the only justification it can have for making us obey it. It would, further, be interesting to show how, in our time, a crisis in the modern state has arisen because the rights protected by it are interpreted too narrowly by the holders of power. I should seek to show, did time permit, how that movement for the equalization of privilege, which is the inevitable outcome of Protestantism, has passed from the sphere of politics and religion to that of economic life. The movement of course, is one towards greater freedom, in the sense of giving to the average man far wider opportunities of self-realization than he has been able, so far, to secure. It is the end of *laissez faire* in economic arrangements, the introduction therein of a conscious control of the means of living by the organized community. Put briefly, it is the movement from the authoritarian to the functional state.

Clearly, all this is a matter of profound and passionate controversy. I do not think it is, or ought to be, avoided. I know no place where, as I believe, social problems can be better or more fitly studied than within the walls of a university. We can introduce there, as we cannot in the conflicts of the market-place, the doubts and hesitations, the quantitative estimates, the limited certainties that necessarily appertain to all solutions. I am tempted to argue that while statesmen, who have to convince vast multitudes, must necessarily live by purveying undistributed middles, the student in an academic atmosphere has a unique opportunity of examining creeds and hypotheses in entire indifference to the results of his examination. He can take questions like the right of private property, the limits of toleration, the sovereignty of the state, and examine them as a zoologist examines his specimens in a laboratory. And he must teach what he believes to be the results of his inquiry so long as he is careful to base those results upon the widest induction that is open to him, and with an insistence upon the large margin of probable error which attaches to all social theorems.

This view drives us back at once to my original hypothesis about method. For the largest induction which is open to the student of politics is one to be made only upon the basis of historical investigation. Take a single instance. Suppose that he believes in freedom of speech. What better way of proof lies open to him than the investigation of the painful record to the acquisition of such freedom as we have? He would show how Catholic persecuted Calvinist, how Calvinist persecuted Socinian, how Socinian persecuted Atheist, all in the name of supposed truths which did not win one genuine convert by being enforced at the point of the sword. He could describe how the heresies of one generation become the orthodoxies of the next. He could explain how, on the record of history, the minds of men are so little receptive of novelty, as to make it urgent that ideas be welcomed because they are ideas, and be left to survive or perish by competition among themselves. He could take shibboleths like the famous phrase 'liberty but not licence', and show how the persecutor always means by the latter the idea that causes him acute discomfort, and against which he cannot make the headway his own clear possession of ultimate truth suggests as desirable. The controversy is admirably summarized in the dispute between Bayle and Jurieu about the limits of toleration. Both, as Protestants, were horrified at the Revocation of the Edict of Nantes, and the fiendish cruelties which accompanied it; but while Bayle drew therefrom the inference that all religions should be tolerated, Jurieu argued that only Calvinists had a right to be free from oppression. For Calvinism was true; and if Catholics did not suffer for their faith, it would be assumed that things untrue were as pleasing to God as things that are true, which is absurd. I will not trouble you with Bayle's magnificent reply. But you can see how the historic event may be used to illuminate Bagehot's sage remark that even if 'the ideas of the very wisest were by miracle to be fixed on the race, the certain result would be to stereotype monstrous error'.[5]

I turn to a very different aspect of politics. It is one to which I am anxious to draw your attention for several reasons, not least because its investigation has been a special feature of this School. One of the great changes we are witnessing in the present century is what may be termed the emergence of the positive state. Governments to-day are compelled by the necessity of things to undertake functions qualitatively different from those assumed in any previous age. Where earlier states were typified by the policeman, the modern state is typified by the administrator. The understanding of his art is now central to the understanding of political science; and with its recognition as important there have come into view a whole range of problems unconsidered by the classical writers. You will search Bagehot in vain for a discussion of the civil service as an integral part of the British Constitution. You will not find in Dicey any illustration of that *droit administratif* which is now one of its permanent features. Yet upon the work of the administrator to-day depends the success or failure of the institutions under which we live.

There are few fields of politics in which so much research and so much inventiveness are necessary. Administrators, as a rule, have the natural secrecy about their art which comes from men who live by the exercise of a mystery; and in England especially, the sacred doctrine of ministerial responsibility operates to enforce upon them a somewhat unnatural silence. I believe myself that the investigation of their function, and its reduction to the body of general principles, is one of the most necessary tasks before us. It is extraordinarily difficult and delicate, partly because so little of the ground has been broken, and partly because administrators are themselves busy men who have rarely the time to translate their experience into rules. Yet we must, if our institutions are to work satisfactorily, learn the principles which underline such matters as delegated legislation, the relation of consultative bodies to departmental experts, the relations between executive discretion and judicial control, the right to form associations, and, inferentially, to strike, in public departments, the appointment of officials. Luckily there has come into being an important body, the Institute of Public Administration, which is seeking to organize scientifically the experience of public servants; and there is no omen I more gladly welcome than its desire to have close relations with the University of London. So much of political philosophy depends upon the power to indicate the necessary institutions for its purposes that it is urgent to have with us the men who operate those institutions. For it is a commonplace that those who execute measures are they who in fact control them. If the real rulers of a country are, as a great American lawyer said, undiscoverable, I believe myself that to know its civil service is to come fairly near to the heart of the mystery.

I doubt whether any of the social sciences offer such prospects to the students as the field it is our task to cultivate. So little has already been accomplished, so much remains to be done! Yet it would be wrong on my part not to emphasize the difficulties of the task. The collection of materials is arduous; the provision of texts is by no means satisfactory; and there are whole epochs in which little is known save the fact of our ignorance about their essential features. Let me venture here upon some illustrations. Any one who desires to study what may be called the natural history of the House of Commons, to assess, in the light of its working, the things that have made it a successful representative body, will be surprised to discover how little has been done to cut a path through the jungle. Gleams of light, indeed, there are, as in Professor Notestein's quite admirable study of the way in which the initiative in law-making passed from the Crown to the lower chamber.[6] But if we inquire into matters like the frequency of re-election, the relationship between economic change and parliamentary representation, the period of time which elapsed between election to the House and membership of the Cabinet, we find that there is practically no knowledge available. Yet it is obvious enough that in the place of large-sounding generalizations that have never been tested we badly require quantitative answers to those problems, the proper solution of which can alone make possible the understanding of representative government.

Or, again, take the question of texts in the history of political philosophy. If one thing can be postulated of its study it is that the great men of each epoch do not stand alone, but are, so to say, simply the peaks of a gradually ascending curve, each item of which it is important to know. Every one knows the *Utopia* of Sir Thomas More; few realize that what influenced his own generation were his polemical works, and that most of these can be read only in a public library if one is not a rich man. Gierke has made the work of Althusius a topic of common discussion. Most of us take his word for Althusius's importance without having read him, since only half-a-dozen copies of the *Politica* are in existence; and I hazard the judgement that acquaintance with the book itself would make many who now echo Gierke's eulogy feel that the book was far less influential than he suggested. There are, moreover, thinkers of quite first-rate ability, of whom the English Benedictine Roger Widdrington is an example, the rarity of whose books had meant their almost complete suppression in literature. There are other books of seminal importance, Jurieu's *Lettres Pastorales* is a good example, which ought to be as accessible to the student as Locke or Montesquieu; yet they are available only to the collector who can afford to pay a high price. I do earnestly plead, above all with the presses of our great universities, for the provision of necessary texts for scholar and student. Althusius, Widdrington, Jurieu, Ponet, are surely not less worthy of careful editing than the remoter writers of the Latin silver age. Yet the problem of obtaining attention for them has, so far, proved almost insoluble. Here, let us hope, the work that has been done by Mr. Previté-Orton on Marsiglio of Padua may be the beginning of a better time. But we want a series as helpful to the study of English and French ideas as the *Monumenta* has been to the study of German ideas.

Whole epochs also, I have said, remain unknown. That is not an emphasis by way of paradox. Despite the immense body of work that has been done on the Reformation, we know less of Tudor political ideas than of any comparable epoch in English, indeed in European, history. I need not stress the importance of the period; I would emphasize my conviction that there awaits the historian of this aspect of it revelations as important, and discoveries as exciting, as it has ever fallen to the scholar to make. We have, for instance, in this age a group of sceptics who are no whit less interesting even than the great Montaigne and his disciples. Again, it is surprising, in view of its importance, how little we really know of the eighteenth century in

France. The great men, Voltaire, Montesquieu, Rousseau, Condorcet, have been studied and discussed almost to exhaustion; but we do not yet know them in perspective simply because their roots and filiations have not been studied. I think, for example, of great Conservative writers like Linguet, whose *Théorie des Lois Civiles* is a fascinating combination of Burke and Marx. Yet his place in the great succession, despite what attention he has attracted, remains undetermined. Something in recent years has been done for Holbach; but Fréron, Moreau, Lambert, to take names merely at random still await critical treatment. And the writer, to throw out a hint, who studies French constitutionalism under the last half-century of the *ancien régime* will find that he can throw a totally unexpected light upon the character of the Revolution.

I am anxious, further, that the study, from our angle, of institutions should not be neglected. Here let me confine my observations to England and note certain obvious lacunae. The three outstanding institutions of our own day still await adequate treatment. We have no history, at least worth the name, of the Cabinet; we have none upon local government in the nineteenth century; we have no satisfactory treatment of the civil service. The critical study in the light of history would, I venture to believe, illuminate the whole field of political philosophy. To those who read the great work of Mr. and Mrs. Webb upon Local Government before the Municipal Corporations Act, this emphasis will be the merest commonplace. Yet I am not convinced that the lesson has been widely learned. For any one who studies either the history of our political life or our political thinking in the nineteenth century can hardly fail to be struck by the degree to which it remains narrowly biographical in character. I would not be taken as denying the importance of leadership in politics; but I would still dare to believe that it is in the study of the institution as idea and instrument that the most fruit is to be gathered.

One other grave need should, I think be noted. The sister social sciences have all of them the media of discussion and publication; we have been the Cinderella of the family. The economists have their great journal, the Political Economy Club, their section at the British Association. The historians have a review which is known wherever scholarship is cherished, and a number of societies which can even induce Prime Ministers to offer them their reflections. The sociologists have their journal and a club which, it is pleasant to reflect, this School has done much to foster. Only political science remains neglected. I am not unmindful of the gallant effort made before the War by my friend Professor Adams to found a journal; but it did not survive the difficulties of the post-war epoch. France,

America, Germany and now Canada, have all of them the full instruments of organized research at their disposal. Cannot we emulate their example and that, as I have shown, of kindred studies? Could we not persuade, let us say, the British Association to experiment with our subject and so centralize the interest in its discussion we so sorely need? Cannot we political scientists do what the economists have done and dine together? Post-prandial fellowship in English history has not seldom been the parent of intellectual discovery.

To some of you, perhaps, I may appear to be too ambitious for my subject. Yet I would urge two pleas in mitigation. The thirst for conquest in the realm of intelligence is not the least noble of human aims. To make a chart of this great hinterland of knowledge is, even if it be but partial, still something won for the amelioration of man's lot. And it is particularly important in our own time that the effort should be made. Our civilization is being tested by a strain as great as ever led to the destruction of past empires. Its margins are haunted by the conflict of races, the struggle of classes, the clash of colour. If we are in the end to survive, we must, above all things, bend our energies to the discovery of knowledge. There is no other road to salvation. We are not less destined than our forefathers to earn our livelihood in the sweat of our brow. We have, do not let us forget, the overwhelming task of giving to the common man that access to his inheritance of which he has hitherto been deprived. He tests our effort not by the thought and pain that have gone into its making so much as by the results it achieves. He remembers not its fragility, but its power. We have to discover both what he wants and how with justice and wisdom, we may meet those wants. Only as we possess that knowledge can we await his judgement with confidence.

I do not, believe me, minimize the difficulty of the task. I realize full well how little we shall ever know, compared to what we desire to understand. I am, I hope, only too dismally aware to how few of us it will be given to account our achievement either significant or rare. Yet I have some measure of confidence. The highest of all joys, after all, perhaps because it is the most difficult, is the effort to show the connexion between the facts one studies and the structure of the universe. I quoted Spinoza earlier in this lecture; and I am reminded here of another phrase of his, not less noble—'omnia praeclara tam difficilia quam rara sunt'. The very difficulty of our problems only makes the pursuit more ardent and the results more precious.

The pursuit, moreover, is conducted here in an atmosphere peculiarly suitable to the task. This School is old enough to have a tradition and young enough to have avoided dogmas. It works in an atmosphere that is eager only that inquiry should be made, and regardless of, even if it be interested in, the conclusions of the inquiry. As a laboratory of investigation it is very happily placed. The libraries are at our elbow; the great departments of State, the House of Commons, the government of London, can be observed and analysed at first hand. may I add that I particularly, am fortunate in a body of colleagues who make the work of teaching and research less a labour than a privilege? In the years that lie ahead we shall seek additions to knowledge as worthy as we can make them of the trust that has been confided to us. We shall do that, not with the thought or hope of impressing upon students any special doctrines or convictions, but, as we desire, with the power to live their lives more fully by reason of the ferment created in them. It is our ambition to inspire in them a silent devotion to the great subject we serve. We are still young enough to believe that the service of thought is the noblest calling to which a man can devote himself. We ask to be judged by the measure of our effort to make others think likewise.

1. Laski was correct in nominating Oxford as the first such university but computes mistakenly in saying (in 1926) that the chair was established 'seventeen years ago'. The Oxford Professorship was established in 1912, not 1909. although W. G. S. Adams was then lecturing in the subject there. (Ed.)
2. *Works* (ed. Bowering), x. 73.
3. Cf. the very interesting essay of Geoffroy Atkinson, *Les Relations des Voyages du XVIIe Siècle et l'Évolution des Idées* (Paris, 1925).
4. Meinecke, *Weltbürgertum und Nationalstaat* (Berlin, 1911), p. vii.
5. *Collected Works,* vol. vi, p. 225.
6. *The Winning of the Initiative by the House of Commons in the Seventeenth Century,* Oxford University Press, 1925.

2

Professor E. Barker

THE STUDY OF POLITICAL SCIENCE

I

A preliminary modesty becomes a new professor; and a deprecatory
preface to his inaugural discourse is not only a decency, but also a
debt, when the new professor is sitting uneasily in a new chair to
expound a subject which, he well knows, many of his hearers will
regard as certainly nebulous, probably dubious, and possibly
disputatious. Happy is the Cambridge man, with history bred in his
very bones, who returns to Cambridge, after years of devotion and
service, to declare the ascertained mysteries of the muse Clio;[1] but
unhappy, thrice unhappy, is the Oxford man, who comes to
Cambridge for the first time, dripping from seven years of immersion
in the bewildering complications of the University of London, to
profess an uncertain subject about which he has already forgotten
more than he ever knew. To come to Cambridge—the home of exact
knowledge, where men walk on the razor's edge of acute analysis—
and to come, with such an equipment, for the exposition of such a
subject, is a bold and desperate thing. I can only promise, as I do with
a genuine sincerity, to attempt to ascertain the nature of my subject:
to seek to discover the facts, if such there be, which form its basis; and
to try to analyse, as best I can, their significance and implications.
And I may perhaps be allowed to take some measure of comfort from
the reflection that such experience of affairs as I have had in London
during the last seven years may give to my lectures that tang of reality
which my subject especially needs. No philosophy of human life can
live by books alone; and political philosophy, no less than other
forms, must study the busy hum of affairs in the cave before it can
move into the upper light of contemplation.

17

You will not expect me, after what I have said in my preface, to begin the body of my discourse by any precise definition of my subject. It is a subject which has come to be known in this place by the name of Political Science. I am not altogether happy about the term 'Science.' It has been vindicated so largely, and almost exclusively, for the exact and experimental study of natural phenomena, that its application to politics may convey suggestions, and excite anticipations, which cannot be justified. If I am to use the designation of Political Science, I shall use it, as Aristotle used πολιτικὴ ἐπιστήμη, to signify a method, or form of inquiry, concerned with the moral phenomena of human behaviour in political studies. I should prefer to call such a method or form of inquiry by the name of Political Theory, because I should hope, by the use of that name, to avoid the appearance of any excessive claim to exactitude, and I should be indicating more precisely the nature of the inquiry, as simply a 'speculation' (θεωρία) about a group of facts in the field of political action, a speculation intended to result in a general scheme which connects the facts systematically with one another and thus gives an explanation of their significance. If that name be adopted, a respectable and honourable antiquity may readily be vindicated for the subject I have to profess. It was studied by Aristotle: it was expounded by St Thomas Aquinas: it was discussed by the venerable Paley, a light of this University, in his *Principles of Moral and Political Philosophy;* and it has been treated continuously, during the last seventy years, by a succession of distinguished men in both of the older Universities.

In the cultivation of political theory as a subject of University study Oxford has perhaps been more systematic, if less many-sided, than Cambridge. The Oxford school of Literae Humaniores, the glory of my old University, has produced what itself may almost be called a school of thinkers (for Oxford naturally runs to 'schools' and 'movements' of thought) in T. H. Green and F. H. Bradley and Bernard Bosanquet. Nurtured on a double inspiration, the ancient oracles of Greek philosophy and the modern mysteries of German idealism—blending Plato· with Hegel, and Aristotle with Kant— these Oxford thinkers have advanced to the creation of original philosophies on the principles of political obligation, the duties of social station, and the general theory of the State. Their influence on generations of Oxford men has been profound; some who have sat at the feet of their political wisdom have in after days been called to handle the political destinies of their country; and they have shown that they had not forgotten the lessons which they once learned.

Cambridge, always more individualistic, has never produced a single dominant mode or prevalent body of opinion in the field of political theory. But Cambridge has none the less been the nursing-mother of a rich and various speculation. Now it has fostered a philosopher, and now an historian—now a lawyer, and now a churchman—who has turned to the study of politics and made, from his own particular angle, some new and vigorous contribution to its development. There is the honoured name of Henry Sidgwick, a philosopher who took both politics and economics for his province, and who, steeped in the teaching of John Stuart Mill, expounded with a rigorous integrity, and a scrupulous analysis, the purely English tradition which makes the utility of individuals the canon of all institutions and the criterion of every policy. There is Sir John Seeley, Regius Professor of Modern History, one of the earliest discoverers of the existence of the British Empire, a scholar of masculine vigour and a robust realism, who regarded political science as the fruit on the branches of history, and, drawing his principles of politics from a study of the modern working of the English constitution, turned the attention of Cambridge scholars towards that study of political institutions which has continued to be endemic. There is Lord Acton, Seeley's successor, *clarum et venerabile nomen,* a profound and pregnant thinker on all European affairs 'as well civil as ecclesiastical,' who cherished a delicate and fastidious love of liberty, believing that the independence of the Church in the State had been, and should continue to be, its bulwark, and dreading those nationalist enthusiasms which seek to make a national State into a destructive tyrant 'crushing all natural rights and all established liberties for the purpose of vindicating itself.' No influence has been more profound in this place than that of Acton; and I would commemorate among those who felt and propagated that influence the name of Neville Figgis, whom I was proud to call a friend; who adorned with incisive wit and industrious scholarship all the themes of political theory which he touched; who loved and prophesied the cause of liberty, both political and religious (I shall never forget his taking me round the garden of the house of the community in which he lived at Mirfield, and suddenly exclaiming, 'Barker, I really believe I'm a syndicalist'); and who, if he had lived, would have been an occupant as proud as he would have been worthy of the chair to which, in his stead, I am called. I cannot but glow as I think of his memory. Admiration and affection were his due; and he had his due from many. And there is another name which comes last, but is very far from being least—a name which also kindles a glow in the minds of those who have heard his voice and fed on his thought— the name of one who was worthy, in his field, to be counted by the side of Acton, and who, along with Acton, filled the mind and determined the thought of Figgis—the name of Maitland. I can cite no greater name. I can only record the measure of the debt which I owe to the man who wrote, in his own inimitable style, the opening chapters of the *History of English Law*, the introduction to *Political Theories of the Middle Ages*, and the essays which deal with or touch on the problems of politics in the three volumes of his *Collected Papers*. How massive was the monument which he erected; how stately and delicate was the style of its architecture; and how far-reaching has been the influence which his teaching, and in particular his teaching about the character of associations and the nature of their personality, has exerted.

I cannot but reflect, as I think of the writings of these Cambridge scholars, how many of them were vowed to the cause of liberty. If Oxford, with its strong corporate sense, about the origin of which I have often wondered, has professed the cause of the body politic, Cambridge, once the apostle of Protestantism and always the apostle of freedom, has followed the banner of individual autonomy. It is the banner which claims my allegiance; and I am proud and comforted to think of the great men who formed the tradition which I shall follow. The chair of Political Science is a new chair; but behind it stretches a line of solemn and majestic shadows. There is Sidgwick, with his scrupulous regard for the canon of individual liberty: there is Acton, for whom history was above all the history of freedom: there is Maitland, whose dissertation for his fellowship at Trinity was 'a historical sketch of liberty and equality as ideals of English political philosophy,' and whose theory of associations has nerved both defenders of the liberties of Trade Unions and champions of the rights of churches in the modern State. Thinking of these things, and seeing behind me these great figures, I may say of my efforts, as with infinitely less reason Ranke said of his in his inaugural lecture, *Non attingunt metam, sed meta posita est.*

II

Among the precursors whose names I have mentioned there were at least four—Seeley and Acton, Figgis and Maitland—who had devoted themselves to the study of history; and Sidgwick himself, philosopher as he was, had studied the development of European polity. There is an obvious affinity between history and political theory; and it may well be a way to the better understanding of the nature of political theory if I turn to consider how far it proceeds on the ground of history, and how far it takes wing and transcends the bounds of historical study. Herodotus, the most garrulous and lovable of story-tellers, could not tell the story of the Persian wars without passing into political reflections; and in his third book he makes a number of Persian grandees, after compassing the death of the false Smerdis, proceed straight from assassination to a calm discussion of the inherent merits, and the inevitable defects, of monarchy, aristocracy, and democracy. The austere Thucydides mingles a pithy and astringent philosophy with his severe narrative of the Peloponnesian war; and alike in the Melian Dialogue, the funeral speech of Pericles, and the passage on sedition in his third book, he gravely attempts *rerum cognoscere causas*. As the historians of Greece became philosophers, so the philosophers became, if not historians, at any rate students of history. Plato himself, idealist as he was, and however cavalier he might generally be in his treatment of history, attempts a review of the lessons of the past, in the third book of the *Laws,* before he proceeds to build an ideal State. The *Politics* of Aristotle is built on the solid foundations of Greek experience; and its political theory was compacted and corroborated from a study of 158 constitutions, of which we possess an example in the treatise on the Constitution of Athens. The practice of the Greeks may seem to confirm the theory which Seeley expressed in a well-known jingle, 'History without Political Science has no fruit: Political Science without History has no root.' And if this be so, history will be but philosophy—political philosophy— teaching by examples; and political philosophy in turn will be simply history precipitated in a patterned shape of generalities.

But I take leave to doubt whether Professor Trevelyan should be termed a root, and, still more, whether I deserve the appellation of fruit. History and political theory march together for all the length of their frontiers; but they are separate and independent studies. Let us assume, for the purpose of argument, the truth of Croce's proposition that 'every true history is contemporary history'—that it is a history of the present regarded as contained the past, or, if you will, of the past regarded as constituting the present. Let us further assume the truth of another saying of Croce, that 'dead history revives, and past history again becomes present, as the development of life demands them,' or, in other words, that in a given present some element of a distant past, acquiring a new vitality from a new congruity with the life of that present, may become once more a creative force, as the Greek past did at the Renaissance. On these assumptions we may proceed to admit that there is much political theory which has been bred partly from the stimulus of present experience, but partly also from the study and stimulus of some congruous past which has become alive and present from its congruity with present experience. The political theory of Rousseau, for example, was born of Rousseau's experience of the Republic of Geneva and of his study of the parallel city-states of the Greek past in the biographies of

Plutarch and the dialogues of Plato. The political theory of the Whigs in the seventeenth century sprang equally from a mixture of contemporary political experience and the study of precedents and analogies in a congruous past— particularly, perhaps, the reign of Richard II, which was affected by the Whigs for its records of constitutional opposition and its example of a king's deposition. But while we may readily admit the debt of such political theory to the study of history, we must equally admit the possibility of a great and influential theory of politics which has no definite basis in history. It may be the method of a political thinker to assume as his axiom certain views about the nature of the human mind and the end of human life, and to deduce a systematic theory from those views. This was the method of Spinoza; it was the method of Plato when he wrote the *Republic;* and it is fundamentally the method of Aristotle, who— however historical, and even empirical, he may appear—was none the less purely philosophical in his explanation of the existence, his conception of the purposes, and his derivation of the institutions, of the true or normal State. In this way, and in this sense, history and political theory may be independent, if conterminous, powers. You may have a political theory which is a good theory without being rooted in historical study, just as you may have history which is fine history without issuing in any fruit of political science. For to relate what actually occurred, *wie es eigentlich gewesen ist,* is a task worthy of the greatest historian; and he who tells some noble and stirring story in noble and stirring prose may mix true art with genuine history and carry every vote.

Not only is political theory a study which is, or may be, independent of the study of history. We may go further, and say that it is a study which loses its true nature, and puts its neck unnecessarily under the yoke of happening and the routine of historic sequence, if it occupies itself largely with problems of history. It is concerned with questions of being rather than with those of becoming: it has to discuss what the State is *semper et ubique,* rather than what it was at this time or in that place, or how it developed from one form into another. It is true that John Stuart Mill once wrote that the fundamental problem of all social speculation was 'to find the laws according to which any state of society produces the state which succeeds it.' He was following Comte and the Positivist theory of successive stages in a superseding process of development, by which, for example, the industrial regime ejects the military as 'positive' thought ousts 'metaphysical.' But to anatomize the history of society and thought into separate sections divided by deep abysses—as if it were a desert of Arizona traversed and split by great cañons—is to forget the continuous eternities both of society and of thought. There are questions of political theory which are the same yesterday, today, and for ever. Why does the State exist? What are the purposes for which it exists? What are the best and most congruous means for their realization? These are the fundamental problems; and it is thus concerned less with historic processes (however generally and even abstractly they may be conceived) than with the fundamental realities—essence, purpose, and value—which transcend the category of time. We must admit, indeed, that the state exists in time, and may vary in form, if not in substance, from age to age. We must equally admit that political speculation has often dressed itself in historical language, and that the theory of the Social Contract, for instance, has sometimes been expressed in terms which suggest an historical account of the actual genesis of the State. But even the theory of the Social Contract is, at bottom, a philosophical theory rather than an historical narrative. It is an attempt to explain, not the chronological antecedents, but the logical presuppositions, of the State—to show, not how it came to be, but on what assumptions we can explain its being. Hobbes himself, after an account of the state of nature which imposes the necessity of a social contract, remarks 'It may peradventure be thought that there never was such a time . . . and I believe it was never generally so . . . howsoever it may be perceived what manner of life *there would be,* where there were no common power to fear.' In a word, the whole theory is a matter of an hypothesis, or assumption, on which the existence of the State and its government can be explained; and it does not profess or claim historical validity. There is a profound remark of Hobbes which may serve as the conclusion of the whole matter. Philosophy 'excludes history as well natural as political, though most useful—nay necessary—to philosophy; because such knowledge is but experience, and not ratiocination.'

'Most useful—nay necessary.' Nurtured as I have been in history, I should be the last to decry its utility, and, indeed, its necessity, for the purposes of my subject. Any true philosophy must be one which has been immersed in experience—and yet has escaped the peril of submersion in its wide and brimming flood. A philosophy of politics must especially be immersed in a double experience—that of the past and that of the present. It must be based, in the first place, on a knowledge of what Sidgwick called 'the development of European polity'—a knowledge of Greek democracy, of Roman imperialism, of mediaeval institutions both feudal and ecclesaistical, and of the mingled parliamentarianism and nationalism of modern Europe. It must be founded, in the second place, on a real acquaintance, deeper than can be derived from the study of books alone, with the forms— and not only the forms, but also the spirit and working—of

contemporary institutions. The parallel chair in the sister University
bears a double designation: it is a chair of political theory and
institutions. In this University too the study of political institutions
has been cultivated, for many years past, by a number of lecturers;
and one of the papers set in the first part of the Historical Tripos is
primarily concerned with 'a comparative survey of Political
Institutions and their development, with some reference to the
history of Political Theory.' Such study, and such survey, has a
natural and obvious fascination. Who is there who cannot read with
delight the memorable works of Bryce on *The American
Commonwealth* and *Modern Democracies,* or President Lowell's lucid
treatises on *Governments and Parties in Continental Europe* and *The
Government of England*? From this point of view I can well
understand why the University, even if it has not specifically used the
word institutions in the designation of the new chair, has included in
the Professor's terms of appointment a generous clause which
permits his absence, during one term in every three, in order that he
may study abroad the actual working of institutions or the actual
development of theory. I have thought how I could best take
advantage of this permission, and while I may take some liberty to
myself, I am inclined to think that I shall not fly away much, or for
long, from the cage in which I am more than content to sit and sing.
There are some far flights (I can think of three) which I desire to
undertake during my tenure of the chair; but I believe that I may
occasionally desire to spend the academic year in the company of my
colleagues. For one thing, my own bias leans towards the side of
theory, and it is probably best for me to run with the bias. Other
professors will contribute, in time to come, what I have failed to give;
and the subject of the chair is vast enough to permit some measure of
selection and specialization. Meanwhile I am happy to think that a
number of University lecturers in the field of history are lecturing,
and will continue to lecture, on political institutions. I will help
whenever I can, and wherever I have fresh knowledge to contribute;
and though it may not be given to me to survey mankind in China and
Peru, I will remember that Capetown and Delhi and Washington are
not inaccessible, that vacations are sometimes long, and that
continental journeys are often short. For the rest, I will cultivate my
garden in Cambridge, and I will comfort myself with the austere
reflection that though absence might endear me more, presence may
make for greater continuity of study and instruction. The
uninterrupted movement of a University's life, as I have had some
occasion to observe, does not pause for the absence of any Professor;
nor does the business of any other body or society in which he may be
interested. And I feel it the duty of a Professor of Political Science to

interest himself, as far as he may, in the life and affairs of the community in which he lives. It is difficult, I confess, for a professor to practise what he professes; but χαλεπὰ τὰ καλά—all good things are difficult.

I seem to have diverged from history into an autobiography of the future; and I must return from green fields into the dusty road. I have spoken of history and political theory as separate things: let me put them together and treat of the history of political theory— or, as it is often called, the history of political ideas. It is a fascinating subject, just as the history of philosophy is a fascinating subject. And just as, I imagine, you must know something of the history of philosophy to be a good philosopher, so you must certainly know a good deal of the history of political ideas to be a tolerable political theorist. In thought, as well as in action, the roots of the present lie deep in the past; and Hegel had his foundations in Plato, as Bosanquet, in his turn, had his foundations in both. The more the development of political ideas is studied, the richer will be the development of political theory—provided, I hasten to add, that it is studied as a means and not as an end, and provided again that it is studied in its breadth as well as its depth. Let me explain these two provisos. The first is simple. To study and to understand previous theories about a subject does not absolve a teacher from the duty of himself understanding the subject itself. It is possible, but not perhaps very useful, to know all political theories without attaining a theory; and there may be more wisdom in less knowledge, if it is brought to a point and used as a tool of original thought. The danger of some subjects of speculation—I would cite in evidence literary criticism as well as political theory— is that they may be choked, as it were, by the history of their own past. The second proviso which I have made raises larger considerations. When I speak of considering breadth as well as depth, I mean that besides political theory there is what I would call political thought, which is as broad and wide as the general community from which it proceeds, and which, in any study of political ideas, must be considered no less than political theory, however deeply such theory may delve. Political theory is the speculation of individual minds, self-conscious and analytic; political thought is the thought of a whole society, often but dimly concious of itself, and yet pervading and shaping political life and growth. The complex of political ideas which we may call by the name of political thought is implicit in, and has to be gathered from, its own actual and historical results—the development of Athenian democracy, the growth of the English constitution, the general unfolding of national ideas and aspirations in modern Europe. It is embedded in institutions, from which it must be disengaged; and it may even be, as it were, interred in the political vocabulary of a language, from which it may be exhumed, as Professor Myres has shown in a recent work on *The Political Ideas of the Greeks,* by a patient study of etymologies and the nuances of meaning attached to political terms. Whatever the sources from which it may be discovered, it is a matter of profound moment; and no history of political ideas can be complete which does not reckon with *Staatsgedanke* as well as with *Staatslehre.*

I have spoken long of history in its relation to political theory. If I speak but briefly of a study cognate to history—the study of law—my brevity must be regarded less as the measure of my respect than as the index of my ignorance. But I hasten to say how readily I admit that political theory can never afford to neglect the study of legal ideas, and how gratefully I recognize the debt which my subject owes to a succession of great legal thinkers. Legal ideas have formed, or contributed to form, the institutions of the state; and they are still the bony substance, or supporting *vertebrae,* of its subtly compacted organs. The family is a legal rather than a natural institution—an institution which was thought into existence by the primitive lawyers who made its rules, rather than brought to birth by innate instincts[2]: property, too, is a conception of the lawyers; and the State itself, in one of its aspects, is a legal framework which lawyers have largely built and whose anatomy they have discussed in treatises on *Staatsrecht.* In England, indeed, with its unwritten constitution and its conception of the general sovereignty of a single law, there has never been any separate *Staatsrecht;* and the study of constitutional law has been part and parcel of the general study of common law. But perhaps for that reason, and because there has been no separate compartment of study, but only a disengaging of broad constitutional principles from the body of our law, the thought of the lawyers has exercised all the more influence on political ideas and speculation. Blackstone is justly famous; the name of one of his successors in the Vinerian Chair—that of Dicey—deserves to be had in lasting remembrance; and I have already celebrated the name of a great occupant of the Downing Chair of the Laws of England in this University, Maitland, who not only showed that the history of English Law was an essential part of the history of English politics and political ideas, but made his exposition, by his style and his genius, a part of English literature. In the more general field of Jurisprudence Cambridge produced Maine, if Maine adorned Oxford; and Maine, pursuing an historical method of inquiry, made the general history of law at once illustrate and check political theories, whether of the patriarchal origin of society or of the formation of the State by a Social Contract. Nor, outside England, and not to mention other English names, such as that of Austin, can I

forget the work on my subject done by the lawyers of the Continent—
Bodin, Grotius and Montesquieu, Gierke and Jellinek, Duguit and
Esmein. The debt is profound; and I cannot, even at the risk of
egotism, forbear to mention what I owe to the teachers of law in my
own old University with whom I have had discussions, or, I had
perhaps better say, from whom I have had expositions. I will only add
that I hope to be allowed to renew the indebtedness here. Political
theory and its teachers must consort not only with history and
historians, but also with law and the lawyers.

III

Before I turn from history and the cognate study of law to consider
philosophy, I desire to say some few words about psychology, which
is, as it were, a half-way house on the road I am travelling. If in the
days of Seeley, and in the general tradition of Cambridge, the study of
politics has been mainly connected with the study of history; if again
in the days of T. H. Green and his successors, and in the general
tradition of Oxford, it has been connected with the study of
philosophy—in the world outside it has come more and more to
connect itself with the growing study of psychology. Political theory
would sometimes seem to be turning itself before our eyes into social
psychology. Theorists of an older type are censured for basing their
theory on a very imperfect observation of the human mind and the
tendencies of human conduct, and the new science of mental and
moral behaviour is promising to supply the defect. There is some
justice in the censure, and some actual delivery accompanies the
promise; nor can I be blind, even if in this matter my eyes are a little
held, to the new substance and new inspiration brought into social
studies by writers such as Tarde, MacDougall, and Graham Wallas.
But I cannot but say to myself—it may be from hardness of heart and
an obstinate clinging to the gospel I once received—that psychology
is a fashion (I have seen, in my lifetime, more than one fashion of
thought): that fashions change; and that the quiet hodden grey of
philosophy endures.

In its modern form psychology runs into the mould of natural
science. Like physics, it decomposes its subject-matter into atoms and
electrons which it calls by the name of instincts. Like biology, it works
from the primitive to the present; it explains the present in terms of
evolution from the past; and it may be led to refer the behaviour of
civilized man to the instincts developed in man's rude beginnings.
Decomposing the mind into instincts, it may miss the unity secured to
the mind by a pervading and freely moving reason which 'passeth and

goeth through all things by reason of her pureness,' and makes the mind move freely as a whole towards its chosen purpose. Referring the present to the past, and explaining social behaviour to-day by primary and primitive instincts, it may forget any standard of value, and blend the high with the low in a common continuous substance. The dignity of man may suffer, and he may become not a little lower than angels, if the study of his mind is treated as the study of so much mechanism. On the other hand there can be no doubt that the study of psychology in its various forms—and there are very various and divergent forms of the study—has added new substance to political theory. If the study of political institutions and legal principles brings us face to face with what Hegel would call Mind Objective—mind concrete and deposited in a solid and stable fabric—the study of psychology presents us with mind subjective, the subtle spinning of mental processes which forms the living stuff of Society and the State, the play of emotions, sentiments, instincts, and habits, which lies behind and peeps through political and legal systems. Nor does social psychology only add to knowledge: it may also claim to be a practical and applied science. I have been told that its aim is entirely practical; that it might be described as a sort of social therapeutics; that just as the doctor studies physical processes with a view to stimulating or inhibiting or modifying those processes, so the social psychologist studies psychical processes with a view to similar control. In a word, he wishes to know how normal man behaves in the presence of a given stimulus in order that he may discover how far you can change his behaviour by changing the stimulus. Perhaps there may be a remedy for the evils of states if psychologists are kings, or kings have the spirit and power of psychology; and a statesman who has studied psychology may be the better aware both of the difficulties which he has to face in men's instincts and modes of behaviour, and of the methods by which he may overcome those difficulties. But there is a certain danger in that form of applied psychology, not unknown to statesmen, which leads to spell-binding and *réclame*; and there is also a tendency even in pure students of the subject to let their view of human nature suffer from their observations of the working of the human mind. The political theorists who used psychology even before it existed—and one may perhaps speak in such terms of Machiavelli and Hobbes and Bentham—were apt to think that mankind was a little breed. Greater knowledge has bred greater respect; but even now the observation of mass-behaviour may lead the psychological student of 'human nature in politics' to feel—half in sadness, and more than half in kindness—how little real wisdom goes to the government of the world.

The affinities of psychology, when it is regarded or studied as a branch of natural science, are affinities with biology. If it be true that psychology has added new content to political theory—and of that, whatever else may be said, there cannot be any doubt—it is also true that biology has laid it under a debt. It is not only a matter of the theory of evolution, which has influenced all thought in every field, and has turned political theory to the study of social development; nor is it a matter merely of the idea of adaptation to environment, which has led some political thinkers to regard a people's political ideas and institutions as a way of life adjusted to suit regional features and needs. The service which biology can render to political theory goes farther than these things. What has happened in the past is that biologists have elaborated their own theories in their own field, and that students in other fields have borrowed these theories and applied them to their subject without adequate consideration of their relevance or validity in the study of that subject. Ideas of struggle for life and survival of the fittest, which have their value in the domain for which they were elaborated, have thus been, as it were, lifted and transported to the alien domain of human society. It is the natural fate of new and seminal theories that, by being applied too generally—as if they were panaceas or universal 'open sesames'— they should again and again be misapplied; but neither Darwin nor Einstein can be blamed for the indiscriminate zeal of those votaries of novelty who find the secret of the universe in each new discovery. I need not, however, linger over what has happened in the past. What has now begun to happen in the field of Biology, and what is likely to go farther, holds far more promise. Instead of sustaining a sort of theft, biologists are beginning to lend. They have turned their attention to 'the biological foundations of society.' if I may quote the title of a work by an old colleague of mine, the late Professor Dendy: they have taken into their province (to quote again, and this time from the title of a lecture by a great Cambridge biologist, Dr. Bateson) the study of the relation between 'biological fact and the structure of society.' The growth of Eugenics—a subject of profound importance for political theory—is an example of the contribution which biology may make when it turns to the study of biological fact in its connexion with social structure; and that is perhaps only one example of what we may justly expect. Biology has perhaps greater contributions to make to the study of human welfare than any other science. And in this place, celebrated by the names of great biologists, it is fitting for a Professor of Political Science to acknowledge existing debt, to anticipate further obligation, and to promise neither to neglect biological fact in his own inquiries nor to be slow in grasping any chance of co-operation with students of biology in the general field of social investigation.

IV

I come in conclusion, and I come with a genuine feeling of modest stillness and humility, to the great subject of which I conceive the subject of this chair to be a province, a border-province, if you will, but none the less a province. That subject is philosophy, and especially moral philosophy. As I see it, political theory is primarily concerned with the purpose, or purposes, which man proposes to himself as a moral being, living in association with other moral beings, who at once desires and is forced to pursue his purpose or purposes in the medium of a common life. It is a study of ends, and of the modes of realization of those ends; and since ends have supreme value, and determine the value of other things which serve as their means, it is a study of value or values. Here it may be said to touch the sister science or theory which is called economics. Economics is also concerned with values; and if originally it concerned itself only with money value, it has been led inevitably to the study of social value and the measurement of the difference between the one and the other. 'This consideration,' Marshall has remarked, 'will be found to underlie nearly all the most serious modern economic studies.' Economics and politics thus run up together into philosophy; and moral philosophy (or moral science) is the basis, or apex, common to both. For such philosophy is a study of ultimate value; and that is a necessary criterion for those who pursue the study of social value, whether in the field of political life and institutions, or in that of economic life and production.

It is here, and in this conception of political theory as moral philosophy applied to the life of the whole community, that Plato and Aristotle still remain masters. Plato combined ethics and politics in a single dialogue which he entitled, 'polity, or concerning righteousness'—the dialogue which we call the *Republic*. Aristotle wrote separate treatises on *Ethics* and *Politics;* but the one is related to the other, and both are concerned with the study of the human good, which is 'the same for the individual and the state,' though it 'appears a greater and more perfect thing to have and to hold' when it is exhibited in the life of a good community. In the *Elements of Politics* and the *Principles of Political Obligation* the method of Henry Sidgwick and T. H. Green is fundamentally similar. Whatever the difference of their views, both of these thinkers postulated a conception of the human good, and both of them attempted to determine, on the basis and by the criterion of that conception, the system of relations which ought to be established in a political community. In its essentials the problem of political theory is a constant. It has to determine the end, or ultimate value, which governs and determines the life of political society: it has to discover the appropriate and congruous means by which that end may be realized, that ultimate value actually enjoyed. But in one age one aspect of the final good may be emphasized, and in other another; and the means of realization also vary, not only with variations in the aspect of the final good selected for emphasis, but also with the variations of the medium—by which I mean the congeries of contemporary institutions, customs, conditions, and problems—in which realization has to be achieved. That is why political theory is always new as well as always old, and why it is constantly changing even while it remains the same.

Is there any aspect of social well-being which particularly needs emphasis to-day, and is there any means for its attainment which offers particular promise and demands particular study? If I can answer these questions, I shall have given some clue to the prepossessions with which I start and the lines which I hope to follow. I will say at once that there is one aspect of social well-being which lies heavily on my mind at the present time. I assume that the general end of society is the development in each member of a full personality, which on the one hand issues in the individual doing or enjoying of things worth doing or enjoying, and on the other hand flows in the channels of harmonious co-operation with other and like personalities. The human good, in the form in which it is pursued in the state, is the energy of individual moral wills acting for their own appropriate objects in a regular system of organized co-operation. On the one hand individual energy, on the other social co-operation; on the one hand free initiative, on the other organization. The pendulum swings slowly from this side to that in the development of humanity; and now it may seem to pause here, and now there. Yet freedom remains a precious thing; and an individual moral will, even when it has to act in harmony with other and similar wills, must essentially be free if it is to be moral—for free action only is moral. The cause of liberty was proclaimed by Mill, as it was proclaimed by Milton: it seemed a cause which was accepted: it is a cause which is being threatened. Its enemies wear no ignoble faces. There is the puritanism of administrative zeal, concerned for the setting in order of a thickly populated and sadly complicated society, full of contacts and conflicts of interest which seem to cry for adjustment. There will always be men who would fain leave the world a tidier place than they found it; and we cannot readily blame them for a misguided zeal. There is, again, the passion of social enthusiasm, aflame for a creed and consumed by desire for grasping quickly the sorry scheme of things and remoulding it instantly new. Such passion will not readily stay to gain consent, and it may move to its end like a rushing impatient wind, taking ultimate acceptance for granted, and ready to impose a dictatorship until it comes. Liberty is thus threatened alike from the right and the left—at once by the sober administrator and by the ardent reformer. And meanwhile the methods by which men once thought that liberty could be made secure have themselves fallen into discredit. It is not so long ago since democracy was a word of power, and men were ready to suffer for the cause of free parliaments and free suffrage. To-day the word and the cause are under suspicion; and there is a feeling abroad that the people, too vast to be moved except in moments of passion, when movement may become a tyrannical frenzy, are a managed multitude which the controllers of the machine can manipulate at their will. We have to face a reaction against the old faith in liberty and popular government; we have to admit that the political hopes in which men once dressed themselves were sanguine. But the faith and the hopes abide. There is no better way for the management of men than the way of self-management; and in the long run it is only possible way. It is true that the burden of self-government is heavy. It makes great demands on the intelligence and the interest of every citizen. But the demands which it makes are its justification. A form of government which elicits and enlists the mental and moral energy of a whole civic body for its working is a good form of government. Yet the justification will only be theoretical unless the energy is really present. And it will only be really present if electorates can develop an instructed and interested public opinion, which is neither tyrannical in its occasional pressure nor apathetic in its general laxity. The formation of such a public opinion is the crux of our politics.

If liberty is the aspect of social well-being which needs emphasis to-day, and if liberty demands a living body of public opinion for its realization, is there any means for attaining such a body of opinion which offers particular promise and demands particular study? There is an answer which is painfully obvious, but which in the hope that the obvious may also be true, I shall none the less venture to give. That answer is 'education.' It is an old saying that we must educate our masters. It is an older saying repeated again and again in the *Politics* of Aristotle, that the citizen must be educated in the spirit of the constitution under which he lives. That saying, with a new application, and, it may be, with a new depth of interpretation, is one which may well be repeated to-day. The theory of education is essentially a part of political theory. It is not so much a matter of psychology, with which it has been generally connected in the Universities and Training Colleges where it is taught (though I admit that the study of psychology has a value for the theory of education, as it has for political theory in general): it is rather a matter of social theory—of grasping and comprehending the purposes, the character, and the needs of Society and the State, and of discovering the methods by which the young can best be trained to achieve these purposes to maintain and even improve that character, and to satisfy those needs. To Plato the State was essentially an educational society, and its activity was first and foremost a training of its members to understand, and understanding to fulfil, the duties of their station in the community. I believe that we shall come to take the same view. A national system of education is a comparatively new thing with us; and we only see in part the services it can render and the significance it may assume, in the scheme of our national life. That it may give us the instructed and interested public opinion which we need for the safety of democracy is only one of the expectations we may perhaps legitimately form. It may also help to form, and even to strengthen, civic character, banishing some of those shadows—the shadow of a restless instability; the shadow of a gregarious and imitative habit—which have been cast upon it by the urbanization of our life. It may train men not only to do their work in the world, but also to use the time of their leisure—that time which is the growing-time of the spirit; that time in which the spirit of man, casting aside its shackles, can expand and exult in the free play of its faculties, released, and at the same time realized, in the delight of music and literature, the joy of thought and discussion. For to bring the matter to a clear and simple point, I cannot but believe that it may well be part of the function of the state, and a part which ought to be emphasized in political theory, that it should promote from its own funds, and encourage by its own institutions, not only education in the narrower sense in which we habitually use the word, but also (if I may use a word soiled by some dubious use) that broader and more general culture which includes among many other things, the hearing of good music and the seeing of good plays.

But this is too exciting a theme for the end of a lecture; and I must fall into a quiet final cadence. I know enthusiasts who would call the theory of education the core and centre of social theory; and I am almost persuaded to be such an enthusiast myself. I do not wish, in devoting myself to political theory, to relinquish the interest which I have more and more come to feel in the matter of education. I believe, on the contrary, that in virtue of that very devotion I am likely, and indeed bound, to feel an even greater interest. Any scheme, therefore, that may be launched in this University, either for its fuller participation in the training of teachers, or for its sharing in other ways, in the preparation of social workers (and are we not all such?) in other fields—any plan intended to secure, in the noble words of the Bidding Prayer, 'that there may never be wanting a succession of persons duly qualified for the service of God in Church and in State'—must necessarily command the fullest measure of my attention. Not that I come with any scheme which I wish to press. μὴ γένοιτο. I only come with a desire to learn and wish to help.

NOTES

1. Professor G. M. Trevelyan, who had only the term before delivered his Inaugural Lecture as Regius Professor of Modern History.
2. Eduard Meyer, *Geschichte des Altertums*, I. i. (3rd edition), p. 17.

3

Professor D. W. Brogan
THE STUDY OF POLITICS

There is something incongruous, possibly impertinent, in offering to give an inaugural lecture more than six years after this university had done me the signal honour of electing me to succeed so great a scholar as Sir Ernest Barker in the chair of Political Science. My main, my only effectual excuse, must be the stress and strain of war, the claims of other authorities than the university on what services I could perform. The alternative was not the giving of an inaugural lecture earlier but the not giving of it at all.

Yet that alternative, which has its attractions for human idleness and timidity, was rejected by me and, I think, rightly rejected. For there is a special duty incumbent on a professor in a field like mine to declare the faith, or the doubt, that is in him. He is not professing an exact science in which his opinions, prejudices, views of his field of study matter little. There may, indeed, be no such fields of study, but if there are, the academic study of politics is most certainly not one of them. To claim for it the austerity and exactness, the freedom from the passions of the hour that is the peculiar glory of those studies of which this university is the most famous academic home, would be absurd.

This seems to me to be a truth self-evident, but in academic fashion, I fall back on the greatest name in the long list of those who have written on politics in the English tongue. It is true political science, true realism to assert with Burke that 'no reasonable man ever did govern himself by abstracts and universals'. Neither does nor did any society, and the study of a field of human action in which passion and faith must play a great part must call, at any rate, surely may call for a modicum of passion and faith in the student?

If this be admitted, it is right that I should declare that I do not come to the study or teaching of politics a complete neutral, ready to believe that nothing has yet been decided or that all is eternally in question. I do not, so far, see my duties as those of a political seismologist content to note an earthquake here and a mere tremor there. Like Sir Ernest Barker, I think that the theme of politics is closely connected with ethics and especially 'with liberty as a part or element of the social aspect of goodness'. Such a confession will seem naïve to many, but to those who hold beliefs like mine it is some consolation to notice how hard it is for the adherents of more realist creeds, tied by first principles to more material concepts, to purge their vocabularies of the seductive words. And if those words are only used to seduce because of the resonance imparted to them by so many centuries of history, the mere habit of using them may not be without unforeseen results. For as Elie Halévy used to say, from the point of view of the statesman, of the public moralist, the homage of hypocrisy, paid by vice to virtue, is a real homage and may end in the conquest of the hypocrite by the virtues he has practised so long. To talk continually of liberty is dangerous, for the word may ask to be examined, and if examined may be found to have its old appeal. Be that as it may, the study of politics, as seen by me, is first of all and, perhaps, last of all, the study of the means whereby liberty and authority may be best combined, whereby the dignity of the free man is made compatible with the highest and richest forms of co-operation. For the art or science of politics, if it be more than a device for the acquisition of coercive power, must I think terminate in the creation or augmentation of men, not of things.

Had this chair been founded a century ago, the old Cambridge of mathematics tempered by classics might have been scandalized by the intrusion, but there would have been less scepticism as to the existence of a field of study called political science, although there might have been strong feeling that the proper place for such study was London or even Oxford. It may be surmised that there would have been fairly general agreement with the Society for the Diffusion of Useful Knowledge which began a lengthy work on *Political Philosophy* with a chapter entitled 'Advantages of Political Science'. True, in that chapter was admitted, handsomely, the superior precision of other disciplines.

'Mathematicians who run hardly any risk of error—naturalists who run but little more—have never been so bigoted and so uncharitable as those whose speculations are fated to be always involved more or less in doubt.' Having, from time to time, listened to the professional conversation of practitioners of these disciplines, I am a little inclined to see in this handsome testimonial an illustration of the well-known contrast between the reverence of the laity and the ironical levity of the priesthood. But the contrast with 'political reasoners' in whom 'we find beside the intolerance of metaphysicians, a new source of error and of fault in the excitement which the interests of men, real or supposed, lend to their passions', has still its old force. Indeed, it has more than its old force, for we may doubt to-day whether any such academic discipline as political science exists, a doubt practically unknown to earlier ages.

There is, it must be admitted, in the title of this chair, an ambiguity or a pretension that many find repellent. The direct connection of science with politics is infrequent, and that politics can be, in any but the most special sense, a science, may well be doubted. We can, of course, regard the whole of human experience as an unplanned biological experiment, providing data which, in their different ways, the historian, the economist, the sociologist, the political scientist studies and systematizes. And many, many books have been written on some such assumption. With few exceptions, however, the world has willingly let them die, and the rulers of the world have not been willing to go to school to such masters. So it was when Lemuel Gulliver happened to mention to the King of Brobdingnag that 'there were several thousand books among us written upon the *Art of Government;* it gave him (directly contrary to my intention) a very mean opinion of our Understandings'.

The King's opinion is widely shared and until a Darwin or Mendel comes among us to give a few general laws of political behaviour true of all species of political societies and of men in all their political relations, there is not much hope of changing this judgment of the world. In this sense 'political science' *is* a pretentious term, since its students and teachers do not acquire any such mastery of the political world as do physical scientists of the material world. Politics may have all the potentialities of the atomic bomb, but those potentialities are not the result of the activities of political scientists, as Plutonium or Neptunium are of the activities of the physicists.

When the whole problem of politics was the combination of liberty and effective authority and while there was still apparent agreement on the meaning, both of liberty and of effective and legitimate authority, the mechanisms of politics could be studied with the same optimistic attention as the mechanics which were transforming the industry and commerce of nations. Representative government was as happy and imitable an invention as the steam engine. Henry Hallam would have agreed with James Madison in admiration for the discovery of 'this great mechanical power in government, by the simple agency of which the will of the largest political body may be concentrated, and its force directed to any object which the public good requires'. This discovery relieved the optimistic political thinkers of the early nineteenth century from the fears of the incompatibility of power and freedom which had haunted

Montesquieu and Rousseau. The fall of the Roman Empire was as much due to the failure of the Roman Republic to find this solution of its imperial problem, as to the incursion of the Barbarians, the influence of Christianity, or any accidents of history of the type of the length of Cleopatra's nose. The desperate remedy of Caesarism was made necessary by the failure to find the mild remedy of a representative Senate.

Dwelling in this climate of opinion, it was easy to de-limit the field of political science, to put excessive faith (as even John Stuart Mill did) in mechanical devices like proportional representation, and see in the formal spread of representative government a ground for rejoicing and an invitation to study the ways in which the new Prussian or Japanese parliamentarism was imperfect though hopeful, the ways in which the congressional government of the United States diverged from a norm of which the House of Commons, or the total English system as described by Bagehot, was the exemplification.

The study of politics became, especially in the United States, a study of the mechanics of a society whose general character was taken for granted. Political mechanisms and ideas were added to a social structure; either they were forcibly imported and imposed as by the British in India, or were adopted by an awakening state as in Japan. If the adoption of western political principles and practices did not seem to give uniformly good results, or indeed uniform results of any kind, there were apparently adequate explanations to hand: race conflicts, illiteracy, backward religious beliefs and practices, debilitating climates, mere intellectual failure to grasp the rules of the game. So could the state of Mexico, of Italy, of Spain be accounted for. This type of explanation survived down into very recent times. It would be easy, but unkind, to exemplify it, to refer to a modern map illustrating the close correlation between illiteracy and dictatorial government, or to arguments assuming that once the Prussian military and civil bureaucracy was put under parliamentary control, the mere virtues of the parliamentary democratic system would work wonders, above all the wonder of replacing an old and deep-rooted German tradition with a new and foreign tradition. But to put it that way is to be unjust to the optimists who hardly considered the question of tradition at all, but saw the problem simply as the replacement of one mechanically conceived system of political organization by another.

We are, for the most part, cured of that illusion to-day. We have seen that universal literacy was no proof against the imposition of tyranny and that the most ingenious imitations of our political methods often, very often, failed to work. It has been seen that the question was not one of making minor modifications like the adjustment of a ship's piano to sail through the tropics, but of pondering the question, in no very optimistic frame of mind, 'Can any political mechanisms be usefully exported at all?' It was a useful reaction but it was too complete a reaction.

For the failures and the disillusionments of the old methods of comparative politics came from their too limited definition of the content of 'politics' and their failure to notice the relevance of other fields of comparative study. We have come to see the profound relevance of economic problems. We can see, for example, that the main Irish problem of the nineteenth century was the economic problem of the land system. We can see that the mere verbal imitation of the constitution of the United States of America by the United States of Mexico was bound to be a parody as long as the Mexican social structure was so different from the American, as long as there was no equivalent of the 'We the People of the United States', the concept and the political reality on which the constitution of the United States rested and rests.

It was and it is an easy reaction to dismiss the whole political apparatus as irrelevant and so its study as time-wasting pedantry. But such a view would be as far from realism as that of Broadbent in *John Bull's Other Island*. Broadbent, you will remember, could 'see no evils in the world—except, of course, natural evils—that cannot be remedied by freedom, self-government, and English institutions'. It was and is proper to laugh, but we can laugh too heartily and fail to notice that Broadbent was only exaggerating grossly, not talking mere nonsense. For freedom, self-government and English institutions have in practice cured or moderated very serious evils, from Suttee in India to child labour in England. The modern history of the Ireland in which Broadbent was pontificating would have been very different if there had not been English political institutions in England—and in Ireland. If you doubt that look at the very different history of Poland under the rule either of Prussia or of Russia. Because in Ireland the rulers and ruled talked the same political language, which both assumed was universally valid, they had a common ground on which to fight and argue and, on the stronger side, an increasing moral but none the less real compulsion to diminish the strain caused by the conflict between words and practice. Because there was a common political language and, if you will, a common superstition that political language mattered, the mere preponderance of power on one side was not given full weight. If you think that the matter of the dispute between England and Ireland was, once the basic land question was settled, of no real moment anyway, it is surely a very academic doctrine indeed that, in the name of realism, ignores what passions really move men to action!

And if the 'People of the United States' has become more and more a reality behind the text of the American constitution, it is because the constitution has proved, in practice, to be an effective environment for the real body politic to grow in.

When we laugh at the superstitious reverence of past generations for 'freedom, self-government and English institutions', we are in our right when we are laughing at an absurd and dangerous complacency, but we are not so much in our right when we laugh at the idea that freedom and self-government are or have been either good or important, or when we ignore the fact that they have been, in practice, associated with English institutions or colourable imitations of them. For the next stage is not to dismiss political institutions as unimportant, but to regard as virtues in other political institutions the mere absence of those qualities which Broadbent exalted with such complacency but not without good reason. Those qualities of a political system which Broadbent and an overwhelming majority of his countrymen prized for so long are, perhaps, not to be prized to-day. If this be so, I can only say with a Cambridge poet:

> 'Men are we and must grieve.'

I shall borrow, without permission but, I am certain, without objection from my predecessor, a justification of the university study of politics which Sir Ernest Barker applied to the general situation of democracy.

He listed among what he called the 'works of justification', the 'strengthening of the power of discussion—the broadening of civic intelligence and the extension of civic knowledge'. We must, in the university, do what is rightly declared to be the function and opportunity of the democratic state, 'enlist the effective thought of the whole community in the operation of discussion'.[1]

Here we are confronted with the difficulty that, whatever may be the case of the whole community of Britain, our university system, with its specialization and segregation, makes the 'enlistment of the whole community in the operation of discussion' difficult, perhaps impossible. It is likely, indeed, that as far as we attain any enlistment of the university community 'in the operation of discussion' it will be by reflecting back from the national community such degree of candour and unity as the nation may have attained. There is nothing, alas, in the history of universities, even of this university, that suggests any immunity from passion inherent in the institution or in its teachers and students. But that weakness has arisen, in part at least, from the tacit acceptance of the view that politics was not a fit subject for university discussion or for the application of university standards or methods.

In such a frame of mind it was easy to admire the attitude of the Warden of Judas in the other place, 'year following year in ornamental seclusion from the follies and fusses of the world'. But the world has a way of forcing its follies and fusses on us, even on the two ancient universities. And in the home of the Cavendish laboratory, it is not irrelevant to point out that the universities have their way of intruding, decisively, on the fusses and follies of the world.

At this moment in world history, when the contrast between man's command over nature, almost over the processes of creation, and his power of command over his own society has never been so great or so terrifying, it is unnecessary to stress the importance of politics. It is politics that fills the world with fear; it is political failure that is the greatest menace to 'life, liberty and the pursuit of happiness'. In bad politics is our doom; in good politics is our only hope of salvation.

What can a university do to encourage what I have called good politics? It cannot and it should not attempt to train statesmen; they are artists, no more to be produced by universities than are great painters by the multiplication of art schools. Yet great artists have come out of art schools none the worse for it, and great statesmen have come out of universities possibly even the better for it. Nor is the idea of making a university education part of the foundation on which the future politician and ruler builds, really novel. To go no further back than the last great century, it was an admitted function of the mathematical tripos in this university, of the school of *Literae Humaniores* in Oxford, to give to the future member of Parliament, cabinet minister, ruler of India, a view of the world of state that would, it was hoped, raise them above the mere 'bustle of local agency' deprecated by Burke. It may be objected that any good university education will do that, and that the more exact and traditional academic studies do it better than those too much mingled with the business of the day. The first thesis I should not, for a moment, deny; the second I am, in a sense, debarred from accepting as long as I draw the stipend of this chair. But even did I hold the older academic view, I should feel myself bound to notice that the world expects the universities to have wider interests than the teaching of the young; they exist for the advancement of learning as well as its transmission. And we must also notice that the taught have their choices and if denied the gratification of them, if forced to accept the old fortifying curriculum, will not thereby be prevented from seeking the food they crave elsewhere. It is then too late to rebuke the young for being

'swoln with wind, and the rank mist they draw'

or even, to amend Milton, reproach them that they

'rot outwardly and foul contagion spread'.

It is now too late to save the university 'from the contagion of the world's slow stain'; it always has been. And it is to be noted that Shelley wrote this after being sent down for extra-curricular politics.

If the university is to teach politics, it is sufficient justification and sufficient guide to its methods of teaching that the job is in any case being done by others, outside the university, and so it had better be done inside it. I have already suggested that it is vain to expect of the teaching or teachers of politics that they should be as exact or neutral as the traditional teacher of mathematics or grammar. We must not try to impose on the teaching of politics a degree of abstractness or bogus neutrality which it cannot stand. But we *can* bring to its study auxiliaries that are not so easily called on by the outside world. First of all we must bring the aid of history. This university has wisely provided for the case of any professor holding this chair who might be tempted to deny this, by attaching him to the History Board in the first place as well as to the Board of Economics and Politics. But even were there not this legal bond, there is the bond imposed by the nature of the study. 'History is past politics', said a Cambridge professor. He was only very partially right, but present politics is always at least half history. It is natural and, indeed, right that we should regret this, for the history that is present politics is mainly composed of envy, malice and all uncharitableness. But we must understand the world before we can hope to change it and that is our world. It is useless merely to rail against it. We must use good history, scholarly history, to drive out bad; we may be sure that there are all the devils possible already in possession and that the broom of historical scholarship will do something to make the house of nations more habitable.

Then we must bring to our students' minds—and perpetually recall to our own—those great minds of the past who have pondered the perennial problems of man in society and in the state. Their relevance is not that they give us blue prints, but that they make us see, and feel, and think in a fashion that our unaided faculties would not enable us to do. The young are more likely to appreciate the dictum of a late master of Trinity that denies infallibility even to youth, when that lesson is taught them by Plato or Burke, than when it is taught them by a living and palpably misguided mortal like a professor.

The mind of a great thinker of the past may suddenly illuminate the mind, not only of the average man, but of the very exceptional man as, on their own testimony, the *Republic* did for Mr Shaw and Mr Wells. And when these great minds of the past are illuminated by a great scholar in the present, as Plato and Aristotle were by my predecessor, there is hardly any need to justify the teaching of politics in this exalted and elevating sense.

But there are other academic aids to breeding in the young more understanding of the world they very reasonably want to change. Although it was necessity, not any prevision of self-improvement, that led to the postponement to 1945 of an inaugural lecture that should have been delivered in 1939, that delay has been, for me at any rate, of great value. I held then the general views I hold now, but my views as to the scope and method of the study of politics have been altered and, I naturally think, improved. I am by equipment, by temperament and by limitations a student of political institutions. I am incapable of changing, of becoming a political philosopher or a philosophical historian. But I have learned in the past six years, by non-academic work, by reflection and by reading, even by writing, that the student of political institutions must be much more than that. He must be purged of the idea that political institutions exist in a vacuum or that they can be understood apart from other institutions. That, as I have suggested, was the great error of the public-spirited, highly intelligent, and highly effective makers of the modern liberal tradition. Politics could not be separated from many non-political habits and institutions. New political institutions could at best be grafted, they could not merely be soldered on.

The realization of this truth would not be helpful or encouraging if we had no more means of studying these related social institutions than we had a hundred years ago, in the prematurely confident days of Bentham, Comte, Marx and other founders of great and influential schools of political and social doctrine. But we are, in fact, much better equipped to understand society and mankind than our great predecessors were. It is only necessary to turn to the anthropology, the psychology, the sociology of a century ago to see how much that seems commonplace to us was then unknown. For good or ill, Freud and Frazer, Marx and Darwin, Maine and Maitland have passed by. The organization of primitive society is far better known; the survival in our society of primitive elements is far better realized. We shrink from the simply rational explanation; we shrink too much I feel, but we have learned that we see (all philosophical scepticism apart) very darkly indeed through the imperfect glass left us by our ancestors. The full enlightenment, we know to-day, is still far ahead of us; it may be permanently ahead of us.

But this 'scepticism of the instrument', to borrow a phrase from Mr Wells, should not and need not reduce us to a resigned acceptance of our inheritance. We can, if we like, fall back on what American sociologists call the 'mores' or, more pedantically, the 'folkways' and, in a new and debased form of determinism, assume readily that we cannot alter them, we can only accept them, describe them, classify and explain them. So Indian sociologists a century ago (had they existed then) might have passively regarded Suttee or Thuggee. So did not Lord William Bentinck or his energetic 'brains trust', young Mr Macaulay late of Trinity.

There is no need for passivity or pessimism and it is my suspicion that the passivity or pessimism, in most exponents of the doctrine of the practical impossibility even of gradualness, has more temperamental than strictly intellectual roots. But the study of society and of man, of the institutions, the traditions, the historical conditions that limit and impose direction on purely political activity, is certainly far more possible to-day than it has ever been in human history. And a university school of politics, should one come into existence, would be bound to take a far wider view of the content of its teaching and researches than a mere professor of Political Science can afford to do. All that he can do is to avert his eyes from the lavish provision for such related studies in the great American universities, and return to his own narrower field.

Politics in the university sense can be taught, can be researched on. The politician in the university sense has the duty, in his teaching and writing, in his encouragement of the teaching and writing of others, to import into this double activity as much of the standards of university teaching and research as the mixed and troublesome nature of his subject will permit. As the politician himself is the specialist in not being a specialist, the academic politician must suffer the qualms that beset the practitioner of a slightly suspect mystery. He must not worry if he is called a bone-setter, *if* he can be sure that he has at least once set even a small bone. He may be well advised to stay out of politics, national or university, and I gather from the late Professor Cornford that the rigours of the game are as great in King's Parade or the Senate House as in Westminster or Tammany Hall.

But his main duty will be to teach and exemplify a view of politics once advanced by a then obscure, practising politician in face of a great national crisis. 'If we could first know where we are, and whither we are tending, we could better judge what to do, and how to do it.' What Abraham Lincoln said, in his first great speech, seems banal enough. But platitudinous as it is, it is a platitude to be repeated and insinuated into the public mind in every generation and in every crisis. If, as Chesterton said, 'the world will never be made safe for democracy, it is a dangerous trade', the main reason is that the platitudes of politics are forever being forgotten, the forts of folly being rebuilt with formidable speed. The university contribution to politics must often take the dull form of reiterating old truth; it can also take the form of developing new and deeper understanding of those truths and, lastly, it can take the form of teaching, by example, that it matters a great deal with what cannon and what ammunition

·you assail the forts of folly. The example of the other studies of this university and of all other true *studia generalia* may, and I hope will, teach this terribly threatened generation that more permanent victories are won by clearer heads and cleaner hands than the world, left to itself, will suggest to the practising politician that he should use.

NOTES

1. Sir Ernest Barker, *Reflections on Government,* p. 414.

4

Professor G. D. H. Cole

SCOPE AND METHOD IN SOCIAL AND POLITICAL THEORY

Social and Political Theory is a subject (or should I say two subjects?) upon which centre great, and sometimes acrimonious, disputes. The very word 'theory' is an attempt to steer a middle course, and is apt to displease the votaries both of 'Social and Political Philosophy' and of 'Social and Political Science'. If I were made to choose between calling my subject 'Philosophy' and calling it 'Science' I should unhesitatingly choose 'Philosophy'; but I am very much happier in being allowed to call it simply 'Theory'. It is my business as Professor to contemplate the world of social and political affairs and the concepts which belong to that world. I am left free to choose my own way of contemplation—my own method—and I have no predecessors in my office, which is a new one, to tie me down or compel me to any act of defiant reinterpretation of my field of study or of the right and proper way of studying in that field. For that very reason, I am under something of an obligation to explain, if I can, what I am trying to do. Such is the purpose of this lecture—not dogmatism about what anyone else ought to do or to attempt, but explanation, as clear and simple as I can make it, of my own notions of how I can best try to make myself useful.

First, then, I am concerned not only with Political but also with Social Theory. What is this word 'Social' intended to mean, and what do I mean it to mean, in relation to my own work? It could be taken to mean something *distinct* from 'Political', in the sense of the one excluding the other; or something *wider* than 'Political', in the sense of including it and much besides; or something *narrower,* in the sense in which social politics are sometimes spoken of as a branch of politics. Which of these meanings am I to take as my starting-point?

I shall take the widest, according to which 'Social' is the adjective of 'society', and 'society' signifies the entire complex of human relations wherever they transcend the purely personal and private

47

sphere, so as to become elements in the life of communities and of that greater community in the making, which is mankind. This does not mean that I shall be able to leave out the sphere of personal and private relations, but that I shall concern myself with it directly only in its institutional aspects, in which it becomes part of the life of 'society', as well as of the lives of the individuals of whom, in their public and private relations, 'society' is made up. Thus I am not concerned with a mother's love for her child except to the extent to which this love is part of the family, an institution with which I am necessarily very much concerned. The extent to which private and personal relations are incorporated into institutions obviously differs from society to society, and from time to time; and there are accordingly no fixed boundaries between the relations which come within and those which remain outside the field of social studies. But the degree of 'institutionalization'—an evil word, but I know not how to avoid it—furnishes a rough-and-ready test.

My subject, then, as 'Social Theory', covers the whole field of institutions—or so I interpret it. But that is not saying much, unless I can make clear what I mean by 'institutions'. Here again the frontiers are undefined, but the general meaning, I hope, is not. I mean by 'institutions' anything that forms part of the effective framework of a 'society', and is recognized as doing so, not necessarily with approval, but in fact. Evidently, as 'societies' change, growing, developing, or decaying, their institutions change too. Some things that were institutions cease to be so: new institutions arise and force their way to recognition, often in face of keen resistances. At any time, if change is coming about, some things are becoming institutions and others ceasing to be institutions. There is, however, a difference between the two processes. A thing that is becoming an institution of a society usually begins by developing as an institution of some element in that society, rather than of the society as a whole; whereas a thing that is ceasing to be an institution of the whole society may retain its institutional character in relation to some elements of that society, but may also live on for a long while as an atrophied institution of the whole society, retaining its status because of its history, but losing all its potency in the society's daily life. I shall confine my examples to quite modern times, though they could be drawn from any age. In the nineteenth century in western Europe Trade Unionism and Co-operation were both becoming institutions of whole societies; but they did this by becoming first institutions of the working classes and only thereafter forcing their way towards recognition by the whole societies in which they grew up. On the other hand, in a number of societies the institution of hereditary nobility shrank from being a recognized institution of the entire society into being one recognized only within certain limited social groups. This applies most of all in France; but to a less extreme degree it applies in a good many other countries.

Institutions are of more than one type. Sometimes the institution takes the form of an association with a definite membership and constitutional structure. In this country Parliament, the Church of England and the various Dissenting Churches, the Trade Union and Co-operative Movements, the main political parties, the universities, and the leading professional institutes are all institutions of this associative type. But there are other institutions which, though they are of course related to persons, are in essence impersonal— monogamous marriage, freedom of inheritance, freedom of association, freedom of the press, monarchy, Bank Holidays, the rule of the road, the pound sterling, to mention only a few. Usually it takes time for a thing to become an institution, of either type. New associations, new ways of acting, become institutions at once only under very exceptional circumstances—for example, on the morrow of a really catastrophic revolution. They become so because a people cannot do without institutions, and if a large proportion of its institutions is swept away, the process of creating new ones has to be speeded up. In the Russian Revolution of 1917 the Soviets became an institution practically at once, though we must not forget that the way had been prepared for them by their appearance in the abortive Revolution of 1905. The Räte which appeared in Germany in 1918 did not become an institution: there was no such holocaust of old institutions in Germany as to make the necessary vacuum.

I have said that institutions are of two types. Perhaps I should have said rather that they are all of one kind, but can incorporate themselves in two different ways. Parliament is not only an institution: it is also part of the machinery of government, based on the principle of association. Marriage is not only an institution, but also a legally sanctioned form of relationship between persons. Certain things are institutions, in the sense of possessing an institutional quality; but that does not prevent them from being what they are in other respects. Indeed, the institutional quality is adjectival rather than substantive. It is a quality attached to certain things which stand significantly for certain elements in the organized habits and values of the society in which they are found.

I take it, then, that, as a 'Social Theorist', I have to study 'institutions'. But so, evidently, does the Social Anthropologist, whose principal field of study they are. He, like me, is concerned to study institutions in relation to the pattern of community living among peoples, especially primitive peoples, in all parts of the world, and to compare the results of his local studies and derive from them any general conclusions that may emerge—or none, if none do emerge. How, then, am I to mark out my field from his? In practice, quite easily; for he is pre-eminently a field research worker and a sort of scientist, which I am not, and he is concerned primarily with studying how men behave, whereas I am concerned much more with their thoughts in relation to their behaviour. Or, to put the matter another way, he is a collector and analyser of social data, chiefly though not exclusively those of the more primitive societies, and his aim is to arrive at scientific judgements about social behaviour without any attempt to consider the value of the values which form part of the data with which he deals; whereas I use his data, and the conclusions, if any, which he draws from them, primarily for the purpose of evaluating the values of the different societies in accordance with conceptions of value which I myself entertain. For the Social Anthropologist, such concepts as justice, liberty, order, aristocracy, democracy, representation, public spirit, toleration, are merely for use as convenient categories for classification, where they are for use at all. He is not concerned to think of any of these things as good or bad, or as having good and bad aspects. 'Good' and 'bad' are words that do not appear in the Social Anthropologist's professional vocabulary, unless they creep in by inadvertence. Coherence, contradiction, unity, confusion—these are concepts which he can apply. He can seek to descry 'patterns of culture' and can find symmetry here and discordance there. But whether the 'patterns' he finds are good or bad it is not for him, he will tell you, to say. For as a scientist he cannot pass judgements of value involving the concepts of 'good' and 'bad'. 'Murder' is, or should be, as neutral a word for him as 'marriage', when he is acting in his professional capacity as a scientist.

Of course, the Social Anthropologist, being a man as well as a scientist, often finds it hard to live up to this austerity of judgement. He has values, just as much as anybody else; and when he meets with some peculiarly revolting savage custom, he condemns it, just as much as anybody else whose values belong to the same moral order. But this is not the point. *Qua* Social Anthropologist, he does not make such judgements.

Should I make them, in my professional capacity as a Social Theorist? Yes, I should. I have, as I see my task, a dual role to fulfil.

irst, as an historian and recorder of Social Theories, past and present, I have to disentangle in them the foundation of values on which they rest. This involves me in trying to put myself, again and again, into other men's minds (and into the mental climates of other peoples and of other ages) in order to discover the principles of coherent valuation which underlie their social judgements and aspirations and to present as clear pictures as I can of the structure of their social thought in its relation to their social practice. I have to explain what they thought and, as far as possible, how they came to think such thoughts, to embody them in such institutions, or to derive them from such environments as I find in being among them. I have to attempt these tasks, not statically, but so as to show thoughts, institutions, and environments all in motion and to bring out the causal and mutually determinative elements in their development. In this capacity, as historian and as recorder, I am not concerned to judge other people's values by my own, but, like the Social Anthropologist, to enter into other people's mental skins, and to analyse and compare what I find. If this were all I had to do, I should be different from the Social Anthropologist only in studying primarily the social thought of other times and peoples and using the study of institutions only as a means of elucidating their thought— and of course also in focusing my attention mainly on developed rather than on primitive societies, because only in developed societies is the content of social thought written down, systematized, and consciously evaluated. I too should follow, if that were my only task, a quasi-scientific method, and though I should be much concerned with other men's values, I should as far as possible avoid proclaiming valuations of my own.

That, however, is not my only, or even my primary, task as a Social Theorist. When I study past Social Theories, or for that matter the contemporary Social Theories of different societies or of schools of thought to which I do not belong, I do so, not primarily as historian or recorder or for the purpose of analysis and comparison— important as all these are—but for the practical purpose of suggesting to anyone I can influence, and above all to the society to which I belong, what is the right pattern of social thought to guide social action in the circumstances of here and now. This is what all the great Social Theorists of the past have attempted to do; and this is what I am attempting to do. It is not my only task; but it is incomparably my most important, and it directs my approach to all the others.

This means that I have to make, throughout, judgements of value. I have to proclaim certain ends as good, and to denounce others as evil. I have to make for myself a certain picture of man as a social animal, not only as he is but also as he is capable of becoming; and this capacity of becoming has to be conceived, not as undifferentiated capacity for good and evil, but as capacity for good. Of course, my picture has to be made *for* man as he is, and in the circumstances in which he is placed: not for a different kind of person in a different world of nature. I have to deal with possibilities, both immediate and ultimate, and betwixt and between; but among possibilities I am concerned to designate some as desirable and others as undesirable, in accordance with my conceptions of what human aims and qualities are good, and what bad.

What are these conceptions of good and bad with which I work? I will try to state the most elementary, which largely govern the rest. First, on the physical plane, health. Secondly, on the intellectual plane, desire for knowledge, respect for truth, rationality, tolerance. Thirdly, on the aesthetic plane, sensibility, appreciativeness, creative imagination. Fourthly, on the plane of conduct, initiative, organizing capacity, self-control, and, in a man's attitude to others, cheerfulness, comradeliness, co-operativeness, consideration, kindness. Fifthly, on the plane of society itself, as goods to be realized for the individuals through social action, democracy, liberty, social security. These goods are of different kinds, and I realize that some of them have their excesses and perversions and are not therefore good in all their manifestations. Nor do I suppose that my list exhausts all the goods that I should accept as such if they were named. However, as far as they go, believing them to be the goods of most practical importance in relation to the social pattern, I believe those societies to be best which achieve the amplest practicable combination of them.

The possibilities of achieving and combining them are, of course, always limited by the circumstances of any particular society, including its inheritance of both mental and material possessions as well as its relation to other societies and to developing factors in its environment. The relative importance which it can afford to assign to different goods depends on these possibilities; and one good can be pursued more easily in some circumstances and another in others. I therefore arrive at no Utopian conception of a single best of all possible combinations of my different goods: nor do I believe that it is feasible to measure in exact quantities how much of any of them a society either possesses or should seek to achieve. Nor, again, do I believe that they can all be resolved into, or caught up into, a single kind of good, which includes them all. On the contrary, I am sure they can and do conflict, and that there are many possible combinations of them that may be equally worthy of respect, but no combination that is clearly and demonstrably superior to all others. Every society represents a limited 'pattern' of values, and into no possible society can all the good in all the patterns be squeezed. Nor can any society be made up wholly of 'goods'; for every pattern involves disadvantages and an admixture of evils at the points where its goods come into conflict.

I am also well aware that my choice of goods is not made in the cool clear light of eternity, but under the influence both of my day and generation and of my personal predilections. Other men might choose very different goods: Hitler manifestly did. His goods, by my valuation, were largely evils; but other men might choose different lists of goods, including some which I should admit to be goods, but should not think important enough to include, and perhaps others which I should regard as fictitious, though not positively evil. My list of goods is both personal to me and drawn up under the influence of the scales of value which exist in the society I have been brought up in, or were made to seem important to me by my education and study. My list will not quite coincide with anyone else's list; nor do I expect anyone at all to find it even moderately satisfactory in a hundred years' time—or indeed any Chinaman or Indian to find it so even now. It is *my* list; but it is also a list which I hope and believe may be *broadly* satisfactory to a good number of my contemporaries in my own society and in other societies not too different from it to be capable of thinking together about social affairs.

But how do I know that any of these things on my list are good? Or rather, even if I do know it, how can I set out to persuade anyone else that I am right? I cannot, unless I can get him to agree to at any rate some common valuations. If I say 'I think we ought to give other people as much pleasure and as little pain as possible', and he says 'Why?', I am at a loss. I can only try again, perhaps by saying 'I think every human being has a right to as much well-being and happiness as is consistent with the well-being and happiness of others', and he again says 'Why?', there is no point in continuing the conversation. I could of course answer 'Because acting on that assumption conduces to biological survival'; but I should be sorry to do so, for if the argument convinced him we should be at worse cross-purposes than ever. I should then have to ask him 'Why do you think it is good to survive?' and that is a question to which I do not myself know any answer.

I know that it is good to be kind, tolerant, co-operative, comradely, creative, and so on because the experience of these things, and of their opposites, in myself and in others, induces in me the sense of goodness and badness; and I am confirmed in these attributions of value by finding that I share them with most of the people I like and respect. Beyond that I cannot go. How important I think any particular one of them to be I can see to depend on the social pattern, and I can imagine, or discover in my studies, social patterns in which any of them are held in scant esteem. I draw a distinction, however, between not esteeming a thing and esteeming its opposite. Some of my goods may not be esteemed in a particular society because that society has chosen a pattern which finds no room for these goods but does find large scope for other things which I recognize as good. I do not therefore condemn it, even if it is not my 'cup of tea'. I do condemn a society whose pattern puts into the forefront of esteem things I regard as evil; but I should not hope to be able to convince a devout admirer of such a pattern that his goods are bads. It was of no more use to argue with Hitler than to 'appease' him.

'Social Theory', then, I regard as an essentially normative study, of which the purpose is to tell people how to be socially good, and to aim at social goods and avoid social evils. It is not, however, for that reason a branch of Ethics; for its concern is necessarily with the means to be employed in seeking social goods through social institutions. It has, therefore, a large technical field of its own to explore; for it has to find out what sorts of social institution and what combinations of social institutions will be most helpful towards the pursuit of social goods in the general environment and climate of values appertaining to the broad civilization to which the theorist belongs, and for which he formulates his doctrine. He can theorize effectively only within the limits set by his climate of values: he can try to modify or develop these values here or there, but I know of only one way—a sort of inversion—by which he can construct a radically different pattern. He must build with the bricks his civilization provides for him, though he can turn the bricks any way up he pleases—and though they are not really bricks, but living things, with a capacity for internal change and development as well as for change of relative position. However we describe them, they are the materials he must use, and it is his task to devise the best institutional instruments for moulding them to serve the advancement of practicable goods.

This, it may be said, is to bring Social Theory very close to the realm of Psychology as well as to that of Ethics; for the materials the theorist must use are in men's minds as well as in the external world in which men live. This is true; and it is a matter of great contemporary importance to mark out, as far as we can, the respective fields of Psychology, Ethics, and Social Theory. Psychology in general is now generally regarded as a scientific study, using the methods of observation and, where it can, experiment to arrive at conclusions about what men (and animals) mentally are, and are capable of, without passing judgements of moral value, but not without taking note of the judgements of moral value which men (and animals?) do actually make. It has a branch, Social Psychology, of which the field and the objectives are much less clearly determined. Social Psychology is most often understood as meaning the study of mental processes in their social aspects; and, if this is what it is, there is evidently no line to be drawn between it and General Psychology, because most mental processes, if not all, have a social aspect and character. There is, however, a quite distinct field, which Social Psychologists sometimes touch upon but seldom explore—the field of group deliberation and action. In this field, though only individuals can think, the thinking individuals think and exchange thoughts with a view to acting not merely individually but together— and often not at all individually, but only as a group. The phenomena of such associated action and group action afford, I believe, no basis at all for the dangerous notion of a 'group mind'; but they are none the less interesting and important. Social acticn is largely, though not exclusively, associative action or group action; and the behaviour of men is undoubtedly different when they act in these ways from what it is when they act individually, however much they may then act from social motives and under social influences.

If we are concerned in Social Theory to consider how the institutional forms of society can be so shaped as to further social goods, it is of the greatest importance for us to understand institutional behaviour, not only as the behaviour of individuals acting under institutional influences, but also as the behaviour of individuals acting together through institutions—which I hope I may be allowed, without exposing myself to the charge of believing in a 'group mind', to call for short the 'behaviour' of the institutions themselves. It is important to know the differences between individual action and the action of committees, boards, cabinets, parliaments, soviets, and other representative or corporate agencies. This ought to be either Social Psychology, or a study on its own, or a part of some other recognized study; but it is still largely an uncharted sea, despite the work of Graham Wallas, Robert Michels, Ostrogorsky, and a few others, and despite many hints about it scattered elsewhere. How far does it fall within the field of Social Theory?

As field work it does not. It is not my job, but, in its political aspects, rather, my colleague's, now that the former Chair of 'Theory and Institutions' has been cut into two. It is, in effect, a vital part of the direct study of institutions, and one which has been hitherto badly neglected. It requires a technique of its own, taking much from Psychology and from Social Psychology in the other sense of the term, but devising its special apparatus of investigation appropriate to the study of group behaviour and especially to that characteristic form of such behaviour in which one man or a few act as the executants of the decisions taken by a number, who are themselves often purporting to decide as the representatives of a still larger number. Study of this kind of 'filtered' action, where the 'filter' has a will of its own, is of peculiar importance in relation to the real efficacy of the mechanisms employed for advancing social goods; and I, as a

Social Theorist, should wish to be provided with data about it as full and as carefully observed and sorted as those which I look to General Psychology to provide me with in the field of industrial behaviour. If these data are not forthcoming, I may have to go and look for them myself, as many a student has had to step outside his subject to enter fields, essential to yield the data he needs, where no adequate provision has been made for specialist exploration.

There is, of course, some provision. The field worker in Social Anthropology does regard it as very much his business to study institutional behaviour. But he does so mainly in the field of primitive society, whereas what I want, for my normative purpose, is primarily a study of such behaviour in the societies belonging to the pattern of civilization in which I live. I can pick up something from the 'Middletown' type of study, but not nearly enough; something also from the students of political institutions who have allowed themselves to be influenced by modern developments in Anthropology and Psychology. I should, I suppose, get even more from the Sociologists of the Mannheim school; but they have not in fact done much about this particular problem, except in relation to the single issue of *élites* and leadership. Furthermore, the students of Political Institutions fail me because they are concentrating their attention on a particular type of institution, whereas my concern as a Social Theorist is with social institutions of every kind.

This brings me at last to the other half of my office, as Professor of *Political*, as well as of *Social*, Theory. There are no doubt some in this University who think I ought to regard myself primarily as Professor of Political Theory, and to treat the 'Social' aspect as a mere frill. I think I have made it clear that this is not my view of what I have been appointed to do. I am well aware that it is part of the traditional climate not only of Oxford, but of academic teaching and thinking in Great Britain, to make the State the point of focus for the consideration of men in their social relations. It is sometimes said that we derive this tradition from the Greeks; but that, I think, is quite untrue. *Polis* does not mean 'State'; and in translating it as 'State' we are twisting Greek thought to suit our own patterns of thinking. Our preoccupation with 'the State' as the central conception in the theory of Society has, I think, arisen rather in this way. In the Middle Ages nobody thought like that. Nobody could; for all social thinking had to take account of two main points of focus, of which one was the Church and the other—not 'the State' or even the Emperor, but the much more complex set of institutions embodying the secular powers. 'The State' emerged as a point (or rather a series of points) for the concentration of these several powers; and thereafter great battles were fought, in the realm of theory as well as in that of practical affairs, between Church and State. In the course of these battles the church was worsted and broken; and first in Machiavelli and again in Hobbes, Political Theory took shape as pre-eminently the Theory of the State. Social thinking was secularized, except among the Catholics, and Protestant determination to repel the 'Kingdom of Darkness' led to an exclusive concentration on the secular State as the repository of Sovereignty and, as it took a more democratic turn, of the people's will. The main course of Political Theory in the eighteenth and nineteenth centuries reflected this attitude, which fitted in well not only with the theories of nationalism and national independence but also with the economico-social theories of *laissez-faire*. For the *laissez-faire* thinkers believed in an order of nature which would shape all things (except a few) for the best if nobody interfered with it; and the only great exception they allowed was the preservation of 'order', which involved the regulation of the rights of property. The State thus stood out, in its police capacity, as an isolated instance of the need for regulation in a world otherwise best left to the 'government' of natural forces; and accordingly 'the State' called for a theory of its own quite apart from any other forms of human association or group action. Indeed, other forms were apt to be looked on with suspicion, as, potentially at least, conspiracies against the 'natural order', and therefore to be kept down and either prevented or strictly circumscribed by the State as the guardian of that order.

That world of *laissez-faire* is dead, and so is the conception which accompanied it of the all but all-embracing natural order, which it was regarded as man's affair to obey and not to mould to the service of his ends. The apartness of the State from all other forms of human grouping and association dies with these notions and historical conditions. Our century requires not a merely Political Theory, with the State as its central concept and the conflict between the Individual and the State as its central problem, but a wider Social Theory within which these concepts and relations can find their appropriate place. We have to start out, not from the contrasted ideas of the atomized individual and of the State, but from man in all his complex groupings and relations, partially embodied in social institutions of many sorts and kinds, never in balanced equilibrium, but always changing, so that the pattern of loyalties and of social behaviour changes with it. This brings us back to a much more real kind of man than the social atom of Hobbes or of Herbert Spencer. It brings us to men who are not isolated individuals, but members one of another in a host of different ways, and behave differently as different loyalties and associations come uppermost. It makes the stuff of society seem much more malleable for good and evil, and emphasizes the diversity of the influences by which society can be moulded, as well as the immense importance of all the mechanisms by means of which the moulding can be done. For this reason, it suggests to some the totalitarian conception—the idea that everything must be captured for the State—because it makes plain that all forms of social organization, and not merely the political forms, are of vital importance in making a society what it is, and as driving forces in settling its future. But it also suggests anti-totalitarianism, which I call 'Pluralism', as a recognition of the positive value of this diversity, and a repudiation of the Idealist notion that all values are ultimately aspects of a single value, which must therefore find embodiment in a universal institution, and not in the individual beings who alone have, in truth, the capacity to think, to feel, and to believe, and singly or in association to express their thoughts, feelings, and beliefs in actions which further or obstruct well-being—their own and others'.

I have no time left to develop this theme now. It will be the central inspiration of everything I have to say as occupant of this chair, except when I am acting as an expositor of other people's views and of their historical development. It has obviously influenced the notions of scope and method which I have put forward in this lecture. I start with people, who are many, in their social relations, which are manifold; and so I end—with the many, and not with the 'One'. 'EK ΔΙΟC 'ΑΡΧωΜΕΘΑ ΚΑΙ ε ΙC ΔΙΑ ΑΗΓΕΤΕ ΜωϹΑΙ. But my Zeus is men.

5

Professor K. C. Wheare

THE MACHINERY OF GOVERNMENT

'The distinctive task of our age is not to extend scientific achievement but to improve the regulative mechanism of government in its widest sense.' With these words my predecessor in this chair concluded his Alfred Marshall lectures at Cambridge in 1933 upon *The Framework of an Ordered Society*. Sir Arthur Salter's training and experience had led him to an understanding of the nature of government more surely than the traditional training of a professor might have done. He had been a distinguished civil servant—but not merely a British civil servant, for he had entered as a pioneer into the field, first of Allied, and then of international administration. And his civil service experience, national and international, had not been confined to the sphere of politics narrowly understood; the principal problems with which he had been concerned were economic. Nor was his experience confined to governmental or inter-governmental administration. He had proved himself an impartial and successful conciliator in disputes arising in the world of trade and industry—I name only his chairmanship of the Road and Rail Conference in 1932.

Sir Arthur Salter brought this great experience to the service of the study of government in Oxford on his election in 1934 to the Gladstone Professorship of Political Theory and Institutions. Succeeding one much loved in this place, W. G. S. Adams, he became the second holder of the chair. And he was to be the last. For in 1940 the University decided that the duties of the Gladstone Professor of Political Theory and Institutions should be divided between two professorships. The scope of the Gladstone chair was restricted and it was renamed the Gladstone Professorship of Government and Public Administration. At the same time, partly by the generosity of All Souls College, there was established a Chichele Professorship of Social and Political Theory, a chair the filling of which was deferred until the appointment of G. D. H. Cole in 1944. In the new Gladstone chair, however, Sir Arthur Salter continued to hold office until 1944. To his varied administrative experience he added, from 1937, that of membership of the House of Commons as the Independent Junior Burgess of Oxford University.

In the years that preceded the war undergraduates and tutors alike admired the clarity and penetration of his analysis of political institutions and respected a judgement founded upon great experience, great common sense, and a great idealism of the most practical kind. When the war came, it was possible to expect that Sir Arthur Salter could be spared for his duties in Oxford, but we have watched with admiration the services—of necessity still but partly known—which he performed once more in that wider range of national and international administration in which he is by nature at home. It was with regret that we learned in 1944 that the claims of these public duties had compelled him to decide that he must resign the Gladstone chair. But he is far from lost to Oxford, for this College has proceeded to re-elect him to a fellowship and the University has re-elected him to the House of Commons. For my own part I hope he may continue long to enjoy both offices, so that I may avail myself to the full of the knowledge and counsel of one who is so distinguished a practitioner of the arts of government and public administration.

I cannot pass to the subject of my lecture without a reference to one who during the greater part of the war years has acted as Deputy for the Gladstone professor in his absence—R. C. K. Ensor, who retires from his fellowship at Corpus on 31 December next. He, more than anyone, has helped to maintain political studies in Oxford during the war, and we regret the great loss of one whose active mind, enormous knowledge, and trenchant manners in speech and argument delighted and instructed us all.

I have chosen as the subject of my Inaugural Lecture a small aspect of that topic of 'the regulative mechanism of government' of which my predecessor spoke in his Marshall lectures. It is with the machinery of government in the United Kingdom that I am mainly concerned, and with but one aspect of that. Yet the subject is so large that in one lecture I may do no more than make a few dogmatic assertions.

The form of government which exists in this country today may be described with substantial accuracy as a parliamentary bureaucracy. It has been parliamentary for many centuries; it has been bureaucratic for little more than half a century. These two predominant elements in our government are not disconnected. They are organically joined by the institution of the Cabinet, whose members have the double function of controlling both Parliament and bureaucracy.

The parliamentary element in our machinery of government extends from the top to the bottom of its structure, from the House of Commons, through county, county borough, district, and parish councils. It embodies at least two great axioms: first, that the ultimate controlling power in the last resort over the operations of government is with the whole body of the people; second, that 'talk' is an essential element to good government.

> I know not how a representative assembly can more usefully employ itself than in talk, when the subject of talk is the great public interests of the country. . . . A place where every interest and shade of opinion in the country can have its cause even passionately pleaded, in the face of the government and of all other interests and opinions, can compel them to listen, and either comply, or state clearly why they do not, is in itself, if it answered no other purpose, one of the most important political institutions that can exist anywhere, and one of the foremost benefits of free government.[1]

The bureaucratic element in our government extends similarly from Whitehall to the county halls, the town halls, and the parish halls. It embodies the maxim that 'every branch of public administration is a skilled business',[2] and it is accepted in our system that at every stage in the transaction of public business—in finding facts upon which policy is to be formulated, in formulating policy, in passing it into law, in applying the law to particular cases, and in reviewing the operation of policy—trained officials, expert in their own branch of government, must be associated with the representatives of the whole body of the people. Parliament without bureaucracy would be halt and lame; bureaucracy without Parliament would be deaf and blind.

I believe that this system of parliamentary bureaucracy, in which both elements are organically integrated and controlled by a cabinet system, is the ideally best form of democratic government for a modern industrial state. I need hardly add that I do not mean by this that the parliamentary bureaucracy is a practicable and eligible form of government for all modern industrial states, but that where the circumstances exist in which it is practicable and eligible—and they are rarely and with difficulty obtained—it is attended with the greatest amount of beneficial consequences. Yet it is also, of all forms of government, the most difficult to work well and the most liable to decline. The balance between the parliamentary and the bureaucratic elements essential to its working is so easy to disturb, and its nature so easily becomes degenerate and perverted.

The machinery of government in a parliamentary bureaucracy must, then, be constantly under review, and never more so than at a time like the present when we emerge from a great war to undertake the formidable tasks of government in a period of reconstruction. We must regret that, so far, we have not had a document comparable to the report of Lord Haldane's Machinery of Government Committee at the close of the last war, which still illuminates the path of the student today. But unofficial students have investigated the subject and disturbed our minds—I mention only one, Dr. C. K. Allen's *Law and Orders*—while the House of Commons itself has set on foot an inquiry into its procedure. In the United States a similar disquiet is apparent, well expressed recently in two books, among many— Thomas K. Finletter's *Can Representative Government do the Job?* and Merlo J. Pusey's *Big Government—Can we Control it?*, not to mention such an extreme attack as Ludwig von Mises's *Bureaucracy*.

In most discussions of the subject it is clear that the prevailing anxiety is lest the bureaucratic is overwhelming the parliamentary element in our government. Indeed, so great is the dislike of these tendencies that to use the word 'bureaucracy' to describe the public service in this country is considered a partial criticism if not an insult. Yet I have chosen the word deliberately. Bureaucracy, pure and simple, is an inferior form of government. Indeed, it is almost the worst. Parliamentary bureaucracy can be a very good form of government, but it can so easily decline. That we may be reminded continually of the dangers of decline always present in this element of our government, I have retained the use of the word 'bureaucracy'.

These dangers are well known. 'The trained official hates the rude, untrained public. He thinks that they are stupid, ignorant, reckless— that they cannot tell their own interest—that they should have the leave of the office before they do anything.' Bureaucracy 'tends to over-government'.[3] Worse even than the trained official is the half-trained or untrained official, so familiar to us in war time. And there is no one who has not experienced some example of the indolence, the incompetence, the obstruction, the arrogance, the ignorance, the unimaginativeness of some bureaucrat in the national or the local civil service. Yet with all this, which I know and admit, I believe I must say a word in defence of the bureaucracy.

To start with, let it be remembered that there are far more bureaucrats outside the government service than inside it. The bureaucrat—the administrator at his desk, the official who directs, organizes, and co-ordinates, the 'manager' of James Burnham's stimulating essay, *The Managerial Revolution*—is an essential element in modern society. The great insurance companies and banks, the transport companies, the fuel and power undertakings, the chemical industry, the organizations of employers and employees, all employ bureaucrats on a large scale. They must if they are to regulate their affairs. The guess has been made that by the end of the war one in every twenty-five adults in this country was a government official;[4] I am prepared to guess that another five out of the twenty-five were bureaucrats not in the government service, but performing duties of the kind which the various grades of state bureaucrats perform. And while I am guessing I would add that it is likely that there are more bureaucrats in the City of London than in Whitehall.

To say this is not to excuse the faults of government officials. It is but to say that bureaucracy is a part and an essential part of our whole social organization; it is not a phenomenon peculiar to government activity and control. Nor are the defects of bureaucracy found only in government officials. The simple citizen who has put a simple question upon the law to his solicitor has received from that arch-bureaucrat, that embodiment of all the virtues and vices of bureaucracy, an answer which rivals in obscurity and qualification any letter which a civil servant has sent. Let it be remembered that, since the civil service began to use white tape,[5] the chief public functionary who uses red tape is the solicitor. Nor would anyone who has dealt with a large economic organization like an insurance company lack experience of those faults which are often thought to be solely exhibited by government officials. The fact is that, with the increased technical complication of modern production and with the growth of monopoly or quasi-monopoly in economic and social life, bureaucracy has grown generally and has begun to exhibit its faults generally.

And it is here that we see the reason why the state must have its bureaucracy. If the state is to be something more than a weak and inferior competitor with the other institutions in society, it must have a bureaucracy large enough and skilled enough to hold its own with, if not to control, these other institutions. For my part I believe the state must be able to control society, and if it is to do so, it must have an appropriate bureaucracy. The history of the last seventy years has seen a rapid growth of bureaucracy in all forms of social institutions in this country, not only economic. It is a development of much greater interest and importance, I believe, even than the development of a state bureaucracy. Yet it has had no detailed study. James Burnham's *The Managerial Revolution* has given us a glimpse of the fascinating field of inquiry that is there. I hope that it will be studied. None the less, the broad picture is clear. There has been admittedly a growth of state bureaucracy, but it is a growth which is consequential upon the wider and fundamental development of bureaucracy in society as a whole.

But the severest critics of governmental bureaucracy are usually ready to admit that some bureaucracy is necessary. They think there should be little of it—too little in my view. They would be inclined to say to me: 'What you say about the wide extent of bureaucracy is true. But remember this: No bureaucrat outside a government department has anything like the power which a government official has.' There is something here. The powers to legislate which Parliament has delegated to government departments in this country are wider than anything that it has given to, say, a railway company—powers even to alter Acts of Parliament themselves. In the light of these powers the state bureaucracy is, among non-state bureaucracies, as a leviathan but as a leviathan among whales.

Yet this great leviathan, even if its task is to control great whales, must itself be controlled, if our government is to be in truth a *parliamentary* bureaucracy. Nothing that I have said so far denies this; it has been intended to put the problem in proper perspective. It is time to ask now: Is our bureaucracy triumphant? Are we, in the phrase of F. von Hayek, on *The Road to Serfdom?* Or, to use less tendentious language, has the fear expressed by the Machinery of Government Committee's Report in 1918 been realized that 'a more efficient public service may expose the State to the evils of bureaucracy unless the reality of parliamentary control is so enforced as to keep pace with any improvement in departmental methods'?[6]

The Cabinet is intended to be the principal instrument of control. Its members are chosen to control the bureaucracy because they have the confidence of the House of Commons. Their function is well established. 'It is not the business of a Cabinet Minister to work his department. His business is to see that it is properly worked.'[7] The ideal Minister is one who corrects, controls, and above all animates his department. He must be a man of sufficient intelligence, enough various knowledge, and enough miscellaneous experience to represent effectually general sense in opposition to bureaucratic sense.[8] That is the ideal. And it is remarkable how often we come near it.

It is well to remember that the good or very good Minister can be such only if he is served by a good or very good bureaucracy. The ideal bureaucrat in our system is not that fabulous man who can prepare an unanswerable case for or against any policy that is proposed. He is the man who can make the best case for and against a policy, who is prepared to indicate his own preference, but who encourages the Minister always to take the initiative and the responsibility for decisions. A bureaucrat who draws out responsibility and initiative from his Minister is near the ideal. Let it never be forgotten that 'energy in the executive is a leading character in the definition of good government',[9] and it is the greatest danger of bureaucracy that it will dissipate its own energy and exhaust or suppress or deflect the energy of its Minister. If the ideal bureaucrat is the man of constructive energy, drawing forth from his Minister or supporting in his Minister initiative and responsibility and courage, the worst bureaucrat is the man of obstructive energy who wears down his Minister with objections and routines. The cardinal sin of bureaucracy is not ignorance, not indolence, not routine, not even timidity or arrogance, but, rivalling even corruption itself, energetic obstruction. Your worst bureaucrat is not an incompetent man but a man of great capacity and energy who devotes those great gifts to the obstruction of policies other than his own and to the destruction of initiative and responsibility. Few Ministers can prevail against him, and he is to be found in all grades of our state bureaucracy, national and local.

Whether individual Ministers succeed or fail in controlling their several departments, there is still the problem of Cabinet control and co-ordination of all the departments. A good Minister and a good bureaucrat may forget the existence of other departments, almost as much as a bad Minister and a bad bureaucrat. The Cabinet must supervise. But this task is not easy. Consider what a Cabinet is like. It consists of a collection of Ministers, most of whom are in charge of departments. Each department is a relatively independent organization, it is strongly organized, its business is great, complicated, and specialized. Its Minister identifies himself with it, be he strong or weak. I believe that we in Oxford can understand the nature of our central government and of the Cabinet more easily than many other people because the departments of that government are, in their independence and corporate spirit, very like our Oxford Colleges, and a Cabinet meeting is much more like a meeting of Heads of Houses with Mr. Vice-Chancellor in the chair than it is like, say, a meeting of a board of directors with the managing director in the chair. The analogy cannot be completely accurate, but it is near the truth.

It has been said that our Cabinets anyhow are too large to provide effective control. In peace time they numbered between twenty and thirty, and the number present, allowing for Ministers not in the Cabinet but summoned for special business, was usually nearer thirty than twenty. How can so large a body effectively and collectively control all government departments? The average Minister will not feel competent to criticize his colleague's affairs, and he will hope that his colleague feels a similar diffidence. And even if it were not so, there is no time for each member of so large a body to take an interest in and discuss his colleague's department. There is much truth in this criticism. The remedy proposed is a smaller Cabinet, to consist, usually, of a few Ministers without departmental duties whose task would be to co-ordinate groups of departments, together with one or two Ministers with departmental duties.

In my view some reduction in the size of the Cabinet from the pre-war figure of between twenty and thirty is advisable, but I do not think that a really small cabinet of from five to seven is practicable or desirable. The analogy between the crisis of war and the crisis of peace-making and reconstruction is not exact. The crisis of war demands a very small Cabinet, because decisions must be taken rapidly, secretly, and frequently. The crisis of peace involves decisions on matters, it may well be, of life and death, but they require deliberation, and they permit of discussion. Nor can it be expected that, when the strain of war is past and party politics have returned, the leaders of any party in power in the House of Commons will submit to decisions being taken on all matters of major importance by half a dozen of their number. Parties in a democratic state will not work in that way.

I believe that a Cabinet of twelve to sixteen is the best number we can choose. It could include the principal leaders of the party and the principal departments of state. Some Ministers not in the Cabinet would be summoned to meetings for particular items of business, and the total number present would come near to twenty. It would be the task of certain members of the Cabinet to co-ordinate the work of a group of departments, not usually as super-Ministers but rather as the chairmen of Cabinet committees of Ministers concerned. It is sometimes suggested that this co-ordinating work should be carried out by Ministers with no or merely nominal departmental duties. There is value in this system, but too much is often expected of it. A Minister without departmental duties is a Minister without a departmental staff, and he confronts on his co-ordinating committee a group of colleagues each one of whom is supported, if not dominated, by a highly organized department, armed to the teeth with arguments and evidence in support of its case. A Minister with great drive and skill may achieve much co-ordination, but there will be a limit to what he can do. Experience of the work of two co-ordinating Ministers, virtually without departments, illustrates this—the Minister for the Co-ordination of Defence in the years from 1936 to 1940, and the Minister of Reconstruction in the years from 1943 to 1945.

In a Cabinet of this smaller size something more like collective responsibility can be attained. Departments can be controlled and co-ordinated; the obstructive bureaucrat or Minister can be overborne or animated; the zealous bureaucrat and Minister can be encouraged, but not too much. The great evil of departmentalism, the refusal to collaborate or co-operate, can be attacked; and that other evil of over inter-departmentalism, the tendency to collaborate and confer too much, can be curbed. There is some chance of this when a Cabinet is small enough for the majority of Ministers, at any rate, to take part in the discussion and preparation of business.

But a further criticism is heard. You may get Cabinet control of the

bureaucracy, but may you not get also an alliance of Cabinet and
bureaucracy against the House of Commons? Is not one
characteristic of our system 'Cabinet Dictatorship'? And will not a
smaller Cabinet be a more effective instrument of this dictatorship?
This interpretation of the working of our machinery of government
is, I believe, incorrect. It is a popular misinterpretation and I will take
time to correct it. If the record of the House of Commons is
considered in the years of this century, it will be seen that at no time
has it been a mere voting machine for the government of the day. It is
true that governments have been rarely defeated. But that is not an
adequate test. The test is the extent to which governments have
adapted themselves to the wishes of the House and have accepted
amendments proposed to them. When this record is considered, the
charge of 'Cabinet Dictatorship' is seen in its true proportions.

Consider first the decade before this last war. In the years from
1929 to 1931 a minority Labour government was in office and the
supremacy of the House of Commons over the Cabinet was only too
apparent. In 1930 a Coal Bill was greatly modified to meet the
objections of the Liberal party; an Education Bill was dropped, later
reintroduced in a different form, and then passed in the House only
after considerable amendment; a Consumers' Council Bill was
introduced, but encountered so much opposition that it was dropped.
In 1931 a similar story can be told. A Trade Unions Bill suffered so
many setbacks in committee that it was withdrawn; and an Electoral
Reform Bill was amended.

Since the general election of 1931 the government of this country
has always had a substantial majority and it might be expected that
Cabinet control would be complete. But the facts show otherwise. In
1932 the government left the Sunday Performances (Regulation) Bill
to a free vote of the House; it was carried, but opposition in the
committee stage became so strong that the Bill was dropped. In the
same year the government accepted amendments of some importance
to the Wheat Bill. In 1933 concessions were made on the budget
proposals, in regard to taxation of heavy fuel oils and the control of
the Exchange Equalization Fund; the contributions of local
authorities proposed under the Unemployment Bill were reduced,
and the provisions of the Newfoundland Bill were amended so that
the constitution of the Dominion was suspended, not abrogated—all
as the result of pressure by the House of Commons. In 1934 the
Incitement to Disaffection Bill was drastically modified as a result, in
part, of pressure in the Commons, and in the same year a whole set of
unemployment assistance regulations proposed by the government
had to be withdrawn and amended through protests in the House. In
1935 the resignation of Sir Samuel Hoare was directly due to

opposition in the House to the proposals for a settlement of the Italo-Abyssinian dispute with which he was connected; the Government of India Bill received a most critical examination in Committee of the whole House for thirty days and the government went far to meet the views of its Conservative critics. In 1936 a Coal Mines Bill was withdrawn after introduction because it was found unacceptable to the Conservative party. In 1937 the government took the unusual step of withdrawing a part of its budget proposals—the National Defence Contribution; in the same year a steady agitation in the House was directed against the administration of civil aviation, and the Secretary of State for Air, who was in the Lords, later resigned. The Regency Bill, a measure of constitutional importance, was amended in important particulars on the suggestion of private members. In 1938 the Population Statistics Bill and a new Coal Mines Bill were substantially amended and a Milk Bill was withdrawn.

Nor is the record in the years of the war much different: The House that was willing to pass nearly fifty Bills in a few days with hardly any discussion in the week of crisis before and after 3 September 1939, refused on 31 October 1939 to accept the drastic regulations proposed by the Home Secretary under the Emergency Powers Act. Considerable modifications were made in the regulations—though in the case of the famous Regulation 18B they were to be shown less effective than was hoped—and the House approved the revised code on 23 November. Throughout the war there was the same vigilance combined with the same readiness to give the government full powers. In 1940 the Bill to establish special war-zone courts in case of invasion was amended in an important respect, and the scope of the purchase tax was considerably limited in the discussions on the Finance Bill. Protests in the House led to an improvement in the conditions of internees, and to the curtailing of such extravagances as the Ministry of Information's 'silent column'. Criticisms in 1940 of the means-test provisions in the Pensions Bill led, in 1941, to their modification in a new Bill, the Determination of Needs Bill. In 1941, too, the War Damage Bill was amended. Throughout the year there was steady criticism of administration, particularly concerning production, and the appointment of a Minister of Production was pressed. Mr Churchill resisted the proposal, but at the beginning of 1942 he accepted it. In 1942, also, a long agitation of the previous year, to increase the allowances to families of serving men, was at last successful. The government's fuel-rationing scheme was withdrawn in face of protests in the Commons. The House secured also an increase in old-age pensions and in the pay of service men, but in neither case were the increases considered satisfactory. Agitation continued, and in 1943 a further increase was made in pensions. The influence of the House was strikingly illustrated in the discussion of the budget proposals of 1943. As originally introduced they had rejected the 'Pay as you Earn' system of collecting income tax. On pressure from the House the Chancellor agreed to examine the system. He then agreed to adopt it on a limited scale; the House pressed him further, and finally he agreed to extend it to all salary earners. In 1944 the government accepted important amendments to the House of Commons Disqualification Bill, the Town and Country Planning Bill, and the Education Bill. It is true that, on this last Bill, the House was forced, in regard to one amendment—that proposing equal pay for men and women—to eat its words. The government's action in this case was high-handed and contrary to usage. Finally, in 1945, important amendments were accepted to the Requisitioned Land and War Works Bill, and the Family Allowances Bill, on the strong pressure of the Commons.

I have given, perforce, a mere catalogue. But it is a catalogue which could be doubled. It may be said: These are exceptions. They *are* exceptions, and they should be. In our system of government the Cabinet is in office because it can command the confidence of a majority in the House of Commons. It should be exceptional, therefore, that it gives way. But there is a further consideration. Bills are framed to pass. By what amounts to a convention of our constitution most major Bills are not introduced into the House until a thorough consultation of the interests affected by the proposed legislation has been undertaken. Advisory councils are attached to many Ministries and their advice on proposed legislation is sought. No Minister and no department would be considered to be doing their work well if they introduced Bills which had not been discussed thoroughly with the major interests concerned and their objections met so far as possible. So also amendments are inserted in the draft of a Bill in *anticipation* of the criticisms of the House of Commons. All these amendments made in draft Bills in anticipation of opposition must be taken into account along with those made after the introduction of a Bill, if a just picture is to be obtained of the influence which the House of Commons has upon the Cabinet and the bureaucracy.

Against this wider background assertions of 'Cabinet dictatorship' and of 'the decline of legislatures' are, in my view, phrases remote from reality in our machinery of government. I believe that the House of Commons has been at least as effective in these last two decades as it has ever been in this last century.

To say this is not to say that the control of the House over the bureaucracy both in the legislative and administrative process is adequate. In my opinion it is necessary to make a wider use of standing committees for the consideration of Bills. My object would not be to increase the output of legislation. It is doubtful how far that is necessary. A review of the Statute Book in the years from 1919 to 1939 shows that, on average, three Bills of major importance—excluding financial legislation—were passed each year, and I believe that record is satisfactory. In times of crisis the House is able to act with speed, as 1931 and 1939 have shown. Nor is it possible to increase output substantially and still retain adequate discussion in the House and in standing committees. What an increased use of standing committees will do is to improve the quality of the House's discussion and control of legislation. In the atmosphere of the committee room, government and private members are ready to learn from each other and the discussion of Bills can be more informed, more responsible, more constructive. But here again too much must not be expected.

The control of the House of Commons over delegated legislation has long been criticized as inadequate or even non-existent. Powers are conferred upon departments in terms so wide and vague that it is difficult to see what powers of control are retained. The mere bulk of delegated legislation makes effective control by the House as a whole impossible. In the years between 1922 and 1939 on an average 1,500 Statutory Rules and Orders were made each year; between 25 July 1939 and 1 October 1944 no less than 8,542 Statutory Rules and Orders were made.[10] And not all these regulations were required to be laid before the House for approval. Of those required to be laid, many went into effect unless a negative resolution of the House was passed. It is only when an affirmative resolution is required that an opportunity must be given for the House to express its views.

It is well to emphasize that the House, when given an opportunity, has frequently criticized and secured modifications in regulations placed before it. I have mentioned its attack upon the regulations, including 18B, in October 1939, and the amendments it secured. During the parliamentary session of 1942-3 ten prayers were moved against various regulations. During the years 1943 and 1944 there was a marked increase in the activities of certain back-bench members, of various parties, in criticizing Orders. One Order, dealing with transport, was withdrawn, and a number of others were contested and in most cases substantial concessions were obtained.[11] On 1 June 1945 the House declined to approve an Order relating to the Purchase Tax.

But the opportunities for this criticism are too few and the House as a whole is not a fit body to give careful consideration to complex regulations. The Committee on Ministers' Powers recommended in 1932 that a Select Committee of the House should be appointed to consider clauses in Bills providing for delegation and also the exercise of the powers so delegated. The Government resisted it consistently, but in 1944 in response to strong pressure from the Back Benches a Select Committee was established. It is too early to say yet whether the Committee will become permanent or what success it will have. What one hopes is that it would obtain, in relation to delegated legislation, that respect from the bureaucracy which it accords, in financial matters, to the proceedings and reports of the Select Committee on Public Accounts.

I have spoken so far of the method by which the parliamentary element in our machinery of government can be made effective in controlling the bureaucratic element in the making of laws. May I add a word on the control of administration? It is not the function of the House of Commons directly to control the administration. That is the function of the Cabinet. The Commons by their control of the Cabinet may indirectly control administration. How effective has this control become? More effective than is sometimes thought. Question-time is generally agreed to provide an opportunity for the members of the House to press Ministers on administrative questions. Departments are nervous of questions—often too nervous—and this institution of question-time undoubtedly provides one effective method by which Parliament controls the bureaucracy. And it may be added that by motions on the adjournment, by debates in committee of supply, and on the address, and, above all, by the work of the Public Accounts Committee and, in the war, the Select Committee on National Expenditure, there are considerable opportunities for criticism and control of administration. But, on a review of the whole situation, they are still inadequate. And in this sphere also it seems to me the use of committees might be extended. I do not advocate anything so formal as that suggested, in 1931, for example, by Mr. Lloyd George or Sir Horace Dawkins, then Clerk of the House—a series of established standing committees attached to groups of departments. What I suggest is a development of the informal system which usually exists in the House of Commons and which has been established in this present Parliament—the setting up of informal committees of members covering the whole range of administrative activity, to keep in touch with Ministers and with each other, and to discuss matters from time to time with departments concerned. At the present time these committees are constituted on a party basis— Labour has its dozen or so committees, the Conservatives have theirs. Already they perform valuable work in educating members and in controlling Ministers. It is doubtful whether they could be improved. I believe that joint all-party committees would be preferable, more educative both to their members and to the departments. Officials would profit by contact with these committees, and the parliamentary control of bureaucracy would be increased through the processes of discussion, exposition and criticism.

I have been able to deal with one aspect only of the method by which bureaucracy may be controlled in our machinery of government—the control by the Cabinet and the House of Commons. Of equal importance is control by the courts of law, and concerning its effectiveness equal anxiety has been expressed. I have not the qualifications to deal authoritatively with this subject, but I feel bound to mention that it is as much upon the courts as upon the House of Commons that the safeguarding of our democratic system of government depends. Nor have I had time to do more than mention a method of controlling bureaucracy which has developed in this country as an adjunct of Parliament—the use of advisory councils. We owe our understanding of the working and effectiveness of these bodies in greatest measure to my predecessor, who instituted in 1937 a co-operative inquiry in Oxford into their use in relation to central government, an inquiry which resulted in the publication of a book entitled *Advisory Bodies* in 1940. In my view these bodies can be of the greatest value in assisting parliamentary bureaucracy to work well and they should be regarded as an essential part of our machinery of government.

There are many other aspects of my subject which I have not even mentioned and which may appear to others more important than those which I have discussed. To some the greatest need in our machinery of government is decentralization, devolution of authority to regional parliaments upon the model of Northern Ireland; to others a reorganization of our local government; to others the secret is found not in controlling bureaucracy but in altering its content, in changing the methods of recruitment in the national as well as in the local civil service.

I can do no more than name these problems. All deserve study and, one may say, all will receive study here in Oxford. Some of us have had experience in the war years in government departments and one may say that we were never so well equipped in Oxford as we are now for the study of the machinery of government. A professor is expected to say something in his inaugural lecture of what he hopes to see done by himself and perhaps by others to advance the study of his subject. For my own part I am drawn to an analysis of the decentralization of government in the United Kingdom in its great variety, for I believe that upon the strength of our parliamentary bureaucracy in its local and regional levels, not less than at the national level, very much depends. Looking to what others may do, I should hope to see the study of war government undertaken by a group, say, of those who have had experience in administration during the war. But on this wider question of research in Oxford there is one thing I should like to stress. The Gladstone Professor has no department; he has no staff; he has not even an Institute! May it continue so. For my part I have no aspiration to see an Institute of Government established in Oxford. I cannot presume to discuss the problem of Institutes in Oxford, of their growth and their place in the University. I wish their objects could be accomplished within the framework of the College system, but I can see that for many subjects that is not possible. The study of government might well have been in that position. But Colleges have steadily recognized the subject as one in which teaching and research are worth doing, and there are now more than a dozen fellowships, in whole or in part devoted to the subject, the most recent of them created in my old College of Oriel. To these is added the new foundations of Nuffield College, where the study of economics and politics is to be conducted in a close association of student and practitioner. What Nuffield will become we cannot say, but I rejoice that it is a College and not an Institute, an association in terms of equality and fellowship, not a staff co-ordinated and animated by a director. The greatest virtue of our College system is this fellowship, in equality and co-operation, of men and women studying their subjects. There is no better system for University work. I rejoice that in the study of government in Oxford there exists already this established and numerous fellowship. I shall hope to continue to study within it in the future in the friendly and cheerful and vigorous companionship we knew in the years before the war.

NOTES

1. Mill, *Representative Government*, chapter 5.
2. *Ibid.*
3. Bagehot, *The English Constitution* (World Classics), p. 172.
4. C. K. Allen, *Law and Orders*, p. 203
5. C. T. Carr, *Concerning English Administrative Law*, p. 160.
6. p. 16.
7. Bagehot, quoting Sir G. Cornewall Lewis *op. cit.*, p. 177.
8. Bagehot, *ibid.*, p. 178.
9. *Federalist* (Everyman), p. 357.
10. Shannon, *Modern Law Manual for Practitioners*, p. 2.
11. Allen, *Law and Orders*, p. 95.

6

Professor Michael Oakeshott
POLITICAL EDUCATION[1]

The two former occupants of this Chair, Graham Wallas and Harold Laski, were both men of great distinction; to follow them is an undertaking for which I am ill-prepared. In the first of them, experience and reflection were happily combined to give a reading of politics at once practical and profound; a thinker without a system whose thoughts were nevertheless firmly held together by a thread of honest, patient inquiry, a man who brought his powers of intellect to bear upon the inconsequence of human behaviour and to whom the reasons of the head and of the heart were alike familiar. In the second, the dry light of intellect was matched with a warm enthusiasm; to the humour of a scholar was joined the temperament of a reformer. It seems but an hour ago that he was dazzling us with the range and readiness of his learning, winning our sympathy by the fearlessness of his advocacy and endearing himself to us by his generosity. In their several ways, ways in which their successor cannot hope to compete with them, these two men left their mark upon the political education of England. They were both great teachers, devoted, tireless, and with sure confidence in what they had to teach. And it seems perhaps a little ungrateful that they should be followed by a sceptic; one who would do better if only he knew how. But no one could wish for more exacting or more sympathetic witness of his activities than these two men. And the subject I have chosen to speak about today is one which would have their approval.

I

The expression 'political education' has fallen on evil days; in the wilful and disingenuous corruption of language which is characteristic of our time it has acquired a sinister meaning. In places other than this, it is associated with that softening of the mind, by force, by alarm, or by the hypnotism of the endless repetition of what was scarcely worth saying once, by means of which whole populations have been reduced to submission. It is, therefore, an

75

enterprise worth undertaking to consider again, in a quiet moment, how we should understand this expression, which joins together two laudable activities, and in doing so play a small part in rescuing it from abuse.

Politics I take to be the activity of attending to the general arrangements of a set of people whom chance or choice have brought together. In this sense, families, clubs, and learned societies have their 'politics'. But the communities in which this manner of activity is pre-eminent are the hereditary co-operative groups, many of them of ancient lineage, all of them aware of a past, a present and a future, which we call 'states'. For most people, political activity is a secondary activity—that is to say, they have something else to do besides attending to these arrangements. But, as we have come to understand it, the activity is one in which every member of the group who is neither a child nor a lunatic has some part and some responsibility. With us it is, at one level or another, a universal activity.

I speak of this activity as 'attending to arrangements', rather than as 'making arrangements', because in these hereditary co-operative groups the activity is never offered the blank sheet of infinite possibility. In any generation, even the most revolutionary, the arrangements which are enjoyed always far exceed those which are recognized to stand in need of attention, and those which are being prepared for enjoyment are few in comparison with those which receive amendment: the new is an insignificant proportion of the whole. There are some people, of course, who allow themselves to speak

> As if arrangements were intended
> For nothing else but to be mended,

but, for most of us, our determination to improve our conduct does not prevent us from recognizing that the greater part of what we have is not a burden to be carried or an incubus to be thrown off, but an inheritance to be enjoyed. And a certain degree of shabbiness is joined with every real convenience.

Now, attending to the arrangements of a society is an activity which, like every other, has to be learned. Politics make a call upon knowledge. Consequently, it is not irrelevant to inquire into the kind of knowledge which is involved, and to investigate the nature of political education. I do not, however, propose to ask what information we should equip ourselves with before we begin to be politically active, or what we need to know in order to be successful politicians but to inquire into the kind of knowledge we unavoidably call upon whenever we are engaged in political activity and to get from this an understanding of the nature of political education.

Our thoughts on political education, then, might be supposed to spring from our understanding of political activity and the kind of knowledge it involves. And it would appear that what is wanted at this point is a definition of political activity from which to draw some conclusions. But this, I think, would be a mistaken way of going about our business. What we require is not so much a definition of politics from which to deduce the character of political education, as an understanding of political activity which includes a recognition of the sort of education it involves. For, to understand an activity is to know it as a concrete whole; it is to recognize the activity as having the source of its movement within itself. An understanding which leaves the activity in debt to something outside itself is, for that reason, an inadequate understanding. And if political activity is impossible without a certain kind of knowledge and a certain sort of education, then this knowledge and education are not mere appendages to the activity but are part of the activity itself and must be incorporated in our understanding of it. We should not, therefore, seek a definition of politics in order to deduce from it the character of political knowledge and education, but rather observe the kind of knowledge and education which is inherent in any understanding of political activity, and use this observation as a means of improving our understanding of politics.

My proposal, then, is to consider the adequacy of two current understandings of politics, together with the sort of knowledge and kind of education they imply, and by improving upon them to reach what may perhaps be a more adequate understanding at once of political activity itself and the knowledge and education which belongs to it.

2

In the understanding of some people, politics are what may be called an empirical activity. Attending to the arrangements of a society is waking up each morning and considering, 'What would I like to do?' or 'What would somebody else (whom I desire to please) like to see done?', and doing it. This understanding of political activity may be called politics without a policy. On the briefest inspection it will appear a concept of politics difficult to substantiate; it does not look like a possible manner of activity at all. But a near approach to it is, perhaps, to be detected in the politics of the proverbial oriental despot, or in the politics of the wall-scribbler and the vote-catcher. And the result may be supposed to be chaos modified by whatever consistency is allowed to creep into caprice. They are the politics attributed to the first Lord Liverpool, of whom Acton said, 'The secret of his policy was that he had none', and of whom a Frenchman remarked that if he had been present at the creation of the world he would have said, '*Mon Dieu, conservons le chaos*'. It seems then, that a concrete activity, which may be described as an approximation to empirical politics, is possible. But it is clear that, although knowledge of a sort belongs to this style of political activity (knowledge, as the French say, not of ourselves but only of our appetites), the only kind of education appropriate to it would be an education in lunacy— learning to be ruled solely by passing desires. And this reveals the important point; namely, that to understand politics as a purely empirical activity is to misunderstand it, because empiricism by itself is not a concrete manner of activity at all, and can become a partner in a concrete manner of activity only when it is joined with something else—in science, for example, when it is joined with hypothesis. What is significant about this understanding of politics is not that some sort of approach to it can appear, but that it mistakes for a concrete, self-moved manner of activity what is never more than an abstract moment in any manner of being active. Of course, politics are the pursuit of what is desired and of what is desired at the moment; but precisely because they are this, they can never be the pursuit of merely what recommends itself from moment to moment. The activity of desiring does not take this course; caprice is never absolute. From a practical point of view, then, we may decry the *style* of politics which approximates to pure empiricism because we can observe in it an approach to lunacy. But from a theoretical point of view, purely empirical politics are not something difficult to achieve or proper to be avoided, they are merely impossible; the product of a musunderstanding.

3

The understanding of politics as an empirical activity is, then, inadequate because it fails to reveal a concrete manner of activity at all. And it has the incidental defect of seeming to encourage the thoughtless to pursue a *style* of attending to the arrangements of their society which is likely to have unfortunate results; to try to do something which is inherently impossible is always a corrupting enterprise. We must, if we can, improve upon it. And the impulse to improve may be given a direction by asking, 'What is it that this understanding of politics has neglected to observe?' What (to put it crudely) has it left out which, if added in, would compose an understanding in which politics are revealed as a self-moved (or concrete) manner of activity? And the answer to the question is, or seems to be, available as soon as the question is formulated. It would appear that what this understanding of politics lacks is something to set empiricism to work, something to correspond with specific hypothesis in science, an end to be pursued more extensive than a merely instant desire. And this, it should be observed, is not merely a good companion for empiricism; it is something without which empiricism in action is impossible. Let us explore this suggestion, and in order to bring it to a point I will state it in the form of a proposition: that politics appear as a self-moved manner of activity when empiricism is preceded and guided by an ideological activity. I am not concerned with the so-called ideological *style* of politics as a desirable or undesirable manner of attending to the arrangements of a society; I am concerned only with the contention that when to the ineluctable element of empiricism (doing what one wants to do) is added a political ideology, a self-moved manner of activity appears, and that consequently this may be regarded in principle as an adequate understanding of political activity.

As I understand it, a political ideology purports to be an abstract principle, or set of related abstract principles, which has been independently premeditated. It supplies in advance of the activity of attending to the arrangements of a society a formulated end to be pursued, and in so doing it provides a means of distinguishing between those desires which ought to be encouraged and those which ought to be suppressed or redirected.

The simplest sort of political ideology is a single abstract idea, such as Freedom, Equality, Maximum Productivity, Racial Purity, or Happiness. And in that case political activity is understood as the enterprise of seeing that the arrangements of a society conform to or reflect the chosen abstract idea. It is usual, however, to recognize the need for a complex scheme of related ideas, rather than a single idea, and the examples pointed to will be such systems of ideas as: 'the principles of 1789', 'Liberalism', 'Democracy', Marxism', or the Atlantic Charter. These principles need not be considered absolute or immune from change (though they are frequently so considered), but their value lies in their having been premeditated. They compose an understanding of *what* is to be pursued independent of *how* it is to be pursued. A political ideology purports to supply in advance knowledge of what 'Freedom' or 'Democracy' or 'Justice' is, and in this manner sets empiricism to work. Such a set of principles is, of course, capable of being argued about and reflected upon; it is something that men compose for themselves, and they may later remember it or write it down. But the condition upon which it can perform the service assigned to it is that it owes nothing to the activity it controls. 'To know the true good of the community is what constitutes the science of legislation,' said Bentham; 'the art consists in finding the means to realize that good.' The contention we have before us, then, is that empiricism can be set to work (and a concrete, self-moved manner of activity appear) when there is added to it a guide of this sort: desire and something not generated by desire.

Now, there is no doubt about the sort of knowledge which political activity, understood in this manner, calls upon. What is required, in the first place, is knowledge of the chosen political ideology—a knowledge of the ends to be pursued, a knowledge of what we want to do. Of course, if we are to be successful in pursuing these ends we shall need knowledge of another sort also—a knowledge, shall we say, of economics and psychology. But the common characteristic of all the kinds of knowledge required is that they may be, and should be, gathered in advance of the activity of attending to the arrangements of a society. Moreover, the appropriate sort of education will be an education in which the chosen political ideology is taught and learned, in which the techniques necessary for success are acquired, and (if we are so unfortunate as to find ourselves empty-handed in the matter of an ideology) an education in the skill of abstract thought and premeditation necessary to compose one for ourselves. The education we shall need is one which enables us to expound, defend, implement, and possibly invent a political ideology.

In casting around for some convincing demonstration that this understanding of politics reveals a self-moved manner of activity, we should no doubt consider ourselves rewarded if we could find an example of politics being conducted precisely in this manner. This at least would constitute a sign that we were on the right track. The defect, it will be remembered, of the understanding of politics as a purely empirical activity was that it revealed, not a manner of activity at all, but an abstraction; and this defect made itself manifest in our inability to find a *style* of politics which was anything more than an approximation to it. How does the understanding of politics as empiricism joined with an ideology fare in this respect? And without being over-confident, we may perhaps think that this is where we wade ashore. For we would appear to be in no difficulty whatever in finding an example of political activity which corresponds to this understanding of it: half the world, at a conservative estimate, seems to conduct its affairs in precisely this manner. And further, is it not so manifestly a possible style of politics that, even if we disagree with a particular ideology, we find nothing technically absurd in the writings of those who urge it upon us as an admirable style of politics? At least its advocates seem to know what they are talking about: they understand not only the manner of the activity but also the sort of knowledge and the kind of education it involves. 'Every schoolboy in Russia,' wrote Sir Norman Angel, 'is familiar with the doctrine of Marx and can recite its catechism. How many British schoolboys have any corresponding knowledge of the principles enunciated by Mill in his incomparable essay on Liberty?' 'Few people,' says Mr. E.

H. Carr, 'any longer contest the thesis that the child should be educated *in* the official ideology of his country.' In short, if we are looking for a sign to indicate that the understanding of politics as empirical activity preceded by ideological activity is an adequate understanding we can scarcely be mistaken in supposing that we have it to hand.

And yet there is perhaps room for doubt: doubt first of all whether in principle this understanding of politics reveals a self-moved manner of activity; and doubt, consequentially, whether what have been identified as examples of a *style* of politics corresponding exactly to this understanding have been properly identified.

The contention we are investigating is that attending to the arrangements of a society can begin with a premeditated ideology, can begin with independently acquired knowledge of the ends to be pursued.[2] It is supposed that a political ideology is the product of intellectual premeditation and that, because it is a body of principles not itself in debt to the activity of attending to the arrangements of a society, it is able to determine and guide the direction of that activity. If, however, we consider more closely the character of a political ideology, we find at once that this supposition is falsified. So far from a political ideology being the quasi-divine parent of political activity, it turns out to be its earthly stepchild. Instead of an independently premeditated scheme of ends to be pursued, it is a system of ideas abstracted from the manner in which people have been accustomed to go about the business of attending to the arrangements of their societies. The pedigree of every political ideology shows it to be the creature, not of premeditation in advance of political activity, but of meditation upon a manner of politics. In short, political activity comes first and a political ideology follows after; and the understanding of politics we are investigating has the disadvantage of being, in the strict sense, preposterous.

Let us consider the matter first in relation to scientific hypothesis, which I have taken to play a role in scientific activity in some respects similar to that of an ideology in politics. If a scientific hypothesis were a self-generated bright idea which owed nothing to scientific activity, then empiricism governed by hypothesis could be considered to compose a self-contained manner of activity; but this certainly is not its character. The truth is that only a man who is already a scientist can formulate a scientific hypothesis; that is, an hypothesis is not an independent invention capable of guiding scientific inquiry, but a dependent supposition which arises as an abstraction from within already existing activity. Moreover, even when the specific hypothesis has in this manner been formulated, it is inoperative as a guide to research without constant reference to the traditions of scientific inquiry from which it was abstracted. The concrete situation does not appear until the specific hypothesis, which is the occasion of empiricism being set to work, is recognized as itself the creature of knowing how to conduct a scientific inquiry.

Or consider the example of cookery. It might be supposed that an ignorant man, some edible materials and a cookery book compose together the necessities of a self-moved (or concrete) activity called cooking. But nothing is further from the truth. The cookery book is not an independently generated beginning from which cooking can spring; it is nothing more than an abstract of somebody's knowledge of how to cook: it is the stepchild, not the parent of the activity. The book, in its turn, may help to set a man on to dressing a dinner, but if his sole guide he could never, in fact, begin: the book speaks only to those who know already the kind of thing to expect from it and consequently how to interpret it.

Now, just as a cookery book presupposes somebody who knows how to cook, and its use presupposes somebody who already knows how to use it, and just as a scientific hypothesis springs from a knowledge of how to conduct a scientific investigation and separated from that knowledge is powerless to set empiricism profitably to work, so a political ideology must be understood, not as an independently premeditated beginning for political activity, but as knowledge (abstract and generalized) of a concrete manner of attending to the arrangements of the society. The catechism which sets out the purposes to be pursued merely abridges a concrete manner of behaviour in which those purposes are already hidden. It does not exist in advance of political activity, and by itself it is always an insufficient guide. Political enterprises, the ends to be pursued, the arrangements to be established (all the normal ingredients of a political ideology), cannot be premeditated in advance of a manner of attending to the arrangements of a society; *what* we do, and moreover what we want to do, is the creature of *how* we are accustomed to conduct our affairs. Indeed, it often reflects no more than a discovered ability to do something which is then translated into an authority to do it.

On August 4, 1789, for the complex and bankrupt social and political system of France was substituted the Rights of Man. Reading this document we come to the conclusion that somebody has done some thinking. Here, displayed in a few sentences, is a political ideology: a system of rights and duties, a scheme of ends—justice, freedom, equality, security, property, and the rest—ready and waiting to put into practice for the first time. 'For the first time?' Not a bit of it. This ideology no more existed in advance of political practice than a cookery book exists in advance of knowing how to cook. Certainly it was the product of somebody's reflection, but it was not the product of reflection in advance of political activity. For here, in fact, are disclosed, abstracted and abridged, the common law rights of Englishmen, the gift not of independent premeditation or divine munificence, but of centuries of the day-to-day attending to the arrangements of an historic society. Or consider Locke's *Second Treatise of Civil Government,* read in America and in France in the eighteenth century as a statement of abstract principles to be put into practice, regarded there as a preface to political activity. But so far from being a preface, it has all the marks of a postscript, and its power to guide derived from its roots in actual political experience. Here, set down in abstract terms, is a brief conspectus of the manner in which Englishmen were accustomed to go about the business of attending to their arrangements—a brilliant abridgment of the political habits of Englishmen. Or consider this passage from a contemporary continental writer: 'Freedom keeps Europeans in unrest and movement. They wish to have freedom, and at the same time they know they have not got it. They know also that freedom belongs to man as a human right.' And having established the end to be pursued, political activity is represented as the realization of this end. But the 'freedom' which can be pursued is not an independently premeditated 'ideal' or a dream; like scientific hypothesis, it is something which is already intimated in a concrete manner of behaving. Freedom, like a recipe for game pie, is not a bright idea; it is not a 'human right' to be deduced from some speculative concept of human nature. The freedom which we enjoy is nothing more than arrangements, procedures of a certain kind: the freedom of an Englishman is not something exemplified in the procedure of *habeas corpus,* it *is,* at that point, the availability of that procedure. And the freedom which we wish to enjoy is not an 'ideal' which we premeditate independently of our political experience; it is what is already intimated in that experience.[3]

On this reading, then, the systems of abstract ideas we call 'ideologies' are abstracts of some kind of concrete activity. Most political ideologies, and certainly the most useful of them (because they unquestionably have their use), are abstracts of the political traditions of some society. But it sometimes happens that an ideology is offered as a guide to politics which an abstract, not of political experience, but of some other manner of activity—war, religion, or the conduct of industry, for example. And here the model we are shown is not only abstract, but is also inappropriate on account of the irrelevance of the activity from which it has been abstracted. This I think, is one of the defects of the model provided by the Marxist ideology. But the important point is that, at most, an ideology is an abbreviation of some manner of concrete activity.

We are now, perhaps, in a position to perceive more accurately the character of what may be called the ideological *style* of politics, and to observe that its existence offers no ground for supposing that the understanding of political activity as empiricism guided solely by an ideology is an adequate understanding. The ideological style of politics is a confused style. Properly speaking, it is a traditional manner of attending to the arrangements of a society which has been abridged into a doctrine of ends to be pursued, the abridgment (together with the necessary technical knowledge) being erroneously regarded as the sole guide relied upon. In certain circumstances an abridgment of this kind may be valuable; it gives sharpness of outline and precision to a political tradition which the occasion may make seem appropriate. When a manner of attending to arrangements is to be transplanted from the society in which it has grown up into another society (always a questionable enterprise), the simplification of an ideology may appear as an asset. If, for example, the English manner of politics is to be planted elsewhere in the world, it is perhaps appropriate that it should first be abridged into something called 'democracy' before it is packed up and shipped abroad. There is, of course, an alternative method: the method by which what is exported is the detail and not the abridgment of the tradition and the workmen travel with the tools—the method which made the British Empire. But it is a slow and costly method. And, particularly with men in a hurry, *l'homme à programme* with his abridgment wins every time; his slogans enchant, while the resident magistrate is seen only as a sign of servility. But whatever the apparent appropriateness on occasion of the ideological style of politics, the defect of the explanation of political activity connected with it becomes apparent when we consider the sort of knowledge and the kind of education it encourages us to believe is sufficient for understanding the activity of attending to the arrangements of a society. For it suggests that a knowledge of the chosen political ideology can take the place of understanding a tradition of political behaviour. The wand and the book come to be regarded as themselves potent, and not merely the symbols of potency. The arrangements of a society are made to appear, not as manners of behaviour, but as pieces of machinery to be transported about the world indiscriminately. The complexities of the tradition which have been squeezed out in the process of abridgment are taken to be unimportant: the 'rights of man' are understood to exist insulated from a manner of attending to arrangements. And because, in practice, the abridgment is never by itself a sufficient guide, we are encouraged to fill it out, not with our suspect political experience, but with experience drawn from other (often irrelevant) concretely understood activities such as war, the conduct of industry, or Trade Union negotiation.

4

The understanding of politics as the activity of attending to the arrangements of a society under the guidance of an independently premeditated ideology is, then, no less a misunderstanding than the understanding of its purely empirical activity. Wherever else politics may begin, they cannot begin in ideological activity. And in an attempt to improve upon this understanding of politics, we have already observed in principle what needs to be recognized in order to have an intelligible concept. Just as scientific hypothesis cannot appear, and is impossible to operate, except within an already existing tradition of scientific investigation, so a scheme of ends for political activity appears within, and can be evaluated only when it is related to, an already existing tradition of how to attend to our arrangements. In politics, the only concrete manner of activity detectable is one in which empiricism and the ends to be pursued are recognized as dependent, alike for their existence and their operation, upon a traditional manner of behaviour.

Politics is the activity of attending to the general arrangements of a collection of people who, in respect of their common recognition of a manner of attending to its arrangements, compose a single community. To suppose a collection of people without recognized traditions of behaviour, or one which enjoyed arrangements which intimated no direction for change and needed no attention,[4] is to suppose a people incapable of politics. This activity, then, springs neither from instant desires, nor from general principles, but from the existing traditions of behaviour themselves. And the form it takes, because it can take no other, is the amendment of existing arrangements by exploring and pursuing what is intimated in them. The arrangements which constitute a society capable of political activity, whether they are customs or institutions or laws or diplomatic decisions, are at once coherent and incoherent; they compose a pattern and at the same time they intimate a sympathy for what does not fully appear. Political activity is the exploration of that sympathy; and consequently, relevant political reasoning will be the convincing exposure of a sympathy, present but not yet followed up, and the convincing demonstration that now is the appropriate moment for recognizing it. For example, the legal status of women in our society was for a long time (and perhaps still is) in comparative confusion, because the rights and duties which composed it intimated rights and duties which were nevertheless not recognized. And, on the view of things I am suggesting, the only cogent reason to be advanced for the technical 'enfranchisement' of women was that in all or most other important respects they had already been enfranchised. Arguments drawn from abstract natural right, from 'justice', or from some general concept of feminine personality, must be regarded as either irrelevant, or as unfortunately disguised forms of the one valid argument; namely, that there was an incoherence in the arrangements of the society which pressed convincingly for remedy. In politics, then, every enterprise is a consequential enterprise, the pursuit, not of a dream, or of a general principle, but of an intimation.[5] What we have to do with is something less imposing than logical implications or necessary consequences: but if the intimations of a tradition of behaviour are less dignified or more elusive than these, they are not on that account less important. Of course, there is no piece of mistake-proof apparatus by means of which we can elicit the intimation most worth while pursuing; and not only do we often make gross errors of judgment in this matter, but also the total effect of a desire satisfied is so little to be forecast, that our activity of amendment is often found to lead us where we would not go. Moreover, the whole enterprise is liable at any moment to be perverted by the incursion of an approximation to empiricism in the pursuit of power. These are features which can never be eliminated; they belong to the character of political activity. But it may be believed that our mistakes of understanding will be less frequent and less disastrous if we escape the illusion that politics is ever anything more than the pursuit of intimations; a conversation, not an argument.

Now, every society which is intellectually alive is liable, from time to time, to abridge its tradition of behaviour into a scheme of abstract ideas; and on occasion political discussion will be concerned, not (like the debates in the *Iliad*) with isolated transactions, nor (like the speeches in Thucydides) with policies and traditions of activity, but with general principles. And in this there is no harm; perhaps even some positive benefit. It is possible that this distorting mirror of an ideology will reveal important hidden passages in the tradition, as a caricature reveals the potentialities of a face; and if this is so, the intellectual enterprise of seeing what a tradition looks like when it is reduced to an ideology will be a useful part of political education. But to make use of abridgment as a technique for exploring the intimations of political tradition, to use it, that is, as a scientist uses hypothesis, is one thing; it is something different and something inappropriate, to understand political activity itself as the activity of amending the arrangements of a society so as to make them agree with the provisions of an ideology. For then a character has been attributed to an ideology which it is unable to sustain, and we may find ourselves, in practice, directed by a false and a misleading guide: false, because in the abridgment, however skilfully it has been performed, a single intimation is apt to be exaggerated and proposed for unconditional pursuit and the benefit to be had from observing what the distortion reveals is least when the distortion itself is given the office of a criterion; misleading, because the abridgment itself never, in fact, provides the whole of the knowledge used in political activity.

There will be some people who though in general agreement with this understanding of political activity, will suspect that it confuses what is perhaps, normal with what is necessary, and the important exceptions (of great contemporary relevance) have been lost in a hazy generality. It is all very well, it may be said, to observe in politics the activity of exploring and pursuing the intimations of a tradition of behaviour, but what light does this throw upon a political crisis such as the Norman Conquest of England, or the establishment of the Soviet *régime* in Russia? It would be foolish, of course, to deny the possibility of serious crisis. But if we exclude (as we must) a genuine cataclysm which for the time being made an end of politics by altogether obliterating a current tradition of behaviour (which is *not* what happened in Anglo-Saxon England or in Russia),[6] there is little to support the view that even the most serious political upheaval carries us outside this understanding of politics. A tradition of behaviour is not a fixed and inflexible manner of doing things; it is a flow of sympathy. It may be temporarily disrupted by the incursion of a foreign influence, it may be diverted, restricted, arrested, or become dried-up, and it may reveal so deep seated an incoherence that (even without foreign assistance) a crisis appears. And if in order to meet these crises, there were some steady, unchanging independent guide to which a society might resort, it would no doubt be well advised to do so. But no such guide exists; we have no resources outside the fragments, the vestiges, the relics of its own tradition of behaviour which the crisis has left untouched. For even the help we may get from the traditions of another society (or from a tradition of a vaguer sort which is shared by a number of societies) is conditional upon our being able to assimilate them to our own arrangements and our own manner of attending to our arrangements. The hungry and helpless man is mistaken if he supposes that he overcomes the crisis by means of a tin-opener; what saves him is somebody else's knowledge of how to cook, which he can make use of only because he is not himself entirely ignorant. In short, political crisis (even when it seems to be imposed upon a society by changes beyond its control) always appears *within* a tradition of political activity; and 'salvation' comes from the unimpaired resources of the tradition itself. Those societies which retain, in changing circumstances, a lively sense of their own identity and continuity (which are without that hatred of their own experience which makes them desire to efface it) are to be counted fortunate, not because they possess what others lack, but because they have already mobilized what none is without and all, in fact, rely upon.

In political activity, then, men sail a boundless and bottomless sea; there is neither harbour for shelter nor floor for anchorage, neither starting-place nor appointed destination. The enterprise is to keep afloat on an even keel; the sea is both friend and enemy; and the seamanship consists in using the resources of a traditional manner of behaviour in order to make a friend of every hostile occasion.[7]

A depressing doctrine, it will be said—even by those who do not make the mistake of adding in an element of crude determinism which, in fact, it has no place for. A tradition of behaviour is not a groove within which we are destined to grind out our helpless and unsatisfying lives: Spartam nactus es; hanc *exorna*. But in the main the depression springs from the exclusion of hopes that were false and the discovery that guides, reputed to be of superhuman wisdom and skill, are, in fact, of a somewhat different character. If the doctrine deprives us of a model laid up in heaven to which we should approximate our behaviour, at least is does not lead us into a morass where every choice is equally good or equally to be deplored. And if it suggests that politics are *nur für die Schwindelfreie,* that should depress only those who have lost their nerve.

5

The sin of the academic is that he takes so long in coming to the point. Nevertheless, there is some virtue in his dilatoriness; what he has to offer may, in the end, be no great matter, but at least it is not unripe fruit, and to pluck it is the work of a moment. We set out to consider the kind of knowledge involved in political activity and the appropriate sort of education. And if the understanding of politics I have recommended is not a misunderstanding, there is little doubt about the kind of knowledge and the sort of education which belongs to it. It is knowledge, as profound as we can make it, of our tradition of political behaviour. Other knowledge, certainly, is desirable in addition; but this is the knowledge without which we cannot make use of whatever else we may have learned.

Now, a tradition of behaviour is a tricky thing to get to know. Indeed, it may even appear to be essentially unintelligible. It is neither fixed nor finished; it has no changeless centre to which understanding can anchor itself; there is no sovereign purpose to be perceived or invariable direction to be detected; there is no model to be copied, idea to be realized, or rule to be followed. Some parts of it may change more slowly than others, but none is immune from change. Everything is temporary. Nevertheless, though a tradition of behaviour is flimsy and elusive, it is not without identity, and what makes it a possible object of knowledge is the fact that all its parts do not change at the same time and that the changes it undergoes are potential within it. Its principle is a principle of *continuity:* authority is diffused between past, present, and future; between the old, the new, and what is to come. It is steady because, though it moves, it is never wholly in motion; and though it is tranquil, it is never wholly at rest.[8] Nothing that ever belonged to it is completely lost; we are always swerving back to recover and make something topical out of even its remotest moments: and nothing for long remains unmodified. Everything is temporary, but nothing is arbitrary. Everything figures by comparison, not with what stands next to it, but with the whole. And since a tradition of behaviour is not susceptible of the distinction between essence and accident, knowledge of it is unavoidably knowledge of its detail: to know only the gist is to know nothing. What has to be learned is not an abstract idea, or a set of tricks, not even a ritual, but a concrete, coherent manner of living in all its intricateness.

It is clear, then, that we must not entertain the hope of acquiring this difficult understanding by easy methods. Though the knowledge we seek is municipal, not universal, there is no short cut to it. Moreover, political education is not merely a matter of coming to understand a tradition, it is learning how to participate in a conversation: it is at once initiation into an inheritance in which we have a life interest, and the exploration of its intimations. There will always remain something of a mystery about how a tradition of political behaviour is learned, and perhaps the only certainty is that there is no point at which learning it can properly be said to begin. The politics of a community are not less individual (and not more so) than its language, and they are learned and practised in the same manner. We do not begin to learn our native language by learning the alphabet, or by learning its grammar, we do not begin by learning words, but words in use; we do not begin (as we begin in reading) with what is easy and go on to what is more difficult; we do not begin at school, but in the cradle; and what we say springs always from our manner of speaking. And this is true also of our political education; it begins in the enjoyment of a tradition, in the observation and imitation of the behaviour of our elders, and there is little or nothing in the world which comes before us as we open our eyes which does not contribute to it. We are aware of a past and a future as soon as we are aware of a present. Long before we are of an age to take interest in a book about our politics we are acquiring that complex and intricate knowledge of our political tradition without which we could not make sense of a book when we come to open it. And the projects we entertain are the creatures of our tradition. The greater part, then—perhaps the most important part—of our political education we acquire haphazard in finding our way about the natural-artificial world into which we are born, and there is no other way of acquiring it. There will, of course, be more to acquire, and it will be more readily acquired, if we have the good fortune to be born into a rich and lively political tradition and among those who are well educated politically; the lineaments of *political* activity will earlier become distinct: but even the most needy society and the most cramped surroundings have some political education to offer, and we take what we can get.

But if this is the manner of our beginning, there are deeper recesses to explore. Politics are a proper subject for academic study; there is something to think about and it is important that we should think about the appropriate things. Here also, and everywhere, the governing consideration is that what we are learning to understand is a political tradition, a concrete manner of behaviour. And for this reason it is proper that, at the academic level, the study of politics should be an historical study—not, in the first place, because it is proper to be concerned with the past, but because we need to be concerned with the detail of the concrete. It is true that nothing appears on the present surface of a tradition of political activity which has not its roots deep in the past, and that not to observe it coming into being is often to be denied the clue to its significance; and for this reason genuine historical study is an indispensable part of a political education. But what is equally important is not what happened, here or there, but what people have thought and said about what happened: the history, not of political ideas, but of the manner of our political thinking. Every society, by the underlinings it makes in the book of its history, constructs a legend of its own fortunes which it keeps up to date and in which is hidden its own understanding of its politics; and the historical investigation of this legend—not to expose its errors but to understand its prejudices—must be a pre-eminent part of a political education. It is, then, in the study of genuine history, and of this quasi-history which reveals in its backward glances the tendencies which are afoot, that we may hope to escape one of the most insidious current misunderstandings of political activity—the misunderstanding in which institutions and procedures appear as pieces of machinery designed to achieve a purpose settled in advance, instead of as manners of behaviour which are meaningless when separated from their context: the misunderstanding, for example, in which Mill convinced himself that something called 'Representative Government' was a 'form' of politics which could be regarded as proper to any society which had reached a certain level of what he called 'civilization'; in short, the misunderstanding in which we regard our arrangements and institutions as something more significant than the footprints of thinkers and statesmen who knew which way to turn their feet without knowing anything about a final destination.

Nevertheless, to be concerned only with one's own tradition of political activity is not enough. A political education worth the name must embrace, also, knowledge of the politics of other contemporary societies. It must do this because some at least of our political activity is related to that of other people's, and not to know how they go about attending to their own arrangements is not to know the course they will pursue and not to know what resources to call upon in our own tradition; and because to know only one's own tradition is not to know even that. But here again two observations must be made. We did not begin yesterday to have relations with our neighbours; and we do not require constantly to be hunting outside the tradition of our politics to find some special formula or some merely *ad hoc* expedient to direct those relations. It is only when wilfully or negligently we forget the resources of understanding and initiative which belongs to our tradition that, like actors who have forgotten their part, we are obliged to gag. And secondly, the only knowledge worth having about the politics of another society is the same kind of knowledge as we seek of our own tradition. Here also *reste la vérité, dans les nuances;* and a comparative study of institutions, for example, which obscured this would provide only an illusory sense of having understood what nevertheless remains a secret. The study of another people's politics, like the study of our own, should be an oecological study of a tradition of behaviour, not an anatomical study of mechanical devices or the investigation of an ideology. And only when our study is of this sort shall we find ourselves in the way of being stimulated, but not intoxicated, by the manners of others. To range the world in order to select the 'best' of the practices and purposes of others (as the eclectic Zeuxis is said to have tried to compose a figure more beautiful than Helen's by putting together features each notable for its perfection) is a corrupting enterprise and one of the surest ways of losing one's political balance; but to investigate the concrete manner in which another people goes about the business of attending to its arrangements may reveal significant passages in our own tradition which might otherwise remain hidden.

There is a third department in the academic study of politics which must be considered—what, for want of a better name, I shall call a philosophical study. Reflection on political activity may take place at various levels: we may consider what resources our political tradition offers for dealing with a certain situation, or we may abridge our political experience into a doctrine, which may be used, as a scientist uses hypothesis, to explore its intimations. But beyond these, and other manners of political thinking, there is a range of reflection the object of which is to consider the place of political activity itself on the map of our total experience. Reflection of this sort has gone on in every society which is politically conscious and intellectually alive. and so far as European societies are concerned, the inquiry has uncovered a variety of intellectual problems which each generation has formulated in its own way and has tackled with the technical resources at its disposal. And because political philosophy is not what may be called a 'progressive' science, accumulating solid results and reaching conclusions upon which further investigation may be based with confidence, its history is specially important: indeed, in a sense, it has nothing but a history, which is a history of the incoherencies philosophers have detected in common ways of thinking and the manner of solution they have proposed, rather than a history of doctrines and systems. The study of this history may be supposed to have a considerable place in a political education, and the enterprise of understanding the turn which contemporary reflection has given to it, an even more considerable place. Political philosophy cannot be expected to increase our ability to be successful in political activity. It will not help us to distinguish between good and bad political projects; it has no power to guide or direct us in the enterprise of pursuing the intimations of our tradition. But the patient analysis of the general ideas which have come to be connected with political activity—ideas such as nature, artifice, reason, will, law, authority, obligation, etc.—in so far as it succeeds in removing some of the crookedness from our thinking and leads to a more economical use of concepts, is an activity neither to be overrated nor despised. But it must be understood as an explanatory, not a practical, activity, and if we pursue it, we may hope only to be less often cheated by ambiguous statement and irrelevant argument.

Abeunt studia in mores. The fruits of a political education will appear in the manner in which we think and speak about politics and perhaps in the manner in which we conduct our political activity. To select items from this prospective harvest must always be hazardous, and opinions will differ about what is most important. But for myself I should hope for two things. The more profound our understanding of political activity, the less we shall be at the mercy of plausible but mistaken analogy, the less we shall be tempted by a false or irrelevant model. And the more thoroughly we understand our own political tradition, the more readily its whole resources are available to us, the

less likely we shall be to embrace the illusions which wait for the ignorant and the unwary: the illusion that in politics we can get on without a tradition of behaviour, the illusion that the abridgment of a tradition is itself a sufficient guide, and the illusion that in politics there is anywhere a safe harbour, a destination to be reached or even a detectable strand of progress. 'The world is the best of all possible worlds, and *everything* in it is a necessary evil.'
1951

THE PURSUIT OF INTIMATIONS

(1) This expression, as I hoped I had made clear, was intended as a description of what political activity actually is in the circumstances indicated, namely, in the 'hereditary, co-operative groups, many of them of ancient lineage, all of them aware of a past, a present, and a future, which we call "states"'. Critics who find this to be so specialized a description that it fails altogether to account for some of the most significant passages in modern political history are, of course, making relevant comment. But those who find this expression to be meaningless in respect of every so-called 'revolutionary' situation and every essay in so-called 'idealistic' politics may be asked to think again, remembering that it is neither intended as a description of the motives of politicians nor of what they believe themselves to be doing, but of what they actually succeed in doing.

I connected with this understanding of political activity two further propositions: first, that if true, it must be supposed to have some bearing upon how we study politics, that is, upon political education; secondly, that if true, it may be supposed to have some bearing upon how we conduct ourselves in political activity—there being, perhaps, some advantage in thinking and speaking and arguing in a manner consonant with what we are really doing. The second of these propositions I do not think to be very important.

(2) It has been concluded that this understanding of political activity reduces it to 'acting on hunches', 'following intuitions' and that it 'discourages argument of any sort'. Nothing I have said warrants this conclusion. The conclusion I myself drew in this connection was that, if this understanding of political activity were true, certain forms of argument (e.g. arguments designed to determine the correspondence of a political proposal with Natural Law or with abstract 'justice') must be considered either irrelevant or as clumsy formulations of other and relevant inquiries, and must be understood to have a merely rhetorical or persuasive value.

(3) It has been suggested that this understanding of political activity provides no standard or criterion for distinguishing between good and bad political projects or for deciding to do one thing rather

than another. This, again, is an unfortunate misreading of what I said: 'everything figures, not with what stands next to it, but with the whole'. Those who are accustomed to judge everything in relation to 'justice', or 'solidarity', or 'welfare' or some other abstract 'principle', and know no other way of thinking and speaking, may perhaps be asked to consider how, in fact, a barrister in a Court of Appeal argues the inadequacy of the damages awarded to his client. Does he say, 'This is a glaring injustice', and leave it at that? Or may he be expected to say that the damages awarded are 'out of line with the general level of damages currently being awarded in libel actions'? And if he says this, or something like it, is he to be properly accused of not engaging in argument of any sort, or of having no standard or criterion, or of merely referring to 'what was done last time'? (Cf. Aristotle, *Analytica Priora*, II. 23.) Again, is Mr N. A. Swanson all at sea when he argues in this fashion about the revolutionary proposal that the bowler in cricket should be allowed to 'throw' the ball: 'the present bowling action has evolved as a sequence, from under-arm by way of round-arm to over-arm, by successive legislation of unorthodox actions. Now, I maintain that the "throw" has no place in this sequence . . .'? Or, is Mr G. H. Fender arguing without a standard or criterion, or is he merely expressing a 'hunch', when he contends that the 'throw' *has* a place in this sequence and should be permitted? And is it so far-fetched to describe what is being done here and elsewhere as 'exploring the intimations' of the total situation? And, whatever we like to say in order to bolster up our self-esteem, is not this the manner in which changes take place in the design of anything, furniture, clothes, motor-cars and societies capable of political activity? Does it all become much more intelligible if we exclude circumstance and translate it into the idiom of 'principles', the bowler, perhaps, arguing his 'natural right' to throw? And, even then, can we exclude circumstance: would there ever be a question of the right to throw if the right to bowl over-arm had not already been conceded? At all events, I may perhaps be allowed to reiterate my view that moral and political 'principles' are abridgments of traditional manners of behaviour, and to refer specific conduct to 'principles' is not what it is made to appear (*viz*. referring it to a criterion which is reliable because it is devoid of contingency, like a so-called 'just price').

(4) It has been asserted that in politics there is no 'total situation': 'why should we presuppose that, inside the territory we call Britain . . . there is only one society, with one tradition? Why should not there be two societies . . . each with its own way of life?' In the understanding of a more profound critic this might be a philosophical question which would require something more than a short answer. But in the circumstances it is perhaps enough to say: first, that the

absence of homogeneity does not necessarily destroy singleness; secondly, what we are considering here is a legally organized society and we are considering the manner in which its legal structure (which in spite of its incoherencies cannot be supposed to have a competitor) is reformed and amended; and thirdly, I stated (on p. 85) what I meant by a 'single community' and my reasons for making this my starting-place.

(5) Lastly, it has been said that, since I reject 'general principles', I provide no means for detecting incoherencies and for determining what shall be on the agenda of reform. 'How do we discover what a society [*sic*] intimates?' But to this I can only reply: 'Do you want to be told that in politics there is, what certainly exists nowhere else, a mistake-proof manner of deciding what should be done?' How does a scientist, with the current condition of physics before him, decide upon a direction of profitable advance? What considerations passed through the minds of medieval builders when they detected the inappropriateness of building in stone as if they were building in wood? How does a critic arrive at the judgment that a picture is incoherent, that the artist's treatment of some passages is inconsistent with his treatment of others?

J. S. Mill (*Autobiography*, OUP pp. 136-7, 144-5), when he abandoned reference to general principle either as a reliable guide in political activity or as a satisfactory explanatory device, put in its place a 'theory of human progress' and what he called a 'philosophy of history'. The view I have expressed in this essay may be taken to represent a further stage in this intellectual pilgrimage, a stage reached when neither 'principle' (on account of what it turns out to be: a mere index of concrete behaviour) nor any general theory about the character and direction of social change seem to supply an adequate reference for explanation or for practical conduct.

NOTES

1. First delivered as an Inaugural Lecture at the London School of Economics, this piece was commented upon from various points of view. The notes I have now added, and a few changes I have made in the text, are designed to remove some of the misunderstandings it provoked. But, in general, the reader is advised to remember that it is concerned with understanding or explaining political activity which, in my view, is the proper object of political education. What people project in political activity, and different styles of political conduct, are considered here, first merely because they sometimes reveal the way in which political activity is being understood, and secondly because it is commonly (though I think wrongly) supposed that explanations are warrants for conduct.

2. This is the case, for example, with Natural Law; whether it is taken to be an explanation of political activity or (improperly) as a guide to political conduct.

3. Cf. 'Substantive law has the first look of being gradually secreted in the interstices of procedure.' Maine, *Early Law and Customs*, p. 389.

4. E.g. a society in which law was believed to be a divine gift.
5. See terminal note, p. 93.
6. The Russian Revolution (what actually happened in Russia) was not the implementation of an abstract design worked out by Lenin and others in Switzerland: it was a modification of *Russian* circumstances. And the French Revolution was far more closely connected with the *ancien régime* than with Locke or America.
7. To those who seem to themselves to have a clear view of an immediate destination (that is, of a condition of human circumstance to be achieved), and who are confident that this condition is proper to be imposed upon everybody, this will seem an unduly sceptical understanding of political activity; but they may be asked where they have got it from, and whether they imagine that 'political activity' will come to an end with the achievement of this condition? And if they agree that some more distant destination may then be expected to disclose itself, does not this situation entail an understanding of politics as an open-ended activity such as I have described? Or do they understand politics as making the necessary arrangements for a set of castaways who have always in reserve the thought that they are going to be 'rescued'?
8. The critic who found 'some mystical qualities' in this passage leaves me puzzled: it seems to me an exceedingly matter-of-fact description of the characteristics of any tradition—the Common Law of England, for example, the so-called British Constitution, the Christian religion, modern physics, the game of cricket, shipbuilding.

7

Professor J. C. Rees

INTERPRETING THE CONSTITUTION

Not everyone looks upon politics as a genuine academic pursuit, but the creation of a new chair in the subject is a reliable sign that doubts about its credentials are gradually being dispelled and that its authenticity is gaining wider recognition. My several months in Swansea have convinced me that it will find at this College fertile soil for steady growth and development. And for this the credit must largely go to the Principal and to Mr. Frank Stacey: to the Principal because he knows from his own experience and from the example of the late Lord Lindsay what a systematic training in politics can do for the young mind, and to Mr. Stacey for showing how the subject can be fruitfully allied with disciplines that differ from it substantially in both content and method.

The title of the chair I now occupy suggests a twofold division of political studies: political theory and political institutions. I have sometimes wondered if the choice of this title was intended to convey that distinction or, in view of the common saying that politics is a dirty game, designed to spare the first incumbent from having to describe himself officially as a professor of politics. However that may be, the distinction itself is familiar enough and is found at least as far back as Aristotle, for he took politics to be an inquiry into the nature of the good life and the ideal state as well as an empirical study of the kinds of constitution there are and how they work. My subject this evening does not fit neatly into either division, but it is related to the second. I propose to discuss a variety of interpretations of the British Constitution put forward in recent times.

I think we can best approach the matter by considering first the sorts of disagreements that occur among authoritative writers on the constitution. If one wanted to be thorough and yet risk being thought facetious one could begin by asking whether we have a constitution at all and cite de Tocqueville's famous remark: 'In England the constitution does not in reality exist'—in favour of a sceptical view. But we do not argue about this any more. The kind of thing we do dispute is the nature of the royal prerogative to dissolve parliament. And this is an example that could be usefully elaborated. It is generally agreed nowadays that the monarch cannot dissolve parliament without advice; that, as it was put in the course of a well-known controversy in *The Times* in 1913, 'The Sovereign cannot act alone, and such an independent decision on his part would almost inevitably be equivalent to a dismissal of his Ministers.'[1] But although the Queen cannot dissolve on her own initiative, is she not entitled to refuse a dissolution to the Prime Minister? Sir Ivor Jennings thinks that although there has been no instance of a refusal in this country for over a hundred years a monarch 'who thought that the power was being put to serious abuse could refuse to allow a dissolution'. Harold Laski, on the other hand, argued that the revival of a prerogative power so long fallen into disuse would open the monarchy to the charge of discriminating between the parties, hence to grant a dissolution automatically was the only way to maintain the neutrality of the Crown—and this, he assumed, was a feature of the constitution everyone wished to preserve. Now the argument here, it will be noticed, is about what *is* or is *not* constitutional, and the constitutionality of any given action or procedure is a question on which opinions can reasonably differ. Other examples of this class would be the part played by George V in the formation of the National Government in 1931. Did he behave with strict constitutional propriety? And what *are* the proprieties in such circumstances? Or again, how far can a resigning minister reveal cabinet secrets in explaining his action before the House of Commons? Another type of question arises from the interpretation to be put upon specific constitutional developments. The dispute in this case is not about the constitutionality of some action or practice but about the significance or meaning of what are generally recognized as new trends in the system of government. Anyone who has read the Donoughmore Report, the works of Lord Hewart, and Professor Robson, will know that there is no agreed verdict on the way we should describe the growth of delegated legislation and administrative tribunals. Whereas some wish to describe delegated legislation as a desirable necessity for coping with the increased demands made on modern government there are others who regard it as 'a serious invasion of the sphere of Parliament by the Executive . . . [which] leads not only to widespread suspicion and distrust of the machinery of Government, but actually endangers our civic and personal liberties'.[2] Clearly in matters of this kind our interpretation of new constitutional trends is often bound up with our attitude to the institutions concerned and so this sort of question shades into that of appraising institutions, estimating their worth and making proposals for their reform should they be thought to need it. Controversy over the reform of the House of Lords or our system of local government, and discussion of the respective merits of our present electoral procedures and proportional representation; these are examples of our third category. Divisions here frequently coincide with party allegiance but not always: the support for, and opposition to, regionalism as a form of local government do not conform to the pattern of ideological attachment.

But my chief interest this evening is in what may be termed the general theory of the constitution or the attempt to view the constitution as a whole and reveal its real meaning or essence. There is a problem here, on the face of it at least, in so far as we are presented with various interpretations of the constitution, interpretations that seem to be quite at odds with each other. Nor can we explain the divergence by the mere passage of time, for it is not a case of comparing de Lolme with Bagehot, or Burke with Dicey. The particular theories I propose to consider have all been propounded within the last two decades and have their devotees at the present time. I shall proceed in this way. I have selected four types of interpretation of the constitution, each expounded by a recognized authority but accepted, perhaps with small modifications in some cases, by wide circles of opinion. To anyone acquainted with them it might seem that they cannot *all* be true accounts of what they are supposed to describe and one will probably be led to ask which of them is right.

The first type of interpretation I shall consider is to be found in the writings of Sir Ivor Jennings,[3] and so influential has it become that people sometimes refer to it as the prevailing orthodoxy. It runs like this. The business of government in this country proceeds in a society where the great Whig principles of liberty and toleration are generally accepted. We also assume that one person's opinion on public policy is as good as another's and so we give one vote, but not more than one, to every adult person. We settle our differences by majority vote, yet encourage the minority to play its part at all stages of our democratic system. It is a *democratic* system because the rulers govern according to the will of the people, in the sense that there is close correspondence between the actions of the government and the opinions of the electorate. In fact the whole machinery of government is keyed to public opinion because the character of the government depends on the results of the last general election, because there must be an election at least every five years and because the electors have a

genuinely free choice between candidates putting forward different policies. And, since public opinion can rouse parliament, and parliament can rouse the cabinet, the close relation between government and public opinion is maintained in the intervals between elections. In short, our government is democratic: that is, the people are free, they choose their rulers, and the rulers govern according to the wishes of the people. All of which Jennings thoroughly approves. As he puts it: 'I have adopted the principles of liberalism and toleration which are implicit in the Constitution.'

Sir Ernest Barker best illustrates the second kind of approach. His concern is with the moral basis of democracy, of which our constitution is an example, and he finds it in the idea of discussion. Government resting solely on the will of the majority is just government by number—in other words, sheer force. To be legitimate it must elicit the capacities of each member of the community by facilitating a mutual interchange of ideas. The essence of democracy, therefore, is free discussion among individuals. It is government by discussion because the ideas which prevail bear the imprint of all members of society. It is a method of achieving a compromise which can be truly described as the national will.

Government by discussion, says Barker, proceeds by stages. In Britain there are four distinct yet interdependent stages: party, electorate, parliament, and cabinet. The function of each stage is different and each is necessary to the system as a whole. The parties formulate the issues for presentation to the electorate. Discussion goes on within and between them. The electorate is engaged in discussion when it chooses a set of party representatives and the programme they stand for. The outcome of their choice is a pattern of parliamentary representation and a set of proposals for legal enactment. But parliament is more than a legislature; it has the task of reviewing the behaviour of the departments, of seeing that they conform to the general spirit of the programme approved by the electorate. Then, finally, at the level of the cabinet, discussion issues in decision. At each level discussion affects discussion at other levels and at the same time every stage has its own peculiar contribution to make: it is a process that combines division of labour with mutual control. What is achieved is the collection and sifting of public opinion, thus ensuring that the ideas which emerge triumphant have the mark of quality and a basis in consent. Moreover, in the grand debate we are all the time developing our personalities as we bring our minds to bear on matters of public concern.[4]

The third account comes from the late Mr. L. S. Amery's *Thoughts on the Constitution*. The essential feature of our constitution, contends Mr. Amery, is that is consists of two independent but interacting elements, the Crown and the Nation. The Crown is represented by the government of the day and is the active and initiating element. The Nation is represented by its members in parliament whose function is to ventilate grievances and discuss the proposals put to them by the government. Parliament itself does not govern, nor does it legislate, still less does it create governments. The Prime Minister is chosen by the monarch and selects his team of ministers without any dictation from parliament. No picture misrepresents our constitution so artlessly as the nineteenth-century Liberal version of it in terms of delegation from the people to parliament and thence to the cabinet, typified by Bagehot's description of the cabinet as a committee of the majority in parliament. In truth the people, as the electorate, exercise a choice within narrow limits because there is already a government in being and the only alternative is Her Majesty's Opposition. The Crown's authority is not derivative and has never rested on a mandate from the people: its power has been enlarged despite the extension of the franchise and the ever-increasing part played by public opinion. It has an independent status such that ministers, who undoubtedly have a responsibility to parliament, owe their first responsibility to the Crown as the embodiment of the unity and continuity of the life of the Nation. Moreover, it is quite alien to the spirit of our constitution to regard a decision by the majority *qua* majority as absolute and unquestionable, for as Burke reminds us, the constitution is something more than a problem in arithmetic.

My fourth and final specimen is the economic interpretation of the constitution of which Harold Laski was the ablest exponent in this country. In the habits and procedure of the House of Commons, which he greatly admired, Laski saw government by discussion at its best. But government by discussion, he argued, was a very rare thing, able to grow and flourish in very special conditions; and its survival depended on the maintenance of those conditions. In Britain the success of liberal democracy has rested on the fundamental unity of the people, itself the function of economic expansion and prosperity. But now it is obvious that the régime of private property in the means of production has outlived its purpose and in seeking to redefine the relations of production we cannot assume the state to be a neutral force which responds objectively to the will of an electoral majority. For our constitution has been adapted to the needs of a specific set of social relationships: the positions of power in the state, in the judiciary, the civil service, the police, and the defence forces are held by reliable servants of the propertied classes. Hence to understand the real nature of our parliamentary system we must recognize that behind the formal processes of liberal democracy there stands a pattern of social power based on the ownership of property. Our political institutions operate within the confines set by that pattern.[5]

Confronted with these four divergent interpretations of our constitution we might be inclined to ask which of them is correct. But this would be taking it for granted that they are all in the same category, that if one is correct then it must be at the expense of the others. Perhaps they are not all trying to do the same thing. To take an obvious example. No one supposes that when Bagehot was writing the *English Constitution* he was engaged on the same sort of task as James Mill had set himself in his *Essay on Government*. Clearly they were doing different things: one *describing* the constitution as he found it in the 1860s, the other seeking to derive the form that government *ought* to take from the laws of human nature and the principle of utility. It would be absurd to regard them as rival accounts of the same phenomenon. I am not saying that we shall be able to make precisely this distinction among our constitutional theories, but we must allow for the possibility that the business of adjudicating between them will prove to be far less simple than merely awarding the prize to the one which portrays the constitution with the greatest accuracy.

Of one thing we can be sure, all four interpretations are in the indicative mood, that is, they are, in varying degrees, concerned with the constitution as it operates in the real world. They have other elements too, but for the present let us consider them solely as attempts to reveal the essence of a working system of government, therefore standing committed to factual assertions about the way we transact our public affairs. Regarded thus we might call them empirical theories of the constitution. Now although I have said they all fall into this category there is an important difference between the type of account given by Laski and those of the other three, for Laski is dealing with the *conditions* of successful parliamentary government rather than its principal features. His is an explanation of the stability of, and widespread support for, our constitutional arrangements together with a prediction of grave difficulties ahead now that the economic system on which they were reared faces a period of decline. Such a prognosis can quite consistently be combined with a preference for liberal values, a willingness to describe our form of government as representative of the people, and a justification of that form of government in exactly the same terms as Sir Ernest Barker's. There would be no logical error in holding all these positions at the same time, any more than in saying in one place, as Laski does, that the state is in essence coercive authority placed at the disposal of the holders of economic power, and in another that it is an organization for enabling the mass of men to realize social good on the largest possible scale.[6] There is no contradiction here, for on the first occasion he speaks as a political scientist or sociologist and on the second as a political philosopher. I grant that if we agreed with Laski about the role of economics in social causation we should want to take the study of political power beyond the limits of law and convention. But that is another story. To return for a moment to Laski's theory of the constitution, on which I shall make only a brief comment. Laski himself was forced to acknowledge its weakness in the years after the first majority Labour Government came to power in 1945 and my evidence for saying this is not confined to what was extracted from him by Sir Patrick Hastings in the difficult circumstances of his libel action.[7] It is true that according to the extreme exponents of this brand of prophecy events have by no means upset the theory, but under examination their version becomes so flexible that its immunity from refutation, far from being a virtue, is in truth a vital defect.

If we can eliminate the economic interpretation as belonging to a separate species our next task is to assess the merits of the accounts that remain, for they appear to operate on the same level and to manifest differences which seem to be definite and irreconcilable. For example, Sir Ivor Jennings and Mr. Amery look as if they hold completely opposed views on the part played by 'the people' in the constitution. Jennings insists that the essential principle underlying the whole constitution is the principle of democracy: it is government by opinion and in accordance with the wishes of the people. Amery, on the other hand, is sure that we do not have government *by* the people, either directly or by delegation. The essential feature of the constitution, he claims, is that there are *two* independent elements, the Crown and the People. He maintains that the authority of the Crown is original and remains intact despite the power of public opinion and the fact that the People's verdict recorded at periodic elections is reflected in a parliament on whose continued support each particular government depends for its existence.

One of the problems here is to decide what would count as evidence for or against either view. How can we determine whether our system of government is correctly described as being in essence 'government by opinion', 'government in accordance with the wishes of the people', *or* whether its essential nature is that of balance between two independent elements, the Crown and the Nation? Is there a real conflict: if so, what facts are relevant to settling it? Or are we wrong in thinking that facts matter in an issue of this sort? It could be that the features of the constitution Amery and Jennings have in mind as justifying these expressions are really not in dispute between them. They might agree about the powers of the monarch, the cabinet, parliament, and so on, yet still choose to look on them in the manner indicated by their central concepts. The question then could not be settled as we may originally have thought it could, and consideration of quite another order would have to enter. So our problem becomes one of discovering the exact nature of the disagreement (if any) between them, and as a contribution to this let us consider Jennings's interpretation on its own merits.

Government in Britain, says Sir Ivor Jennings, is carried on according to the wishes of the people and in close relation to public opinion. What facts does he cite in support? He points out that the character of the government is determined by the results of periodic elections in which the voter has a genuinely free choice, that under our present electoral arrangements a slight shift in opinion (that is, when a relatively small number of voters change their allegiance) can turn out a government or at least considerably reduce its majority, that government leaders are anxious not to have opinion (as defined) move away to the opposition and are thus sensitive to what they take to be signs of movements in opinion, and that government policy is sometimes shaped, modified, or even changed, by outbursts of public opinion as manifested by the attitude of the press, reports from private members on feeling in the constituencies, conversation in the clubs, and so on—what Jennings calls 'vocal public opinion', implying thereby that it need not represent in exact proportion the views of the public as measured by a gallup poll (a frequently quoted example of the influence of public opinion in this sense, which Jennings himself also gives, is the resignation of Sir Samuel Hoare in 1935 after the country had learnt of the plan he had agreed upon with Laval for a peace settlement in Abyssinia). There can be no doubt about the importance of these facts: they would not be denied by most students of the constitution and nothing in the works we have so far mentioned can be construed as denying them. But are they sufficient for the claim that government is carried on according to the wishes of the people, in close relation to public opinion? They are not, if we interpret these phrases in a strict or literal sense. For even when public opinion, in whatever sense, is unmistakably expressed, governments do not always defer to it. Jennings recognizes this when he says that although governments are very sensitive to public opinion it is also true that public opinion follows the lead of governments. Moreover, he points out that if there are some cabinet ministers who adapt their views to the changing currents of opinion, most of them 'place their opinions before their prospects'. And of the relation between public opinion and the foreign policy of the Baldwin Government he remarks: 'Finding public opinion against it in 1933–35, the Government neither changed its policy nor tried to change public opinion.' In foreign policy, however, the public's interest is not close and constant. Indeed the analysis of public opinion polls over a number of years shows that about a third of the electorate admit not having read or heard of important foreign policy questions and that another third have only the most rudimentary knowledge of them. Only a minority of the British people knew about Marshall Aid after we had been receiving it for a whole year, yet the decision to put the Marshall Plan into operation was surely one of the crucial points in the history of the Cold War. It would be reasonable to expect greater interest in and knowledge of domestic affairs, but even here vital decisions are taken of which the bulk of the population is largely ignorant and on which, had it been consulted, it would probably not have bestowed its blessing. As Mr. Amery says, it is very doubtful if a gallup poll would have shown a majority in favour of the creation of the National Government in 1931. And we can be sure that no British government would assign such a low priority to the development of nuclear energy as the public are currently recorded as doing in the opinion polls. If we add to all this such evidence as we have about voting behaviour— like the fact that support for a party at an election is no guarantee that the individual items of the party programme are approved—the qualifications we should have to make to formulas like 'government in accordance with the wishes of the people' are so important that their use cannot be justified by the degree of considered reflection on public policy that takes place or the amount of continuing popular control exercised over the administration. But the attraction of these favoured expressions is not to be accounted for solely in terms of their very limited explanatory power: we must also reckon with the place they occupy in a style of political philosophy going back to at least the seventeenth century, to Locke and the Levellers.

Coming now to Mr. Amery's account of the constitution we find that many of the things he wishes to emphasize would not be disputed at all by those who accept the type of interpretation offered by Sir Ivor Jennings. Parliament, says Amery, is not primarily a law-making body: the government holds the initiative in legislation and parliament's function is to discuss the administrative activity and legislative proposals of the government. He maintains that the starting-point and mainspring of action has always been the government, that our system is not one of delegation from the people to parliament and thence to the cabinet, and that Bagehot's famous description of the cabinet as a committee of the parliamentary majority is false because a committee 'usually implies definite appointment in detail by the parent body'. Compare this with what Jennings has to say. Parliament, he observes, usually approves what the government puts before it—'the last word as well as the first rests with the Government'—and since parliament cannot govern its main job is to criticize. The House of Commons controls the government, but it is equally true to say that the government controls the House. It is difficult to see any significant difference between them. Again, the accounts they give of the stages in the formation of cabinets—the powers of the monarch in the choice of a Prime Minister, the latter's choice of cabinet colleagues, the weapon of dissolution—are virtually identical.[8] But, it may be said, there is surely one contention of Amery's that quite decisively separates his from the Whig approach to the constitution and it is over this that he and Jennings are basically at odds. In Amery's view ministers on taking office accept 'a first and dominant responsibility to the Crown, as representing the unity and continuity of the life of the nation and of the Empire, for defending the wider national and Imperial interest'. Jennings, with so much emphasis on the popular control of our rulers, on government according to the wishes of the people, might be thought to take quite the opposite view. Is not the whole spirit of assertions like, 'The fundamental principle (of the Constitution) is that of democracy' and 'The House of Commons and the Cabinet are the *instruments* of democracy' the very negation of Amery's belief in the independent authority of the Crown? Yet even here, when the difference seems genuine and fundamental, it is hard to see just what the disagreement is, partly because Amery doesn't make it altogether clear what sort of responsibility it is. Plainly it is not a responsibility which the monarch personally can enforce by the dismissal of ministers who seem to be disregarding the national interest. For although there may be circumstances in which the Queen is justified in refusing assent to the policy of her ministers there is no one today who would uphold Disraeli's statement, made in 1878, that 'If your Majesty's Government have . . . not fulfilled their engagements to their Sovereign . . . your Majesty has the clear constitutional right to dismiss them.'[9] I do not remember any suggestion made at the time or since that Mr. Baldwin should have been dismissed from office by the King for neglecting the defences of the nation. But what Amery probably intends to say is that ministers have an overriding duty to promote the national interest, that the interests of the nation come before those of party or pressure group, and that this is recognized in all parties as a constitutional duty. And I think we must agree with Amery, for vague though the idea of promoting the national interest is, it *is* a widely accepted doctrine. In his recent book, *Government and Parliament,* Mr. Herbert Morrison states that in a well-conducted cabinet the main consideration is to do what is right for the nation. It is 'a sound moral principle', he goes on, right in itself but also more likely to bring success than 'if policy were settled by low-down considerations of party advantage'.[10] Now if this is what Mr. Amery means it turns out to be no very startling proposition and it is, as we have seen, one with which there would be scarcely any disagreement. When Sir Ivor Jennings says that 'the main function of government is the provision of services, including the maintenance of external relations and the defence of the country, for the welfare of the people', is he not putting forward essentially the same view?

The key to understanding our constitution, Mr. Amery maintains, is to see it as a 'balance and adjustment between two elements each of independent and original authority, the Crown and the Nation'. We have seen why it is misleading to describe the constitution as one of government according to the wishes of the people. Is this formula of Mr. Amery's an improvement? I fear not. For one thing I find the notion of adjustment and interaction between Crown and Nation somewhat obscure. As these terms are used by Mr. Amery the Crown is the central executive—the cabinet and the departments—and by the Nation is meant the various 'classes and communities' that make up our society, that is, the whole network of interlocking and overlapping associations, classes and localized communities that we often refer to by the word 'society'. Between Crown and Nation, one may suppose, the relation is one of ruler and ruled, and this relationship obtains wherever we find government. The forms such a relationship may assume are many, and there seems no point in saying that the essential feature of *our* constitution is the balance and adjustment that must of necessity be present in every society with a government: the specific nature of that balance needs to be described. Once it is explained that the balance achieved in our system assigns to the government and to parliament distinctive yet interdependent functions, that they are separate entities for all the interaction between them, one wonders why it should be necessary to call our attention to this familiar and essentially simple fact by means of a formula which really tells us nothing about the constitution itself. There is no reason to regard it, outside the context of the delegation theory, as a more important fact than, for example, the legislative sovereignty of parliament.

In parliament, continues Mr. Amery, the Crown and the Nation conduct 'a continuous conference or parley'[11] and so it is 'the centre and focus of the nation's affairs', the arena where 'the great game of politics is played'. And of course it is true that parliament is a principal forum for debating the affairs of state and that it is an organ to which we turn for the redress of grievances. But we must not overlook the other channels of contact between rulers and ruled; the way, for example, the departments of government are approached by those who wish to bring pressure to bear on behalf of the countless interest groups that form part of 'the Nation'. These contacts usually take place outside parliament altogether and although members of parliament act frequently on behalf of associations, either because they belong to them or are sympathetic to their aims, the associations also deal directly with the departments and some are without a single advocate in parliament. Again, to say that parliament is the arena where the Crown and the Nation meet does not sufficiently recognize the importance of the vast amount of extra-parliamentary discussion and protest (in the press, over the radio, at public meetings, in the reports of Royal Commissions or private committees, in the work of experts, and so on), not all of which finds corresponding expression in the House of Commons; yet it is a form of influence that can be successfully exerted without, or not mainly on account of, its being formally recorded in Hansard. Moreover, if we say that the government, and not parliament, is the active and originating element in the constitution, this may be so understood as to ignore the extent to which many of the proposals which issue as legislative enactments are not born in the departments, in the cabinet or any of its committees. The Labour Government of 1945 was committed to and largely succeeded in carrying out a programme which owed very little, apart from the actual drafting of the bills, to anyone in the official machine, and much the same could be said of many of the legislative proposals of other governments. From interest groups, inner-party discussions and research, individual publicists, and committees of inquiry there is a constant stream of recommendations from which any single government has to select when it prepares its legislative programme. However, in using the formula of 'balance and adjustment' Mr. Amery wishes to direct our attention to specific aspects of the constitution which he claims are too often neglected. He wants to emphasize the active, governing role of the Crown, holding as it does the initiative in legislation. He insists that parliament's job is not to govern but to ventilate grievances and discuss the government's proposals, that ministers regard themselves as under a duty to promote the national interest, and that the cabinet and parliament are independent bodies each having its characteristic methods of controlling the other. But we have seen that there is nothing in Jennings's account of the constitution which is at all incompatible with any of these particular assertions. The contrasting terminology of their general theories obscures the fact that they really agree about the working of particular institutions. And whether the working of those institutions should be described as 'a balance and adjustment between two elements . . . the Crown and the Nation' cannot be decided as one would, for example, decide the question of whether the cabinet usually gets its way in parliament.

Why then does one writer wish to speak of the constitution in terms of a balance and adjustment between the Crown and the Nation, while another prefers to regard it as government in accordance with the wishes of the people? (I have been arguing that they need not disagree in any significant way about the actual functioning of political institutions despite the appearance of conflict created by the formulas used to characterize the general nature of the constitution. I shall be dealing with Sir Ernest Barker's interpretation presently but I can say now that there is nothing to suggest that he would dissent from the detailed descriptions of Mr. Amery and Sir Ivor Jennings.) Probably the most important reason—and one long recognized—is that a theory of the constitution is closely bound up with the writer's political philosophy: or you might say that an interpretation of the constitution is *part* of one's political philosophy. When he emphasizes the independent authority of the Crown Amery at the same time repudiates the view that the 'active and originating element' in our constitution is the voter selecting a delegate to carry out his wishes in parliament, which in turn selects an administration to act in conformity to those wishes; that is to say, he is repudiating the delegation theory both as a putative account of our constitution and as a profession of what ought to be, for government by delegation, he claims, carries with it such control by the legislature over the government as to render the latter unstable in its tenure of office and vacillating in its policy. Thus the effect of Amery's espousal of the doctrine of balance between Crown and Nation is to uphold strong government and assign to the popular will its appropriate role of checking and approving, rather than instructing, the government. In this he is quite explicitly following Burke, who said:

> No legislator has willingly placed the seat of active power in the hands of the multitude; because then it admits of no control, no regulation; no steady direction whatever. The people are the natural control on authority; but to exercise and to control together is contradictory and impossible.[12]

According to Burke, and those who follow him, we court disaster if we attempt to rely solely on the meagre 'stock of reason' nature has granted us. And so they exhort us all to 'approach to the faults of the state as to the wounds of a father, with pious awe and trembling solicitude', for we shall find the guidance we need in the accumulated experience of the nation as embodied in the laws and customs passed down from our forbears. They assert the claims of established authority because they deem strong government a necessary price for order and progress. Society being an intricate organism, its health would be in danger if the recurrent upheavals of mass emotion were registered each time as a political mandate, a consequence impossible to avoid when in the constitution there is faithfully reflected the doctrine of popular delegation. This, as I see it, is what Amery is arguing in his theory of balance between Crown and Nation. He is warning us against an executive dependent on the legislature, against a legislature with the power to initiate and which is yet an instrument of popular control. 'Such a system of government', he claims, 'is bound . . . to be weak and unstable, subject to the continual shifting and reshuffling of coalition ministries and to the influence of personal ambitions.' Government by an elected assembly cannot work and it is not the kind of government we have in Britain. We put a high premium on strong and stable government and that is why ours is a 'democracy by consent and not by delegation'.

It is worth digressing here for a short while to notice that Mr. Walter Lippmann in his book, *The Public Philosophy,* published earlier this year, sets out from premises almost identical with those of Mr. Amery. He maintains that there is a correct balance of power between governors and governed, a proper relationship 'between, on the one hand, the governing and executive power, and, on the other hand, the elected assembly and the voters in the constituencies'.

> The executive is the active power in the state, [he says] the asking and proposing power. The representative assembly is the consenting power, the petitioning, the approving and the criticizing, the accepting and the refusing power. The two powers are necessary if there is to be order and freedom. But each must be true to its own nature, each limiting and complementing the other. . . . The health of the system depends upon the relationship of the two powers. If either absorbs or destroys the functions of the other power, the constitution is deranged.

And like Mr. Amery he sees no virtue in the voice of a majority *qua* majority. The opportunities the enfranchised masses have for judging matters of state are so few that we ought not to take their opinions to be expressions of the social good, for 'the public interest may be presumed to be what men would choose if they saw clearly, thought rationally, acted disinterestedly and benevolently'. But whereas Mr. Amery believes the essential character of our constitution has remained intact throughout its history—he quotes Hearn approvingly: it is the 'very constitution under which the Confessor ruled and which William swore to obey'—Mr. Lippmann is convinced that since about 1917 the Western democracies have entered a period of decline due principally to a radical change in the nature of their constitutional systems. I am sure we should all admit that the character and extent of state activity has undergone a massive transformation since 1917. And Mr. Amery recognizes that the Crown has 'enormously increased the sum total of its power and influence' and that public opinion has been exercising ever greater control on the whole process of government. Yet he maintains that the essential principle of the constitution—the balance between Crown and Nation—has been left undisturbed. Mr. Lippmann, on the other hand, is alarmed by the eclipse of the executive branch of government: it has been pushed out of its traditional position in the political structure by the representative assembly, the mass electorate, party bosses, and the agents of pressure groups. Mass opinion, he complains, now exercises irresistible influence on cabinets, but the mass of people lack the knowledge to arrive at wise decisions on the terribly complex and intractable problems of the mid-twentieth century. Mass opinion always chooses the easy alternative when often the national interest requires austerity, determination, or even sacrifice. In our age of mass democracy the constitutional pattern of the West has been shattered and it is in this breakdown of the traditional balance between rulers and subjects that lies the true cause of the decline in Western power and prestige. As Mr. Lippmann puts it: 'This devitalization of the governing power is the malady of democratic states.'

Here then we have two writers, who start off from the same postulates with regard to the proper division of powers in the political system, disagreeing fundamentally in their interpretation of an important phase in our recent constitutional history. The continuity Mr. Amery claims to see is the continuity of a balanced interaction between Crown and Nation, maintained despite the incessant modification and adaptation of the particular instruments of government. And the balance corresponds to what he insists is the right and true allocation of power. For Mr. Lippmann our ills derive from the derangement of the system which at one time exhibited the principle both he and Mr. Amery strongly approve. What has vanished, says Mr. Lippmann, is an equilibrium in government and he is so firmly a believer in the virtues of the equilibrium that he discovers in its demise the prime cause of our predicament. What has survived, says Mr. Amery, is a balance in the constitution and he is so convinced of the rightness of the balance that he attributes the strength and stability of our government to the fact of its survival. The interpretations of both revolve around a cardinal aspect of their political philosophies: 'the relationship between governors and governed which is rooted in the nature of things'.[13]

Before this digression I was saying that Mr. Amery's portrayal of the constitution was a product of the Burkian idea of the state. In the case of Sir Ivor Jennings we are aided by his forthright declaration: 'I have adopted the principles of liberalism and toleration which are implicit in the Constitution.' But we could have inferred from the type of interpretation he provides that his philosophy falls within the great liberal tradition coming down from Locke, a tradition that regards organized coercion as legitimate only when it is based on the free consent of the people. As Jefferson and the revolutionaries of 1776 proclaimed: 'Governments are instituted among Men, deriving their just powers from the consent of the governed, that whenever any form of government becomes destructive of these ends, it is the right of the People to alter and abolish it.' It is a doctrine with a long career: beginning as a justification of revolt against ungodly and despotic power it has roots in the Middle Ages, grows to maturity in the hands of the Monarchomachs, put into classic shape in the seventeenth century, and emerging as part of the enlightened man's outlook in the age of reason. It has had more than one function: at times to sanction rebellion, by others to provide a moral basis for established government and yet again to serve as an abridgement of democracy at work. Nurtured in this tradition men have frequently thought our constitution to be the embodiment of their principles. But it seldom happens that constitutions can be identified from the formulae of their admirers: historically at least they have rarely conformed to the prescriptions of doctrine, liberal or otherwise. The constitution described by Sir Ivor Jennings, we have seen, refuses to fit tidily into the simple categories acquired from the tradition he is heir to, and if we turn to the picture of our democracy painted by Sir Ernest Barker we shall find that he too has composed an idealized version of our political system.

Government in Britain, says Sir Ernest, is government by discussion. And we must agree with him that the widespread discussion of public policy in conditions of freedom is with us a common practice: indeed, this is one of the reasons for calling our state a democracy. Proposals which started life as no more than the schemes of small minorities have passed through ever-broadening circles of critical scrutiny, often benefiting from the clash of views accompanying their journey, and have eventually arrived in parliament supported by the bulk of articulate opinion. Bentham and law reform, the Webbs and the poor law, the later extensions of the franchise, and Eleanor Rathbone and family allowances: it is a plausible reading of our history that would regard them as examples of this kind of process. The more proposals for reform travel this journey the better, for I agree with Barker that a system of government which encourages discussion of public affairs in this spirit has a claim on our loyalty and is to that extent justified. What better reason could there be for respecting the laws and institutions of a state than that its citizens have, and regularly make use of, the opportunity to decide after free and full discussion what those laws and institutions should be like? But even if we suppose that the examples I have quoted are evidence for the claim (and this is what Sir Ernest Barker claims) that our method of government by discussion results in a compromise solution to which *all* ideas contribute and made acceptable because it bears the imprint of *all*—a charitable interpretation I should say—how would measures like the Parliament Acts of 1911 and 1949, the Trades Disputes Act of 1927, or the Iron and Steel Act of 1949 fit into the picture? They were all resisted— some of them bitterly—at every stage of their progress through parliament. Nor were their antagonists reconciled after they had reached the statute book, for the last two were repealed when the opposition came into power. Perhaps some other meaning could be given to the idea of 'a compromise in which all ideas are reconciled and which can be accepted by all because it bears the imprint of all'? It might be said that an act of parliament bears the imprint of all merely in the sense that it has been the subject of discussion on the part of everyone who took part in the debates, but from this we could not draw any conclusions about the national will being embodied in the final enactment. It might also be said that there is a national will for the *procedure* through which all legislative proposals have to go; that is, the three readings and the committee stage in the House of Commons, and the corresponding stages in the Lords. But general approval for a specific form of legislative procedure cannot be stretched to include the proposals which emerge from that procedure; nor does it distinguish a democracy from a totalitarian state, since there might be a real unanimity in the latter for that part of the constitution which prescribes the rules for law-making. The crucial difference here is that in a democracy there are genuine clashes of opinion, sometimes involving the fundamentals of foreign and domestic policy, and— what is equally important—a variety of views on subjects which are not connected with politics at all. Most of us, I think, would wish to emphasize that diversity of opinion was not only a necessary *sign* of democracy but even an argument in its favour. And of course Sir Ernest Barker would wish to do the same. An implied convention of government by discussion, he says, is that there is no sole possessor of the truth: differences of opinion should therefore be tolerated. Moreover, he urges us to be moderate and reasonable 'even in the throes of defeat'. But I do not see how this can be squared with the notion of a national will to which we all contribute or with the idea of law as bearing the imprint of all those who come under it.[14] However, we must attempt to see Sir Ernest

Barker's interpretation of the constitution as part of his general theory of the state, for although liberals have, historically, been champions of free discussion the way it enters into their philosophy has not always been the same.

In political society the many are constrained to obey laws made and administered by the few. Can this be justified? Here is one of the traditional questions of political philosophy. The answer Locke gave was simple. Men set up governments on the understanding that those who govern will protect their rights and in return they promise to obey the laws. Government is therefore justified because it enables men better to enjoy the rights to life, liberty, and property with which they are endowed by nature. The theory was built on the two notions of a contract to establish government and a law of nature apprehended by the faculty of reason, two notions effectively undermined by David Hume in the eighteenth century. Thereafter liberal theory gradually abandoned the ideas of contract and natural rights and in their stead took up the principle of utility. For the utilitarian the duty of government was to promote the greatest happiness of the greatest number: he counselled obedience to law up to the point when the probable pains of resistance were equivalent to the sufferings of continued obedience. It mattered not how happiness was obtained: the pleasures of the intellect assumed no pride of place in his calculus unless they brought with them more enjoyment than was available from any alternative source. But first Mill and then T. H. Green began to insist upon the *quality* of happiness and conceived its content in terms of the moral and intellectual development of man. In this way the goal of state activity became that of enabling each citizen to fulfil his personality. The purpose of the state, says Sir Ernest Barker in his version of the reformed liberalism, is to promote 'the highest possible development of all the capacities of personality in all of its members'. Believing this to be the only basis for state power, how natural that he should see in the constitution those very features required by his philosophy. 'The form of government we have to find', he argues, 'is one which elicits and enlists . . . the thought, the will, and the general capacity of every member. It must be a government depending upon mutual interchange of ideas . . . A government depending on such a process . . . will be self-government: it will square with, and be based upon, the development of personality and individuality in every self.'

It is now time to summarize and draw one or two conclusions. We began with a number of divergent accounts of the constitution and noticed that they did not all operate on the same level. Diversity did not imply incompatibility, so there was no question of choosing between theories of a different type. We found that even when the interpretations were of the same kind the differences which at first seemed basic and irreconcilable turned out to involve no substantial disagreement about the working of specific institutions. I have been maintaining, too, that each theory has a tendency to exaggerate the extent and importance of some aspect of the constitution and convert it in this magnified form into the essential principle of the whole system of government. A constitution, I contend, is a complex set of arrangements whose nature is inevitably distorted by the attempt to compress its leading characteristics into a simple formula. That is why features which figure prominently in the detailed accounts of our authorities are perforce neglected in their general theories.

It may well be objected that it is not possible to describe any constitution without at the same time interpreting it. Some institutions are obviously more important than others and it is one of the jobs of the political scientist to stress those aspects that deserve to be stressed. Are not the theories under discussion just ways of emphasizing certain characteristics of the constitution, of drawing attention to features the significance of which other accounts neglect or underestimate? Mr. Amery, for example, wishes to discredit the theory of popular delegation which, he claims, has been responsible for the widely accepted misconception of the relation between cabinet and parliament, and his idea of a balance between Crown and Nation is at once a denial that parliament instructs the executive and an insistence on the independent role of the modern cabinet. Now I do not want to gainsay the necessarily selective character of any treatise on the constitution. Emphasis is inescapable and desirable, and the sort of emphasis one gives will clearly depend on the context in which one is writing. In face of the popularity of the delegation theory it is indeed proper to stress the powers of the executive, just as it would be legitimate to stress against the opposite view, that governments *do* sometimes bow to pressure from the House of Commons and what is taken to be public opinion, and that their complexion *does* depend on the results of general elections. Similarly, in contrast with government in the totalitarian world, it is surely right to emphasize the role of free discussion in our political life. But all this, I maintain, falls short of the sort of emphasis I have been discussing in this lecture: what may be called *absolute* or *over*-emphasis. I mean that the features stressed are seized on irrespective of context and given an importance quite disproportionate to their actual place in the living constitution.

There have been times when the nature of political activity was conceived in narrow and purely rational terms. We are not all Burkians now but most of us are ready to grant the importance of prejudice and prescription. And it is not as if political behaviour drew on irrational sources as external aids to its own momentum, for the relationship is an internal one with habit and myth as part of the activity itself. Political authority has undoubtedly been fortified by beliefs about its origin and sustained by theories which seem to lend it justification. They may take the form of a general theory of the state or an interpretation of a particular constitution. The growing power of international communism is attributable in part to the enormous attraction Marxian theory has for millions over the world, a theory which appears to explain and support the political régimes in China and the U.S.S.R. That there might be a gulf between deed and doctrine—as, for example, between the specification of the conditions for social revolution in the Marxian texts and what the Bolsheviks actually did in 1917—seems not to matter: the power of the myth endures. Now, it may be asked, does not liberal democracy need to be sustained by myths appropriate to its character? Indeed, could we do *without* a political doctrine of this kind? And if, like Sir Ernest Barker's, it succeeds in *combining* a justification of democracy with a theory of the constitution, is not this an added virtue? True, it embodies an embroidered version of the constitution, but can men be satisfied with less? Is it not the task of the political theorist to strengthen the hold of liberal ideals by maintaining or repairing or perhaps even replacing with others more suitable the ideological constructs without which democracy cannot survive?

These are very large questions to which it is tempting to make the simple and defiant reply, 'Truth must prevail.' I am sure that any plan that would subordinate intellectual integrity to the need for an inspiring myth can never succeed so long as we remain a democratic society. For we should have to state not what we find to be the case but rather what we believe is likely to preserve a system of government whose true nature cannot in fact be concealed if it continues to be what its admirers say it is now—government by free discussion. But is the future of democracy really linked with the fate of the political philosophies which accompanied its growth? For my part, I do not believe—though there is no time to marshall the evidence—that democratic government is endangered by the absence of an inspiring myth. Certainly in my programme for political studies at this College I shall assume that in a democracy such as ours we do not need to distort reality before we can be stirred to defend it.

NOTES

1. Professor J. H. Morgan in a letter to *The Times*, 10 Sept. 1913 (reprinted by Sir Ivor Jennings in his *Cabinet Government*, Appendix IV).

2. Report of the *Committee on Ministers' Powers* (Cmd. 4060, 1932), p. 53, summarizing the arguments of the critics of delegated legislation.

3. The summary that follows is based on *Cabinet Government, Parliament, The British Constitution*, and *The Queen's Government*.

4. I have followed Sir Ernest Barker's account in chap. ii of his *Reflections on Government*.

5. This is a recurring theme in Laski's political writings, but see especially his *Parliamentary Government in England*, chaps. i and ii.

6. Compare *The State in Theory and Practice*, p. 329, and the *Grammar of Politics*, p. 25.

7. See Laski's *Reflections on the Constitution* (published posthumously), and Herbert A. Deane's *The Political Ideas of Harold J. Laski* (1955), pp 270-5 and 290-1.

8. i.e. in *Cabinet Government* and *Thoughts on the Constitution*.

9. Quoted by Jennings, *Cabinet Government*, p. 303.

10. p. 11.

11. The 'Nation', it will be remembered, is made up of classes and communities. It is difficult to see how the Crown could parley with a class. Perhaps Her Majesty's Opposition represents a class? But the suggestion that parties represent classes is contrary both to what Mr. Amery believes about the social basis of our major parties and what we know of the voting behaviour of classes in Britain.

12. Quoted by Amery, *op. cit.*, p. 15.

13. Lippmann, *op. cit.*, p. 34.

14. Another possibility would be to say that there is a general will for the main features of the constitution, for the framework within which we conduct our party battles, and for the principle of abiding by majority decisions to amend the constitution. But here again we are dealing with something quite different from general support for specific acts of the administration or particular items of legislation.

8

Professor Isaiah Berlin

TWO CONCEPTS OF LIBERTY

If men never disagreed about the ends of life, if our ancestors had remained undisturbed in the Garden of Eden, the studies to which the Chichele Chair of Social and Political Theory is dedicated could scarcely have been conceived. For these studies spring from, and thrive on, discord. Someone may question this on the ground that even in a society of saintly anarchists, where no conflicts about ultimate purpose can take place, political problems, for example constitutional or legislative issues, might still arise. But this objection rests on a mistake. Where ends are agreed, the only questions left are those of means, and these are not political but technical, that is to say, capable of being settled by experts or machines like arguments between engineers or doctors. That is why those who put their faith in some immense, world-transforming phenomenon, like the final triumph of reason or the proletarian revolution, must believe that all political and moral problems can thereby be turned into technological ones. That is the meaning of St.-Simon's famous phrase about 'replacing the government of persons by the administration of things', and the Marxist prophecies about the withering away of the state and the beginning of the true history of humanity. This outlook is called utopian by those for whom speculation about this condition of perfect social harmony is the play of idle fancy. Nevertheless, a visitor from Mars to any British—or American—university today, might perhaps be forgiven if he sustained the impression that its members lived in something very like this innocent and idyllic state, for all the serious attention that is paid to fundamental problems of politics by professional philosophers.

Yet this is both surprising and dangerous. Surprising because there has, perhaps, been no time in modern history when so large a number of human beings, both in the East and West, have had their notions, and indeed their lives, so deeply altered, and in some cases violently upset, by fanatically held social and political doctrines. Dangerous,

119

because when ideas are neglected by those who ought to attend to them— that is to say, those who have been trained to think critically about ideas—they sometimes acquire an unchecked momentum and an irresistible power over multitudes of men that may grow too violent to be affected by rational criticism. Over a hundred years ago, the German poet Heine warned the French not to underestimate the power of ideas: philosophical concepts nurtured in the stillness of a professor's study could destroy a civilization. He spoke of Kant's *Critique of Pure Reason* as the sword with which European deism had been decapitated, and described the works of Rousseau as the blood-stained weapon which, in the hands of Robespierre, had destroyed the old régime; and prophesied that the romantic faith of Fichte and Schelling would one day be turned, with terrible effect, by their fanatical German followers, against the liberal culture of the West. The facts have not wholly belied this prediction; but if professors can truly wield this fatal power, may it not be that other professors, and they alone, can disarm them?

Our philosophers seem oddly unaware of these devastating effects of their activities. It may be that, intoxicated by their magnificent achievements in more abstract realms, the best among them look with disdain upon a field in which radical discoveries are less likely to be made, and talent for minute analysis is less likely to be rewarded. Yet, despite every effort to separate them, conducted by a blind scholastic pedantry, politics has remained indissolubly intertwined with every other form of philosophical inquiry. To neglect the field of political thought, because its unstable subject matter, with its blurred edges, is not to be caught by the fixed concepts, abstract models and fine instruments suitable to logic or to linguistic analysis—to demand a unity of method in philosophy, and reject whatever the method cannot successfully manage—is merely to allow oneself to remain at the mercy of primitive and uncriticized political beliefs. It is only a very vulgar historical materialism that denies the power of ideas, and says that ideals are mere material interests in disguise. It may be that without the pressure of social forces, political ideas are stillborn: what is certain is that these forces, unless they clothe themselves in ideas, remain blind and undirected.

This truth has not escaped every Oxford teacher, even in our own day. It is because he has grasped the importance of political ideas in theory and practice, and has dedicated his life to their analysis and propagation, that the first holder of this Chair has made so great an impact upon the world in which he has lived. The name of Douglas Cole is known wherever men have political or social issues at heart. His fame extends far beyond the confines of this university and country. A political thinker of complete independence, honesty, and courage, a writer and speaker of extra-ordinary lucidity and eloquence, a poet and a novelist, a teacher and *animateur des idées* of genius, he is, in the first place, a man who has given his life to the fearless support of principles not always popular, and to the unswerving and passionate defence of justice and truth, often in circumstances of great difficulty and discouragement. These are the qualities for which this most generous and imaginative of English socialists is today chiefly known to the world. Not the least remarkable, and perhaps the most characteristic, fact about him is that he has achieved this public position without sacrificing his natural humanity, his spontaneity of feeling, his inexhaustible personal goodness, and above all his deep and scrupulous devotion— a devotion reinforced by the most prodigious wealth of many-sided learning, and a fabulous memory—to his vocation as a teacher in Oxford and outside it. It is a source of deep pleasure and pride to me to attempt to put on record what I, and many others, feel about this great Oxford figure, whose moral and intellectual character is an asset to his country, and to the cause of justice and human equality everywhere.

It is from him, at least as much as from his writings, that many members of my generation at Oxford have learnt that political theory is a branch of moral philosophy, which starts from the discovery, or application, of moral notions in the sphere of political relations. I do not mean, as I think some Idealist philosophers may have believed, that all historical movements or conflicts between human beings are reducible to movements or conflicts of ideas or spiritual forces, nor even that they are effects (or aspects) of them. But I do mean (and I do not think that Professor Cole would disagree) that to understand such movements or conflicts is, above all, to understand the ideas or attitudes to life involved in them, which alone make such movements a part of human history, and not mere natural events. Political words and notions and acts are not intelligible save in the context of the issues that divide the men who use them. Consequently our own attitudes and activities are likely to remain obscure to us, unless we understand the dominant issues of our own world. The greatest of these is the open war that is being fought between two civilizations and two systems of ideas which return different and conflicting answers to what has long been the central question of politics—the question of obedience and coercion. 'Why should I (or anyone) obey anyone else?' 'Why should I not live as I like?' 'Must I obey?' 'If I disobey, may I be coerced? By whom, and to what degree, and in the name of what, and for the sake of what?'

Upon the answers to the question of the permissible limits of coercion, opposed views are held in the world today, each claiming the allegiance of very large numbers of men. It seems to me, therefore, that any aspect of this issue is worthy of examination.

I

To coerce a man is to deprive him of freedom—freedom from what? Almost every moralist in human history has praised freedom.Like happiness and goodness, like nature and reality, the meaning of this term is so porous that there is little interpretation that it seems able to resist. I do not propose to discuss either the history, or the more than two hundred senses, of this protean word recorded by historians of ideas. I propose to examine no more than two of these senses—but those central ones, with a great deal of human history behind them, and, I dare say, still to come. The first of these political senses of freedom or liberty (I shall use both words to mean the same), which I shall call the 'negative' sense, is involved in the answer to the question 'What is the area within which the subject—a person or group of persons—is or should be left to do or be what he wants to do or be, without interference by other persons?' The second, which I shall call the positive sense, is involved in the answer to the question 'What, or who, is the source of control or interference, that can determine someone to do, or be, one thing rather than another?' The two questions are clearly different, even though the answers to them may overlap.

The notion of 'negative' freedom

I am normally said to be free to the degree to which no human being interferes with my activity. Political liberty in this sense is simply the area within which a man can do what he wants. If I am prevented by other persons from doing what I want I am to that degree unfree; and if the area within which I can do what I want is contracted by other men beyond a certain minimum, I can be described as being coerced, or, it may be, enslaved. Coercion is not, however, a term that covers every form of inability. If I say that I am unable to jump more than 10 feet in the air, or cannot understand the darker pages of Hegel, it would be eccentric to say that I am to that degree enslaved or coerced. Coercion implies the deliberate interference of other human beings within the area in which I wish to act. You lack political liberty or freedom only if you are prevented from attaining your goal by human beings.[1] Mere incapacity to attain your goal is not lack of political freedom.[2] This is brought out by the use of such modern expressions as 'economic freedom' and its counterpart, 'economic slavery'. It is argued, very plausibly, that if a man is too poor to afford something on which there is no legal ban—a

loaf of bread, a journey round the world, recourse to the law courts—
he is as little free to have it as he would be if it were forbidden him by
law. If my poverty were a kind of disease, which prevented me from
buying bread or paying for the journey round the world, or getting
my case heard, as lameness prevents me from running, this inability
would not naturally be described as a lack of freedom at all, least of
all political freedom. It is only because I believe that my inability to
get what I want is due to the fact that other human beings have made
arrangements whereby I am, whereas others are not, prevented from
having enough money with which to pay for it, that I think myself a
victim of coercion or slavery. In other words, this use of the term
depends on a particular social and economic theory about the causes
of my poverty or weakness. If my lack of means is due to my lack of
mental or physical capacity, then I begin to speak of being deprived of
freedom (and not simply of poverty) only if I accept the theory.[3] If, in
addition, I believe that I am being kept in want by a definite
arrangement which I consider unjust or unfair, I speak of economic
slavery or oppression. 'The nature of things does not madden us, only
ill will does', said Rousseau. The criterion of oppression is the part
that I believe to be played by other human beings, directly or
indirectly, in frustrating my wishes. By being free in this sense I mean
not being interfered with by others. The wider the area of non-
interference the wider my freedom.

This is certainly what the classical English political philosophers
meant when they used this word.[4] They disagreed about how wide the
area could or should be. They supposed that it could not, as things
were, be unlimited, because if it were, it would entail a state in which
all men could boundlessly interfere with all other men; and this kind
of 'natural' freedom would lead to social chaos in which men's
minimum needs would not be satisfied; or else the liberties of the weak
would be suppressed by the strong. Because they perceived that
human purposes and activities do not automatically harmonize with
one another; and, because (whatever their official doctrines) they put
a high value on other goals, such as justice, or happiness, or security,
or varying degrees of equality, they were prepared to curtail freedom
in the interests of other values and, indeed, of freedom itself. For,
without this, it was impossible to create the kind of association that
they thought desirable. Consequently, it is assumed by these thinkers
that the area of men's free action must be limited by law. But equally
it is assumed, especially by such libertarians as Locke and Mill in
England, and Constant and Tocqueville in France, that there ought
to exist a certain minimum area of personal freedom which must on
no account be violated, for if it is overstepped, the individual will find
himself in an area too narrow for even that minimum development of

his natural faculties which alone makes it possible to pursue, and even to conceive, the various ends which men hold good or right or sacred. It follows that a frontier must be drawn between the area of private life and that of public authority. Where it is to be drawn is a matter of argument, indeed of haggling. Men are largely interdependent, and no man's activity is so completely private as never to obstruct the lives of others in any way. 'Freedom for the pike is death for the minnows'; the liberty of some must depend on the restraint of others.[5] Still, a practical compromise has to be found.

Philosophers with an optimistic view of human nature, and a belief in the possibility of harmonizing human interests, such as Locke or Adam Smith and, in some moods, Mill, believed that social harmony and progress were compatible with reserving a large area for private life over which neither the state nor any other authority must be allowed to trespass. Hobbes, and those who agreed with him, especially conservative or reactionary thinkers, argued that if men were to be prevented from destroying one another, and making social life a jungle or a wilderness, greater safeguards must be instituted to keep them in their places, and wished correspondingly to increase the area of centralized control, and decrease that of the individual. But both sides agreed that some portion of human existence must remain independent of the sphere of social control. To invade that preserve, however small, would be despotism. The most eloquent of all defenders of freedom and privacy, Benjamin Constant, who had not forgotten the Jacobin dictatorship, declared that at the very least the liberty of religion, opinion, expression, property, must be guaranteed against arbitrary invasion. Jefferson, Burke, Paine, Mill, compiled different catalogues of individual liberties, but the argument for keeping authority at bay is always substantially the same. We must preserve a minimum area of personal freedom if we are not to 'degrade or deny our nature'. We cannot remain absolutely free, and must give up some of our liberty to preserve the rest. But total self-surrender is self-defeating. What then must the minimum be? That which a man cannot give up without offending against the essence of his human nature. What is this essence? What are the standards which it entails? This has been, and perhaps always will be, a matter of infinite debate. But whatever the principle in terms of which the area of non-interference is to be drawn, whether it is that of natural law or natural rights, or of utility or the pronouncements of a categorical imperative, or the sanctity of the social contract, or any other concept with which men have sought to clarify and justify their convictions, liberty in this sense means liberty *from;* absence of interference beyond the shifting, but always recognizable, frontier. 'The only freedom which deserves the name is that of pursuing our own good in our own way', said the most celebrated of its champions. If this is so, is compulsion ever justified? Mill had no doubt that it was. Since justice demands that all individuals be entitled to a minimum of freedom, all other individuals were of necessity to be restrained, if need be by force, from depriving anyone of it. Indeed, the whole function of the law was the prevention of just such collisions: the state was reduced to what Lassalle contemptuously described as the functions of a nightwatchman or traffic policeman.

What made the protection of individual liberty so sacred to Mill? In his famous essay he declares that unless men are left to live as they wish 'in the path which merely concerns themselves', civilization cannot advance; the truth will not, for lack of a free market in ideas, come to light; there will be no scope for spontaneity, originality, genius, for mental energy, for moral courage. Society will be crushed by the weight of 'collective mediocrity'. Whatever is rich and diversified will be crushed by the weight of custom, by men's constant tendency to conformity, which breeds only 'withered capacities', 'pinched and hidebound', 'cramped and warped' human beings. 'Pagan self-assertion is as worthy as Christian self-denial.' 'All the errors which a man is likely to commit against advice and warning are far outweighed by the evil of allowing others to constrain him to what they deem is good.' The defence of liberty consists in the 'negative' goal of warding off interference. To threaten a man with persecution unless he submits to a life in which he exercises no choices of his goals; to block before him every door but one, no matter how noble the prospect upon which it opens, or how benevolent the motives of those who arrange this, is to sin against the truth that he is a man, a being with a life of his own to live. This is liberty as it has been conceived by liberals in the modern world from the days of Erasmus (some would say of Occam) to our own. Every plea for civil liberties and individual rights, every protest against exploitation and humiliation, against the encroachment of public authority, or the mass hypnosis of custom or organized propaganda, springs from the individualistic, and much disputed, conception of man.

Three facts about this position may be noted. In the first place Mill confuses two distinct notions. One is that all coercion is, in so far as it frustrates human desires, bad as such, although it may have to be applied to prevent other, greater evils; while non-interference, which is the opposite of coercion, is good as such, although it is not the only good. This is the 'negative' conception of liberty in its classical form. The other is that men should seek to discover the truth, or to develop a certain type of character of which Mill approved—fearless, original, imaginative, independent, non-conforming to the point of eccentricity, and so on—and that truth can be found, and such character can be bred, only in conditions of freedom. Both these are liberal views, but they are not identical, and the connexion between them is, at best, empirical. No one would argue that truth or freedom of self-expression could flourish where dogma crushes all thought. But the evidence of history tends to show (as, indeed, was argued by James Stephen in his formidable attack on Mill in his *Liberty, Equality, Fraternity*) that integrity, love of truth and fiery individualism grow at least as often in severely disciplined communities among, for example, the puritan Calvinists of Scotland or New England, or under military discipline, as in more tolerant or indifferent societies; and if this is so accepted, Mill's argument for liberty as a necessary condition for the growth of human genius falls to the ground. If his two goals proved incompatible, Mill would be faced with a cruel dilemma, quite apart from the further difficulties created by the inconsistency of his doctrines with strict utilitarianism, even in his own humane version of it.[6]

In the second place, the doctrine is comparatively modern. There seems to be scarcely any consciousness of individual liberty as a political ideal in the ancient world. Condorcet has already remarked that the notion of individual rights is absent from the legal conceptions of the Romans and Greeks; this seems to hold equally of the Jewish, Chinese, and all other ancient civilizations that have since come to light.[7] The domination of this ideal has been the exception rather than the rule, even in the recent history of the West. Nor has liberty in this sense often formed a rallying cry for the great masses of mankind. The desire not to be impinged upon, to be left to oneself, has been a mark of high civilization both on the part of individuals and communities. The sense of privacy itself, of the area of personal relationships as something sacred in its own right, derives from a conception of freedom which, for all its religious roots, is scarcely older, in its developed state, than the Renaissance or the Reformation.[8] Yet its decline would mark the death of a civilization, of an entire moral outlook.

The third characteristic of this notion of liberty is of greater importance. It is that liberty in this sense is not incompatible with some kinds of autocracy, or at any rate with the absence of self-government. Liberty in this sense is principally concerned with the area of control, not with its source. Just as a democracy may, in fact, deprive the individual citizen of a great many liberties which he might have in some other form of society, so it is perfectly conceivable that a liberal-minded despot would allow his subjects a large measure of personal freedom. The despot who leaves his subjects a wide area of liberty may be unjust, or encourage the wildest inequalities, care little for order, or virtue, or knowledge; but provided he does not curb their liberty, or at least curbs it less than many other régimes, he meets with Mill's specification.[9] Freedom in this sense is not, at any rate logically, connected with democracy or self-government. Self-government may, on the whole, provide a better guarantee of the preservation of civil liberties than other régimes, and has been defended as such by libertarians. But there is no necessary connexion between individual liberty and democratic rule. The answer to the question 'Who governs me?' is logically distinct from the question 'How far does government interfere with me?' It is in this difference that the great contrast between the two concepts of negative and positive liberty, in the end, consists.[10] For the 'positive' sense of liberty comes to light if we try to answer the question, not 'What am I free to do or be?', but 'By whom am I ruled?' or 'Who is to say what I am, and what I am not, to be or do?' The connexion between democracy and individual liberty is a good deal more tenuous than it seemed to many advocates of both. The desire to be governed by myself, or at any rate to participate in the process by which my life is to be controlled, may be as deep a wish as that of a free area for action, and perhaps historically older. But it is not a desire for the same thing. So different is it, indeed, as to have led in the end to the great clash of ideologies that dominates our world. For it is this—the 'positive' conception of liberty: not freedom from, but freedom to—which the adherents of the 'negative' notion represent as being, at times, no better than a specious disguise for brutal tyranny.

II

The notion of positive freedom

The 'positive' sense of the word 'liberty' derives from the wish on the part of the individual to be his own master. I wish my life and decisions to depend on myself, not on external forces of whatever kind. I wish to be the instrument of my own, not of other men's, acts of will. I wish to be a subject, not an object; to be moved by reasons, by conscious purposes which are my own, not by causes which affect me, as it were, from outside. I wish to be somebody, not nobody; a doer—deciding, not being decided for, self-directed and not acted upon by external nature or by other men as if I were a thing, or an animal, or a slave incapable of playing a human role, that is, of conceiving goals and policies of my own and realizing them. This is at least part of what I mean when I say that I am rational, and that it is my reason that distinguishes me as a human being from the rest of the world. I wish, above all, to be conscious of myself as a thinking, willing, active being, bearing responsibility for his choices and able to explain them by reference to his own ideas and purposes. I feel free to the degree that I believe this to be true, and enslaved to the degree that I am made to realize that it is not.

The freedom which consists in being one's own master, and the freedom which consists in not being prevented from choosing as I do by other men, may, on the face of it, seem concepts at no great logical distance from each other—no more than negative and positive ways of saying the same thing. Yet the 'positive' and 'negative' notions of freedom developed in divergent directions until, in the end, they came into direct conflict with each other.

One way of making this clear is in terms of the independent momentum which the metaphor of self-mastery acquired. 'I am my own master'; 'I am slave to no man'; but may I not (as, for instance, T. H. Green is always saying) be a slave to nature? Or to my own 'unbridled' passions? Are these not so many species of the identical genus 'slave'—some political or legal, others moral or spiritual? Have not men had the experience of liberating themselves from spiritual slavery, or slavery to nature, and do they not in the course of it become aware, on the one hand, of a self which dominates, and, on the other, of something in them which is brought to heel? This dominant self is then variously identified with reason, with my 'higher nature', with the self which calculates and aims at what will satisfy it in the long run, with my 'real', or 'ideal', or 'autonomous' self, or with my self 'at its best'; which is then contrasted with irrational impulse, uncontrolled desires, my 'lower' nature, the pursuit of immediate pleasures, my 'empirical' or 'heteronomous' self, swept by every gust of desire and passion, needing to be rigidly disciplined if it is ever to rise to the full height of its 'real' nature. Presently the two selves may be represented as divided by an even larger gap: the real self may be conceived as something wider than the individual (as the term is normally understood), as a social 'whole' of which the individual is an element or aspect: a tribe, a race, a church, a state, the great society of the living and the dead and the yet unborn. This entity is then identified as being the 'true' self which, by imposing its collective, or 'organic', single will upon its recalcitrant 'members', achieves its own, and, therefore, their, 'higher' freedom. The perils of using organic metaphors to justify the coercion of some men by others in order to raise them to a 'higher' level of freedom have often been pointed out. But what gives such plausibility as it has to this kind of language is that we recognize that it is possible, and at times justifiable, to coerce men in the name of some goal (let us say, justice or public health) which they would, if they were more enlightened, themselves pursue, but do not, because they are blind or ignorant or corrupt. This renders it easy for me to conceive of myself as coercing others for their own sake, in their, not my, interest. I am then claiming that I know what they truly need better than they know it themselves. What, at most this entails is that they would not resist me if they were rational, and as wise as I, and understood their interests as I do. But I may go on to claim a good deal more than this. I may declare that they are actually aiming at what in their benighted state they consciously resist, because there exists within them an occult entity—their latent rational will, or their 'true' purpose—and that this entity, although it is belied by all that they overtly feel and do and say, is their 'real' self, of which the poor empirical self in space and time may know nothing or little; and that this inner spirit is the only self that deserves to have its wishes taken into account. Once I take this view, I am in a position to ignore the actual wishes of men or societies, to bully, oppress, torture them in the name, and on behalf, of their 'real' selves, in the secure knowledge that whatever is the true goal of man (happiness, fulfilment of duty, wisdom, a just society, self-fulfilment) must be identical with his freedom—the free choice of his 'true', albeit submerged and inarticulate, self.

This paradox has been often exposed. It is one thing to say that I know what is good for X, while he himself does not; and even to ignore his wishes for its—and his—sake; and a very different one to say that he has *eo ipso* chosen it, not indeed consciously, not as he seems in everyday life, but in his role as a rational self which his empirical self may not know—the 'real' self which discerns the good, and cannot help choosing it once it is revealed. This monstrous impersonation, which consists in equating what X would choose if he were something he is not, or at least not yet, with what X actually seeks and chooses, is at the heart of all political theories of self-realization. It is one thing to say that I may be coerced for my own good which I am too blind to see: and another that if it is my good, I am not being coerced, for I have willed it, whether I know this or not, and am free even while my poor earthly body and foolish mind bitterly reject it, and struggle against those who seek to impose it, with the greatest desperation.

This magical transformation, or sleight of hand (for which William James so justly mocked the Hegelians), can no doubt be perpetrated just as easily with the 'negative' concept of freedom, where the self that should not be interfered with is no longer the individual with his actual wishes and needs as they are normally conceived, but the 'real' man within, identified with the pursuit of some ideal purpose not dreamed of by his empirical self. And, as in the case of the 'positively' free self, this entity may be inflated into some super-personal entity— a state, a class, a nation, or the march of history itself, regarded as a more 'real' subject of attributes than the empirical self. But the 'positive' conception of freedom as self-mastery, with its suggestion of a man divided against himself, lends itself more easily to this splitting of personality into two: the transcendent, dominant controller, and the empirical bundle of desires and passions to be disciplined and brought to heel. This demonstrates (if demonstration of so obvious a truth is needed) that the conception of freedom directly derives from the view that is taken of what constitutes a self. a person, a man. Enough manipulation with the definitions of man, and freedom can be made to mean whatever the manipulator wishes. Recent history has made it only too clear that the issue is not merely academic.

The consequences of distinguishing between. two selves will become even clearer if one considers the two major forms which the desire to be self-directed—directed by one's 'true' self—has historically taken: the first, that of self-abnegation in order to attain independence; the second, that of self-realization, or total self-identification with a specific principle or ideal in order to attain the selfsame end.

III

The retreat to the inner citadel

I am the possessor of reason and will; I conceive ends and I desire to pursue them; but if I am prevented from attaining them I no longer feel master of the situation. I may be prevented by the laws of nature, or by accidents, or the activities of men, or the effect, often undesigned, of human institutions. These forces may be too much for me. What am I to do to avoid being crushed by them? I must liberate myself from desires that I know I cannot realize. I wish to be master of my kingdom, but my frontiers are long and vulnerable, therefore I contract them in order to reduce or eliminate the vulnerable area. I begin by desiring happiness, or power or knowledge, or the attainment of some specific object. But I cannot command them. I choose to avoid defeat and waste, and therefore decide to strive for nothing that I cannot be sure to obtain. I determine myself not to desire what is unattainable. The tyrant threatens me with the destruction of my property, with imprisonment, with the exile or death of those I love. But if I no longer feel attached to property, no longer care whether or not I am in prison, if I have killed within myself my natural affections, then he cannot bend me to his will, for all that is left of myself is no longer subject to empirical fears or desires. It is as if I had performed a strategic retreat into an inner citadel—my reason, my soul, my 'noumenal' self—which, do what they may, neither external blind force, nor human malice, can touch.

I have withdrawn into myself; there, and there alone, I am secure. It is as if I were to say: 'I have a wound in my leg. There are two methods of freeing myself from pain. One is to heal the wound. But if the cure is too difficult or uncertain, there is another method. I can get rid of the wound by cutting off my leg. If I train myself to want nothing to which the possession of my leg is indispensable, I shall not feel the lack of it.' This is the traditional self-emancipation of ascetics and quietists, of stoics or Buddhist sages, men of various religions or of none, who have fled the world, and escaped the yoke of society or public opinion, by some process of deliberate self-transformation that enables them to care no longer for any of its values, to remain, isolated and independent, on its edges, no longer vulnerable to its weapons.[11] All political isolationism, all economic autarky, every form of autonomy, has in it some element of this attitude. I eliminate the obstacles in my path by abandoning the path; I retreat into my own sect, my own planned economy, my own deliberately insulated territory, where no voices from outside need be listened to, and no external forces can have effect. This is a form of the search for security; but it has also been called the search for personal or national freedom or independence.

From this doctrine, as it applies to individuals, it is no very great distance to the conceptions of those who, like Kant, identify freedom not indeed with the elimination of desires, but with resistance to them, and control over them. I identify myself with the controller and escape the slavery of the controlled. I am free because, and in so far as, I am autonomous. I obey laws, but I have imposed them on, or found them in, my own uncoerced self. Freedom is obedience, but 'obedience to a law which we prescribe to ourselves', and no man can enslave himself. Heteronomy is dependence on outside factors, liability to be a plaything of the external world that I cannot myself fully control, and which *pro tanto* controls and 'enslaves' me. I am free only to the degree to which my person is 'fettered' by nothing that obeys forces over which I have no control; I cannot control the laws of nature; my free activity must therefore, *ex hypothesi,* be lifted above the empirical world of causality. This is not the place in which to discuss the validity of this ancient and famous doctrine; I only wish to remark that the related notions of freedom as resistance to (or escape from) unrealizable desire, and as independence of the sphere of causality, have played a central role in politics no less than ethics.

For if the essence of men is that they are autonomous beings—authors of values, of ends in themselves, the ultimate authority of which consists precisely in the fact that they are willed freely—then nothing is worse than to treat them as if they were not autonomous, but natural objects, played on by causal influences, creatures at the mercy of external stimuli, whose choices can be manipulated by their rulers, whether by threats of force or offers of rewards. To treat men in this way is to treat them as if they were not self-determined. 'Nobody may compel me to be happy in his own way', said Kant. 'Paternalism is the greatest despotism imaginable.' This is so because it is to treat men as if they were not free, but human material for me, the benevolent reformer, to mould in accordance with my own, not their, freely adopted purpose. This is of course, precisely the policy that the early utilitarians recommended. Helvétius (and Bentham) believed not in resisting, but in using, men's tendency to be slaves to their passions; they wished to dangle rewards and punishments before men—the acutest possible form of heteronomy—if by this means the 'slaves' might be made happier.[12] But to manipulate men, to propel them towards goals which you—the social reformer—see, but they may not, is to deny their human essence, to treat them as objects without wills of their own, and therefore to degrade them. That is why to lie to men, or to deceive them, that is, to use them as means for my, not their own, independently conceived ends, even if it is for their own benefit, is, in effect, to treat them as sub-human, to behave as if their ends are less ultimate and sacred than my own. In the name of what can I ever be justified in forcing men to do what they have not willed or consented to? Only in the name of some value higher than themselves. But if, as Kant held, all values are the creation of men, and called values only so far as they are so, there is no value higher than the individual. Therefore to do this is to coerce men in the name of something less ultimate than themselves—to bend them to my will, or to someone else's particular craving for happiness or expediency or security or convenience. I am aiming at something desired by me or my group, to which I am using other men as means. But this is a contradiction of what I know men to be, namely ends in themselves. All forms of tampering with human beings, getting at them, shaping them against their will to your own pattern, all thought control and conditioning,[13] is, therefore, a denial of that in men which makes them men and their values ultimate.

Kant's free individual is a transcendent being, beyond the realm of natural causality. But in its empirical form—in which the notion of man is that of ordinary life—this doctrine was the heart of liberal humanism, both moral and political, that was deeply influenced both by Kant and by Rousseau in the eighteenth century. In its *a priori* version, it is a form of secularized Protestant individualism, in which the place of God is taken by the conception of the rational life, and the place of the individual soul which strains towards union with Him is replaced by the conception of the individual, endowed with reason, straining to be governed by reason and reason alone and to depend upon nothing that might deflect or delude him by engaging his irrational nature. Autonomy, not heteronomy: to act and not to be acted upon. The notion of slavery to the passions is—for those who think in these terms—more than a metaphor. To rid myself of fear, or love, or the desire to conform is to liberate myself from the despotism of something which I cannot control. Cephalus, whom Plato reports as saying that old age alone has liberated him from the passion of love—the yoke of a cruel master—is reporting an experience as real as that of liberation from a human tyrant or slave owner. The psychological experience of observing myself yielding to some 'lower' impulse, acting from a motive that I dislike, or of doing something which at the very moment of doing I may detest, and reflecting later that I was 'not myself', or 'not in control of myself', when I did it, belongs to this way of thinking and speaking. I identify myself with my critical and rational moments. The consequences of my acts cannot matter, for they are not in my control; only my motives are. This is the creed of the solitary thinker who has defied the world and emancipated himself from the chains of men and things. In this form, the doctrine may seem primarily an ethical creed, and scarcely political at all; nevertheless, its political implications are clear, and it enters into the tradition of liberal individualism at least as deeply as the 'negative' concept of freedom.

It is perhaps worth remarking that in its individualistic form the concept of the rational sage who has escaped into the inner fortress of his true self seems to arise only when the external world has proved exceptionally tyrannical, cruel and unjust. 'He is truly free', said Rousseau, 'who desires what he can perform, and does what he desires.' In a world where a man seeking happiness or justice or freedom (in whatever sense) can do little, because he finds too many avenues of action blocked to him, the temptation to withdraw into himself may become irresistible. It may have been so in Greece, where the Stoic ideal cannot be wholly unconnected with the fall of the independent democracies before centralized Macedonian autocracy. It was so in Rome, for analogous reasons, after the end of the Republic.[14] It arose in Germany in the seventeenth century, during the period of the deepest national degradation of the German states that followed the Thirty Years War, when the character of public life, particularly in the small principalities, forced those who prized the dignity of human life, not for the first or last time, into a kind of inner emigration. The doctrine that maintains that what I cannot have I must teach myself not to desire; that a desire eliminated, or successfully resisted, is as good as a desire satisfied, seems to me a sublime, but unmistakable, form of the doctrine of sour grapes: what I cannot be sure of, I cannot truly want.

Ascetic self-denial may be a source of integrity and spiritual strength, but it is difficult to see how it can be called an enlargement of liberty. If I save myself from an adversary by retreating indoors and locking every entrance and exit, I may remain freer than if I had been captured by him, but am I freer than if I had defeated or captured him? If I go too far, contract myself into too small a space, I shall suffocate and die: The logical culmination of the process of destroying everything through which I can possibly be wounded is suicide. While I exist in the natural world, I can never be wholly secure. Total liberation in this sense (as Schopenhauer correctly perceived) is conferred only by death.[15]

I find myself in a world in which I meet with obstacles to my will. Those who are wedded to the 'negative' concept of freedom may perhaps be forgiven if they think that self-abnegation is not the only method of overcoming obstacles; that it is also possible to do so by removing them: in the case of non-human objects, by physical action; in the case of human resistance, by force or persuasion, as when I induce somebody to make room for me in his carriage, or conquer a country which threatens the interests of my own. Such acts may be unjust, they may involve violence, cruelty, and the enslavement of others, but it can scarcely be denied that thereby the agent is able in the most literal sense to increase his own freedom. It is an irony of history that this truth is repudiated by some of those who practise it most forcibly, men who, even while they conquer power and freedom of action, reject the 'negative' concept of it in favour of its 'positive' counterpart. Their view rules over half our world; let us see upon what metaphysical foundation it rests.

IV

Self-realization

The only true method of attaining freedom, we are told, is by the use of critical reason, the understanding of what is necessary and what is contingent. If I am a schoolboy, all but the simplest truths of mathematics obtrude themselves as obstacles to the free functioning of my mind as theorems whose necessity I do not understand; they are pronounced to be true by some external authority, and present themselves to me as foreign bodies which I am expected mechanically to absorb into my system. But when I understand the functions of the symbols, the axioms, the formation and transformation rules—the logic whereby the conclusions are obtained—and grasp that these things cannot be otherwise, because they appear to follow from the laws that govern the processes of my own reason,[16] then mathematical truths no longer obtrude themselves as external entities forced upon me, which I must receive whether I want this or not, but as something which I now freely will in the course of the natural functioning of my own rational activity. For the mathematician, the proof of these theorems is part of the free exercise of his natural logical capacity. For the musician, after he has assimilated the pattern of the composer's score, and has made the composer's ends his own, the playing of the music is not obedience to external laws, a compulsion and a barrier to liberty, but a free, unimpeded exercise. The player is not bound to the score as an ox to the plough, or a factory worker to the machine. He has absorbed the score into his own system, has, by understanding it, identified it with himself, has changed it from an impediment to free activity into an element in that activity itself. What applies to music or mathematics must, we are told, in principle apply to all other obstacles which present themselves as so many lumps of external stuff blocking free self-development. That is the programme of enlightened rationalism from Spinoza to the latest (at times unconscious) disciples of Hegel. *Sapere aude*. What you know, that of which you understand the necessity—the rational necessity— you cannot, while remaining rational, want to be otherwise. For to want something to be other than what it must be is, given the premisses—the necessities that govern the world— to be *pro tanto* either ignorant or irrational. Passions, prejudices, fears, neuroses, spring from ignorance, and take the form of myths and illusions. To be ruled by myths, whether they spring from the vivid imagination of unscrupulous charlatans who deceive us in order to exploit us, or from psychological or sociological causes, is a form of heteronomy, of being dominated by outside factors in a direction not necessarily willed by the agent. The scientific determinists of the eighteenth century supposed that the study of the sciences of nature, and the creation of sciences of society on the same model, would make the operation of such causes transparently clear, and thus enable individuals to recognize their own part in the working of a rational world, frustrating only when misunderstood. Knowledge liberates by automatically eliminating irrational fears and desires.

Herder, Hegel, and Marx substituted their own vitalistic models of social life for the older, mechanical ones, but believed, no less than their opponents, that to understand the world is to be freed. They merely differed from them in stressing the part played by change and growth in what made human beings human. Social life could not be understood by an analogy drawn from mathematics or physics. One must also understand history, that is the peculiar laws of continuous growth that govern individuals and groups, in their interplay with each other and with nature. Not to grasp this is, according to these thinkers, to fall into a particular kind of error, namely the belief that human nature is static, that its essential properties are the same everywhere and at all times, that it is governed by unvarying natural laws, whether they are conceived in theological or materialistic terms, which entails the fallacious corollary that a wise lawgiver can, in principle, create a perfectly harmonious society at any time by appropriate education and legislation, because rational men, in all ages and countries, must always demand the same unaltering satisfactions of the same unaltering basic needs. Hegel believed that his contemporaries (and indeed all his predecessors) misunderstood the nature of institutions because they did not understand the laws— the rationally intelligible laws, since they spring from the operation of human reason—that create and alter institutions and transform human character and human action. Marx and his disciples maintained that the path of human beings was obstructed not only by natural forces, or the imperfections of their own character, but, even more, by the workings of their social institutions, which they had originally created (not always consciously) for certain purposes, but whose functioning they came to misunderstand, and which thereupon became obstacles in their creators' progress. He offered social and economic hypotheses to account for the inevitability of such misunderstanding, in particular of the illusion that such man-made arrangements were independent forces, as inescapable as the laws of nature. As instances of such pseudo-objective forces, he pointed to the laws of supply and demand, or of property, or the eternal division of society into rich and poor, or owners and workers, as so many unaltering human categories. Not until we had reached a stage at which the spells of these illusions could be broken, that is until enough men understood that these laws and institutions were themselves the work of human minds and hands, historically needed in their day, and later mistaken for inexorable, objective powers, could the old world be destroyed, and more adequate and liberating social machinery substituted.

We are enslaved by despots—institutions or beliefs or neuroses— which can be removed only by being analysed and understood. We are imprisoned by evil spirits which we have ourselves—albeit not consciously—created, and can exorcise them only by becoming conscious and acting accordingly. I am free if, and only if, I plan my life in accordance with my own will; plans entail rules; a rule does not oppress me or enslave me if I impose it on myself consciously, or accept it freely, having understood it, whether it was invented by me or by others, provided that it is rational, that is to say, conforms to the necessities of things. To understand why things must be as they must be is to will them to be so. Knowledge liberates not by offering us more open possibilities amongst which we can make our choice, but by preserving us from the frustration of attempting the impossible. To want necessary laws to be other than they are is to be prey to an irrational desire—a desire that what must be X should also be not X. To go farther, and believe these laws to be other than what they necessarily are, is to be insane. That is the metaphysical heart of rationalism. The notion of liberty contained in it is not the 'negative' conception of a field without obstacles, a vacuum in which I can do as I please, but the notion of self-direction or self-control. I can do what I will with my own. I am a rational being; whatever I can demonstrate to myself as being necessary, as incapable of being otherwise in a rational society—that is in a society directed by rational minds, towards goals such as a rational being would have—I cannot, being rational, wish to sweep out of my way. I assimilate into my substance as I do the laws of logic, of mathematics, of physics, the rules of art, the principles that govern everything of which I understand, and therefore will, the rational purpose, by which I can never be thwarted, since I cannot want it to be other than it is.

This is the positive doctrine of liberation by reason. Socialized forms of it are at the heart of many of the nationalist, Marxist, authoritarian, and totalitarian creeds of our day. It may, in the course of its evolution, have left its rationalist moorings. Nevertheless, it is this freedom that, in democracies and in dictatorships, is argued about, and fought for, in many parts of the earth today. Without attempting to trace the historical evolution of this idea, I should like to comment on some of its vicissitudes.

V

The Temple of Sarastro

Those who believed in freedom as rational self-direction were bound, sooner or later, to consider how this was to be applied not merely to a man's inner life, but to his relations with other members of his society. Even the most individualistic among them—and Rousseau, Kant, and Fichte certainly began as individualists—came at some point to ask themselves whether a rational life not only for the individual, but also for society, was possible, and if so, how it was to be achieved. I wish to be free to live as my rational will (my 'real self') commands, but so must others be. How am I to avoid collisions with their wills? Where is the frontier that lies between my (rationally determined) rights and the identical rights of others? For if I am rational, I cannot deny that what is right for me must, for the same reasons, be right for others who are rational like me. A rational (or free) state would be a state governed by such laws as all rational men would freely accept; that is to say, such laws as they would themselves have enacted had they been asked what, as rational beings, they demanded; hence the frontiers would be such as all rational men would consider to be the right frontiers for rational beings. But who, in fact, was to determine what these frontiers were? Thinkers of this type argued that if moral and political problems were genuine—as surely they were—they must in principle be fully soluble; that is to say, there must exist one and only one true solution to any problem. All truths could in principle be discovered by any rational thinker, and demonstrated so clearly that all other rational men could not but accept them; indeed, this was already to a large extent the case in the new natural sciences. On this assumption, political problems were soluble by establishing a just order that would give to each man all the freedom to which a rational being was entitled. My claim to unfettered freedom can *prima facie* at times not be reconciled with your equally unqualified claim; but the rational solution of one problem cannot collide with the equally true solution of another, for two truths cannot logically be incompatible; therefore a just order must in principle be discoverable—an order of which the rules make possible correct solutions to all possible problems that could arise in it. This ideal, harmonious state of affairs was sometimes imagined as a Garden of Eden before the Fall of Man, from which we were expelled, but for which we were still filled with longing; or as a golden age still before us, in which men, having become rational, will no longer be 'outer-directed' or frustrate one another. In existing societies justice and equality are ideals which it is still necessary to obtain with some measure of coercion, because the premature lifting of social controls might lead to the oppression of the weaker and the stupider by the stronger or abler or more energetic and unscrupulous. But it is only irrationality on the part of men (according to this doctrine) that leads them to wish to oppress or exploit or humiliate one another. Rational men will respect the principle of reason in each other, and lack all desire to fight or dominate one another. The desire to dominate is itself a symptom of irrationality, and can be explained and cured by rational methods. Spinoza offers one kind of explanation and remedy, Hegel another, Marx a third. Some of these theories may perhaps, to some degree, supplement each other, others are not combinable. But they all assume that in a society of perfectly rational beings the lust for domination over men will be absent or ineffective. The existence of oppression will be the first symptom that the true solution to the problems of social life has not been reached.

This can be put in another way. Freedom is self-mastery, the elimination of obstacles to my will, whatever these obstacles may be—the resistance of nature, of my ungoverned passions, of irrational institutions, of the opposing wills of others. Nature I can, at least in principle, always mould by technical means, and impose my will upon it. But how am I to treat recalcitrant human beings? I must, if I can, impose my will on them too, 'mould' them to my pattern, cast parts for them in my play. But will this not mean that I alone am free, while they are slaves? They will be so if my plan has nothing to do with their wishes or values, only with my own. But if my plan is fully rational, it will allow for the full development of their 'true' natures, the realization of their capacities for rational decisions as a part of the realization of my own. All true solutions to all genuine problems must be compatible: more than this, they must fit into a single whole: for this is what is meant by calling them all rational and the universe harmonious. Each man has his specific character, abilities, aspirations, ends. If I grasp both what these ends and natures are, and how they all relate to one another, I can, at least in principle, if I have the knowledge and the strength, satisfy them all, so long as the nature and the purposes in question are rational. Rationality is knowing things and people for what they are: I must not use stones to make violins, nor try to make born violin players play flutes. If the universe is governed by reason, then there will be no need for coercion; a correctly planned life for all will coincide with full freedom—the freedom of rational self-direction—for all. This will be so if, and only if, the plan is the true plan—the one unique pattern which alone fulfils the claims of reason. Its laws will be the rules which reason prescribes: they will only seem irksome to those whose reason is dormant, who do not understand the true 'needs' of their own 'real' selves. So long as each player recognizes and plays the part set him by reason—the faculty that understands his true nature and discerns his true ends— there can be no conflict. Each man will be a liberated, self-directed actor in the cosmic drama. Thus Spinoza tells us that 'children, although they are coerced, are not slaves', because 'they obey orders given in their own interests', and that 'The subject of a true commonwealth is no slave, because the common interests must include his own.' Similarly, Locke says 'Where there is no law there is no freedom', because rational laws are directions to a man's 'proper interests' or 'general good'; and adds that since such laws are what 'hedges us from bogs and precipices' they 'ill deserve the name of confinement', and speaks of desires to escape from such laws as being irrational, forms of 'licence', 'brutish', and so on. Montesquieu, forgetting his liberal moments, speaks of political liberty as being not permission to do what we want, or even what the law allows, but only 'the power of doing what we ought to will', which Kant virtually repeats. Burke proclaims the individual's 'right' to be restrained in his own interest, because 'the presumed consent of every rational creature is in unison with the predisposed order of things'. The common assumption of these thinkers (and of many a schoolman before them, and Jacobin and Communist after them) is that the rational ends of our 'true' natures must coincide, or be made to coincide, however violently our poor, unreflective, desire-ridden, passionate, empirical selves may cry out against this process. Freedom is not freedom to do what is irrational, or stupid, or bad. To force empirical selves into the right pattern is no tyranny, but liberation.[17] Rousseau tells me that if I freely surrender all the parts of my life to society, I create an entity which, because it has been built by an equality of sacrifice of all its members, cannot wish to hurt any one of them; in such a society, we are informed, it can be nobody's interest to damage anyone else. 'In giving myself to all, I give myself to none', and get back as much as I lose, with enough new force to preserve my new gains. Kant tells me that when 'the individual has entirely abandoned his wild, lawless freedom, to find it again, unimpaired, in a state of dependence according to law', that alone is true freedom, 'for this dependence is the work of my own will acting as a lawgiver'. Liberty, so far from being incompatible with authority, becomes virtually identical with it. This is the thought and language of all the declarations of the rights of man in the eighteenth century, and of all those who look upon society as a design constructed according to the rational laws of the wise lawgiver, or of nature, or of history, or of the Supreme Being. Bentham, almost alone, doggedly went on repeating that the business of laws was not to liberate but to restrain: 'Every law is an infraction of liberty.'

If the underlying assumptions had been correct—if the method of solving social problems resembled the way in which solutions to the problems of the natural sciences are found, and if reason were what rationalists said that it was, all this would perhaps follow. In the ideal case, liberty coincides with law: autonomy with authority. A law which forbids me to do what I could not, as a sane being, conceivably wish to do is not a restraint of my freedom. In the ideal society, composed of wholly responsible beings, laws, because I should scarcely be conscious of them, would gradually wither away. Only one social movement was bold enough to render this assumption quite explicit and accept its consequences—that of the Anarchists. But all forms of liberalism founded on a rationalist metaphysics are less or more watered-down versions of this creed.

In due course, the thinkers who bent their energies to the solution of the problem on these lines came to be faced with the question of how in practice men were to be made rational in this way. Clearly they must be educated. For only the uneducated are irrational, heteronomous, and need to be coerced, if only to make life tolerable for the rational, if they are to live in the same society and not be compelled to withdraw to a desert or some Olympian height. But the uneducated cannot be expected to understand or co-operate with the purposes of their educators. Education, says Fichte, must inevitably work in such a way that 'you will later recognize the reasons for what I am doing now'. Children cannot be expected to understand why they are compelled to go to school, nor the ignorant—that is, for the moment, the majority of mankind—why they are made to obey the laws that will presently make them rational. 'Compulsion is also a kind of education.' You learn the great virtue of obedience to superior persons. If you cannot understand your own interests as a rational being, I cannot be expected to consult you, or abide by your wishes, in the course of making you rational. I must, in the end, force you to be protected against smallpox, even though you may not wish it. Even Mill is prepared to say that I may forcibly prevent a man from crossing a bridge if there is not time to warn him that it is about to collapse, for whatever his behaviour may indicate, I know that he cannot wish to fall into the water. Fichte knows what the uneducated German of his time wishes to be or do, better than he can possibly know them for himself. The sage knows you better than you know yourself, for you are the victim of your passions, a slave living a heteronomous life, purblind, unable to understand your true goals. You want to be a human being. It is the aim of the state to satisfy your wish. 'Compulsion is justified by education for future insight.' The reason within me, if it is to triumph, must eliminate and suppress my 'lower' instincts, my passions and desires, which render me a slave; similarly (the fatal transition from individual to social concepts is almost imperceptible) the higher elements in society—the better educated, the more rational, those who 'possess the highest insight of their time and people'—may exercise compulsion to rationalize the irrational section of society. For, so Hegel, Bradley, Bosanquet have often assured us, by obeying the rational man we obey ourselves—not indeed as we are, sunk in our ignorance and our passions, sick creatures afflicted by diseases that need a healer, wards who need a guardian, but as we could be if we were rational; as we could be even now, if only we would listen to the rational element which is, *ex hypothesi,* within every human being who deserves the name.

The philosophers of 'Objective Reason', from the tough, rigidly centralized, 'organic' state of Fichte, to the mild liberalism of T. H. Green, certainly supposed themselves to be fulfilling, and not resisting, the rational demands which, however inchoate, were to be found in the breast of every sentient being. Alternatively I may break away from the teleological determinism of the Hegelians towards some more voluntarist philosophy, and conceive the idea of imposing on my society—for its own betterment—a plan of my own, which in

my rational wisdom I have elaborated; and which, unless I act on my
own, perhaps against the permanent wishes of the vast majority of my
fellow citizens, may never come to fruition at all. Or, abandoning the
concept of reason altogether, I may conceive myself as an inspired
artist, who moulds men into patterns in the light of his unique vision,
as painters combine colours or composers sounds; humanity is the
raw material upon which I impose my creative will; even though men
suffer and die in the process, they are lifted by it tó a height to which
they could never have risen without my coercive—but creative—
violation of their lives. This is the argument used by every dictator,
inquisitor, and bully, who seeks some moral, or even aesthetic,
justification for his conduct. I must do for men (or with them) what
they cannot do for themselves, and I cannot ask their permission or
consent, because they are in no condition to know what is best for
them; indeed, what they will permit and accept may mean a life of
contemptible mediocrity, or perhaps even their ruin and suicide. Let
me quote from the true progenitor of the heroic doctrine, Fichte, once
again: 'No one has . . . rights against reason.' 'Man is afraid of
subordinating his subjectivity to the laws of reason. He prefers
tradition or arbitrariness.' Nevertheless, subordinated he must be.[18]
Fichte puts forward the claims of what he called reason; Napoleon, or
Carlyle, or romantic authoritarians may worship other values, and
see in their establishment by force the only path to 'true' freedom.
     The same attitude was pointedly expressed by Auguste Comte,
who asked 'If we do not allow free thinking in chemistry or biology,
why should we allow it in morals or politics?' Why indeed? If it makes
sense to speak of political truths—as asserting social ends which all
men, because they are men, must, once they are discovered, agree to
be such; and if, as Comte believed, scientific method will in due course
reveal them; then what case is there for freedom of opinion or
action—at least as an end in itself, and not merely as a stimulating
intellectual climate, either for individuals or for groups? Why should
any conduct be tolerated that is not authorized by appropriate
experts? Comte put bluntly what had been implicit in the rationalist
theory of politics from its ancient Greek beginnings. There can, in
principle, be only one correct way of life; the wise lead it
spontaneously, that is why they are called wise. The unwise must be
dragged towards it by all the social means in the power of the wise; for
why should demonstrable error be suffered to survive and breed? The
immature and untutored must be made to say to themselves: 'Only
the truth liberates, and the only way in which I can learn the truth is
by doing blindly today, what you, who know it, order me, or coerce
me, to do, in the certain knowledge that only thus will I arrive at your
clear vision, and be free like you.'

We have wandered indeed from our liberal beginnings. This argument, employed by Fichte in his latest phase, and by Hegel, and after them by other defenders of authority, from Marx and the Positivists to the latest nationalist or communist dictator, is precisely what the Stoic and Kantian morality protests against most bitterly in the name of the reason of the free individual following his own inner light. In this way the rationalist argument, with its assumption of the single true solution, has led from an ethical doctrine of individual responsibility and individual self-perfection, to an authoritarian state obedient to the directives of an élite of Platonic guardians.

What can have led to so strange a reversal—the transformation of Kant's severe individualism into something close to a pure totalitarian doctrine on the part of thinkers who, after all, claimed to be his disciples? This question is not of merely historical interest, for not a few contemporary liberals have gone through the same peculiar evolution. It is true that Kant insisted, following Rousseau, that a capacity for rational self-direction belonged to all men; that there could be no experts in moral matters, since morality was a matter not of specialized knowledge (as the utilitarians and *philosophes* had maintained), but of the correct use of a universal human faculty; and consequently that what made men free was not acting in certain self-improving ways, which they could be coerced to do, but knowing why they ought to do so, which nobody could do for, or on behalf of, anyone else. But even Kant, when he came to deal with political issues, conceded that no law, provided that it was such that I should, if I were asked, approve it as a rational being, could possibly deprive me of any portion of my rational freedom. With this the door was opened wide to the rule of experts. I cannot consult all men about all enactments all the time. The government cannot be a continuous plebiscite. Moreover, some men are not as well attuned to the voice of their own reason as others: some seem singularly deaf. If I am a legislator or a ruler, I must assume that if the law I impose is rational (and I can only consult my own reason) it will automatically be approved by all the members of my society so far as they are rational beings. For if they disapprove, they must, *pro tanto,* be irrational; then they will need to be repressed by reason: whether their own or mine cannot matter, for the pronouncements of reason must be the same in all minds. I issue my orders, and if you resist, take it upon myself to repress the irrational element in you which opposes reason. My task would be easier if you repressed it in yourself; I try to educate you to do so. But I am responsible for public welfare, I cannot wait until all men are wholly rational. Kant may protest that the essence of the subject's freedom is that he, and he alone, has given himself the order to obey. But this is a counsel of perfection. If you fail to discipline yourself, I must do so for you; and you cannot complain of lack of freedom, for the fact that Kant's rational judge has sent you to prison is evidence that you have not listened to your own inner reason, that, like a child, a savage, an idiot, you are not ripe for self-direction or permanently incapable of it.[19]

If this leads to despotism, albeit by the best or the wisest— to Sarastro's temple in the *Magic Flute*—but still despotism, which turns out to be identical with freedom, can it be that there is something amiss in the premisses of the argument? that the basic assumptions are themselves somewhere at fault? Let me state them once more: first, that all men have one purpose, and one only, that of rational self-direction; second, that the ends of all rational beings must of necessity fit into a single universal, harmonious pattern, which some men may be able to discern more clearly than others; third, that all conflict, and consequently all tragedy, is due solely to the clash of reason with the irrational or the insufficiently rational— the immature and undeveloped elements in life— whether individual or communal, and that such clashes are, in principle, avoidable, and for rational beings impossible; finally, that when all men have been made rational, they will obey the rational laws of their own natures, which are one and the same in them all, and so be at once wholly law-abiding and wholly free. Can it be that Hume is right, and Socrates mistaken, that virtue is not knowledge, and freedom not identical with either? that despite the fact that it rules the lives of more men than ever before in its long history, not one of the basic assumptions of this famous view is demonstrable, or, perhaps, even true?

IV

The search for status

There is yet another historically important approach to this topic, which, by confounding liberty with her sisters, equality and fraternity, leads to similarly illiberal conclusions. Ever since the issue was raised towards the end of the eighteenth century, the question of what is meant by 'an individual' has been asked persistently, and with increasing effect. In so far as I live in society, everything that I do inevitably affects, and is affected by, what others do. Even Mill's strenuous effort to mark the distinction between the spheres of private and social life breaks down under examination. Virtually all Mill's critics have pointed out that everything that I do may have results which will harm other human beings. Moreover, I am a social being in a deeper sense than that of interaction with others. For am I not what I am, to some degree, in virtue of what others think and feel me to be? When I ask myself what I am, and answer: an Englishman, a

Chinese, a merchant, a man of no importance, a millionaire, a convict—I find upon analysis that to possess these attributes entails being recognized as belonging to a particular group or class by other persons in my society, and that this recognition is part of the meaning of most of the terms that denote some of my most personal and permanent characteristics. I am not disembodied reason. Nor am I Robinson Crusoe, alone upon his island. It is not only that my material life depends upon interaction with other men, or that I am what I am as a result of social forces, but that some, perhaps all, of my ideas about myself, in particular my sense of my own moral and social identity, are intelligible only in terms of the social network in which I am (the metaphor must not be pressed too far) an element. The lack of freedom about which a man or a nation complains amounts, as often as not, to the lack of proper recognition. I may be seeking not for what Mill would wish me to seek, namely security from coercion, from arbitrary arrest, tyranny, deprivation of certain opportunities of action, or for space within which I am legally accountable to no one for my movements. Equally, I may not be seeking for a rational plan of social life, or the self-perfection of a dispassionate sage. What I may seek to avoid is simply being ignored, or patronized, or despised, or being taken too much for granted—in short, not being treated as an individual, having my uniqueness insufficiently recognized, being classed as a member of some featureless amalgam, a statistical unit without identifiable, specifically human features and purposes of my own.[20] This is the degradation that I am fighting against—not equality of legal rights, nor liberty to do as I wish (although I may want these too), but for a condition in which I can feel that I am, because I am treated as a responsible agent, whose will is taken into consideration as being entitled to this, even if I am attacked and persecuted for being what I am, or choosing as I do. This is a hankering after status and recognition: 'The poorest he that is in England hath a life to live as the greatest he.' I desire to be understood and recognized, even if this means to be unpopular and disliked. And the only persons who can so recognize me, and thereby give me the sense of being someone, are the members of the society to which, historically, morally, economically, and perhaps ethnically, I feel that I belong.[21] My individual self is not something which I can detach from my relationship with others, or from those attributes of myself which consist in their attitude towards me. Consequently, when I demand to be liberated from, let us say, the status of political or social dependence, what I demand is an alteration of the attitude towards me of those whose opinions and behaviour help to determine my own image of myself. What oppressed classes or nationalities as a rule demand is neither simply unhampered liberty of action for their members, nor, above everything, equality of social or economic opportunity, still less assignment of a place in a frictionless, organic state devised by the rational lawgiver. What they want, as often as not, is simply recognition (of their class or nation, or colour or race) as an independent source of human activity, as an entity with a will of its own, intending to act in accordance with it (whether it is good, or legitimate, or not), and not to be ruled, educated, guided, with however light a hand, as being not quite fully human, and therefore not quite fully free. This gives a far wider than a purely rationalist sense to Kant's 'paternalism is the greatest despotism imaginable'; paternalism is despotic, not because it is more oppressive than naked, brutal, unenlightened tyranny, nor merely because it ignores the transcendental reason embodied in me, but because it is an insult to my conception of myself as a human being, determined to make my own life in accordance with my own (not necessarily rational or benevolent) purposes, and, above all, entitled to be recognized as such by others. For if I am not so recognized, then I may fail to recognize, I may doubt, my own claim to be a fully independent human being. For what I am is, in large part, determined by what I feel and think; and what I feel and think is determined by the feeling and thought prevailing in the society to which I belong, of which, in Burke's sense, I form not an isolable atom, but an ingredient (to use a perilous but indispensable metaphor) in a social pattern. I may feel unfree in the sense of not being recognized as a self-governing individual human being; but I may feel it also as a member of an unrecognized or insufficiently respected group: then I wish for the emancipation of my entire class, or nation, or race, or profession. So much can I desire this, that I may, in my bitter longing for status, prefer to be bullied and misgoverned by some member of my own race or social class, by whom I am, nevertheless, recognized as a man and a rival—that is as an equal—to being well and tolerantly treated by someone from some higher and remoter group, who does not recognize me for what I wish to feel myself to be. This is the heart of the great cry for recognition on the part of both individuals and groups, and in our own day, of professions and classes, nations and races. Although I may not get 'negative' liberty at the hands of the members of my own society, yet they are members of my own group; they understand me, as I understand them; and this understanding creates within me the sense of being somebody in the world. It is this desire for reciprocal recognition that leads the most authoritarian democracies to be, at times, consciously preferred by its members to the most enlightened oligarchies, or sometimes causes a member of some newly liberated Asian or African state to complain less today, when he is rudely treated by members of his own race or nation, than when he was governed by some cautious, just, gentle, well-meaning administrator from outside. Unless this phenomenon is grasped, the ideals and behaviour of entire peoples who, in Mill's sense of the word, suffer deprivation of elementary human rights, and who, with every appearance of sincerity, speak of enjoying more freedom than when they possessed a wider measure of these rights, becomes an unintelligible paradox.

Yet it is not with liberty, in either the 'negative' or in the positive' senses of the word, that this desire for status and recognition can easily be identified. It is something no less profoundly needed and passionately fought for by human beings—it is something akin to, but not itself, freedom: it is more closely related to solidarity, fraternity, mutual understanding, need for association on equal terms, all of which are sometimes—but misleadingly—called social freedom. Social and political terms are necessarily vague. The attempt to make the vocabulary of politics too precise may render it useless. But it is no service to the truth to loosen usage beyond necessity. The essence of the notion of liberty, both in the 'positive' and the 'negative' senses, is the holding off of something or someone—of others, who trespass on my field or assert their authority over me, or of obsessions, fears, neuroses, irrational forces—intruders and despots of one kind or another. The desire for recognition is a desire for something very different: for union, closer understanding, integration of interests, a life of common dependence and common sacrifice. It is only the confusion of desire for liberty with this profound and universal craving for status and understanding, further confounded by being identified with the notion of social self-direction, where the self is no longer the individual but the 'social whole', that makes it possible for men, while submitting to the authority of oligarchs or dictators, to claim that this in some sense liberates them.

Much has been written on the fallacy of regarding social groups as being literally persons or selves, whose control and discipline of their members is no more than self-discipline, voluntary self-control which leaves the individual agent free. But even on the 'organic' view, would it be natural or desirable to call the demand for recognition and status a demand for liberty in some third sense? It is true that the group from which recognition is sought must itself have a sufficient measure of 'negative' freedom—from control by any outside authority— otherwise recognition by it will not give the claimant the status he seeks. But is the struggle for higher status, the wish to escape from an inferior position, to be called a struggle for liberty? Is it mere pedantry to confine this word to the main senses discussed above, or are we, as I suspect, in danger of calling any adjustment of his social situation favoured by a human being an increase of his liberty, and will this not render this term so vague and distended as to make it virtually useless? And yet we cannot simply dismiss this case as a mere confusion of the notion of freedom with those of status, or solidarity, or fraternity, or equality, or some combination of these. For the craving for status is, in certain respects, very close to the desire to be an independent agent.

We may refuse this goal the title of liberty; yet it would be a shallow view that assumed that analogies between individuals and groups, or organic metaphors, or several senses of the word liberty, are mere fallacies, due either to assertions of likeness between entities in respects in which they are unlike, or simple semantic confusion. What is wanted by those who are prepared to barter their own and others' liberty of individual action for the status of their group, and their own status within the group, is not simply a surrender of liberty for the sake of security, of some assured place in a harmonious hierarchy in which all men and all classes know their place, and are prepared to exchange the painful privilege of choosing—'the burden of freedom'—for the peace and comfort and relative mindlessness of an authoritarian or totalitarian structure. No doubt, there are such men and such desires, and no doubt such surrenders of individual liberty can occur, and, indeed, have often occurred. But it is a profound misunderstanding of the temper of our times to assume that this is what makes nationalism or Marxism attractive to nations which have been ruled by foreign masters, or to classes whose lives were directed by other classes in a semi-feudal, or some other hierarchically organized, régime. What they seek is more akin to what Mill called 'pagan self-assertion', but in a collective, socialized form. Indeed, much of what he says about his own reasons for desiring liberty—the value that he puts on boldness and non-conformity, on the assertion of the individual's own values in the face of the prevailing opinion, on strong and self-reliant personalities free from the leading strings of the official law-givers and instructors of society—has little enough to do with his conception of freedom as non-intereference, but a great deal with the desire of men not to have their personalities set at too low a value, assumed to be incapable of autonomous, original, 'authentic' behaviour, even if such behaviour is to be met with opprobrium, or social restrictions, or inhibitive legislation. This wish to assert the 'personality' of my class, or group or nation, is not wholly unconnected with the answer to the question 'What is to be the area of authority?' (for the group must not be interfered with by outside masters), and is even more closely related to the question 'Who is to govern us?'—govern well or badly, liberally or oppressively—but above all 'who?' And such answers as: 'by

representatives elected by my own and others' untrammelled choice',
or 'all of us gathered together in regular assemblies', or 'the best', or
'the wisest', or 'the nations as embodied in these or those persons or
institutions', or 'the divine leader', are answers that are logically, and
often also politically and socially, independent of what extent of
'negative' liberty I demand for my own or my group's activities.
Provided the answer to 'Who shall govern me?' is somebody or
something which I can represent as 'my own', as something which
belongs to me, or to whom I belong, I can, by using words which
convey fraternity and solidarity, as well as some part of the
connotation of the 'positive' sense of the word freedom (which it is
difficult to specify more precisely), describe it as a hybrid form of
freedom; at any rate as an ideal which is perhaps more prominent
than any other in the world today, yet one which no existing term
seems to fit. Those who purchase it at the price of their 'negative'
Millian freedom certainly claim to be 'liberated' by this means, in this
confused, but ardently felt, sense. 'Whose service is perfect freedom'
can in this way be secularized, and the state, or the nation, or the race,
or an assembly, or a dictator, or my family or milieu, or I myself, can
be substituted for the Deity, without thereby rendering the word
'freedom' wholly meaningless.[22]

No doubt every interpretation of the word liberty, however
unusual, must include a minimum of what I have called 'negative'
liberty. There must be an area within which my wishes are not
frustrated. No society literally suppresses all the liberties of its
members; a being who is prevented by others from doing anything at
all that he wishes to do is not a moral agent at all, and could not either
legally or morally be regarded as a human being, even if a
physiologist or a biologist, or even a psychologist, felt inclined to
classify him as a man. But the fathers of liberalism—Mill and
Constant—want more than this minimum: they demand a maximum
degree of non-interference compatible with the minimum demands of
social life. It seems unlikely that this demand for liberty has ever been
made by any but a small minority of highly civilized and self-
conscious human beings. The bulk of humanity has certainly at most
times been prepared to sacrifice this to other goals: security, status,
prosperity, power, virtue, rewards in the next world; or justice,
equality, fraternity, and many other values which appear wholly, or
in part, incompatible with the attainment of the greatest degree of
individual liberty, and certainly do not need it as a pre-condition for
their own realization. It is not a demand for *Lebensraum* for each
individual that has stimulated the rebellions and wars of liberation
for which men were ready to die in the past, or, indeed, in the present.
Men who have fought for freedom have commonly fought for the

right to be governed by themselves or their representatives—sternly
governed, if need be, like the Spartans, with little individual liberty,
but in a manner which allowed them to participate, or at any rate to
think that they were participating, in the legislation and
administration of their collective lives. And men who have made
revolutions have, as often as not, meant by liberty no more than the
conquest of power and authority by a given sect of believers in a
doctrine, or by a class, or by some other social group, old or new.
Their victories certainly frustrated those whom they ousted, and
sometimes repressed, enslaved, or exterminated vast numbers of
human beings. Yet, such revolutionaries have usually felt it necessary
to argue that, despite this, they represented the party of liberty, or
'true' liberty, by claiming universality for their ideal, which the 'real
selves' of even those who resisted them were also alleged to be
seeking, although they were held to have lost the way to the goal, or to
have mistaken the goal itself owing to some moral or spiritual
blindness. All this has little to do with Mill's notion of liberty as
limited only by the danger of doing harm to others. It is the non-
recognition of this psychological and political fact (which lurks
behind the apparent ambiguity of the term 'liberty') that has,
perhaps, blinded some contemporary liberals to the world in which
they live. Their plea is clear, their cause is just. But they do not allow
for the variety of human wishes. Nor yet for the ingenuity with which
men can prove to their own satisfaction that the road to one ideal also
leads to its contrary.

VII

Liberty and sovereignty

The French Revolution, like all great revolutions, was, at least in
its Jacobin form, just such an eruption of the desire for 'positive'
freedom of collective self-direction on the part of a large body of
Frenchmen who felt liberated as a nation, even though the result was,
for a good many of them, a severe restriction of individual freedoms.
Rousseau had spoken exultantly of the fact that the laws of liberty
might prove to be more austere than the yoke of tyranny. Tyranny is
service to human masters. The law cannot be a tyrant. Rousseau does
not mean by liberty the 'negative' freedom of the individual not to be
interefered with within a defined area, but the possession by all, and
not merely by some, of the fully qualified members of a society of a
share in public power, which is entitled to interfere with every aspect
of every citizen's life. The liberals of the first half of the nineteenth
century correctly foresaw that liberty in this 'positive' sense could
easily destroy every 'negative' liberty that they held sacred. They

pointed out that the sovereignty of the people could easily destroy that of individuals. Mill explained, patiently and unanswerably, that government by the people was not, in his sense, necessarily freedom at all. For those who govern are not necessarily the same 'people' as those who are governed, and democratic self-government is not the government 'of each by himself' but, at best, of 'each by the rest'. Mill and his disciples spoke of the tyranny of the majority and of the tyranny of 'the prevailing feeling and opinion', and saw no great difference between that and any other kind of tyranny which encroaches upon men's activities beyond the sacred frontiers of private life.

But no one saw the conflict between the two types of liberty better, or expressed it more clearly, than Benjamin Constant. He pointed out that the transference by a successful rising of the unlimited authority, commonly called sovereignty, from one set of hands to another does not increase liberty, but merely shifts the burden of slavery. He reasonably asked why a man should deeply care whether he is crushed by a popular government or by a monarch, or even by a set of oppressive laws. He saw that the main problem for those who desire 'negative', individual freedom is not who wields this authority, but how much authority should be placed in any set of hands. For unlimited authority in anybody's grasp was bound, he believed, sooner or later, to destroy somebody. He maintained that usually men protested against this or that set of governors as oppressive, when the real cause of oppression lay in the mere fact of the accumulation of power itself, wherever it might happen to be, since liberty was endangered by the mere existence of absolute authority as such. 'It is not the arm that is unjust', he wrote, 'but the weapon that is too heavy—some weights are too heavy for the human hand.' Democracy may disarm a given oligarchy, a given privileged individual or set of individuals, but it can still crush individuals as mercilessly as any previous ruler. Equality of the right to oppress—or interfere—is not equivalent to liberty. Nor does universal consent to loss of liberty somehow miraculously preserve it merely by being universal, or by being consent. If I consent to be oppressed, or acquiesce in my condition with detachment or irony, am I less oppressed? If I sell myself into slavery, am I the less a slave? If I commit suicide, am I the less dead because I have taken my own life freely? 'Popular government is a spasmodic tyranny, monarchy a more efficiently centralised despotism.' Constant saw in Rousseau the most dangerous enemy of individual liberty, because he had declared that 'by giving myself to all I give myself to none'. Constant could not see why, even though the sovereign is 'everybody', it should not oppress one of the 'members' of its indivisible self, if it so decided.

I may, of course, prefer to be deprived of my liberties by an assembly, or a family, or a class, in which I am a minority. It may give me an opportunity one day of persuading the others to do for me that to which I feel I am entitled. But to be deprived of my liberty at the hands of my family or friends or fellow citizens is to be deprived of it just as effectively. Hobbes was at any rate more honest: he did not pretend that a sovereign does not enslave: he justified this slavery, but at least did not have the effrontery to call it freedom.

Throughout the nineteenth century liberal thinkers correctly maintained that if liberty involved a limit upon the powers of any man to force me to do what I did not wish to do, then whatever the ideal in the name of which I was coerced, I was not free; that the doctrine of absolute sovereignty was a tyrannical doctrine in itself. If I wish to preserve my liberty, it is not enough to say that it must not be violated unless someone or other—the absolute ruler, or the popular assembly, or the King in Parliament, or the judges, or some combination of authorities, or the laws themselves—for the laws may be oppressive—authorizes its violation. I must establish a society in which there must be some frontiers of freedom which nobody should ever be permitted to cross. Different names or natures may be given to the rules that determine these frontiers: they may be called natural rights or the word of God, or Natural Law, or the demands of utility or of the 'deepest interests of man'; I may believe them to be valid *a priori,* or assert them to be my own subjective ends, or the ends of my society or culture. What these rules or commandments will have in common is that they are accepted so widely, and are grounded so deeply in the actual nature of men as they have developed through history, as to be, by now, an essential part of what we mean by being a normal human being. Genuine belief in the inviolability of a minimum extent of individual liberty entails some such absolute stand. For it is clear that it has little to hope for from the rule of majorities; democracy as such is logically uncommitted to it, and historically has failed to protect it, while remaining faithful to its own principles. Few governments, it has been observed, have found much difficulty in causing their subjects to generate any will that the government wanted. 'The triumph of despotism is to force the slaves to declare themselves free.' It may need no force: the slaves may proclaim their freedom quite sincerely: but they are none the less slaves. Perhaps the chief value for liberals of political—'positive'—rights, of participating in the government, is as a means for protecting what they hold to be an ultimate value, namely individual—'negative'—liberty.

But if democracies can, without ceasing to be democratic, suppress freedom, at least as liberals have used the word, what would make a society truly free? For Mill, Constant, Tocqueville, and the liberal tradition to which they belong, no society is free unless it is governed by at any rate two interrelated principles: first, that no power, but only rights, can be regarded as absolute, so that all men, whatever power governs them, have an absolute right to refuse to behave inhumanly; and, second, that there are frontiers not artificially drawn, within which men should be inviolable, these frontiers being defined in terms of rules so long and widely accepted that their observance has entered into the very conception of what it is to be a normal human being, and, therefore, also of what it is to act inhumanly or insanely; rules of which it would be absurd to say, for example, that they could be abrogated by some formal procedure on the part of some court or sovereign body. When I speak of a man as being normal, a part of what I mean is that he could not break these rules easily, without a qualm of revulsion. It is such rules as these that are broken when a man is declared guilty without trial, or punished under retroactive law; when children are ordered to denounce their parents, friends to betray one another, soldiers to use methods of barbarism; when men are tortured or murdered, or minorities are massacred because they irritate a majority or a tyrant. Such acts, even if they are made legal by the sovereign, cause horror even in these days, and this springs from the recognition of the moral validity—irrespective of the laws—of some absolute barriers to the imposition of one man's will on another. The freedom of a society, or a class or a group, in this sense of freedom, is measured by the strength of these barriers, and the number and importance of the paths which they keep open for their members—if not for all, for at any rate a great number of them.[23]

This is almost at the opposite pole from the purposes of those who believe in liberty in the 'positive'—self-directive—sense. The former want to curb authority as such. The latter want it placed in their own hands. That is the cardinal issue. These are not two different interpretations of a single concept, but two profoundly divergent and irreconcilable attitudes to the ends of life. It is as well to recognize this, even if in practice it is often necessary to strike a compromise between them. For each of them makes absolute claims. These claims cannot both be fully satisfied. But it is a profound lack of social and moral understanding not to recognize that the satisfaction that each of them seeks is an ultimate value which, both historically and morally, has an equal right to be classed among the deepest interests of mankind.

VIII

The One and the Many

One belief, more than any other, is responsible for the slaughter of individuals on the altars of the great historical ideals—justice or progress or the happiness of future generations, or the sacred mission or emancipation of a nation or race or class, or even liberty itself, which demands the sacrifice of individuals for the freedom of society. This is the belief that somewhere, in the past, or in the future, in divine revelation, or in the mind of an individual thinker, in the pronouncements of history or science, or in the simple heart of an uncorrupted good man, there is a final solution. This ancient faith rests on the conviction that all the positive values in which men have believed must, in the end, be compatible, and perhaps even entail one another. 'Nature binds truth, happiness and virtue together as by an indissoluble chain', said one of the best men who ever lived, and spoke in similar terms of liberty, equality, and justice.[24] But is this true? It is a commonplace that neither political equality nor efficient organization is compatible with more than a modicum of individual liberty, and certainly not with unrestricted *laissez-faire;* that justice and generosity, public and private loyalties, the demands of genius and the claims of society can conflict violently with each other. And it is no great way from that to the generalization that not all good things are compatible, still less all the ideals of mankind. But somewhere, we shall be told, and in some way, it must be possible for all these values to live together, for unless this is so, the universe is not a cosmos, not a harmony; unless this is so, conflicts of values may be an intrinsic, irremovable element in human life. To admit that the fulfilment of some of our ideals may in principle make the fulfilment of others impossible is to say that the notion of total human fulfilment is a formal contradiction, a metaphysical chimaera. For every rationalist metaphysician, from Plato to the last disciples of Hegel or Marx, this abandonment of the notion of a final harmony, in which all riddles are solved, all contradictions reconciled, is a piece of crude empiricism, an abdication before brute facts, an intolerable bankruptcy of reason before things as they are, a failure to explain and to justify, to reduce everything to a system, which 'reason' indignantly rejects. But if we are not armed with an *a priori* guarantee of the proposition that a total harmony of true values is somewhere to be found—perhaps in some ideal realm the characteristics of which we can, in our finite state, not so much as conceive—we must fall back on the ordinary resources of empirical observation and ordinary human knowledge. And these certainly give us no warrant for supposing (or even understanding what would be meant by saying) that all good things, or all bad things for that matter, are reconcilable with each other. The world that we encounter in ordinary experience is one in which we are faced with choices between ends equally ultimate, the realization of some of which must inevitably involve the sacrifice of others. Indeed, it is because this is their situation that men place such immense value upon the freedom to choose; for if they had assurance that in some perfect state, realizable by men on earth, no ends pursued by them would ever be in conflict, the necessity and agony of choice would disappear, and with it the central importance of the freedom to choose. Any method of bringing this final state nearer would then seem fully justified, no matter how much freedom were sacrificed to forward its advance. It is, I have no doubt, some such dogmatic and *a priori* certainty that has been responsible for the deep, serene, unshakeable conviction in the minds of some of the most merciless tyrants and persecutors in history that what they did was fully justified by its purpose. I do not say that the ideal of self-perfection— whether for individuals or nations or churches or classes—is to be condemned in itself, or that the language which was used in its defence was in all cases the result of a confused or fraudulent use of words, or of moral or intellectual perversity. Indeed, I have tried to show that it is the notion of freedom in its 'positive' sense that is at the heart of the demands for national or social self-direction which animate the most powerful public movements of our time, and that not to recognize this is to misunderstand the most vital facts and ideas of our age. But equally it seems to me that the belief that some single formula can in principle be found whereby all the diverse ends of men can be harmoniously realized is demonstrably false. If, as I believe, the ends of men are many, and not all of them are in principle compatible with each other, then the possibility of conflict—and of tragedy—can never wholly be eliminated from human life, either personal or social. The necessity of choosing between absolute claims is then an inescapable characteristic of the human condition. This gives its value to freedom as Acton had conceived of it—as an end in itself, and not as a temporary need, arising out of our confused notions and disordered lives, a predicament which a panacea could one day put right.

I do not wish to say that individual freedom is, even in the most liberal societies, the sole, or even the dominant, criterion of social action. We compel children to be educated, and we forbid public executions. These are certainly curbs to freedom. We justify them on the ground that ignorance, or a barbarian upbringing, or cruel pleasures and excitements are worse for us than the amount of restraint needed to repress them. This judgement in turn depends on how we determine good and evil, that is to say, on our moral, religious, intellectual, economic and aesthetic values; which are, in their turn, bound up with our conception of man, and of the basic demands of his nature. In other words, our solution of such problems is based on our vision, by which we are consciously or unconsciously guided, of what constitutes a fulfilled human life, as contrasted with Mill's 'cramped and warped', 'pinched and hidebound' natures. To protest against the laws governing censorship or personal morals as intolerable infringements of personal liberty presupposes a belief that the activities which such laws forbid are fundamental needs of men as men, in a good (or, indeed, any) society. To defend such laws is to hold that these needs are not essential, or that they cannot be satisfied without sacrificing other values which come higher—satisfy deeper needs—than individual freedom, determined by some standard that is not merely subjective, a standard for which some objective status— empirical or *a priori*—is claimed.

The extent of a man's or a people's liberty to choose to live as they desire must be weighed against the claims of many other values, of which equality, or justice, or happiness, or security, or public order are perhaps the most obvious examples. For this reason, it cannot be unlimited. We are rightly reminded by Mr. Tawney that the liberty of the strong, whether their strength is physical or economic, must be restrained. This maxim claims respect, not as a consequence of some *a priori* rule, whereby the respect for the liberty of one man logically entails respect for the liberty of others like him; but simply because respect for the principles of justice, or shame at gross inequality of treatment, is as basic in men as the desire for liberty. That we cannot have everything is a necessary, not a contingent, truth. Burke's plea for the constant need to compensate, to reconcile, to balance; Mill's plea for novel 'experiments in living' with their permanent possibility of error, the knowledge that it is not merely in practice, but in principle, impossible to reach clear-cut and certain answers, even in an ideal world of wholly good men and wholly clear ideas, may madden those who seek for final solutions and single, all-embracing systems, guaranteed to be eternal. Nevertheless, it is a conclusion that cannot be escaped by those who, with Kant, have learnt the truth that out of the crooked timber of humanity no straight thing was ever made.

There is little need to stress the fact that monism, and faith in a single criterion, has always proved a deep source of satisfaction both to the intellect and to the emotions. Whether the standard of judgement derives from some future perfection, as was done by the *philosophes* in the eighteenth century and their technocratic successors in our own day, or is rooted in the past—*la terre et les morts*—as was done by German historicists or French theocrats, or neo-Conservatives in English-speaking countries, it is bound, provided it is inflexible enough, to encounter some unforeseen and unforeseeable human development, which it will not fit; and will then be used to justify the *a priori* barbarities of Procrustes—the vivisection of actual human societies into some fixed pattern dictated by our fallible understanding of a largely imaginary past or a wholly imaginary future. To preserve our absolute categories or ideals at the expense of human lives offends equally against the principles of science and of history; it is an attitude found in equal measure on the right and left wings in our days, and is not reconcilable with the principles accepted by those who respect the facts.

The 'negative' liberty that they strive to realize seems to me a truer and more humane ideal than the goals of those who seek in the great, disciplined, authoritarian structures the ideal of 'positive' self-mastery by classes, or peoples, or the whole of mankind. It is truer, because it recognizes the fact that human goals are many, not all of them commensurable, and in perpetual rivalry with one another. To assume that all values can be graded on one scale, so that it is a mere matter of inspection to determine the highest, is to falsify our knowledge of men as free agents, to represent moral decision as an operation which a sliderule could, in principle, perform; to say that in some ultimate, all-reconciling, yet realizable synthesis, duty *is* interest, or individual freedom *is* pure democracy, or an authoritarian state, is to throw a metaphysical blanket over either self-deceit or deliberate hypocrisy. It is more humane because it does not (as the system builders do) deprive men, in the name of some remote, or incoherent, ideal, of much that they have found to be indispensable to their life as human beings.[25] In the end, men choose between ultimate values; they choose as they do, because their life and thought are determined by fundamental moral categories and concepts that are as much a part of their being and conscious thought and sense of their own identity, as their basic physical structure.

It may be that the ideal of freedom to live as one wishes—and the pluralism of values connected with it—is only the late fruit of our declining capitalist civilisation: an ideal which remote ages and primitive societies have not known, and one which posterity will regard with curiosity, even sympathy, but little comprehension. This may be so; but no sceptical conclusions seem to me to follow. Principles are not less sacred because their duration cannot be guaranteed. Indeed, the very desire for guarantees that our values are eternal and secure in some objective heaven is perhaps only a craving for the certainties of childhood or the absolute values of our primitive past. 'To realise the relative validity of one's convictions', said an admirable writer of our time, 'and yet stand for them unflinchingly, is

what distinguishes a civilised man from a barbarian.' To demand
more than this is perhaps a deep and incurable metaphysical need;
but to allow it to guide one's practice is a symptom of an equally deep,
and far more dangerous, moral and political immaturity.

NOTES

1. I do not, of course, mean to imply the truth of the converse.
2. Helvétius made this point very clearly: 'The free man is the man who is not in
    irons, nor imprisoned in a gaol, nor terrorized like a slave by the fear of
    punishment . . . it is not lack of freedom not to fly like an eagle or swim like a
    whale.'
3. The Marxist conception of social laws is, of course, the best-known version of this
    theory, but it forms a large element in some Christian and utilitarian, and all
    socialist, doctrines.
4. 'A free man', said Hobbes, 'is he that . . . is not hindered to do what he hath the
    will to do.' Law is always a 'fetter', even if it protects you from being bound in
    chains that are heavier than those of the law, say, arbitrary despotism or chaos.
    Bentham says much the same.
5. Freedom for an Oxford don', others have been known to add, 'is a very different
    thing from freedom for an Egyptian peasant.'
    This propositon derives its force from something that is both true and
    important, but the phrase itself remains a piece of political claptrap. It is true that
    to offer political rights, or safeguards against intervention by the state, to men
    who are half-naked, illiterate, underfed, and diseased is to mock their condition;
    they need medical help or education before they can understand, or make use of,
    an increase in their freedom. First things come first: there are situations, as a
    nineteenth-century Russian radical writer declared, in which boots are superior
    to the works of Shakespeare; individual freedom is not everyone's primary need.
    For freedom is not the mere absence of frustration of whatever kind; this would
    inflate the meaning of the word until it meant too much or too little. The Egyptian
    peasant needs clothes or medicine before, and more than, personal liberty, but the
    minimum freedom that he needs today, and the greater degree of freedom that he
    may need tomorrow, is not some species of freedom peculiar to him, but identical
    with that of professors, artists, and millionaires.
    What troubles the consciences of Western liberals is not, I think, the belief that
    the freedom that men seek differs according to their social or economic
    conditions, but that the minority who possess it have gained it by exploiting or, at
    least, averting their gaze from the vast majority who do not. They believe, with
    good reason, that if individual liberty is an ultimate end for human beings, none
    should be deprived of it by others; least of all that some should enjoy it at the
    expense of others. Equality of liberty; not to treat others as I should not wish
    them to treat me; repayment of my debt to those who alone have made possible
    my liberty or prosperity or enlightenment; justice, in its simplest and most
    universal sense—these are the foundations of liberal morality. Liberty is not the
    only goal of men. I can, like the Russian critic Belinsky, say that if others are to be
    deprived of it—if my brothers are to remain in poverty, squalor, and chains—
    then I do not want it for myself, I reject it with both hands, and infinitely prefer to
    share their fate. But nothing is gained by a confusion of terms. To avoid glaring
    inequality or widespread misery I am ready to sacrifice some, or all, of my
    freedom: I may do so willingly and freely: but it is freedom that I am giving up for
    the sake of justice or equality or the love of my fellow men. I should be guilt-
    stricken, and rightly so, if I were not, in some circumstances, ready to make this
    sacrifice. But a sacrifice is not an increase in what is being sacrificed, namely

freedom, however great the moral need or the compensation for it. Everything is what it is: liberty is liberty, not equality or fairness or justice or human happiness or a quiet conscience. If the liberty of myself or my class or nation depends on the misery of a vast number of other human beings, the system which promotes this is

shame of such inequality, and do not thereby materially increase the individual liberty of others, an absolute loss of liberty occurs. This may be compensated for by a gain in justice or in happiness or in peace, but the loss remains, and it is nothing but a confusion of values to say that although my 'liberal', individual freedom may go by the board, some other kind of freedom—'social' or 'economic'—is increased. But it remains true that the freedom of some must at times be curtailed to secure the freedom of others. Upon what principle should this be done? If freedom is a sacred, untouchable value, there can be no such absolute principle.

6. This is but another illustration of the natural tendency of all but a very few thinkers to believe that all the things they hold good must be intimately connected, or at least compatible, with one another. The history of thought, like the history of nations, is strewn with examples of inconsistent, or at least disparate, elements artificially yoked together in a despotic system, or held together by the danger of some common enemy. In due course the danger passes, and conflicts between the allies arise, which often disrupt the system, sometimes to the great benefit of mankind.

7. See the valuable discussion of this in Michel Villey, *Leçons d'Histoire de la Philosophie du Droit*, who traces the embryo of the notion of subjective rights to Occam.

8. Christian (and Jewish or Moslem) belief in the absolute authority of divine or natural laws, or in the equality of all men in the sight of God, is very different from belief in freedom to live as one prefers.

9. Indeed, it is arguable that in the Prussia of Frederick the Great or in the Austria of Joseph II, men of imagination, originality, and creative genius, and indeed, minorities of all kinds, were less persecuted and felt the pressure, both of institutions and custom, less heavy upon them than in many an earlier or later democracy.

10. 'Negative liberty' is something the extent of which, in a given case, it is difficult to estimate. It might, *prima facie,* seem to depend simply on the power to choose between at any rate two alternatives. Neverthless, not all choices are equally free, or free at all. If in a totalitarian state I betray my friend under threat of torture, perhaps even if I act from fear of losing my job, I can reasonably say that I did not act freely. Nevertheless, I did, of course, make a choice, and could, at any rate in theory, have chosen to be killed or tortured or imprisoned. The mere existence of alternatives is not, therefore, enough to make my action free (although it may be voluntary) in the normal sense of the word. The extent of my freedom seems to depend on (*a*) how many possibilities are open to me (although the method of counting these can never be more than impressionistic. Possibilities of action are not discrete entities like apples, which can be exhaustively enumerated); (*b*) how easy or difficult each of these possibilities is to actualize; (*c*) how important in my plan of life, given my character and circumstances, these possibilities are when compared with each other; (*d*) how far they are closed and opened by deliberate human acts; (*e*) what value not merely the agent, but the general sentiment of the society in which he lives, puts on the various possibilities. All these magnitudes must be 'integrated', and a conclusion, necessarily never precise, or indisputable, drawn from this process. It may well be that there are many incommensurable degrees of freedom, and that they cannot be drawn up on a single scale of

magnitude, however conceived. Moreover, in the case of societies, we are faced by
such (logically absurd) questions as 'Would arrangement X increase the liberty of
Mr. A more than it would that of Messrs. B, C, and D between them, added
together?' The same difficulties arise in applying utilitarian criteria. Nevertheless,
provided we do not demand precise measurement, we can give valid reasons for
saying that the average subject of the King of Sweden is, on the whole, a good deal
freer today than the average citizen of the Republic of Rumania. Total patterns of
life must be compared directly as wholes, although the method by which we make
the comparison, and the truth of the conclusions, are difficult or impossible to
demonstrate. But the vagueness of the concepts, and the multiplicity of the
criteria involved, is an attribute of the subject-matter itself, not of our imperfect
methods of measurement, or incapacity for precise thought.

11.   'A wise man, though he be a slave, is at liberty, and from this it follows that
      though a fool rule, he is in slavery', said St. Ambrose. It might equally well have
      been said by Epictetus or Kant.

12.   'Proletarian coercion, in all its forms, from executions to forced labour, is,
      paradoxical as it may sound, the method of moulding communist humanity out
      of the human material of the capitalist period.' These lines by the Bolshevik
      leader Nikolai Bukharin, in a work which appeared in 1920, especially the term
      'human material', vividly convey this attitude.

13.   Kant's psychology, and that of the Stoics and Christians too, assumed that some
      element in man—the 'inner fastness of his mind'—could be made secure against
      conditioning. The development of the techniques of hypnosis, 'brain washing',
      subliminal suggestion, and the like, has made this *a priori* assumption, at least as
      an empirical hypothesis, less plausible.

14.   It is not perhaps far-fetched to assume that the quietism of the Eastern sages was
      similarly, a response to the despotism of the great autocracies, and flourished at
      periods when individuals were apt to be humiliated, or at any rate ignored or
      ruthlessly managed, by those possessed of the instruments of physical coercion.

15.   It is worth remarking that those who demanded liberty for the individual or for
      the nation in France at this period did not fall into this attitude. Might this not be
      precisely because, despite the despotism of the French monarchy and the
      arrogance and arbitrary behaviour of privileged groups in the French state,
      France was a proud and powerful nation, where the reality of political power was
      not beyond the grasp of men of talent, so that withdrawal from battle into some
      untroubled heaven above it, whence it could be surveyed dispassionately by the
      self-sufficient philosopher, was not the only way out?

16.   Or, as some modern theorists maintain, because I have, or could have, invented
      them for myself, since the rules are man made.

17.   On this Bentham seems to me to have said the last word: 'Is not liberty to do evil,
      liberty? If not, what is it? Do we not say that it is necessary to take liberty from
      idiots and bad men, because they abuse it?' Compare with this a typical statement
      made by a Jacobin club of the same period: 'No man is free in doing evil. To
      prevent him is to set him free.'

18.   'To compel men to adopt the right form of government, to impose Right on them
      by force, is not only the right, but the sacred duty of every man who has both the
      insight and the power to do so.'

19.   Kant came nearest to asserting the 'negative' ideal of liberty when (in one of his
      political treatises) he declared that 'the greatest problem of the human race, to the
      solution of which it is compelled by nature, is the establishment of a civil society
      universally administrating right according to the law. It is only in a society which
      possesses the greatest liberty . . .—with . . . the most exact determination and
      guarantee of the limits of [the] liberty [of each individual] in order that it may co-

exist with the liberty of others—that the highest purpose of nature,which is the development of all her capacities, can be attained in the case of mankind.' Apart from the teleological implications, this formulation does not appear very different from orthodox liberalism. The crucial point, however, is how to determine the criterion for 'the exact determination and guarantee of the limits' of individual liberty. Mill, and liberals in general, at their most consistent, want a situation in which as many individuals as possible can realize as many of their ends as possible, without assessment of the value of these ends as such, save in so far as they may frustrate the purposes of others. They wish the frontiers between individuals or groups of men to be drawn solely with a view to preventing collisions between human purposes, all of which must be considered to be equally ultimate, uncriticizable ends in themselves. Kant, and the rationalists of his type, do not regard all ends as of equal value. For them the limits of liberty are determined by applying the rules of 'reason', which is much more than the mere generality of rules as such, and is a faculty that creates or reveals a purpose identical in, and for, all men. In the name of reason anything that is non-rational may be condemned, so that the various personal aims which their individual imagination and idiosyncracies lead men to pursue—for example aesthetic and other non-rational kinds of self-fulfilment—may, at least in theory, be ruthlessly suppressed to make way for the demands of reason. The authority of reason and of the duties it lays upon men is identified with individual freedom, on the assumption that only rational ends can be the 'true' objects of a 'free' man's 'real' nature.

I have never, I must own, understood what 'reason' means in this context; and here merely wish to point out that the *a priori* assumptions of this philosophical psychology are not compatible with empiricism: that is to say, any doctrine founded on knowledge derived from experience of what men are and seek.
20. See above, n.12.

21. This has an obvious affinity with Kant's doctrine of human freedom; but it is a socialized and empirical version of it, and therefore almost its opposite. Kant's free man needs no public recognition for his inner freedom. If he is treated as a means to some external purpose, that is a wrong act on the part of his exploiters, but his own 'noumenal' state is untouched, and he is fully free, and fully a man, however he may be treated. The need spoken of here is bound up wholly with the relation that I have with others; I am nothing if I am unrecognized. I cannot ignore the attitude of others with Byronic disdain, fully conscious of my own intrinsic worth and vocation, or escape into my inner life, for I am in my own eyes as others see me. I identify myself with the point of view of my *milieu:* I feel myself to be somebody or nobody in terms of my position and function in the social whole; mine is the most 'heteronomous' condition imaginable.

22. This argument should be distinguished from the traditional approach of some of the disciples of Burke or Hegel who say that, since I am made what I am by society or history, to escape from them is impossible and to attempt it irrational. No doubt I cannot leap out of my skin, or breath outside my proper element; it is a mere tautology to say that I am what I am, and cannot want to be liberated from my essential characteristics, some of which are social. But it does not follow that all my attributes are intrinsic and inalienable, and that I cannot seek to alter my status within the 'social network', or 'cosmic web', which determine my nature; if this were the case no meaning could be attached to such words as 'choice' or 'decision' or 'activity'. If they are to mean anything, attempts to protect myself against authority, or even to escape from my 'station and its duties', cannot be excluded as automatically irrational or suicidal.

23. In Great Britain such legal power is, of course, constitutionally vested in the

absolute sovereign—the King in Parliament. What makes this country free,therefore, is the fact that this theoretically omnipotent entity is restrained by custom or opinion from behaving as such. It is clear that what matters is not the form of these restraints on power—whether they are legal, or moral, or constitutional—but their effectiveness.

24.   Condorcet, from whose *Esquisse* these words are quoted, declares that the task of social science is to show 'by what bonds Nature has united the progress of enlightenment with that of liberty, virtue, and respect for the natural rights of man; how these ideals, which alone are truly good, yet so often separated from each other that they are even believed to be incompatible, should, on the contrary, become inseparable, as soon as enlightenment has reached a certain level simultaneously among a large number of nations'.He goes on to say that: 'Men still preserve the errors of their childhood, of their country, and of their age long after having recognized all the truths needed for destroying them.' Ironically enough, his belief in the need and possibility of uniting all good things may well be precisely the kind of error he himself so well described.

25.   To this also Bentham seems to me to have provided the answer: 'Individual interests are the only real interests . . . can it be conceived that there are men so absurd as to . . . prefer the man who is not to him who is; to torment the living, under pretence of promoting the happiness of them who are not born, and who may never be born?' This is one of the infrequent occasions when Burke agrees with Bentham; for this passage is at the heart of the empirical, as against the metaphysical, view of politics.

9

Professor Max Beloff

THE TASKS OF GOVERNMENT

'If we could first know where we are, and whither we are tending, we could better judge what to do, and how to do it.' Abraham Lincoln's words are true of homely matters as of great ones. But to know where we are, it is necessary to know whence we have come; and it is this fact, along with a proper sense of piety towards our predecessors, that justifies our convention that an inaugural lecture should look behind at what has been done, as well as forward to the work in hand.

The history of the Gladstone Chair goes back to a meeting of the General Committee of the National Memorial to Mr. Gladstone, held at Crewe House in London on 23 July 1912. The trustees of the fund, having fulfilled their various original purposes, found themselves in possession of a considerable surplus, and were met to approve a scheme for its use. The proposal before them was explained by Sir William Anson, M.P., Warden of All Souls College, who said that 'the idea was to apply the surplus towards raising the readership in political science already established at Oxford to the status of a professorship, to be called the Gladstone Professorship of political theory and institutions'. He had reason to believe, he said 'that there would be no difficulty in obtaining the assent of the University'. This is not surprising. No university that I know of has ever thought of 'Timeo Danaos et dona ferentes' as a possible motto. 'If the proposal were carried', continued Anson, 'the name of Mr. Gladstone would be permanently connected with Oxford, a place to which he was loyal to the very day of his death.'

But if the history of the chair begins in London, its pre-history belongs to Oxford, to an Oxford in which the founding of Ruskin College on the one hand, and the creation of the Rhodes scholarships on the other, had created a new demand for what we have come to call social studies. By a decree of 4 May 1909 the University had met a part of this demand by the creation of a lectureship in political

163

science, and to it on 5 February 1910 there was appointed a man who had already made for himself a name both in the academic world and in the world of affairs, a Mr. W. G. S. Adams. In June of the same year, the lectureship was raised to a readership; and two years later, as we have seen, the action of the Gladstone Committee enabled the University to raise the readership to the status of a full professorship. On both occasions, Mr. Adams was reappointed to the higher post so that the rise of his subject in the University was in one respect a testimony to the importance of his personal contribution to it.

Indeed, as the *Oxford Magazine* pointed out, the second change was 'really nominal in a way' since Mr. Adams, as Reader, had 'generously taught and lectured in all three terms', though only required by statute to do so in two of them. 'Meanwhile', continues the *Magazine's* comment: 'we can congratulate ourselves that the Committee for the National Memorial have enabled the University to recognise, what is common knowledge, the great services rendered by Mr. Adams and the important work already done by him for the scientific and liberal study of political theory and institutions, and the stimulus that his knowledge, personality and zeal have given to an essential branch of study in three of our Final Honour Schools, Literae Humaniores, Modern History and Law.'[1]

During the twenty-one years of Mr. Adams's tenure of the chair, a further development of social studies in Oxford had already made the concluding observation of the *Magazine* sound slightly old-fashioned. In 1912 Mr. Adams was to be found lecturing on representative government for students drawn from both 'Greats' and Modern History. By 1933, when he resigned his chair upon his election as Warden of All Souls, representative government was, I suspect, no longer a prominent concern of those undergraduates who elected to read 'Greats'. It is certainly true today that the Gladstone Professor would be regarded as more than presumptuous if he were to suggest the inclusion of his lectures upon the Lit. Hum. list. Again, whereas in continental universities the growth of political studies has been, and still is, severely limited by their subordination to the dictates of faculties of law, in this University the lawyers have not interfered with them, but have on the whole, and with some exceptions, tended to ignore them as largely irrelevant to their own professional concerns. And even though political science is retained as a subject in the Modern History school, it is not I think now regarded as of primary interest to those who adopt that severe and narrow discipline. It would not become the Gladstone Professor to speculate upon what these Honour Schools may have suffered by the total or partial extrusion of his own subject; but he can say that he believes that he at least—and his subject—are bound to be losers.

Between the study of government and the study of history, ancient and modern, and the study of law, there is in my view a necessary and permanent connexion.

But if by 1933 political science in Oxford was in the process of severing these earlier links, it may be held that this was more than compensated for by its new position as part of the triad of social studies, then ambitiously styled 'Modern Greats' and now, more modestly, P.P.E. When in the following year Mr. Adams was succeeded by Sir Arthur Salter (as he then was), it was natural that the choice should have fallen upon someone with so distinguished a record in the administration of national and international economic affairs. For it was with economics (and modern philosophy) that the study of politics in Oxford now seemed to have found its appropriate resting place.

It was certainly true that the new partnership made increasing demands upon the teachers of political science and when in 1940 the University made its decision to divide the duties of the Chair, the *Oxford Magazine* in approving the change commented that the Gladstone Professor had always had 'two men's work'.

It is perhaps to the particular direction of Lord Salter's interests rather than to any consideration of what Mr. Gladstone might have said, that we owe the fact that the study of 'government and public administration' was assigned to the chair to which Gladstone's name was still attached, while 'social and political theory' was placed under the aegis of Henry Chichele.

But before these changes could be carried into effect, Lord Salter had been called back into public life and for four years of war, Sir Robert Ensor, then a fellow of my own college, Corpus Christi, carried on as his deputy the work of the still undivided professorship—a notable contribution to the continuity of our studies in difficult and trying years. Only in 1944 did the two new chairs receive their first incumbents.

It is said, Mr. Vice-Chancellor, that when Paul Valéry succeeded Anatole France as a member of the Académie Française, he performed the feat of pronouncing the customary *éloge* without once mentioning his predecessor's name. This is not an example I propose to follow. If I do not dwell upon the contribution of the Rector of Exeter to political studies in this University and in the country and Commonwealth at large, it is not through any failure to recognize its importance, but for the happier reason that the Rector is still an active teaching member of our fraternity, so that his translation in mid-career is no appropriate moment at which to evaluate his achievement. I can only say for myself that the knowledge that he is not abandoning his close concern with our affairs is the best reason I have for facing their future with confidence. If I cannot hope to emulate Dr. Wheare's unique combination of theoretical severity with practical common sense, I can at any rate continue to profit by it.

For in at least two respects it is clear that the years ahead are hardly likely to make a sinecure of the Gladstone Chair. The first reason is one which, with your permission, I do not propose to treat today. That is the future relation of political studies with the other main disciplines of P.P.E., or if you will, of Cinderella with her sisters. It is a matter of common knowledge that in one sense at least the hopes of the founders of 'Modern Greats' have been disappointed. It does not look now as though the combination of philosophy, politics, and economics can provide that general introduction to the problems of the modern world that was expected of it, and that this is so is because the three subjects, so far from contributing to each other's growth, have tended increasingly to diverge from one another in their scope and methods. The student of politics is not obviously and immediately at home with an economics that verges towards the status of pure mathematics, or with a philosophy largely preoccupied with problems of language. Since the dissatisfaction with the present position is even more strongly felt among the economists and philosophers themselves, it is clear that we are in for a period during which the whole assumptions of our current curriculum will have to be re-examined. I will at this juncture confine myself to expressing the hope that those upon whom the burden of this re-examination falls will not too easily lose sight of the essentials of the original inspiration. For there is a modern world; it has its problems; and if universities can give no guidance as to the methods by which they can be solved, that guidance will be sought elsewhere, and to our disadvantage.

What I wish to concentrate upon now is the second of the reasons which give me cause to look with some apprehension upon the task that has fallen to my lot—namely the problem of defining the proper contemporary scope of the study of government itself, and of deciding towards what aspects of it to direct my own attention. I find some warning against too much certainty here, when I look at my predecessor's inaugural lecture delivered just over twelve years ago within a few months of the ending of the war. On that occasion the Rector told us that he felt 'drawn to an analysis of the decentralisation of government in the United Kingdom in its great variety'.[2] No-one would argue that the author of *Government by Committee,* who has until recently been an active participant in our own municipal affairs, has done nothing to justify the expectations that these words created. But it will readily be admitted that much of the Rector's activity, and much of his increasing renown, has been due to the part he has played in forwarding the constitutional development of countries whose problems are far removed from those of the United Kingdom itself. The commentator on the Statute of Westminster was not elbowed out by Councillor Wheare.

I do not allude to this fact simply to give a new example of the vanity of human wishes, but because it illustrates one lesson that I think emerges from the entire story at which I have been looking— namely, that in the end, the direction of our teaching and of our research is set for us not by our personal preferences, nor by the momentum generated by our own studies, but by the harsh winds that blow upon our ivory towers from every quarter of the globe— and perhaps soon from other globes as well.

I have already hinted at the fact that but for the demands of Ruskin College and of the Rhodes Scholars, formal provision for the teaching of government in Oxford might not have been made when it was; and the foundation of Ruskin and that of the Rhodes trust symbolized in their different ways the important social changes at home and new relationships overseas that were so rapidly and powerfully to transform that mid-Victorian England which laid the foundations of our present-day University, and which still conditions so much of our thinking about its proper role. Similarly, in the last two decades we have seen the adaptation of the University's oldest unit, the college, to new purposes. In some sense, Nuffield College represents part of the University's contribution to handling the problems of the modern welfare state; whereas St. Antony's helps us to tackle those that arise from the growing interdependence of the nations of Europe and beyond. While I owe much myself to work in which I have taken part at St. Antony's, my debt to it is overshadowed by that I owe to Nuffield College where I have had the privilege of a decade of participation in an intellectual adventure at almost its initial and certainly its most exciting stage. Were it not for what Nuffield has taught me, I should, as a mere historian, hardly have the effrontery to present myself in my present role.

What then, in the light of these experiences, are the particular problems in the study and teaching of politics with which we in Oxford now find ourselves confronted, or at least what are those that fall within the proper sphere of 'government and public administration'? And the first question might be: does this phrase itself cover one subject or two?

As Sir Henry Taylor long ago pointed out, there has been a tendency to put this in the poet's words:

> For forms of government let fools contest,
Whate'er is best administered is best.

My own view like Sir Henry Taylor's is almost precisely the opposite. There are some problems of administration that occur under all forms of government and that have obvious analogies in large-scale organizations of a non-governmental kind. But the idea that this means that in some sense administration is politically a neutral activity, functioning with equal effectiveness not only under the leadership of any particular party within a governmental system, but under quite different governmental systems, is an obvious fallacy.

On the contrary, the way a particular measure is translated into action, and the impact it has upon those intended to be affected by it, will necessarily depend upon the frame of government into which the particular administrative devices in question have to be fitted. The general preference as between pure 'statism' and free association, the existence and shape of any popular controls, the extent to which individual decisions are taken in a quasi-judicial or purely administrative context—all these are as much problems of government itself, in the wider sense, as of public administration in the narrower one. Conversely, the idea that governmental institutions can be translated unchanged into a foreign environment is untrue not only because of the importance of such relative intangibles as social structure or national character, but because these intangibles will influence the extent to which the administrative pattern can also be transferred, and because without this, the mere adoption of governmental institutions of a particular kind is most unlikely to bring about the looked-for results. It is this close interdependence of the form of government and the pattern of administration that gives one the right to question some of the solutions for administrative questions that acquire a vogue when our customary methods do not seem to be effective. To say that one should govern on 'business principles', or to attempt to organize the executive branch of a government as though it were the staff of an army in the field, is to overlook the fact that government is an activity subject to quite different criteria from either business or war.

In other words, those forms of government for which in the poet's view only fools contest, turn out upon examination to be inseparable from administration itself. The Gladstone Professor has one subject, not two.

The second question that confronts our study and teaching today, while not unrelated to this one, is a great deal harder to answer, and that is the question of how far in fact very different systems of government should come within our scope, and of what conceptual framework is available to us if we decide that our present scope requires extending. Our present limitations are best illustrated by the rubric governing the study of political institutions in the P.P.E.

school, which includes 'the study of the structure and functions of modern government, international, national and local, with special reference to the constitutional systems of the United Kingdom, the United States of America, and France'.

Now it is obvious that our own institutions must furnish the starting-point of our studies just as it is the possibility of improving them that gives to these studies their pragmatic justification. Nor would I, of all people, be likely to suggest any reduction in the attention we devote to the very different political institutions of the other great section of the English-speaking world, and to the very different political philosophy by which they are justified. Of France it is harder to speak at a time when so much in her political life is obscure, and when it would be so easy to say that the only reason for studying her political arrangements would be that they might teach us what to avoid. I do not share this view. Whatever may be the outcome of the trials that France is now undergoing, nothing can obliterate the fact that the history of France for the past two hundred years provides the student of government and politics with a richness of material not easily to be matched elsewhere, and material given even greater significance by the depth and luminosity of the reflections to which it has given rise. Of the two paths that have so far been followed in the effort to find a way of harmonizing the unprecedented demands of modern government with respect for the individual and his claims, the Anglo-Saxon way of the common law is one—the other, the combination of popular sovereignty with a centralized yet controlled administration, is still easiest for us to grasp through the experience of our nearest neighbour.

Furthermore, since the broad objectives of all three systems are to a great extent the same, and since at different removes they derive their intellectual and moral sanctions from the common Western stock, each illumines the peculiarities of the other in a way which comparisons taken from farther afield could not possibly match.

Nevertheless, this restriction will no longer do, however convenient it may appear. When the scope of P.P.E. was worked out after the First World War it was still possible to believe that those countries that had not already modelled their institutions upon the British or the American or the French systems would sooner or later do so. It was still possible to believe that the then recent revolution in Russia was either a transitory phenomenon, or would itself develop those aspects of its own ideological inheritance most likely to cause its institutions to evolve in a direction at least roughly analogous to that taken by our own.

Today such confidence is no longer reasonable. Something like one-third of humanity is governed, and successfully governed, by means of institutions whose inspiration is different from that which we recognize as valid for us, and whose shape and functioning do not lend themselves to description merely as aberrations from a central tradition of which we like to think ourselves the custodians. Even so, one could in some circumstances argue in favour of ignoring such experience in the way in which Aristotle ignored the barbarian and semi-barbarian empires in his concentration upon the city-state, though the future was with the empires and not with the city-states. But there is no need to argue by historical analogy. We cannot, in this sphere at least, practise mere co-existence by concentrating upon what is proper to us and regarding the rest as irrelevant to our own concerns. For it is not just Russia and China or their immediate satellites that are in question—other countries, the pattern of whose political life has not yet hardened, are balancing one model as against another, comparing shall we say the smooth finish of one with the economy in performance claimed for its competitor, for all the world like clients at some transcendental motor-show. And among these clients now so open-mindedly scanning the catalogues are some whom a few years ago we thought safely committed to the British or the American or the French exemplar. As an historian of Asia has written: 'At the end of the era of Western colonialism and despite the introduction of parliamentary governments of various kinds, the political leaders of the Orient are still greatly attracted by a bureaucratic-managerial policy which keeps the state supremely strong and the non-bureaucratic and private sector of society supremely weak.'[3]

We cannot, then, safely embark upon studying the political development of countries with whose welfare our own is most intimately and traditionally connected, still less offer them our assistance or advice in their problems, unless we fully understand the nature of the rival claims made upon their attention, and ultimately upon their allegiance.

It is not an answer to say, as will be said, that there is an undoubted place for such studies, but not in the undergraduate school; that the accepted limits for political studies within the P.P.E. school are already broad enough, and the burden on the student heavy enough; nor is it sufficient to point to the fact that at the research level we have already made considerable progress (thanks largely to St. Antony's College) in filling this particular gap in Oxford's intellectual armament. For to give an answer of this kind means to miss the central point of the argument I have been putting before you. It is not just that there is an important field of knowledge that is being neglected, it is rather that what is being studied already cannot properly be understood without this accretion. How can one understand what is specific to liberal and democratic forms of government and administration without understanding also their opposites? In our classic texts this is done by contrasting them with older forms of government, with monarchical or clerical absolutism. But except in a few remote and outlandish parts of the world this contrast is now irrelevant; it is not the claims of le Roi Soleil, or of the Holy Roman Emperor, or of the great potentates of Asia that we have to meet, but those of the Duce, the Führer, the Party Secretary. And further, the inquiries that we do make into the totalitarian forms of government are themselves hampered, I believe, through being carried out by specialists largely for specialists, and in circumstances that tend to isolate them to some extent from the central stream of political studies. Oxford being what it is, and what I hope it will remain, no branch of study has properly arrived until it has been found its niche in the scheme of undergraduate studies, until someone has set a paper on it in the 'schools'.

I do not suggest that this is going to be an easy thing to do, but I do think that people often mistake the nature of the difficulty. It is sometimes said that we cannot teach the political institutions of these non-democratic countries because we are ignorant about them; because we do not know the facts: because the literature does not exist. It is even said that one cannot study them with profit without a knowledge of Russian or Chinese. I do not believe that this objection has much force. There are aspects of the politics of a totalitarian country that we cannot know intimately; but this is true of all contemporary studies. And for the purposes I have in mind, we know enough and more; on the aspects that concern us most, there is already a considerable literature in English where Russia is concerned, and a fast-growing if smaller body of writing about China and the other countries concerned. It is true that we are, and will for some time remain, largely tributary in this respect to the United States; New York has done more to help us than London, and Cambridge, Mass. more than Cambridge, England. But this fact should be a stimulus as well as a reproach; and if our own output in Oxford on contemporary Russia and China is small, we have recently contributed not a little to the study of other totalitarian or near-totalitarian systems of the immediate past in Germany and in Japan.

The real difficulty is not in getting access to information, it is in finding the proper concepts for its classification and a terminology which assists comparison instead of provoking mental and political confusion. This difficulty always exists in social studies; it is rendered particularly grave in the present case by the fact that the terminology used by these régimes themselves is derived at first- or second-hand from a revolutionary tradition once common to most of Europe, even though the reality has long ceased to be that which the words and phrases themselves suggest.

In order to avoid such confusion, it is in my view necessary to step farther back from the current controversies and to view the study of government not in the light of particular institutions or their sustaining theories but rather in the light of the tasks that government imposes upon itself. It may then be found that the differences between governmental systems are in fact largely the product of the differences between what those who govern elect to do, or feel themselves bound to undertake. It is this approach that may enable us to give an answer to our questions about the undoubted attractiveness of totalitarian ideas in so much of the world, and particularly in Asia. For the historian I have quoted, the main reason would seem to lie in the power that, in early times, necessarily fell to the authorities responsible for irrigation in societies dependent for their very life upon the artificial control of a precarious supply of water. We may feel that this is an over-simplification and that durable concentrations of bureaucratic power may be found in societies to which the term 'hydraulic' can only be applied with difficulty. Nevertheless, it remains true that only by accepting the limitations of theories based entirely upon what is contemporary with ourselves, or upon the very recent past, can we hope to achieve an understanding of the crucial relationship between the tasks of government, and its shape and spirit. Only so can we see how infrequent have been the combinations of circumstances making for a wide diffusion of property and of power, and how precarious and precious an artifact is any system of political liberties.

So far from free institutions being taken as the norm and all other modern systems of government as perversions, we may find it more useful to our studies to look at it the other way, and to see what particular limitations upon the role of government, and what particular distribution of its functions has made possible the existence of free institutions. And if I regret the severance of the Gladstone Chair from its former link with classical studies it is not so much because of the relevance of the study of the Greek city-states or of the Roman Republic to the understanding of later forms of free government, but because I feel that our ability to comprehend the drift towards the modern varieties of despotic government might be greater were students of government more deeply versed in the history of the great empires of antiquity.

It may be held that this line of argument overlooks the immense advantages that modern technology has conferred upon those who hold political power, that the despots of antiquity had at their disposal neither the same physical instruments of coercion nor the same capacity for influencing the minds of their subjects. But these things seem to me less important in reality than they are sometimes made out to be. Political power even in an industrial age still depends in the last resort not on its physical instruments but on the organization of human beings: indeed, the more complicated the physical instruments, the more their use will depend upon such organization. Individual human beings still have only one body to destroy and one soul to lose—and the kinds of political behaviour revealed by our earliest records are, as one might expect, not significantly different from those we can witness among our contemporaries. One might hazard a guess that the incentives that held together a praetorian guard or kept the wheels of the administration of the Empire turning were not far removed from those affecting their modern counterparts. It is therefore to be expected that the past should reveal to us systems of government as hierarchic and as bureaucratic as anything the twentieth-century world can show. Political problems are affected by the development of technology— political methods and contrivances much less so.

But if the subject-matter of political studies is the same in all periods, can we be equally certain of the effectiveness of traditional methods? Those of us working in this field who have frequent contacts with out American colleagues—and which of us, thanks to the great generosity of American foundations and universities, has not?—are aware of the increasingly critical eye with which they regard our own entrenched academic habits. New sciences of man— sociology, social anthropology, the analysis of 'communications-media'—all that goes by the barbarous designation of the 'behavioural sciences'—these, they assert, we neglect, or even despise, and to our peril. What is our answer?

I do not myself believe that the development of political studies in Oxford in the forty-five years since the foundation of my chair does in fact reveal the degree of academic conservatism which our critics profess to find. It seems to me, on the contrary, that where the needs of some new field of study or the attractions of some new technique have been established, the necessary facilities have usually been forthcoming. Twelve years' work at Nuffield College in the field of electoral studies has, for instance, done a great deal to add depth to our understanding of the electoral process, and has had its effect on such studies not in this country alone, but in Europe and even farther afield. On the other hand, it is true that towards some of the new techniques we have shown a certain shyness: either because, being by comparison with the United States a poor country, we cannot afford to divert resources, particularly scarce human resources, to time-consuming projects of speculative utility; or else, because we genuinely feel that there are no questions set to us by the direct experience of political life itself, to which such new techniques offer the prospect of new and useful answers. I feel myself that our Oxford organization for postgraduate studies is sufficiently flexible to give each of the new sciences of man its own 'day in court'; and one of the great services which Nuffield College and St. Antony's can render is by acting, if I may so put it, as a kind of filter through which novelties must pass before they are stamped with the seal of respectability through inclusion in the University's examination statutes.

I think it necessary to distinguish fairly carefully between those new social sciences that help us in defining our political problems and those that claim to be a part of the study of politics itself. It is, for instance, obvious enough that the framing of political institutions for particular peoples is likely to go astray if we do not take into account what the economist, the anthropologist, or the sociologist have to teach us about their capacity to use them. And it is indeed one of the main objections that could be argued against the P.P.E. school with its intense compartmentalism, and its relative neglect of such 'bridge-subjects' as economic history and the history of economic and social doctrines, that nowhere in it is the student given a proper conspectus of the whole range of social studies, or any account of their relationship to each other. But this is not to say that the study of politics is not an independent and autonomous branch of knowledge, distinct in purpose and method from the rest.

I believe this to be worth saying because I feel that there is a dangerous tendency nowadays to minimize the importance of this distinction; and one gets the impression that not only other social scientists regard themselves as competent, without any specialized knowledge, to make pronouncements that are in fact political pronouncements, whether those who make them admit it or not. Scientific advance does indeed as I have said, create political and administrative problems, both international and domestic. Turning again to the tasks of government one could, for example, reasonably inquire as do those concerned for our scientific progress, whether responsibility for the entire machinery through which the British Government sponsors or aids research in the sciences should ever be left to a minister who doubles with this immense assignment the perhaps more congenial one of the chairmanship of a political party.

These are not only reasonable questions, they are very important ones: but they are not questions that the scientist as such is qualified to answer; any more than a student of government is qualified to pronounce on the technical issues involved in the choice of alternative lines of scientific research, or on the allocation of resources between them.

But to return to the new techniques of research in the social sciences themselves; it will follow from what I have said of the usefulness of some sort of probationary period, that I do not believe it possible to prophesy which of them are likely to justify themselves in the long run; I can only repeat in other words what I have already said—namely that we should concentrate primarily on those that look like helping with the solution of practical problems. For the same line of thought underlies another reservation of mine, which should not be thought due only to a natural over-estimation of the importance of my own subject. My impression is that most of the new techniques of inquiry concern themselves more with the governed than with government. There is consequently a danger that political studies which give them a preponderant role will tend to neglect the detailed analysis of formal political institutions. And at a time when, as I have suggested, the choice of new institutional forms and the modification of old ones, are such burning issues in so much of the world, this does not seem to me at all desirable. I sometimes feel that American political scientists throw themselves into these inquiries about political behaviour because of their hopes of being able to reform a constitutional structure now dangerously obsolescent.

Finally, from the point of view of teaching, I still hold to the traditional Oxford belief that it is the consideration of the great issues of political organization that provides the most fruitful exercise for the mind, and the best form of training for public affairs.

So far, Mr. Vice-Chancellor, I have been taking advantage of the usual freedom accorded to an incoming professor, that of saying what work it is that others should do, or not do—and with no more than the usual expectations as to the degree of influence that such opinions may have. For my own part, it is from quite a different point of view that I should like to concern myself with the tasks of government, in such opportunities for research as the importunities of administration may allow me. And I should like, again according to tradition, to conclude with some indication as to my own personal agenda.

If we take another look at the tasks of government as we see them today, the outstanding fact about them—except for their mere growth—is the extent to which national policies can no longer be framed in isolation. Almost every government today, and not least our own, is deeply committed through a multitude of institutions, and of less formalized but equally compelling habits of consultation, to take into account the views and requirements of other governments in determining its own policies. Whatever may be the legal attributes of sovereignty which the nation-states of today possess, and however strong the belief of electorates that their own governments are responsible to them and to them alone, international interdependence whether in the military or the economic sphere is a fact of political life that no student of government can afford to disregard.

For someone working in this country, these problems present themselves with an intensity that could hardly be paralleled anywhere else. There is in the first place the Commonwealth itself—and the extraordinarily complex series of arrangements through which are co-ordinated the policies of its member-nations in various fields; arrangements that the British student of government finds impossible to classify and which a foreign student may be pardoned for finding almost unintelligible. There is the peculiar nature of our relationship to the United States, where we seem to have accepted as permanent a degree of military and economic dependence, without having been able so far to ensure the intimacy of joint consultation that was needed to make this permanently palatable. And finally, there is the growing recognition, however reluctant, of our responsibilities as Europeans.

In all these three respects the intermingling of our affairs with those of our partners has gone much too far to be handled under the cover of 'international relations'. Unfortunately, this fact is obfuscated by the plan of our studies where our lectures are arranged and our courses planned as though 'government' were one subject and 'international relations' another. And in fact only a minority of those doing P.P.E. actually come into contact with international government, despite the fact that the relevant rubric talks of 'modern government, international, national and local'.

The failure to indicate that the two subjects of national and international government are today inseparably related may have wider implications than those affecting the teaching of under-graduates. It could be argued that our constitutional arrangements and administrative devices were thoroughly appropriate to a period when separate governments kept each other at arm's length, and when their mutual relations were regulated by the simple procedures of classical diplomacy and, when these broke down, by the clash of armed force; but it could be added with equal truth that these arrangements and devices call for a fundamental remodelling now that the affairs of legally separate governments are in fact inextricably intermixed, and now that decisions vital to the wefare of the communities they are supposed to rule are taken by processes not wholly under their own control.

The theorist of institutions has for the past century-and-a-half managed with the convenient set of classifications by which governments were either wholly independent, wholly subordinate or else linked together by some form of federal (or quasi-federal) structure. But this classification may be positively misleading if we attempt, for instance, to assess the kind of relations that already exist in certain respects with regard to the member-nations of the Coal and Steel Community, and that will be increasingly significant if, and when, the Common Market and Euratom treaties are implemented. Nor should we imagine that the British Government as a member of the O.E.E.C. and of N.A.T.O., to look no farther, is as free an agent politically as it well may be in law.

While the nature and functions of the international institutions themselves are the province of students of international relations, the problem of their impact upon the constitutional structure of individual countries would seem properly to belong to the sphere of government, and indeed to that of public administration as well. For the unity of the two branches of my subject is well illustrated by the kind of questions to which this situation gives rise.

On the administrative side, there is the question as to how departments of state designed either, as with our Foreign Office, for dealing with 'foreign affairs' as such, or as with the other great offices, for dealing with domestic policies, have succeeded in rearranging their activities so as to take into account the obsolescence of this distinction? What effect upon recruitment to, and training in, the civil service has been made by the realization that in almost every major department problems may arise involving collaboration with servants of foreign governments, or participation alongside them in the work of an international institution? And if we may proceed to the intangibles of administration, how far are the habits of work and the atmosphere of confidence generated in the relatively intimate and personal world of Whitehall transferable to the much wider international setting within which so much of the work of government now proceeds?

But no less important are the wider issues of constitutional practice and theory that now confront us. It is surely unhealthy that politicians and the electorate should both proceed upon assumptions that are to a significant extent unrealistic. It is surely wrong that statesmen should suggest that they are able to carry out policies which are in fact dependent for their success upon conditions largely outside their control. The anxiety that has been expressed within this country as to the respective responsibilities of the British and United States governments for the eventual use of the weapons of mass annihilation now located among us is an indication that mere understandings even among friends are no substitute for the proper allocation of constitutional responsibilities. If in defence, and in economic policy, and even in our ability to provide for the social welfare of our people, we have to look to international agreements and international action, then it would surely be preferable to know who our rulers are, and to try to establish new constitutional devices to enforce their responsibilities to the electorate, rather than to accept an ever-increasing delegation of authority to anonymous soldiers and anonymous civil servants.

If it is objected that to seek for definitions and for codes of conduct is un-British, and out of place in a community whose own constitution has broadened down from 'precedent to precedent', I can only comment that arguments of this kind suggest a quite singular capacity for selective oblivion. For the precedents through which Britain came to possess the blessings of constitutional government include, if I remember aright, the decapitation of one monarch, the expulsion of another into life-long exile, and ultimately the calling to our ancient throne of the representative of an alien dynasty. If this is the result of having an unwritten constitution, there might be something to be said for writing it down.

At all events, I have perhaps said enough to make it clear that there is at least room for investigation as to how far the propositions I have put forward do in fact correspond to the existing state of affairs. Translating this into a programme for research, it is my purpose to devote myself to the investigation of the adaptation of government and administration in the Western countries to the fact of their increasing dependence upon each other. It is essentially a comparative study and I have no illusions about its being an easy one. Indeed, one could argue that only an investigator with the wide human sympathies of the first Gladstone Professor, the great practical experience of the second, and the analytical gifts of the third, could adequately perform the task I have set myself. But perhaps this is one of the things better done very inadequately than not at all.

One final word. It is obvious that the starting-point for such a scheme of research must be on the home front. Now, the academic study of one's own government in any of its aspects is a peculiarly delicate operation. On the one side, there is the possibility that one's activities may be so deplored by government that the facilities that one requires are simply not made available. On the other side, there is the possibility of a welcome so warm that the investigator is, as it were, swallowed up by the institution that he is investigating, and becomes ruled in his writing by the administration's own credos and taboos. I should hope with tact and luck to steer a course between these two opposite dangers; but I should like to make it clear, at the outset, that it is the latter that I regard as the more lethal. The quality that a student of government requires most is the quality of independence, of being able to set his own standards of evidence and of relevance. He must no more accept *a priori* the views of officialdom because he studies the contemporary, than a medieval historian would feel bound to respect the standpoint of the chamber or the wardrobe. And it is indeed the good fortune of a professor of government in a great university that he has around him scholars in other major fields, and can use their standards rather than external ones, as the measuring rods for his own. Collective academic research, such as our transatlantic colleagues sometimes urge upon us, is, in my view, a contradiction in terms; but happy is he who can pursue his own individual research, not in isolation, but as the member of a collective, of the community of his college and university, and who is fortified, if he also has the good fortune to be Gladstone Professor, by the strength of an established tradition and the distant reverberation of a great name.

NOTES

1   *Oxford Magazine,* 28 Nov. 1912.
2   K. C. Wheare, *The Machinery of Government* (Oxford, 1945), p. 19.
3   Karl A. Wittfogel, *Oriental Despotism* (Yale University Press, 1957), p. 9.

10

Professor Howard Warrender

THE STUDY OF POLITICS

Under the Charter of Queen's College, a professor was required to make a declaration promising, *inter alia,* that he would not 'introduce or discuss . . . any subject of politics or polemics, tending to produce contention or excitement . . .' Later modified, this political clause was finally abandoned with the establishment of The Queen's University. Thus the danger was at least reduced that a Professor of Political Science might lecture himself out of his Chair in the act of lecturing himself in. But, lest the original statute casts a long shadow, may I assure you that, though I must introduce politics, I shall not produce 'excitement', for I intend to deal mainly with the use of reason and empirical knowledge in the study of politics.

Classes in Political Science were first introduced at Queen's in the year 1910, with a syllabus recognizably close to the one we have today for the Pass Degree. In this year a lecturer was appointed in Economic History and Political Science (to be divided into two separate lectureships in 1948). When I came to Queen's, therefore, I was by no means obliged to begin at the beginning. I found a numerous group of students already reading the subject and have also met many graduates who remembered the course here with gratitude. I should like to pay tribute to the work of the former lecturers in Political Science and to the members of the Departments of Philosophy and Social Studies, and of the Faculty of Law, who carried on these classes in an intervening period when the lectureship was vacant. The main change we have so far introduced into the teaching of Political Science is to extend the courses at the Honours level. For this purpose three degree groups have been established— Politics and History, and Politics and Philosophy in the Faculty of Arts; and Economics and Politics in the Faculty of Economics.

This lecture marks in a formal way the beginning of my term as

Professor of Political Science, and may I take this opportunity to say how much I esteem the honour that has been done me in this. Of more concern than the occupant of the Chair, this lecture marks also, and only too inadequately, the beginning of the office itself. Under these circumstances it seemed to me proper that I should follow the practice of giving some general account of the scope and prospects of the subject and of its relations to neighbouring fields of study, rather than develop a specialized topic. Political science is related to, and dependent upon, many subjects and our problems are so much greater than our intellectual resources for solving them that we cannot afford to refuse help from whatever direction it might come. I shall not be able to deal with many of these inter-relationships today. I propose, however, to examine three connected themes which lie on the border of politics and history, politics and philosophy, and politics and economics, respectively. As these fields of study correspond to our new honours groups, there is something appropriate in this plan.

II

A considerable branch of political science and one that is expanding rapidly concerns government and administration, where the main task at present is to provide an account of contemporary political institutions and the way they work in practice. It is clearly desirable that the citizen should have available a description of the mechanism under which he is governed that is as accurate and impartial as it can be made.[1]

In the field of institutions, academic interest has changed with different views concerning the focal points of political power. As far as British Government is concerned, for example, in the nineteenth century there was great interest in the legislature and the Cabinet. Of recent years, the most notable extension of our knowledge has concerned elections and political parties. The movement is already spreading outwards, to look beyond the executive to the increasing importance of the professional administrator, and beyond the electorate and party system to the nomination of candidates and to the pressure groups[2] that operate below the party level. In this political scientists may have been influenced by a desire to find the lever which operates the political machine. It is most unlikely that there is any single source of control for all purposes. There seems little doubt that the major complexion of British Government is settled by the electorate (though this is not always true of systems that have free elections), and clearly this is only the beginning of an investigation, as we must still ask what influences the electorate. It is equally clear that, in our system of government, important decisions can often be taken by a very few people, and we need look no further than the Munich crisis or the Suez crisis for cases of this kind. Government, in fact, is rarely a matter of dictators and mere cyphers. This search for the centre of influence, nevertheless, has had the benefit of bringing the different aspects of the problem successively under examination.

In the field of political institutions, we are of course heavily dependent upon historical studies. A student of the British Constitution who had no knowledge of its historical evolution could hardly begin to understand its working. It is not usual, however, for political scientists to deny their debts to history, though they may sometimes neglect them in practice. In such cases the historians must correct them, and this I do not think they will hesitate to do.

A more important question, however, is whether the study of political institutions is not so dependent upon history that it cannot itself become more than a form of contemporary history. Such a study, it is true, would be useful at present to the people living under these forms of government; useful also in that it leaves to the future historian a more copious and, we trust, a more accurate record in the governmental field. But this would exhaust its scope, and it is implied that there would be little to be expected from comparing the governments of different countries because each form of government is so much a piece of the history and circumstances of the people it serves, nor could we hope to arrive at a body of general principles. Many of my colleagues who study political science would take such a view. Some of them maintain that the comparative study of political institutions is invalid; others that it is useless in practice.

I do not myself agree with this view, and hold that the political scientist must aim eventually at producing principles of comparative politics. On the question of validity—the enunciation of principles of comparative politics depends upon drawing analogies in human affairs that are not essentially different from those employed by the lawyer or by the historian himself. It is always true, of course, that men who are negligent or ill-informed may draw misleading analogies and these have to be corrected by those who know better, but this is not in any way a problem special to comparative politics.

On the question of usefulness—it is quite true that states are not disposed to borrow principles of government from each other in quiet times.[3] Nevertheless, when states are first established or when they fall into difficulties that are really serious, they are very ready to make use of the experience of others. So much has this been the case that there are scarcely half a dozen forms of government in the modern world that are to any significant degree original.

Perhaps the clearest way to see political institutions is as devices concerned with the solution to a particular kind of problem—a political problem. A political problem is one which in the normal sense does not have an answer at the first level. Unlike a problem in mathematics or natural science where in cases of disagreement one would bring in a better mathematician or conduct more experiments until agreement was reached, a political problem is a case of disagreement with no one answer. A political problem is solved at second level by reaching agreement, not upon the original issue, but upon a mechanism or means of deciding the issue. To take a simple model: suppose there are two friends who always go to the cinema together and on a given occasion they disagree as to which film they should see. After all misunderstandings and defects of knowledge about the nature of the films have been cleared up, they may persist in this disagreement. There may be no answer to the residual problem of personal taste, but they may agree to a device for deciding the issue, such as spinning a coin or something of the kind. If this becomes accepted by them as a regular way of solving their differences, it is a rudimentary political institution. Clearly, a great deal depends upon how fair the mechanism is supposed to be; one of the friends would doubtless regard the matter differently if he discovered that his colleague had used a coin with two 'heads'. The devices used in political institutions for producing agreement in this way are more elaborate—they may divide some spheres of activity off for treatment at a third or fourth level, as in some federal or international systems; also some political devices are less humane than our example. Nevertheless, the methods invented by men for producing agreement in this way have been limited, and it is not surprising that political institutions are variations upon a few main themes.

The similarities between forms of government become more pronounced if we turn from the machinery of government to the functions of government. I am very impressed by the fact that government is developing along remarkably parallel lines in the face of the pervasive forces of modern industrial society. Just as in the nineteenth century there was a lateral swing towards liberalism, so in the twentieth century there has been a similar overall swing towards some kind of socialism, whether countries have been disposed to acknowledge this movement or not. In large modern industrial society there is an increasing demand that the state shall interfere in social and economic affairs to produce some form of the Welfare State and to tackle large-scale unemployment. In even such an affluent society as that of the United States of America, there is an increasing insistence that the individual be protected against such hazards as unemployment and the expense of medical treatment. It is by now a commonplace speculation that by the end of the century the government of the United States and that of Soviet Russia may differ in little but terminology. These forces may not alter dramatically the external shape of political institutions, but they alter considerably their scope and the way they work. It is now generally true that elected representatives cannot control or supervise the policy of the executive at its inception, but must turn more to securing a remedy for specific grievances in administration as they show themselves. Whether this is met, as in Britain, mainly by the use of Question Time in the House of Commons or, as in the United States, by the specialized committees, is by comparison only a matter of second order. It would be a mistake if we spent so much time on the roots and the twigs of modern government that we forgot the branches. We may rightly be suspicious of large-scale philosophies of history or of principles of government that span continents, but it is possible to fall into a specific historical determinism that is just as dogmatic and as far from the facts.

I see nothing invalid, therefore, in trying to discover principles of comparative political institutions and merit in making the attempt. Such a study, one suspects, could never produce a body of knowledge that could be applied mechanically. The most one could hope for would be a knowledge approaching some branches of medicine, where one has a series of likely prescriptions that could be tried on the patient. There are also other difficulties; one of these is to find a sufficiently large number of comparable cases. The student may well envy Aristotle, who was able to investigate over 150 constitutions, many operating under comparable conditions. His *Politics* was the first notable exercise in the quest for comparative principles, and remains the most interesting example of this kind of political science. Many new states are now being established. They will not all adopt or maintain the models of government with which we are familiar. Nevertheless, there seems to be a levelling-out process at work in the world as far as political institutions are concerned, and it may well be that we are moving towards a time when forms of government in general can be more fruitfully compared than they have been in the past.

III

I turn now to the philosophical side of the subject, to which it is more important that I direct attention. Here at present we are not so well circumstanced. A number of factors have thrown into question the whole validity and usefulness of discussing the wider principles and aims of politics, as apart from details of governmental machinery.

It must be remarked in the first place that there is a very worthwhile branch of political theory that is occupied with the history of political ideas. Here the student is concerned to analyse the political notions of the past and to trace their influence through the development of our civilization. Since the problem of the state has exercised some of the ablest men of their time and their views are closely connected with formative ideas in other fields, the student can be offered a very rewarding literature that has little difficulty in defending itself. As this branch of the subject is concerned primarily with the ideas and beliefs that men have as a matter of fact held and the consequence of such ideas, it does not meet in an acute form the question of their validity and can be exempted from our inquiry. But what of the present?

We must note in the first place a number of factors that are not strictly relevant to the validity of political theory, but have so far affected our attitude to it that they had better be cleared out of the way. We must admit that there are many men who dare not discuss political principles at the present time because of the reprisals which their governments or societies may visit upon them if they show any independent spirit of enquiry in these matters. There are also many who are not prepared to discuss political principles because they hold their political views as articles of faith which must not be seriously examined but must be squared with the facts whatever the facts may be. There is clearly a very great difference, for example, in holding Marxism as a hypothesis regarding the ways in which societies develop, which must be continuously set alongside events and whose abandonment or modification in the light of such events should occasion no surprise; and holding this doctrine as a form of religion which must not be seriously questioned or verified. Likewise with other political beliefs, including, of course, the belief in Representative Democracy. It is clear that these cases have nothing to do with the validity of political discussion; they are all cases where there is something wrong with the persons involved or the circumstances in which they find themselves, and do not as such bear upon the character of political principles. They are all problems which have been with us in varying degree throughout our history and have affected the pursuit of knowledge in all fields.

It must also be conceded that in the present period there has been a general dearth of non-academic philosophy. Marxism is a hundred years old and with the exception, perhaps, of a few remarks by Lenin, little has been added to it since then beyond applications that have been transparently opportunist and often self-contradictory. Fascism, a mixture of political slogans and bogus history, hardly deserves the name of a political theory, and on the doctrinal side is not being extended except in the racial doctrine in South Africa. Democratic Socialism has also apparently run out of new ideas. The present period in fact is one in which more attention is being given to the details of administration or to the vices of civil servants (sometimes even set to music) than to the overall political principles that should regulate our affairs. The growth of non-academic political theory appears to depend upon two main factors, namely *(a)* the existence of severe tensions within a society, and *(b)* an audience which reasonably covers the parties to these tensions. On the whole, British society and the Western societies we know best seem at present to be in a period of low tension, compared, for example, with the pre-war period. There are, it is true, plenty of international tensions, but here we have not the stimulus of a suitable audience. The political pamphleteer may well regret the disappearance of the international public opinion of the eighteenth century, though this was largely aristocratic and confined to Europe. The democratic phase which began with the French Revolution and which is still with us, does not so far appear to have been able to generate a world public opinion suitable for political discussion, and on so many important problems has condemned political writers to address their remarks to the converted.[4]

Generally speaking, the present dearth of new non-academic political theory does not appear to me to be in itself a matter for regret. Political theory of this kind is normally generated by serious social disturbances, and as such is a branch of pathology; it is not itself something to be wished for in unlimited amounts. It does give rise, however, to a type of study that it is worth while to cultivate even in times of comparative quiet. It would be a poor doctor who gave up the study of medicine except during an epidemic.

None of the factors I have so far mentioned affects the validity of political discussion, though they have unobtrusively influenced our attitude to it and are as well recognized for what they are.

We come finally to academic political philosophy or political theory (I shall not attempt here to distinguish the two) where we find a crisis that has spread from the field of philosophy as a whole. The main current school of philosophy has drawn its inspiration from the logical positivists, a salient feature of whose doctrine is the application of the verification principle. Such a principle can be stated in more or less extreme ways, but it will suffice for our present purpose to state one of its milder formulations: thus 'a proposition is meaningless unless one can specify a method of verification'; in other words, we must be able to indicate a state of affairs in which we could say that the proposition was true or false as the case may be. It is not necessary that we should be able to verify the proposition in practice, as technical difficulties may intervene; but it is necessary to be able to verify the proposition in principle. Thus the proposition 'there are canals on Mars' has a meaning because it is verifiable in principle; we can specify circumstances under which we would say that the proposition was true, though we may not in practice have the technical ability to make the necessary observations. (I hope that I am just in time with this example.) This is to be compared with a proposition such as 'cruelty is wrong', where we cannot specify the crucial circumstances in which we should regard the proposition or its negative as verified. Such a proposition is to be regarded as unverifiable in principle and so meaningless.

The main critical activity of this school of thought has been directed towards showing that the propositions of traditional metaphysics and of moral philosophy are, in this sense, meaningless. These propositions it is conceded may be useful in all sorts of ways. They may be explained as expressions of approval or disapproval, exhortations or dehortations and the like, but they are not strictly meaningful assertions. By the time it had despatched metaphysics and moral philosophy the logical positivist movement was tiring and did not give political philosophy a very detailed examination. Still it purported to throw fundamental doubt upon the validity of political discussion of the kind relevant to political philosophy. It was claimed that there was no way of verifying a proposition of the form 'a specified type of government is best' or 'one type of government is better than another' and one was often left to conclude that political philosophy, as nearly as matters, was meaningless also. As a result there have come into currency a number of tenets about the nature of political philosophy that are extremely misleading, and students of the subject are often confused as to what they are about.[5]

On the question of applying the verification principle to political philosophy, I wish to make two points: (1) that a large part of political philosophy is made up of propositions that are verifiable in principle, and (2) systems of political philosophy do not depend primarily upon their metaphysical assumptions nor even upon their value judgments, but upon their verifiable propositions.

A political philosopher may be regarded as a person who conducts political discourse with unusual precision. It is one of his main tasks to take the terms which men in fact use in political discussion and to clarify them. Only within strict limits can he invent political terms, for he is concerned with the practice of men and must be able to start from their vocabulary, though this vocabulary is used so extensively for non-philosophic purposes that it must continually be rescued. The clarification of political terms requires, among other things, that the philosopher make a verifiable 'parody' of them. The purpose of this parody is to mark out such aspects of these terms as can be applied to politics, for politics can only concern itself finally with an external social environment.[6] It is also the task of the political philosopher to make apparent the structure of political arguments or political systems and the kinds of knowledge that are relevant to their several parts. I hope to make these functions of political philosophy clearer with a few examples.

Let us look at the word 'freedom'. There is a sense of the word 'freedom' which does not describe any tangible external state of affairs. A man in jail may suddenly feel that he is completely free despite his imprisonment and that his impediments have somehow become irrelevant. Such a meaning of freedom is the concern of the poet or the mystic; it is not a part of political philosophy, which must deal with terms having some external implication.

Turning to the political meanings of freedom; if we look back over some 200 years of European political thought, we find that the term has reached some complexity. In the seventeenth and much of the eighteenth centuries political freedom was thought of very much in terms of the absence of governmental interference. Government was thought of as different from the citizen, and what it enforced was *ipso facto* a diminution of the individual's freedom of action. In diagrammatic terms, therefore, the amount of freedom the individual had against the state could be represented as inversely proportional to what we will call the volume of governmental restrictions:

$$\frac{1}{r}$$

With the French revolution and the growth of democratic theories, it became more common to modify this position. To be free was not so much to be free of all law and restriction, but to be subject only to laws which were in some sense self-made and self-imposed. The citizen could become a part of the state by sharing in the making of laws to which, as an individual, he would then be subject. This meant that the volume of state restrictions had to be qualified by a factor we will call participation in government:[7]

$$\frac{\frac{1}{r}}{p}$$

This conception in turn fell under criticism, mainly from Marxist and socialist directions. It was pointed out that freedom must include a positive capacity to do things. Under nineteenth century liberal notions one was free to stay at the Ritz Hotel, *if* one could afford it; one was free to become Prime Minister *if* one's poverty, malnutrition and lack of education would allow it. There was therefore introduced an economic factor, or more accurately a factor of social welfare and economic means, reflected in a demand for the public provision of education, health services, relief from primary poverty, unemployment, and so on. This we can represent as a material factor in terms of money and leisure.

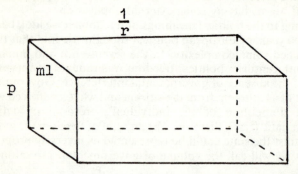

From the above illustration, which is a great simplification of the problem, it is clear that for some people, to speak about more or less freedom is to speak about the increase or decrease of something that is at least three-dimensional.[8]

Compare, for instance, the position before and after the war regarding foreign travel. Before the war there were in this country singularly few impediments to foreign travel in the form of passport requirements, visas, or currency rules. In the years immediately after the war, by contrast, there were many controls, but owing to a distribution of wealth far more people who wanted to travel abroad did so. Comparing these two periods, was the freedom to travel increased or diminished? The problem is clearly complex but not insoluble. Likewise, if you were to say to a Chinese intellectual, for example, that British government was superior to his own on the ground that it gave more freedom, he would think that you were making propaganda, and rightly so. But if even a first order attempt at precision were made, in which account were taken of the volume of governmental restrictions and also what freedom could arise from tackling problems of famine and flood, the discussion could be more fruitful, granted any readiness on both sides to examine the question.

Thus there are some propositions which look at first sight as though they are unverifiable in principle and therefore as though they would make political discussion impossible. Nevertheless, they have this appearance because of their ambiguity and, as we have noted, it is part of the task of the political philosopher to indicate the process of verification that is relevant to them. It should finally be added that I have been concerned here, not with the advisability of using the word 'freedom' in the ways mentioned, and it may be the case that some terms are so badly used that they should be omitted from serious political discourse. I have been concerned simply with the fact that the term 'freedom' has been used in these ways, and that its empirical character becomes much more evident when its complexity is made apparent.[9]

Let us turn from the case of isolated propositions in political philosophy, as in our example of freedom, to the case of a political theory as a system of thought. We may divide a political theory into a number of parts, and here the following diagram will be of assistance:

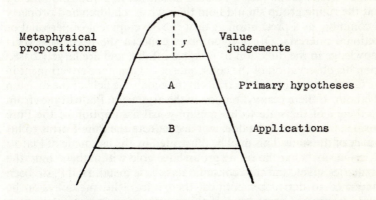

| Metaphysical propositions | x | y | Value judgements |

A — Primary hypotheses

B — Applications

It is common to think of a system of thought as being capable of being represented as a pyramid, and to regard the validity of the system as depending upon the validity of the apex. On such a view and in terms of our diagram, the given political theory will depend upon the region xy, metaphysical and value assertions (which we need not separate here). You will see that on this supposition, if the region xy is taken up by meaningless propositions, the implication is that the entire theory is meaningless in the sense under consideration.

In spite of appearances, however, this is a wrong way of looking at many systems of thought. Political theories, and I believe many comparable theoretical systems, do not begin or depend upon the region xy, but are based essentially upon the middle section A. In other words, what we think of most easily as the presuppositions of the system are more accurately regarded as consequences, though they may be consequences of rather a peculiar kind. In terms of our diagram, this means that the region *xy* and B are both dependent upon A. We are so readily persuaded to the view that if the presuppositions of a system are untenable, the system as a whole is untenable, that it is well to take extra care about what we call presuppositions.

A few examples may make' the point clearer. Even such a 'metaphysical' theorist as Plato bases his system upon a number of primary hypotheses all of which are verifiable in principle, though they may be in need of clarification and will often be difficult to verify in practice. (We must remember, moreover, that we are not here concerned with the question of whether these hypotheses may be said to be true [probable] or not.) Plato considers that revolutions in society begin mainly through divisions within the ruling class, and many features of his ideal state are directed towards ensuring that such divisions cannot arise. Hence Plato is led to his startling theory that the ruling group should hold their wives, children and property in common, as a precaution against the development of personal or sectional interests. Other hypotheses concern the need for expert knowledge in the direction of political affairs, and are largely based upon his observation of the consequences of amateur government in the Greek city state and the fruits in the economic field of the division of labour. If there is any direction in the argument, Plato argues from his theory of the state to his metaphysical assumption of the Pure Forms of knowledge; he does not argue from the Pure Forms to his theory of the state. This may be illustrated by the use made of Plato's myth—a story that the ruling group have gold within their souls, the auxiliaries silver, and the economic class base metal. Had Plato been concerned to derive his political theory from his metaphysics, he would have used something of this nature as an argument to pass from his theory of pure essences to the social stratification of the state. In fact, he proceeds otherwise. Plato's argument that the ruling class will more or less breed true is based upon eugenics—an empirical type of knowledge derived from farming methods; and his story of the ruling class with gold in their natures is explicitly described as a 'noble lie', the purpose of which is to make men satisfied with their station in society. Indeed, if we were to exclude Plato's theory of the state and of education which begin from empirical bases, his metaphysical theory of the Pure Forms would then be grounded only upon a metaphor (the cave) and a mathematical parable. To refute or to declare to be meaningless Plato's metaphysics, therefore, is not to refute his political theory, the origin of which lies elsewhere.

Similarly in the case of Marxism: the Marxist theory of the development of human history, which is essentially a story of economic forces and the social classes they throw into prominence, is based by Marx upon a number of primary hypotheses concerning the factors of history which he elaborated as a result of many years' study in the library of the British Museum and elsewhere. There are, it is true, metaphysical propositions in Marxism. As an example of these, we may take the assertion that the universe is material. Of meaningless propositions this is probably one of the most meaningless.[10]

Now I do not think that if Marx were confronted by a person who denied his theory, he would try to convince him that the universe was essentially material. He would rather try to demonstrate that the course of human history showed the characteristics he had emphasized. Here again, the Marxist metaphysical position is a consequence of his theory of history and of the state; his political theory is not a consequence of his metaphysical position. Thus, what may easily be taken as presuppositions of a political theory and logically prior to it are more accurately regarded as consequences of the system, being projected out backwards as it were. The role of these metaphysical propositions is a considerable and important study to which I cannot do justice here. There is a sense, I think, in which they are meaningless, but this does not mean that they have no function. As far as political theories are concerned, they do operate in various ways as mental catalysts and they supply overtones to the theory itself. But, compared with the body of the theory, so far is it from being true that the theory is decapitated if they are removed, their loss is barely perceptible.[11]

It may be helpful if I give two examples from outside the field of political theory. I hope you will not try my physics too hard, but when I was a very elementary student in the subject it was useful sometimes to have some picture of the fundamental nature of matter. One could take the body of doctrine in physics with its primary hypotheses and its more detailed implications, and, as an addition to this system, matter could be regarded as being made up either of particles or of waves. In other words, these pictures could be introduced into the section I have called x and nothing was changed in sections A and B; such pictures were to some extent irrelevant in that they were equally consistent with all observations. In this way they worked purely as mental catalysts (important perhaps for invention, etc.). Superficially, however, it might have looked as though, being concerned with the fundamental character of matter, they were logically prior to, and the basis of, the body of physical knowledge. Whereas, in fact, anything we can elaborate from physics about the ultimate nature of matter can only proceed in the direction from A towards x and never the other way.

In a similar manner, the so-called psychological presupposition of classical economics regarding the utilitarian motive of economic man, is not strictly a presupposition of the body of classical economic doctrine, but a peculiar kind of consequence which comes out from the doctrine itself and functions mainly as a catalyst. In fact, to remove it and substitute another kind of language here, as has since been done, produces no revolution in economic doctrine. The revolution that took place in the change from classical to Keynesian economics, by contrast, occurred when the primary hypotheses regarding the self-regulating character of supply and demand, etc., had to be revised because the discrepancy between these hypotheses and the world had become too acute. But I shall have to speak about economics in another context later.

In short, the logical structure of a system of thought is the way that system of thought must be built up. It is not the way it pleases us to put it down on paper afterwards. Many of our systems of thought, including political theories, look like simple deductive systems and analogous to the systems of reasoning found in mathematics. In point of fact, however, they are inductive systems, elaborated and presented in a deductive form. And what look like presuppositions or factors logically prior in such cases, may well be factors which are logically subsequent in so far as they are relevant at all.

It is not unusual for us to prefer to set out information in a way which does not make apparent cardinal features in its structure. You may like to consider, for example, the practice of accountants, bank-managers and so on, in their presentation of balance sheets. These documents always seem to be basically optimistic in form. To read them through from the top of the page to the bottom is reminiscent of Pilgrim's Progress, where, after many trials and tribulations, everything comes right at the end and the whole matter balances. Nevertheless, as you will know, the important part of these documents is not the last line but the piece in the middle, and, unfortunately, although the trumpets sound at the end, one may still have to go to jail.

So much for the difference between the logical structure of an argument and the order in which it pleases the mind to set it down.

The position of value judgments is covered to some extent by what has been said about metaphysical propositions.[12] But a brief comment should be added. As noted above, it is part of the task of the political philosopher to show the structure of a political theory. This requires that the values presupposed or advocated in a given political theory should be separated from statements of fact. Further, the political philosopher is required to evaluate a system of values in that he must indicate whether it is self-consistent when its implications are taken into account. He may also attempt to educate the reader in what might be called a sense of values, as we use the expression when we speak of educating people's aesthetic taste. This process of education consists mainly in showing the implications and consequences of given values, and to a less extent, in holding values side by side to indicate differences, as one does, for example, with the shades of a colour.

In the last resort, it is true, one value cannot be demonstrated to be superior to another. In other words, after we have made clear what values are held in a particular system and after we have explained questions of consistency, implication and consequence, there is a final choice of ends which the individual can only make for himself. If he likes, he can take the decision of an authority; but then he must accept responsibility for choosing the authority he follows unless he consents to be something less than a human being. This situation respecting judgments of value has been tolerably clear since David Hume examined the problem in the middle of the eighteenth century, and I do not see that any new problem has arisen here. It means that political philosophy, like any other knowledge, is concerned principally with means and leaves the final choice of ends unspecified. This seems to be so satisfactory a state of affairs, and I find it so difficult to understand what those who would have it otherwise would wish the condition of man to be, that I cannot see how this situation is to be used against either political philosophy or any other branch of knowledge. The fact that political philosophy cannot pronounce about the relative merits of ultimate ends is not itself a matter which affects its validity. It is simply a reminder that the scope of the subject is limited and rightly so. But this still leaves it a very considerable task to perform, and the effect of such an operation upon most discussions in the political field should not be minimised.

If we turn to traditional political theories, we find that the part played in them by value judgments is surprisingly small. Statements of the form 'X is wrong' or 'X is right' rarely make an appearance. Similarly, expressions to the effect that one particular value is superior or inferior to another have also little place. As a general rule, political theories are concerned with the *realization* of values rather than the *justification* of these values and are to be refuted on the same basis. They are written with a view to a specific purpose or set of values, known to be in demand, and to show that such values can best be realized by the form of government prescribed. Hence a given type of state may be defended as being superior in its capacity to produce stability or freedom or individuality or social justice, such values being made explicit or being understood from the context.

With the exception, perhaps, of Hegel, who was a great destroyer of the meaning of words, I do not think that any well-known political theorist has tried to say that his recommendations will give a state that is the best for all possible values. It would be difficult to know what this could mean. Even Plato, for example, does not claim that his state would be the best for poetic or artistic invention, which are to be restrained in the interests of political stability. Marx does not try to show that his socialist state would be best for the capitalist. Political theorists, therefore, have been mainly concerned to put forward empirical hypotheses about the state and society, and to relate them to values in demand. The essential *argument* in their work, in consequence, concerns the probability of these hypotheses and their relevance to the *realization* of given values; it has little to do with the attempt to show that one ultimate value is superior to another.

A more interesting question arising in this connexion is that of whether there can be a political theory which has no values. A political theory *completely* without values would be meaningless. Nevertheless, it is possible to construct a form of *neutral* political theory that is concerned solely with stability and the preservation of men. We may, for example, study the present Welfare State in Britain in two ways: (1) in terms of a whole series of values and aspirations which men hoped to realize or which are being realized in it, or (2) we may stand outside these valuations and see it as a form of order. Before the last war, the social division in Britain had almost produced two nations. It has become apparent that the Welfare State represents, approximately, the terms upon which the class war has been terminated or can be terminated in our society for the foreseeable future. In this connexion the Welfare State can be considered simply in its capacity of resolving conflict. It will be worthwhile to look futher into this question of a neutral theory of politics, and this brings us to the border of politics and economics.[13]

IV

We are being constantly reminded of the relationship between economics and politics. Whether Marxist or not, we have all become increasingly conscious of the pervasive effects upon society of economic forces. Contrariwise, economists are being compelled to take more and more into account institutional factors—in particular, the extent to which economic consequences are following from political decisions. Even so, there has been little contact between economics and politics on the theoretical plane and the similarities between the subjects have not been sufficiently cultivated. There is a good case for trying to elaborate a political theory that would be similar to economic theory and would perform approximately the same function.

In order to think about reality it is necessary to make abstractions, and in response to this need economic theory generated the concept of economic man. On this analogy in politics, if we are to proceed beyond intuitive judgments where we are forced to do simply what we think best, some attempt must be made to form a concept of 'political man' though we have generally been very reluctant to do so. A theory of politics of this kind would, as I have suggested, be concerned mainly with a neutral value of order or stability. The values and aspirations which men set themselves would enter into its equations because these occasion the forces of struggle in society, but the theory would be concerned with conflict and its resolution as such, and not itself with furthering any of the values that gave rise to the conflict.

Let us look back briefly to the beginning of economic theory, often held to originate with Adam Smith. (Coming here as I do from Glasgow where I have many friends, I do not think that it would be safe for me to deny this proposition even if I were disposed to do so.) The question of immediate concern is what it means to begin economic theory or economic science.

I think the feature of the economy that struck Smith with the force of a revelation was the character of the economic exchange, where the individual may, in exchanging goods, further the interests of others at the same time as his own without specifically intending to do so. He was led to his theory of the world market and his thesis of the Natural Harmony of Interests. This conclusion was no doubt optimistic and superficial to a degree which would satisfy few present students of the subject; but it was this which caused, almost accidentally perhaps, an alteration in the whole style of economic theory. Smith and the classical economists began to frame their statements of economic policy in a universal form—that is to say, in principles which, correct or not, were intended to be capable of being followed by all men to their mutual benefit. If we compare such principles with those enunciated by the Mercantilist economists who preceded them, we see that Mercantilism, though it had many features which we are coming to appreciate particularly in the field of economic development, was nevertheless concerned with rules by which one party could benefit to the detriment of other parties. In this way Mercantilism was concerned with how to *exploit* the economy, whereas Smith and the classical economists had begun the study of how the economy could be *rationalized,* and economics has never since completely lost this core of universal rationalistic advice.

If we now turn to the study of politics, we see the beginnings of something like a similar movement taking place approximately a century before. The Renaissance and Reformation had undermined customary and religious authorities, and men began to look for a new source of advice in political affairs. Machiavelli was, perhaps, the first serious writer to attempt this in terms of an examination of political power. Machiavelli's political writings as a whole contain many reservations, but he was essentially concerned with the problem of power on principles which cannot be universalized—with the question of how to *exploit* political power though this may be for good purposes as well as for bad. when we come to the writings of Thomas Hobbes, however, we see the beginnings of the conversion of these principles along the lines already noted with regard to economic theory. Hobbes was concerned with the *rationalization* of power—with principles to which men could simultaneously agree. If there is possible a political theory analogous to economic theory, Hobbes is, in short, the Adam Smith of that theory.

Hobbes's account of human nature runs briefly as follows. Dominated by a restless seeking for satisfaction of their desires, men are engaged in a search that cannot be concluded, as they take more pleasure in prospering than in having prospered. The chief characteristics of men as Hobbes portrays them are pride, avarice, ambition and fear of death, and in their natural state they must be continuously in conflict. Each man wishes not merely to excel his fellows but also to preserve what he has, and will take preventive measures against others lest he should be caught at a disadvantage on another occasion. Each man is the enemy of other men, and men are sufficiently equal in that any man can kill or be killed by another. Hobbes compares life to a race, in which human emotions are essentially connected to victory or frustration in that race, and in a notable passage he describes the natural life of man as 'solitary, poor, nasty, brutish and short'. Fortunately, man's fear of death, though completely self-regarding, is capable of being used to preserve men and provides a motive for the formation of society. Hobbes's theory is essentially the quest for a number of rational principles which, given the motivation of men, will provide a political power strong enough to control their natural tendency towards destruction.

Man is clearly both more noble and less rational than Hobbes's model—a matter which Hobbes himself freely recognizes.[14] Nevertheless, he thought that he had described the character of man as it is essential for the study of politics.

On this basis Hobbes tries to show that it is rational to set up and sustain a governmental agency sufficiently strong to hold men in awe, and further that such a power is essentially uncontrollable. There is, however, a kind of morality connected with the erection of this political power. Though Hobbes has the reputation of being a 'tough' philosopher, he was one of the first people to see very clearly that political power is essentially a power over men's minds. The state can deal with a few criminals, but it cannot be sustained unless a large body of people are prepared to fulfil their civic duties without coercion. In the last resort, therefore, political power must be connected in some way to men's rational or moral convictions.

We do not need to consider Hobbes's theory in detail on this occasion, nor to pursue its shortcomings. Briefly, the principles employed by Hobbes as a basis for his political theory follow, with some innovations, the tradition of Natural Law, in that they are valid for all men of right reason. Hobbes's laws of nature, it is true, have usually been regarded simply as rules of expediency or self-interest. This is, however, to underestimate their status. They are not rules for the preservation of particular men—men may preserve themselves by the most dubious means; they are rules for the preservation of men in general—seek peace, keep covenants, avoid arrogance, and principles of this kind. Just as, for the economists, the individual may acquire wealth by robbery, but this is not a part of economic theory; so for Hobbes the individual may preserve himself by force or fraud but this is not a part of political theory. The reason for this is not essentially that the individual may be discovered and so robbery or fraud may turn out to be against his interest after all; it is because such behaviour cannot be made to fit into any system for the acquisition of wealth or for the preservation of men in general.

To regard Hobbes's principle simply as rules of expediency is to give too little weight to the consideration that they have a universal form, and that, as Hobbes explains, they all fall under the rubric of doing to others as you would have them do to you. Hobbes's system is most clearly seen perhaps as a system of morality, though of an unusual kind—a morality relating to a specialized concept of political man.

It is often said that since Machiavelli morals and politics have been separated, but so far as Hobbes is implicated in this judgment it would appear to be misleading. The position is rather that there are two main kinds of theory relating to personal morals and Hobbes's style of political system belongs to one of these but not to the other.

One tradition of moral theory, which we may call for convenience *motivational ethics,* is concerned mainly with the motives from which actions are done and the moral worth of the agent. The other tradition, which we will call *utilitarian ethics,* is mainly concerned with the results of actions, its interest in motives being ultimately derivative from the results they produce. These two systems of ethics never meet,[15] but one is a permanent criticism of the other.

This morality of results in the political sphere serves as a criticism of intuitionism. In ordinary personal ethics, for example, we should very often regard the so-called Machiavellian as one of the worst types of humanity; whereas in politics from the point of view of the morality of results, a statesman who in a cold and calculating way served the best interest of his state would not be by any means the most serious liability. A much more dangerous figure in politics is what we might call the desperate romantic, who is prepared to blow up himself and take the rest of the world with him, and who in private morality may even get some sympathy. Nevertheless, from the point of view of an ethic of results, it is much less immoral to start wars that you can win than it is to start wars that you cannot win. If states behave no worse than the position of being realistic about their own capacities, there does at least begin to arise the possibility of rationalizing the power relationships in the world and thin ice begins to form over the uncertainty of international politics.[16]

By way of conclusion, I can do little more than indicate the main consequences of using something like a Hobbesian model in politics.

It focuses attention upon means rather than ends—a useful corrective to the last century and a half of political thinking. A Hobbesian model is concerned with the preservation of men in general and has no other serious purpose. This follows from a recognition of the fact that the great values which men commonly regard as worthwhile for their own sake turn out to be diverse, subjective and incompatible, and Hobbes recommends that they be subordinated to the second-order value of survival, where they conflict with it. Historically, this has been the general response of thinking men in the period of fatigue following disastrous wars and Hobbes has written it into a political theory. In a world divided as ours now is between communism and western democracy, not to mention many other forms of politics, morals and religion, all regarded as axioms by their adherents—if we are to avoid catastrophic solutions, we must attempt in some way Hobbes's quest for what concerns all men more or less equally. As the economist sidestepped many ultimate problems in order to concentrate on the question of what rational man would do to increase his material wealth, the political scientist (in the special sense I have outlined) would concentrate upon the problem of what rational man would do to preserve his life.

On this interpretation political man, like economic man, is no doubt a mean creature. Nevertheless, he has his uses and it is well to remember, in the first place, that preserving one's life is not put forward as an objective worthwhile in itself; it is that in order to pursue what is worthwhile, it is generally first necessary to survive (as it is necessary to solve the basic economic problem). Thereafter, it is left to the individual to use his life or his wealth for good purposes or for bad. In the second place, political science would not be concerned merely with the preservation of an individual but with rational principles of preservation—that is with principles enjoining the preservation of men in general. Hence, it is not, for example, concerned with the defence of existing governments. Some governments bolster up their regimes with systems that are not consistent with order in general (a point which Hobbes himself was inclined to overlook), and so may secure order today at the price of disorder tomorrow, or disorder in other communities.[17]

An implication of the Hobbesian model is that we empty out of politics all we can—in particular, what is not related to some concrete condition of our external environment. This is not to belittle in any way the great forces that inspire men's actions such as nationalism or the practice of religion or artistic creation. These forces represent needs in men that are of the greatest significance, and the political scientist would not be offended if their protagonists maintained that they were more important than politics. He would, however, point out at the same time that where these great movements clashed with his model they had a perfectly adequate means of expression and fulfilment outside politics, and that personal problems, as far as possible, should find personal and not political solutions.[18]

A further implication of the Hobbesian model is that we rely upon an empirical evaluation of results rather than upon an evaluation of motives. As such, this tends to be a criticism of our instinctive reactions to moral and political problems and a criticism of tradition.

The problems of the modern world are so new and complex that our instinctive reactions to them, unaided, may well be considerably at fault. To take an example from the economic field: it is instinctive for a family that falls upon poor times to think that it will improve its position by economising. In a similar way western governments first met the great inter-war depression by restrictive measures. There are, however, few people today who would not condemn such a policy, though they may argue about the details. Yet, even now we still feel that there is something 'unnatural' about Keynesian solutions; this does not mean that they are not correct.[19]

A notable defence has recently been made of political tradition as a guide to conduct. It is not clear, however, that this does not fall under the same objections that I have raised to our instinctive reactions in the political sphere. In internal affairs, tradition is useful enough in stable societies when all is going well. But we cannot overlook the fact that a society often has a number of traditions, and the problem may be to escape from them.[20] Before the last war, for instance, there were almost two nations in Britain on the social question, and there were two nations in France. I need hardly tell an Irish audience that tradition would not solve a serious conflict here because there are at least two very different traditions and they are in disagreement. If we turn to the international sphere, tradition seems even more inadequate and needs to be supplemented by a rationalistic or utilitarian enquiry of the kind we have indicated.

International affairs are dominated by two main factors: the emergence of weapons of great destructive force, and a prodigious increase in world population. In this situation, we may easily reach the position that men of all creeds would be prepared to seek a private solution to 'ideological' problems if only the question of continued physical survival could be solved. And in any case, there are certainly a large number of people in all countries who are more interested in what we will call the basic economic and political problem than they are in the nostrums of their political leaders. The growth of large-scale methods of destruction such as the atomic bomb has raised the conjecture that in the international sphere we may soon reach the position that the smallest states could be a fatal menace to the largest. In such an event, we shall have reached, between nations, the position that holds between Hobbes's natural men—a saturation of power or an equality of fear. On Hobbes's assumptions, it would then be rational to form a world state, though whether men would in fact do this is, of course, another question.

Finally, it is necessary to recall the inescapable limitations of the model I have outlined. It is essentially an academic device—a means of connecting theoretical and institutional studies in politics for a specific purpose. Like all models, it is based upon an abstraction and deals only with a slice of life, though it is a very important slice. Nevertheless, the excellence of such a model does not depend primarily upon its intellectual elegance, nor even upon its logical consistency, but upon the quality of the empirical observation which is written into it. I am not suggesting that we should necessarily act as political man would act; but that we should push this unattractive but rational creature before us through the remainder of the twentieth century to see what we can learn from him.

Beyond this model, of course, there remains as before the general field of political science, where we are obliged to take account of the doings of men whatever they may be. There the desperate romantic, whose greatest fear is to be a nobody, will still have his page; though before he decides that he must express himself in a political rather than some other medium, let us hope that he will at least listen first to what political man has to say.

NOTES

1. A present problem, for example, is that there is no adequate up-to-date account of the government of Northern Ireland—a deficiency which I hope that we shall remedy in the near future.
2. These may be mainly economic or social. Before the last war, economic pressure groups were usually regarded as sinister. It is interesting to note that since the war such groups (including trade unions) tend to be regarded as respectable; it is the *social* pressure groups (e.g. the 'Establishment') that are now seen as underhand forces.
3. In Northern Ireland, for example, where for special reasons one party has been in permanent control, the narrowing effects upon political discussion might be mitigated by giving the citizen a greater part to play in the nomination of candidates, so that if the election were a foregone conclusion he might still have some interest in deciding the official party candidate. We could borrow from the United States some system of primary elections but it is normally said that to borrow in this way, even from a country with an Anglo-Saxon heritage, is a political impossibility.
4. The significance of social tensions is readily observable to the teacher of political theory. At the present time, as a rule, it is easier for Irish students to interest themselves in many problems of political theory than it is for their counterparts in England. An Irish student, for example, who reflects that if Marx is correct the divisions of Ireland must be basically economic and not religious, has a hypothesis which he may or may not accept, but easily realizes the difference such a hypothesis might make to his attitude. By contrast, the English student is much more inclined to regard the matter as so much theory and to forget how readily practical problems of great dimension can reappear. Likewise, many of our overseas students, coming from underdeveloped territories where new forms of government are being erected and disputed, can find that nearly all the great discussions in the history of political theory are relevant in some way to their experience.
5. I can deal only briefly on this occasion with the general school of logical positivism and its descendants. My own view is that it is best to regard verification as a philosophical technique. That this technique has its value, I would be one of the last to deny, having found it useful on many occasions and indispensable on others. At the same time, taken as identical with philosophy, it has limitations and gives rise to serious difficulties. In the first place, it is not clear that the logical positivists themselves are freed from metaphysics, preserving certain logical constants isolated from their context and left in the place of Plato's Pure Forms. The ceremonial sweeps with Occam's razor, which are mandatory in their discourse, are manifestly insufficient to ensure this escape. In the second place, and more seriously and unaccountably, their movement has tended to insulate the philosopher from serious empirical enquiries, despite the fact that the whole school begins ostensibly as a criticism of metaphysics to make way for empirical science.
6. Those who seek in politics the satisfaction of basic needs which can only be satisfied, perhaps, in music or in religious practice will condemn themselves to frustration, and politics to something very much worse.

7. Thus during much of the nineteenth century governmental activity was often on the increase, but extensions of the franchise towards universal suffrage enabled people to think that their political freedom was expanding.

8. There are many other types of statement made about freedom—for example, theories of the Hegelian or idealist kind tend to equate the freedom of the individual with obedience to the will of the state. Such a proposition would require a lecture in itself. It may be noted here, however, that it is more accurately regarded as a proposition about the state than it is about freedom, and to unravel it one would have to begin with the meanings of the word 'state'. For the moment, it can be consigned to the poetic and mystical uses of the word 'freedom', in that it has in its existing form no verifiable reference.

9. Since the diagram on freedom produced above has been given a mathematical appearance, we may, perhaps, comment upon the use of mathematical techniques in political studies. There are occasions when such techniques (as in the study of election results) can be introduced as a matter of course and raise no special problem. But would there be any point in applying algebraic or arithmetical methods to something like our problem of freedom?

    I do not think that students of the subject should be discouraged from making the attempt. At present we are suffering from a lack of adventurousness of this kind rather than the contrary. In any event, a person who tried to use mathematical methods on the problem would have first to achieve a much greater level of precision. What, for example, is one to do with the factor of 'participation in government'? How, if at all, does this depend upon whether you have a vote or not in a general election?; whether you are in a constituency where there is a real choice of parties or one where there is always one party that succeeds or even only one party in existence?; whether it depends upon what share the citizen has in nomination? What weights are to be given to all these, and so on? The mathematics may not come out after all, but in the process the student would stand to learn more about political theory and institutions in a few hours than he might otherwise learn in years—if only because of the number of times he would have to re-examine the field of study in order to reach the required precision.

10. According to current philosophical discourse, there are so many meaningless propositions that to call a proposition meaningless is not necessarily to insult it. Propositions of the form, the universe is material or the universe is mental, do however seem to be meaningless in quite a further sense; mind and matter can only be given a meaning in terms of the distinction between them.

11. The loss of these metaphysical propositions affects the pervasiveness of the overtones, the growth or ease of future inventiveness in a theory, etc., rather than the theory itself.

12. Some concepts give rise to particular difficulties. The Historicist assumptions in the works of Hegel or Marx, for example, can be treated as types of metaphysical statements or types of value judgments. To say that a given state of affairs is bound to happen in the end, is very like saying that such a state of affairs has absolute value. Thus Hegel's claims for the nation state and Marx's claims for the classless society can be taken as statements of absolute value.

13. We have so far made little use of the term Political Science—a name which has no precise implication regarding method or validity and whose adoption has been largely accidental. It could, however, be conveniently used for a neutral theory of politics of the type indicated above.

14. In speaking of magnanimity, he allows that there are some noble characters who would scorn to base their lives on fear and he clearly admires such people. But he

maintains that they are either too few or that it is too risky to assume that there will be enough of them to sustain the state. Similarly, men may in a trivial way throw away their lives out of boastfulness or provocation on a mere insult.

15. By this I mean that in resolving their competing claims on any specific occasion the individual must make his own decision as he must do in choosing ultimate ends, and no knowledge could demonstrate the choice that must be made. A valiant attempt was made to draw these two branches of ethics together by Kant, whose theory, nevertheless, was a confusion of the issue. To note one aspect of this confusion, Kant tried to make the universalization principle in ethics a matter of logical consistency and contradiction. Here, Hobbes seems to have been on better ground—the universalization principle behind moral philosophy is of the form 'do as you would be done by'; it is not a logical principle.

16. One of the chief elements of stability in the post-war world has been the fact that Russia has behaved as though she would not start a war unless she thought she could win, and her statesmen have seemed sufficiently realistic in their estimates on this matter.

17. In regimes, for example, which are inherently discriminatory on grounds of race, etc., order is based upon a principle that cannot be universalized.

18. This in no way hinders that men may solve such problems in associations other than the state. During the present century, the state has so far sapped the vitality of churches and other voluntary associations that there is a great deal to be said for reversing the process.

19. Underlying this situation there is a general problem of adjusting our instinctive moral reactions to new and 'unnatural' situations. We may note, for example, the difficulty we have had in feeling the morality of the problem of road accidents— so much so that no fundamental experiment has been made in our society in an attempt to reduce them. This is partly because road accidents are largely unintentional (it would clearly be very different if people were run down on purpose), and most of our instinctive morality is attached to questions of motive and intention. Nevertheless, if we look at the matter from the point of view of an ethic of results, in terms of casualties it is about as serious a moral problem as the problem of peace and war has been up to date in the twentieth century.

Another aspect of the difference between looking at ethical problems from the point of view of a system of motives and from the point of view of a system of results may be illustrated from our treatment of poverty. In the nineteenth century, poverty was a considerable field for voluntary associations and for acts of personal charity, and one cannot but be impressed by the great moral endeavour which went into it. In the twentieth century, by contrast, one pays to the Chancellor of the Exchequer his due in the most appalling frame of mind, and yet the problem of poverty is met more efficiently and systematically.

20. In this respect, it is as well to remember that the tyranny of the past is often a tyranny to which we are, as it were, attached from the outside. You will recall the story of the inebriate who, grasping the railings of the park, went round and round the outside until, concluding that he was locked in, he settled down for the night. If we are shackled to the past, it is often because we are holding on to it from the outside, and if we would only let go the railings we could walk away in freedom.

11

Professor J. H. Burns

THE FABRIC OF FELICITY: THE LEGISLATOR AND THE HUMAN CONDITION

In this inaugural lecture I have chosen to explore a specific (though admittedly a broad) theme, rather than to issue a manifesto expounding the nature or justifying the academic existence of my subject. What kind of subject I take it to be will, I hope, be implicit in what I say about my theme. But, lest my capacity for intellectual innuendo be unequal to my intentions I begin with some brief indications of a more explicit character.

The historical investigation of political ideas cannot lead to a scientifically or philosophically valid theory of politics. Lord Acton was of the opinion that 'the science of politics is the one science that is deposited by the stream of history like grains of gold in the sands of a river'.[1] But Acton was neither the first nor the last prospector to be mistaken about deposits of gold. Neither from history itself nor (most certainly) from the history of political thought, can we hope to derive a satisfactory theory of politics. It is perhaps hardly less true today than it was for David Hume two centuries ago that 'the world is still too young to fix many general truths in politics'.[2] More probably Edmund Burke was even closer to the truth when he doubted whether our collective experience could ever be an adequate basis for 'a sure theory' of political society.[3] It is, happily, not my present responsibility to seek and indicate the way towards a science of politics. My point is that the history of political thought would indeed be as odd a subject as some of its critics have suggested, if it were pursued in quest of such a science.

The subject must be true to its name. It is genuinely historical or it is nothing. By this I mean that it must contribute effectively to our understanding of human experience in so far as that experience is vouchsafed to us historically, through documents preserved from past times. Now the extent of this contribution would be much more limited than I believe it to be, if the range of investigation were confined to systematic philosophical analysis of political phenomena. 'Pure philosophy' is a rarity in this field; and the relationship between political ideas and political experience is seldom adequately, and hardly ever exhaustively, understood by thinking in terms of philosophical, or scientific, or even technological validity. For an analogy to illuminate the relationship of ideas and action here, we might say that it is more like the relationship between religion and liturgy than it is like that between religion and theology. Religious experience is indeed independent of both liturgical forms and theological formulae. Yet without some kind of liturgy we should hardly know that religion was there, whereas we can very well appreciate the reality of religion without theological expositions of its nature. Similarly political theory in the strict sense is not a condition of awareness of political experience. But it is very hard to separate the experience of political activity from some kind of political thinking. Even amid the most furious activities of practical politics,

> . . . men at whiles are sober
> And thinks by fits and starts,[4]

and whenever they do, they are engaging, however spasmodically, in political thought.

The importance of such thought to the historian and its interest for the historian's audience do not depend on its systematic grasp or philosophical soundness. What matters is that it should have been a living part of the political experience of the past. Whatever form it takes, whatever the precise relationship in one case or another between political ideas and political events, these ideas retain their significance for us as the ways in which men have envisaged the actualities and the potentialities of their situation as political animals. Our interest in such ideas is in the end the same as our interest in all historical phenomena—that they deepen and enrich our imaginative awareness of the condition of man. It need hardly be said that the full rigour of historical discipline is needed if imagination is not to degenerate into the indulgence of fantasy or the perversions of the propagandist. But to my mind imagination remains the focus of the enterprise. The function of history, including the history of ideas, is to sustain the imaginative resources of the intellect. If we have not walked down to the Piraeus with Plato's Socrates and his friends and entered into their debate; if we have not trembled with Thomas Hobbes before the dread alternatives of Chaos and Leviathan; if we have not with Jean-Jacques Rousseau sought to lose our self-frustrating liberty as isolated individuals to find it again as free citizens of a free society—then I do not claim that we shall be any farther than we should otherwise be from devising an adequate technology for the elaborate political machine which we operate under the shadow of such paralysing dangers. I do say that we shall live with some dimensions of our minds foreshortened. The history with which my subject is concerned can do little or nothing for the structure and internal comforts of the room we inhabit. It can help to make that room a room with a view.

In approaching the theme I have chosen to illustrate these assumptions, I must begin, however briefly, with the words of my title. In quoting Jeremy Bentham's phrase 'the fabric of felicity' I was moved less by piety than by irresistible impulse. The sentence in which Bentham defines the object of his system as being 'to rear the fabric of felicity by the hands of reason and of law',[5] is one that I have found peculiarly haunting. The legislator who will bring harmony and happiness to the human condition was, of course, no new figure when Bentham brought him into the utilitarian dream. The notion is very old, and I shall have time here to examine only limited parts of a long and complex tradition of ideas. My concern will be to show how that notion has contributed to men's understanding (and, no doubt, to their misunderstanding) of their political situation.

It is a platitude to say that *law* is a key-word for our civilization. But it is remarkable how peripheral, in comparison, is the word *legislator* for the maker of the law. There have indeed been times when this too was a word to conjure with; but it is hardly part of the small change of our political currency. When we see the title of an exquisite novel by Turgenev rendered in one English version as *A Nest of Hereditary Legislators,* we sense an inappropriateness not far removed from the well-worn humours of the foreign-language phrase-book. We may well feel something like embarrassment in recalling the once familiar notion that poets are 'the unacknowledged legislators of mankind'. (When Mr. Day Lewis, dedicating to Mr. Spender his translation of Virgil's *Georgics,* writes of himself and his fellows as

> . . . the unacknowledged rump
> Of a long parliament of legislators,[6]

the irony of that wry comment is not lost upon us.) You will hardly find the word *legislator* indexed as such in a modern encyclopaedia. Yet in the exemplar of them all, the *Grande Encylopédie* of Diderot and his colleagues, the term *Législateur* is the subject of an important and substantial article. From this point, in fact, it is possible to derive a simple formulation of the question with which I am concerned: why does the notion of the legislator as the essential instrumant for contriving human happiness reach, during the eighteenth century, a climax in its long growth, and what legacy did the legislator bequeath to later conceptions of the nature of politics and government?

It is important to recognize at the outset an ambiguity in the very concept of the legislator. The term may be used in two basic meanings, which are not always clearly distinguished. Yet the difference between them profoundly affects the role of the legislator in political thinking. On the one hand, the legislator may be seen mainly or wholly as the founder-figure—the man, or god, or demigod, or prophet, who lays the foundations of the state and then is seen no more save through the thickening mist of pious legend. On the other hand, the legislator may be a continuously active figure, modifying, regulating, sustaining the dynamic structure of political life. To understand the history of the idea we must distinguish within it the legislator as founder from the legislator as governor.

The legislator as governor has certainly played the larger part in shaping our own political understanding; but the legislator as founder has by far the longer history. It has seemed as natural for many human societies to attribute their existence to the work of a 'founding father' as it has seemed for many religions to attribute the existence of the world itself to a creative god. The legislator in this sense is indeed a creator. He may himself, it is true, be subject to still higher powers, so that he does not so much make law for his people as bring law to them. So Prometheus brought fire from heaven, and so Moses—the great archetypal figure here—brought the tablets of the law down from Mount Sinai. Even so, this law-bringer or lawgiver is more than an errand-boy, more even than the essential mediator with the authority this implies. He must after all apply and interpret the divine or quasi-divine message, and as the interpreter of a higher wisdom he will naturally (if not quite logically) be deemed wise himself. For ordinary mortals indeed, his will be the effectively creative wisdom, and the line may be hard to draw between the superhuman role and the functions of a tutelary deity. The foundation-myths of the states of the ancient world illustrate this. Philosophically, it may perhaps be said, the same tendency is reflected in Plato's *Republic,* where the lineaments of an ideal human society are derived from the creative understanding of those few men who have it in them to live the life of reason in a world of eternal and unchanging Ideas. And in Plato's *Laws,* concerned as it is with the detailed construction of a constitution, the philosophical legislator is still more clearly to be seen at work. If we pass from Plato to Aristotle, we find—fragmented indeed but not the less significant—an attempt to theorize generally about 'nomothetics' or the art of legislation. Aristotle, here as elsewhere, shows himself a master of seminal ambiguity, and it is not easy to see whether he regarded legislation as a branch of politics or politics itself as a science subordinate to the more general science of nomothetics. A further problem arises because Aristotle is less clear than Plato as to the positively creative action of legislative wisdom. He is much more inclined to see the legislator as one who brings philosophical criteria to bear upon a given body of laws and institutions, discriminating among and selecting from these rather than himself substituting a new creation for them. But enough has been said to indicate that the political ideas and experience of the Greek *polis* embodied a sufficiently complex conception of the legislator and his art.

There is no wilful paradox in turning at this point from Plato and Aristotle to Machiavelli. At a later stage I shall be concerned with something of what the Middles Ages were to make of the classical tradition in this matter, especially, of course, the reflection of that tradition in Aristotle. But it was the Renaissance that brought about a peculiarly direct return to the historical myth of the legislator and carried this concept, like so many others, into the modern world; and Machiavelli is pre-eminent among those who perpetuated the vision of a lawgiver of herioc virtue and wisdom. His Prince, indeed, lives in a world remote from that of Plato's philosopher-kings, a world with little scope for truly creative wisdom. Nor does the *virtu* of the Prince take the Platonic form. Yet in his ceaseless struggle by force and fraud and calculated ruthlessness against the imprisoning and chaotic circumstances of his world, the Prince does in some measure at least ape the essence of something more exalted. In carving out his transitory clearing of order in the jungle of human greed and treachery, he is, within the narrow limits of what is possible in a corrupt age, doing what the true legislator—Moses, Lycurgus, Solon—did on a grander scale and with far more durable results. To bring order out of chaos is always in Machiavelli's view, a task for one man:

> . . . we must take it as a rule to which there are very few if any exceptions, that no commonwealth or kingdom ever has salutary institutions given it from the first or has its institutions recast in an entirely new mould, unless by a single person. On the contrary, it must be from one man that it receives its institutions at first, and upon one man that all similar reconstruction must depend.[7]

The man who fuses the essential qualities of *virtù* into a truly heroic amalgam is the legislator, the 'providential man', as Pierre Mesnard has called him,[8] of Machiavelli's vision.

The details of that vision—the balanced constitution which the legislator should contrive so as to deliver the state from the otherwise ineluctable cycle of changes and decay—need not concern us here.

But two points must be emphasized. First, the legislator does indeed have to do with what in my title I have called the human condition. His task is to make possible for men what Machiavelli calls a *vivere* civilized happiness because the law established by the legislator is the essence of liberty. In a free state men are at liberty to pursue civilized happiness because the law established by the legislator affords them security of person and property and privacy. At the same time—and this is my second point—the disciplined order of life under these laws makes it possible for men to develop their own civic virtuous and public-spirited citizens must maintain it. They must do not so, the legislator's work would perish with his life. There is nothing inert or inevitable about the life of Machiavelli's free state. The legislator founds, creates; he does not govern or sustain. If the fabric of felicity as Machiavelli understands it is to be maintained, virtuous and public-spiritied citizens must maintain it. They must do this, moreover, in a world of tension and conflict. Concepts such as 'competitive pressure' and 'countervailing power' were in essence entirely familiar to Machiavelli: his legislator's task was to devise a framework within which these forces could work creatively, not destructively. This Machiavelli believes to be possible, and he therefore believes that laws can 'make men good'[9] and that these good men can in turn sustain the structure which makes their goodness possible—but not certain. Aristotle too had believed that 'Legislators make citizens good by forming their habits. This is what all legislators wish to do . . . .'[10] And Aristotle's concern with factors of instability and degeneration in political life show that he, like Machiavelli, knew how hard it was for even the wisest legislators to safeguard men against their own inherent tendencies and impulses.

This Aristotelian and Machiavellian legacy had many beneficiaries. For two centuries and more after Machiavelli's death the same concept of the legislator recurs—often in writers who are otherwise most diverse in character and outlook. But there is perhaps a special sense in which Rousseau is Machiavelli's heir in this respect. The chapter of *Du contrat social* in which Rousseau develops his own theory of the legislator is possibly the most famous single item in all the literature of that concept. It is a chapter resonant with Machiavellian echoes. Here again is the heroic, indeed the divine figure. 'It would take gods to give men laws,' says Rousseau;[11] and the godlike legislator brings to men the law which will confer justice and morality upon their actions, which will release their ethical potentialities, which will enable 'each while uniting himself with all' to remain, none the less, 'as free as before'.[12] Rousseau may be less realistically aware than Machiavelli of the inevitable competing pressures within even the best society: certainly he would doubt the feasibility of building a free society with these tensions as its very foundation. But he shares Machiavelli's understanding that law and liberty must do their civilizing work in a world of conflict. Rousseau's society is not made up of men whose self-interest has been dissolved by some kind of moral chemistry. It is a society where men are taken 'as they are,' but where institutions 'as they might be'[13] liberate enough of men's potential goodness to make moral civilization possible.

Yet there remains of course, an immense difference of outlook between Machiavelli and Rousseau. Machiavelli's republic was, like Rousseau's, to depend for survival upon the virtue and public spirit of its citizens, who in turn were in both systems to derive their best qualities from the discipline of the law. But by definition the Machiavellian citizens were not to make the law for themselves: 'A people . . . is apt to err in judging of things and their accidents in the abstract. . .';[14] and again, 'princes surpass peoples in the work of legislation'.[15] The people were to maintain and run the machine, but the machine did not depend on them either for its design or for its momentum. Law was not simply presented to the people: it was made for them. But for Rousseau liberty itself—the quality without which men lose their very humanity—consists in 'obedience to a law which we have prescribed to ourselves'.[16] To obey the mere fiat of even the wisest legislator is to lose the autonomy which is moral freedom. Thus for Rousseau the *making* of laws, the sovereign act by which a law receives its binding force, must be an act of the whole people and of no one else. The legislator guides, instructs, inspires: he may not and must not impose his will in the sphere which belongs exclusively to the general will of the whole community.

Such a theory is already moving away from the concept of legislation as a creative process belonging essentially to the foundation of the state. The legislator as founder is a single historical or quasi-historical figure, fixed in time, working to achieve his objectives within the limits of a single life-span. But the people labour under no such limitations. A community is a continuing entity, its life transmitted from one generation to another. No doubt the collective lawmaking authority of the people might be supposed to have been wielded once and for all in the generation by which the state was established. Burke may have had some such notion in mind when he said, 'We wish to derive all we possess as *an inheritance from our forefathers'.*[17] Ancestor-worship is after all as viable a form of religious veneration as the deification of a mythical legislator. But to think of 'the people' or 'the community' is almost inevitably to think in terms of more than any single generation, however time-hallowed or however strident in its immediate presence. Burke himself, when he appealed from the folly of the individual and of 'the multitude for the moment' to the wisdom of 'the species' was appealing to something that does not belong exclu .vely to any one generation or epoch.[18] And Rousseau—in so many ways closer to Burke than either of them would have thought credible or creditable—is still more clearly committed to a view in which the community has a continuing and active function in the making of law. Only when every individual, as a full, free, and equal member of the sovereign people, plays his own part in adopting the laws which he is to obey can liberty be a living reality. For Rousseau the legislator can be the law*giver;* but the law*maker* is the individual citizen himself in the legislative assembly of the whole people.

Rousseau's theory in fact brings us face to face with that ambiguity in the concept of legislation which I mentioned early in this lecture. Legislating as an activity of fundamental creation here meets legislation as a continuing and sustaining process. Why the latter concept emerged, and what became of the notion of a legislator in relation to it, are questions shortly to be discussed. But first, something more remains to be said about the role of the legislator as founder in eighteenth-century thought.

The continuing strength of the classical tradition in which the concept was so deeply rooted is, of course, a partial explanation of its hold upon so many eighteenth-century minds. The influence on Rousseau of Machiavelli's version of the classical concept is merely one illustration of this. But factors of a new and different kind were also at work. The *philosophes* of the Enlightenment, heirs and continuators of the Renaissance were heirs also of the new science, children of what A. N. Whitehead called the 'historical revolt' of the seventeenth century.[19] In the study of society and the science of man, as in the sciences of nature, the quest for Whitehead's 'stubborn irreducible facts' was coming to be seen as fundamental. In this intellectual climate the legislator need no longer be restricted to divinely revealed or metaphysically excogitated wisdom. An empirical basis for his work was possible: the legislator could be the exponent and practitioner of legislative science. Too much must not be made of a notoriously ambiguous word; but it is at least interesting to find Rousseau himself, in a passage drafted for *Du contrat social* though not included in the published text, referring explicitly to the idea of a *science* of legislation:

> The original act by which this Body [politic] is formed and unified still leaves indeterminate all that it must do with a view to self-preservation. This is the great object towards which the science of legislation is directed.[20]

Nor is there any doubt as to the basis of this science: it is in Montesquieu that Rousseau finds his model of legislative empiricism, finds a host of instances to show 'the art whereby the legislator directs the institution towards each of its objectives'.[21] The pervasive influence of *De l'esprit des loix* is seen again in the Encylopaedia's *Législateur* article, with its emphasis on climate among the factors which the legislator must consider carefully in adjusting his arrangements so as to maximize security and happiness at the least possible cost in liberty and equality. At this point, then, the figure of the legislator is associated with what might be called circumstantial empiricism—a cautious and in the end an essential conservative approach to social institutions: these institutions should, in this view, be the product of a careful adjustment to the needs created by a number of complex variables in the social situation of each community.

Now it has been argued that in the evolution of a science of society the eighteenth-century legislator was not only an anachronism but a positive obstacle to progress. This was Emile Durkheim's view, and recently Mr Duncan Forbes, citing Durkheim, has suggested that the pioneering social scientists of the Scottish Enlightenment—Adam Ferguson, Adam Smith, John Millar—achieved what he called 'their most original and daring *coup*' by destroying the myth of the legislator.[22] Ferguson, for instance, argued that 'nations stumble upon establishments, which are indeed the result of human action, but not the execution of any human design'.[23] Certainly much of the social science that was to evolve in the nineteenth and twentieth centuries depends essentially on the postulate that institutions are characteristically the product, not of individual genius, but of complex 'states of society'. In such a view the legislator becomes indeed a mythical and stultifying figure.

Yet may this not be a typical instance of a point made in my preliminary remarks? Certainly the kind of social analysis pioneered by writers like Ferguson may claim an historical and scientific validity necessarily denied to the concept of the legislator. But if we are endeavouring to trace, not merely the evolution of valid scientific concepts, but the development of the effective ways in which men have actually thought about society, then we cannot so easily dismiss the legislator. It is true that the effectiveness of the concept was narrowly limited so long as it remained imprisoned in the mould of classical myth given it by the Renaissance, Lycurgus and Romulus were all very well as classical motifs; but, like Robert Clive, they were no longer alive, and there was not a great deal to be said for being dead in this context. I doubt whether Machiavelli, for instance, ever seriously believed that a new Romulus would appear to restore the glories of republican Rome, though he might appeal and hope for a Prince who would free Italy from the barbarians. The famous phrase used by Burckhardt—'the state as a work of art'[24]—can be misleading here. Statecraft in its Renaissance form might indeed be conceived as something for a *virtuoso* performance; but it remained at best a set of brilliantly improvised variations upon set themes. The performer was not a composer. As a mere mythological misunderstanding of the origins of societies, the notion of a legislator could contribute little to the actual political life of modern man.

Within the myth, however, lay the germ of something else. To believe (or write as though one believed) that laws and institutions had once been ordained in the light of reason and wisdom was in effect to say that where reason and wisdom were, there was the possibility of ordaining good laws and institutions. And there was a growing conviction that from admiring the recovered wisdom of the classical past men could now advance to knowledge and power such as the ancients had never had. The age which looked back to the achievements of Galileo and Newton had no reason to think that in the science of man and of society the last word had been said by Plato or the Stoics. Nor, it must be noted, was there any reason why the new social science should be restricted to what I have called circumstantial empiricism. The Newtonian model led rather towards a concept of the social universe in which the behaviour of individuals was explicable, predictable, and thus controllable by means of elementary psychological forces. Sir Karl Popper has criticized this psychologism (to use his term), which he finds surviving in John Stuart Mill's *System of Logic*, as an unsound basis for social science.[25] But here again we may argue that this kind of criticism, however valid, does not dispose of the historical importance of an idea. It seems to me that the belief in the possibility of devising a science of society—and specifically a science of legislation—grounded in the laws of individual psychology was one of the principal liberating factors in the intellectual life of late eighteenth-century Europe. More than anything else, that belief enabled the legislative scientist to take over from the godlike legislators of the past with no sense of inferiority. It led directly to the belief that rational institutions could, here and now, be substituted for the irrational, inefficient, and often oppressive tangle of the existing order, and thus it gave a new dimension to an old dream. The legislator had passed from the world of ancient myth to the world of modern Enlightenment.

This transition was not simply a matter of intellectual fashion. Concrete opportunities for the exercise of the legislator's art were emerging. The Corsican struggle, the effort to preserve Poland as a visible political entity despite the pressures of dynastic power, these created in Europe itself a real if transient need for legislative wisdom. America was soon to provide both an opportunity and an example on a far grander scale and to inaugurate a new phase in Western political experience—the phase of constitution-making. To many who lived through those last thirty years or so of the eighteenth century there need have been nothing visionary in the idea that new political institutions could be rationally contrived to facilitate the pursuit of happiness and 'to endure for ages to come'.[26]

It is true that with the new idea of a constitution as something made rather than inherited there emerged also the belief that this constitution should be made by the whole people. Tom Paine was perhaps the first to attempt a theoretical formulation of this principle,[27] though it is in essence part of what is implied in Rousseau's theory of the general will. But here Machiavelli's teaching came practically to bear. How could a whole people frame a constitution? The constitution-makers might have only a delegated, representative authority; the ratifying power of the people might be safe-guarded. But the legislative enterprise itself must surely be the work of a select few. So it is not surprising to find that the concept of a single legislator survives vigorously. Sometimes, no doubt, it was merely shorthand for a group of legislators; but Jeremy Bentham is there to prove that the strictly monocratic principle did not quickly disappear. Still in the 1820s Bentham was defending the view that the drafting of fundamental laws in a codified form should properly be the work of one man.[28] Bentham learned to admire the American constitution; but the compromises and balance achieved by the play of forces and ideas at Philadelphia in 1787 must lack the logical unity of conception which he, like so many others in the age of Enlightenment, looked for in a legislative system. The need for a single shaft of rational analysis to penetrate the encrusted growth of privilege and vested interest—this is surely one reason why the belief in a single legislator persisted.

In any case Bentham's legislator is far more than a constitution-maker. Bentham provides in his own *Constitutional Code* not only for a representative legislature but also for a Legislation Minister. Legislation is to be a continuous wide-ranging process; and though Bentham now (in the 1820s) thought in terms of representative democracy, he had all through his long life thought of legislation as something far more than a once-for-all creative act. With Bentham we are fully in the presence of the legislator as governor. Now Bentham is, here as elsewhere, representative of a broader and longer tradition of ideas than his own utilitarianism; and we may therefore ask whence and with what credentials the eighteenth century derived this conception of the legislator's art as something concerned with the detailed and continuous regulation of the human condition.

This question involves us in looking at a factor in legislation so far taken for granted without analysis. We have seen the legislator endowed with wisdom, with knowledge, with scientific skill. What we have not yet considered is his power, the power to make law in the form of binding enactments backed by adequate sanctions. We have encountered the legislator as demigod, as philosopher, as scientist; but not yet as sovereign. This is not surprising, for the classical concept with which we have been chiefly concerned had neither need nor motive to regard the legislator as sovereign. He stands outside the system he has created; and in Aristotle's version the sovereign element within the system should be the very law the legislator has devised or selected. Similarly, Rousseau's legislator is outside the system he helps to found, neither sovereign over it nor magistrate within it. Machiavelli (predictably) shows more concern for the realities of power—even in a mythical situation. His legislator is to secure absolute authority without too many scruples as to how he does so. Yet even here the authority is not sovereign within the system: it is power to create the system and set it going. This tradition of thought afforded no basis for a sovereign legislative power continually operative *within* a political society.

This does not mean, of course, that the idea of legislative sovereignty has no classical roots. Inasmuch as sovereignty itself— *imperium, maiestas*—is a concept embodied alike in Roman political practice and in Roman law, its classical origins are well-established. Yet the Roman tradition in this matter had its ambiguities; and whatever its Roman antecedents, the modern concept of legislative sovereignty could not, I think, have been what it is if it had not evolved through the centuries of medieval Christendom.

Christianity itself, rooted in Judaism, is in certain respects preoccupied with law: one of its central concepts is the notion of God as the supreme lawgiver. Upon the classical (especially the Stoic) picture of a world governed by a law, at once natural and divine, of reason and order, the Judaeo-Christian tradition superimposed the figure of a God who made law by will and by commandment. From the first chapter of Genesis onwards sovereign power is always among the attributes of the God of Israel, who was to be the God also of the new Israel, the Christian Church. And here on earth God had his vicegerents, who must act for him no less in the making of law than in other respects. Kings (as sixteenth- and seventeenth-century royalist writers never tire of reminding us) were called gods in the Scriptures,[29] and the power to make law was prominent among their godlike—and God-given—powers.

It is true, of course, that the idea of *making law* is itself ambiguous and that in medieval society it was often scarcely if at all distinguished from the judicial power. It could be regarded, in the words of

Nicholas of Cusa, as a *postestas statuendi dependens a potestate judicandi*—the power to ordain flowing directly from the power to determine cases judicially.[30] The notion of a clearly distinct power to legislate by command emerged only gradually. But much recent scholarly work on the political ideas of the middle ages has tended to confirm the view that the essential notion of legislative sovereignty was emerging clearly well before the end of the period conventionally called medieval. Carolingian ideas of kingship, that part of St Thomas Aquinas's theory of law which emphasizes the authority of the wise legislator, the evolving concept of papal monarchy—all these, in their very different ways, tend towards the same conclusion. The crystallizing of sovereignty in its sixteenth-century form—asserted by Henry VIII in England, analysed by Jean Bodin in France—was the climax of processes running far back into medieval society.

Medieval society made its greatest intellectual effort to come to terms with the problems of law and government in the light of the rediscovered works of Aristotle from the late twelfth century onwards. In this massive rethinking we can see, among so many other things, the Aristotelian concept of legislation meeting and fusing with the medieval experience of kingship. To illustrate this I cite a very late representative of the scholastic tradition in its medieval form. John Mair (or Major as he has commonly been known) was perhaps the last scholastic thinker of originality and distinction. He lived until 1550—a date which is in itself a salutary reminder of the late persistence of creative scholastic thinking. Mair's historical importance was recognized by Acton; more recently tribute has been paid by Professor Trevor-Roper.[31] But I fancy that I need not fear the reproach of rehearsing trite material if I refer to Mair's voluminous but little-read works. In his commentaries on the third book of Peter Lombard's *Sentences* and on Aristotle's *Ethics* we find an instructive illustration of the fusion I have mentioned of Aristotelian and medieval concepts. It is more instructive because Mair in general is far from taking an 'absolutist' view of monarchy. Loyal to the conciliarist and Gallican traditions of Paris, he sees the king as *persona publica,* wielding authority for the good of the community from which he received it and to which he is ultimately subordinate in that his subjects can in extreme circumstances depose him for misgovernment. Yet the king's authority is real and emphatic. No mere magistrate or executive officer, he is 'every inch a king'. And his royal power manifests itself not least in legislation.

Facing the classic question, whether a society is better ruled by a good law or by a good man, Mair has little hesitation in deciding for personal rule, preferring its flexibility to even the best law. In any case, he argues, the dichotomy is false, for there can be no good law that is not itself made by a wise man—*lex non est bona nisi quae a prudenti viro lata.*[32] The skill and wisdom of the 'good legislator' are carefully distinguished from the specifically different kinds of moral wisdom required in private life, in the government of a household, or in the duties of citizenship and subordinate political office. *Prudentia legis positivae*—the wisdom needed for the making of law—is superior to all these, its status being architectonic, concerned with the structure of social life—with, in fact, the fabric of felicity.[33] What makes all this more than a repetition of Aristotle is Mair's consistent identification of the legislator with the king. It is for the king to establish wholesome laws for his people's well-being; and Mair at once links this with the biblical view of kingship by citing the book of Jeremiah in support.[34] More than wisdom is involved here: it is the king's undoubted authority that must be brought into play. In another, earlier work, Mair had insisted that the king *auctoritiatiue condit leges positiuas in quibus dispensat*—he authoritatively makes positive laws and dispenses from them.[35] The king who legislates is at the same time *princeps* and *gubernator* of the realm: his skill and sagacity are backed by power.

The subsequent development of this conception of the sovereign legislator needs little elaboration. What does perhaps need special emphasis is the continuity of the notion that the sovereign as legislator is concerned for the human condition, that he is never merely the man with the big stick, whose function is the purely negative one of keeping order. The picture of the harmonious realm governed by a wise king with which Bodin ends his *Six Livres de la République* is evidently far more than a juristic order of command and obedience.[36] And Hobbes, in a sometimes neglected chapter of *Leviathan*—'Of the Office of the Sovereign representative'—though he begins by defining 'the procuration of *the safety of the people*' as the essential office or duty of the sovereign, goes on at once to add that

> by Safety here, is not meant a bare Preservation, but also all other Contentments of life, which every man of lawfull Industry . . . shall acquire to himself.
>
> And this is intended should be done . . . by a generall Providence, contained in Publique Instruction, both of Doctrine, and Example: and in the making, and executing of good Lawes . . . .[37]

So we return to the eighteenth century, bearing in mind that the sovereign legislator as we have seen him in Mair, in Bodin, in Hobbes, was for much of Europe no mere concept but a substantial part of political reality. In one sense, I think, too much has been made of what is called 'enlightened despotism' (better called 'enlightened absolutism') in the eighteenth century. Taken as generally as its name warrants, the concept does not belong specially to that century. Only if we link it to the specific eighteenth-century notion of Enlightenment can we associate 'enlightened absolutism' narrowly with the era of Frederick the Great in Prussia, Catherine the Great in Russia, Joseph II in Austria, and so on. And if we are to seek a narrow definition in this context, then I suggest that the idea of legislative science has an important part to play. What was new in the latter part of the eighteenth century was neither the concept of the wise legislator nor the notion of legislative sovereignty; it was the possibility of devising legislative techniques which would establish and sustain by constant adjustment and reform the fabric of felicity in the shape of laws which would enable men to find the happiness they all desire and seek.

Like Mair in the sixteenth and Hobbes in the seventeenth century, the theorists of the eighteenth century turned to the sovereign as the only source from which effective law could be derived. But they turned to him in the conviction that they possessed a skill beyond Mair's *prudentis legis positivae* and Hobbes's civil philosophy. They did not all profess quite the same science, though they all perhaps shared a characteristic fusion of rationalism and empiricism. I believe that the form of legislative science we call utilitarianism has a special importance here, though this is not the occasion for a detailed examination of that belief.[38] But it is interesting to observe how Bentham, who above all other English writers represents the Enlightenment concept of the legislator, began by seeing the absolute monarchs of late eighteenth-century Europe as the most likely builders of the fabric of felicity—with himself, no doubt, as planning consultant. We have noticed already that in later years Bentham turned from absolute monarchy to radical democracy; but we have seen also the survival into the phase of Bentham's thinking of the legislator as a single, special intelligence. I would suggest that the essence of that idea survived in other quarters too. In 1832 John Stuart Mill wrote that 'When the value of knowledge is adequately felt, a man will choose his legislator as he chooses his physician';[39] a year later he was arguing that there could be no real reform 'till the real waking minds of the country renounce money-getting, and till they are paid for devoting their time to legislation';[40] in 1846 he wished to see the laws made by 'a skilled Senate, or Council of Legislation'.[41] In all this, surely, Mill was carrying into the age of democracy the legislator whose ancestry I have tried to scrutinize in this lecture. Mill never lost the conviction that this was both possible and necessary; and Mill represents an element in political life which has never been wholly lacking in the modern state. In some such sense as this, the legislator is still with us: in the continuing conviction that the trained mind of the specialist has something essential to contribute to the shaping and governing of a society where human happiness is possible.

An inaugural lecture is in one aspect a very personal occasion; and I hope it will not seem inappropriate if I close with a personal statement of my own reactions to the dreams and destinations I have been examining this evening. I belong to a generation which drank deeply of the sour wine of political illusion. For this reason I find that I must be on my guard against luxuriating too much in the comfort and consolations of political cynicism. It is already not far short of a quarter of a century since I used as an epigraph a lapidary interchange between James Boswell and Samuel Johnson: 'So Sir, you laugh at schemes of political improvement?'—'Sir, most schemes of political improvement are very laughable things!'[42] But Johnson was not a cynic and political cynicism is a dangerous corrosive. None of us is entitled to despise what has been done by legislation in the past century and a half to fashion the social world we so comfortably inhabit. Of course many of the hopes that centred in the legislator were delusive. But if men had not believed that law could do more for them than it ever could, they would never have done as much by law as they have in fact done. Where caution is needed I think, is in our extrapolation from what has been done to what may be done in the future. There is almost certainly a law of diminishing returns to be observed here. And even if there were not, there are frontiers of human misery—and happiness—which no law, no legislator, can cross. Bentham, for one, was well aware that legislation could not regain paradise for us. And speaking personally, as I have said I wish to do in concluding, I find myself led yet again to call on Samuel Johnson to speak for me. Prejudiced, crotchety, neurotic as he was, always honest and often wise, his wisdom is of the kind, I think, which we value because it comes to us from a total human personality, warts and all. My closing words are his, then—and perhaps I am not alone in finding the second, positive couplet less familiar than the negative opening lines:

> How small of all that human hearts endure
> That part which laws or kings can cause or cure!
> Still to ourselves in every place consigned,
> Our own felicity we make or find.[43]

NOTES

1. 'Inaugural Lecture on the Study of History', in *Lectures on Modern History* (London, 1906), p. 2.
2. 'Of Civil Liberty', in *Essays Moral, Political, and Literary: Philosophical Works* (Edinburgh, 1866), III, 98.
3. *Three Letters . . . on the Proposals for Peace with the Regicide Directory of France, Works* (London 1801), VIII, 5: 'I doubt whether the history of mankind is yet complete enough, if ever it can be so, to furnish grounds for a sure theory of the material causes which necessarily affect the fortunes of a State.'
4. A. E. Housman, *Last Poems*, x: *Collected Poems* (London, 1939), p. 109
5. *An Introduction to the Principles of Morals and Legislation* (London, 1789), p. i.
6. *The Georgics of Virgil*, trans. by C. Day Lewis (London, 1940), p. 9.
7. *Discourses on the First Decade of Titus Livius*, trans. from the Italian by Ninian Hill Thomson (London, 1883), I, IX, p. 42.
8. *L'Essor de la Philosophie Politique au XVIe siècle*, 2nd ed. (Paris, 1952), pp. 69 ff. The phrase quoted occurs on p. 76; cf. also the summary on p. 698: 'Nécessité d'un homme providentiel pour instituer la République'.
9. *Discourses, ed. cit.*, I, iii, p. 20.
10. *Ethics*, II.i.5: 1103 b 2.
11. *Du contrat social*, II.vii: 'Il faudroit des Dieux pour donner des loix aux hommes.'
12. cf. *op. cit.*, I.vi: ' "Trouver une forme d'association . . . par laquelle chacun s'unissant à tous n'obéisse pourtant qu'à lui-même et reste aussi libre qu'auparavant." Tel est le problème fondamental . . .'.
13. cf. *op. cit.*, I, preamble: 'Je veux chercher si dans l'ordre civil il peut y avoir quelque règle d'administration légitime et sûre, en prenant les hommes tels qu'ils sont, et les loix telles qu'elles peuvent être.'
14. *Discourses, ed. cit.*, I, xlvii, p. 147.
15. *Ibid.*, I, lviii, p. 179.
16. *Du contract social*, I.viii: '. . . l'obéissance à la loi qu'on s'est prescrite est liberté.'
17. *Reflection on the Revolution in France, Works* (London, 1801), v, 125.
18. Speech on Parliamentary Reform, 1782, in *Works* (London, 1841), II, 487.
19. *Science and the Modern World* (Cambridge, 1926), pp. 11 ff.
20. *The Political Writings of Jean-Jacques Rousseau*, ed. C. E. Vaughan (Cambridge, 1915), 1,477: '. . . l'acte primitif par lequel ce Corps se forme et s'unit, ne détermine rien de ce qu'il doit faire pour se conserver. C'est à ce grand objet que tend la science de la législation.
21. *Du contrat social*, II.xi: 'L'auteur de l'esprit des loix a montré dans des foules d'exemples par quel art le législateur dirige l'institution vers chacun de ses objets.'
22. Introduction to *An Essay on the History of Civil Society*, by Adam Ferguson (Edinburgh, 1966), p. xxiv: cf. E. Durkheim, *Montesquieu and Rousseau: Forerunners of Sociology* (Ann Arbor, 1960), pp. 11-12.
23. *Essay on the History of Civil Society, ed. cit.*, p. 122.
24. The title of Pt. 1 of *Die Kultur der Renaissance in Italien* (1860).
25. K. R. Popper, *The Open Society and its Enemies*, 2nd ed. (1952), II, 87 ff.
26. The phrase is Chief Justice John Marshall's in *McCulloch v. Maryland* (1819), 4 Wheaton 316.
27. cf. *The Rights of Man*, Pt. 1, *Writings*, ed. M. D. Conway (New York, 1896-98), II, p. 310: 'The constitution of a country is not the act of its government, but of the people constituting its government.'
28 cf. *Codification Proposal addressed by Jeremy Bentham to All Nations professing Liberal Opinions*, 1822, esp. §§ 7 ff., *Works* (Edinburgh, 1838-43), iv, 554 ff.

29 cf., e.g., King James VI and I, *The Trew Law of Free Monarchies: The Political Works of James I,* ed. C. H. McIlwain (1918), pp. 54-5.

30. *De Concordantia Catholica,* II.xiii.

31. Acton, *Lecturers on the French Revolution* (1910), pp. 16-17; H. R. Trevor-Roper, *George Buchanan and the Ancient Scottish Constitution,* 1966 *(English Historical Review,* Suppl. 3), p. 22.

32. *In Tertium Sententiarum Disputationes Theologicae Ioannis Maioris Hadyngtonani denuo recognitae et repurgatae* (Paris, 1528), dist. xxxiii, q. xxviii, f. lxxxv r°, col.2.

33. *op. cit.,* dist. xxxiii, q. vi, f. lxvii v°, col. 1: 'Prudentia legis positivae ad principem vel gubernatorem reipublicae spectat ad recte dirigendos subditos.'

34. *Ethica Aristotelis Peripateticorum principis, cum Ioannis Maioris Theologi Parisiensis commentariis* (Paris, 1530), Lib. VI, cap. viii v°: 'Regis enim est leges saluteres populo condere. Hieremiae xxiii. scribitur Regnabit rex et sapiens erit, & faciet iudicium `& iustitiam in terra.'

35. *Joannes Maior in secundum sententiarum* (Paris, 1510), dist xliv, q. v, f. c v°, col. 1.

36. cf. *Six Books of a Commonwealth,* abr. and trans. by M. J. Tooley (Oxford, 1955), VI, vi, pp. 204 ff.

37. *Hobbes's Leviathan reprinted from the edition of 1651* (Oxford, 1909), ch. xxx, p. 258.

38. I have developed some part of the argument in a paper on 'Utilitarianism and Reform: Social Theory and Social Change, 1750-1800' read to the fourth Conference of British and Soviet Historians at Moscow in September 1966.

39. *The Examiner* (4 July 1832), p. 417.

40. Letter to John Pringle Nichol, 10 Jul. 1833: *The Earlier Letters of John Stuart Mill,* ed. F. E. Mineka (Toronto and London, 1963), I, 167.

41. *Dissertations and Discussions,* 2nd ed. (1867), II, 83; reprinted from *Edinburgh Review,* LXXXIII (Apr. 1846), 466.

42. Boswell, *Life of Johnson,* 26 Oct. 1769.

43. Lines added to Goldsmith's *Traveller: The Poems of Samuel Johnson,* ed. D. Nichol Smith and E. L. McAdam (Oxford, 1941), p. 380.

12

Professor W. H. Greenleaf

THE WORLD OF POLITICS

The study of politics in this University College was introduced relatively recently, as was the case in most universities in this country. But, of course, here as elsewhere aspects of the subject were taught from the very beginning as part of the instruction given in more orthodox fields of learning such as classics, history, philosophy, and literature. The first specific appointment of a lecturer in politics was not made until 1949, the chair of political theory and government being established four years later. And the 1950's were the period in which political studies very firmly came into their own in British universities. So, despite this late start as compared with more traditional subjects, when I arrived in Swansea I found an already large and very flourishing department. And my first, and most gratifying, task on this occasion is to express my esteem and my thanks to all those who created and tended this thriving development in the face of real, if sometimes transient, difficulties.

My subject tonight is the 'world of politics' and the broad theme of the remarks I shall make concerns the nature and differentia of politics as an object of academic study. And I must begin with an apology because, although this is a big field, it is also one in which an army of reapers has already been at work. Nevertheless, I think that the harvest is so abundant that even the rather negligent search of a straggling gleaner like myself may be rewarded. Yet, somewhat ungratefully perhaps at the prospect of so generous and easy yield, I want to begin by, apparently, throwing a certain doubt on the status of the subject I profess. For political theory and government is not (in the strict sense) an academic discipline at all: it is a subject-matter or area of attention. There is no special technique or method by which political science can be distinguished, and in this the labours of its votaries are, of course, unlike the work of the natural scientist or the historian, the philosopher or literary critic. In fact, the suggestion that the student of politics is an eclectic is very well observed, for he

225

draws on so many ways of analysis as seem to suit his purpose. And if the current fashion is to try to emulate the methods and employ the categories of the natural sciences (as is, indeed, the case in the field of social studies generally) it is not to be supposed that this is a unique, or necessarily a desirable, trend or one beyond the possibility of reversal. I shall make some comments later on about this political scientism. But this will be in the context of the general issue I wish to put forward for your consideration, which is: if political theory and government is not itself a traditional academic discipline, then how should its area of interest be described, and how may it be explored and made intelligible? These are simple questions but not necessarily easy to answer. As the immortal Pickwick observed to Count Smorltork. 'The word politics, sir, comprises, in itself, a difficult study of no inconsiderable magnitude.'

I

First of all, then, how can we seize on politics as a specific form of activity in some way distinct from the other areas of connected action we talk about? In everyday life and language we commonly refer (for example) to the world of sport, to the financial or business world, to the world of education, of the theatre and so on. And in each of these cases there seems to be implied a set of institutions, activities and persons linked in a particular and recognizable way. What do we mean when we talk about the world of politics as one such aspect of our affairs?

I imagine the common-sense view would be that there is no real problem here at all because everyone knows what politics is. The matter is wholly familiar and is grasped at once. It is true, perhaps, that its nature may not be sharply established because (as Hume says somewhere) we do not annex distinct and complete ideas to every term we make use of; and when we talk about (say) government or law we may not spread out in our minds all the simple notions of which these complex ones are composed. Nevertheless, we know whether or not we are talking within the proper frame of reference. We recognize politics as we recognize a familiar handwriting or voice: the act of apprehension is undoubted even though the particular signs are unspecified.

I suppose that this is so. But 'all true knowledge contradicts common-sense', and it will hardly do to rest content with this implicit point of view, with what Hegel calls 'uncomprehended immediacy'. For one thing, it may be based on a limited or esoteric experience. More importantly, what is apparently apprehended tacitly in this way is never in fact simply given. It hides quite complicated processes of perception and (in Collingwood's phrase) bristles with conceptual inferences. It invariably masks, too, a considerable diversity (or even inconsistency) of ideas. Politics is observed at work in so many ways. If we should try to articulate the position and list a series of ostensive descriptions (as they might be called) we would point out that politics has to do with running the community's affairs, with protecting persons and property, with authority, leadership, influence, pressure groups, government, law parties, monarchs, presidents, cabinets, armies, assemblies (freely elected and otherwise), police, civil servants and so on. Clearly, it embraces a very wide range of reference to persons or offices or activities of many sorts any of which might be quite reasonably invoked as the heart of the matter, as the central feature which gives a degree of conceptual consistency to the world of politics.

At this point, then, we may be driven to a further effort of conscious reflection and to ask how such elementary determinations, all of them, in effect, different aspects of the world of politics, can be held together in some synthesis of the whole. And, at this level of inquiry, what is demanded is some focal direction of attention which accords recognition to all of these partial representations of the political scene. The search is for a general statement which tries to describe what is universal in politics and to bring speculative unity to this very varied range of phenomena, thereby distinguishing the world of politics from related areas. It is this kind of intellectualist enterprise that has often been attempted by academic students of politics. Building on the sphere of popular opinion and common-sense, yet trying to systematize and transcend it, they weave an understanding of politics around crucial concepts or principles which are formulated as precisely as possible. In this way, there have been extensive discussions of: power; legitimacy and coercion; the state and sovereignty; the authoritative allocation of values; the making and obeying of rules; attending to the inherited arrangements of a set of public institutions; maintaining equilibrium by the conciliation and adjustment of interests; and such like.

There are many instances of this kind of thing at varying levels of sophistication. And always there are difficulties, ambiguities and omissions that limit the value of these lapidary generalizations. There is always someone who will point out that really there are one hundred and fifty or more different definitions of the term 'state' (that is, as many as there are independent countries); or that whatever organizing concept is favoured fails to take account of what was once true of politics in the past, or of the manifestly political arrangements of some obscure exotic tribe or region today. Or that it covers too much that is really not political at all. Even that the whole definitional exercise is tautological, no more than a roundabout way of saying that politics is politics.

But the central fact is that this whole reductionist procedure rests on a mistake. And it is simply misleading to assert that, sooner or later, some attempt has to be made to define politics. The error is to suppose that when, as with politics, we are faced with a wide variety of institutions, events and activities, we must look for the identical and recurring feature which is common to them all, that we must analyse these more or less familiar situations to discern their unifying attribute and express this in a universal form. It is clear that the identity this achieved depends on dissection and separation, on the winnowing out of one (or a few) major aspects of the thing examined, and is thus partial and superficial; it is necessarily indifferent to other features of the situations in view. It may be even that the likeness pursued amid these contexts is, in some cases, less important than their differences. In either event, concentration on common qualities is at the expense of a full knowledge of each individual situation and by itself yields no insight into the diversity displayed by each instance and by the range of instances. General statements of this kind are, in a word, merely abstract. And the more general they are, the more empty they become, the less in touch with the real, and less instructive. It follows, therefore, that it would be to compound this kind of error to try to establish a super-definition which encapsulates all the features elicited and stressed by a partial analysis. So it is a great mistake to suggest as, for example, Duverger does, that in discussing the ideas of the social sciences, it is necessary, in the face of a variety of definitions, concepts, classifications and methods that prevail, 'to look for features common to them all'.[1]

The point is, we should not look for a designation of this kind at all: it is a waste of time and a diversion of effort. In political situations, the number of recurring characteristics is so great, so diverse, and connected in such a complex and interlocking way that it is not feasible to reduce them to a single formula. And students of politics who are bewildered at their inability to establish the nature of their subject in this fashion concern themselves unnecessarily.

It is true that rational reflection requires the achievement of some form of universality. But what is needed is not reduction based on the abstraction of residual likenesses only but rather a conception formed by concretion of both similarities and differences.

If, therefore, it is not appropriate to delimit the area of political studies in terms of a definition, in what other way can this task be attempted? In what manner should we approach the job of grouping political data?

An interesting suggestion is to be found (in one of its most recent expressions) in the late Professor Wittgenstein's discussion of 'family resemblance'. He was concerned with the analysis of language, and denied that all its forms have any one quality in common, suggesting instead that linguistic phenomena should be seen as related to one another in many different ways. And he illustrated his point of view further by reference to 'the proceedings that we call "games"'. There are so many different kinds of game (board games, card games, ball games, parlour games, olympic games, and so on) that it is difficult to see that they all share a common attribute. Rather if they are looked at carefully, what will be remarked (he says) is 'a complicated network of similarities, overlapping and criss-crossing: sometimes overall similarities, sometimes similarities of detail'. And Professor Wittgenstein added that he could think of 'no better expression to characterize these similarities than "family resemblances"; for the various resemblances between members of a family: build, features, colour of eyes, gait, temperament, etc., etc. overlap and criss-cross in the same way.'[2] Some members of the family have the same way of holding their head when they talk, others have the same nose or the same build, and so on. And, of course, it is not necessary for any one feature to be common to them all so long as this range of characteristics is widely distributed. It is in this sense, then, that 'games' or 'forms of language'—or 'politics'—constitute a family group.

Now this is certainly a most interesting (if not original) idea and it points us in the right direction even if it does not itself go far enough for our purposes. Granted that the interrelationship is complex and the whole likely to be blurred at the edges, and that it is not appropriate to search for unity in terms of a common and unvarying attribute, it nevertheless seems reasonable to ask what degree and type of grouping is implied by the concept of 'family resemblance'.

And one obvious point is that the identity concerned embraces both similarities and differences. Members of a family are like and unlike one another in various ways and both the similarities and the contrasts are necessary, in the sense of being given, aspects of the whole. Further, as the family identity is not segregated from differences but contains and dominates them, alteration is not excluded either. While recognizably the same (in some sense), the group can (within limits) accommodate changes whether of size, components or features. It alters over time. So in this respect it is rather like one of its own members who, while changing his form or activity in many ways, is nevertheless the same person.

And this directs our attention to the nub of the matter. In what sense is an individual or group or activity or institution, the same thing even through its variations and even though it alters? What sort of identity is it of which the differences are part? The philosophical idealists used to call this a 'concrete universal'; but without raising the controversies surrounding this particular expression, I think an answer may be found in the alternative concept of 'character'.

Now, when we talk of character in this way we are not, of course, referring to anything wholly exact. But (as with definition in its literal sense) we do have in mind, I think, the idea of limits, even though these may be rather hazily formulated. When we discuss the character of a given concrete individual (whether the individual is a person, institution or activity) we mean, not that its personality can be precisely designated in terms of a recurrent attribute, but that it has a certain range, falls within given bounds which are opposites but which the character nevertheless embraces. For instance, when we say that a person does something 'out of character' we imply that he has gone beyond the pales within which his behaviour is normally restricted.[3] I should like to illustrate this notion by a passage I happened to read recently and which occurs in a letter Macaulay wrote in 1828, in which he is describing Lord Jeffrey, the famous Scottish lawyer and critic, and which indicates the kind of consideration I have in mind. When, Macaulay writes, Jeffrey is

> absolutely quiescent, reading a paper, or hearing a conversation in which he takes no interest, his countenance shows no indication whatever of intellectual superiority of any kind. But as soon as he is interested, and opens his eyes upon you, the change is like magic. There is a flash in his glance, a violent contortion in his frown, an exquisite humour in his sneer, and a sweetness and brilliancy in his smile, beyond anything I ever witnessed. A person who had seen him in only one state would not know him if he saw him in another.

And Macaulay goes on to say how this assemblage of dissimilar qualities was united in other ways, and concludes: 'I can easily conceive that two people who had seen him on different days might dispute about him as travellers in the fable disputed about the chameleon.'[4] This is an extreme case perhaps. But it does indicate the ambivalence (or even many-sidedness) to which I refer.

What I am suggesting, therefore, is that if the nature of the world of politics is to be adequately determined then it is not enough to designate this world in terms of one or a few recurring attributes which are seen as common to all the contexts observed. This is a defective procedure so far as it involves abstraction from a total situation which it is desired to understand as a whole. Nor is it sufficient to note the complex set of interrelationships that links these varied instances. This is simply to raise the problem of the nature of the aggregate concerned. Rather what is required is a concrete identity that encompasses without elimination both the manifold differences and the similarities and which in addition is not indifferent to the process of change involved in this variety of connexions. And this unity in diversity may be achieved by establishing the limits which indicate the range of character revealed by the world of politics.

II

The question that now arises, then, is how best to explore this character and to make it intelligible.

In everyday life, as we know, it is already sufficiently understood for the practical purposes involved. But a more precise representation is required in the context of systematic reflection on its nature and differentia. We want to know in terms of what categories and pre-suppositions, and by what method of inquiry, the character of the political world may be most specifically and adequately determined. And there appear to be two possible approaches that are relevant to the study of politics. We have, in fact, to nourish ourselves, like Tennyson's

> youth sublime,
> With the fairy tales of science, and the long result of Time.

In other words, with the naturalistic and the historical modes of understanding. I should like to say something about both of these ways of seeing the world of politics. Each one is rather like a pair of spectacles the lenses of which only permit certain ideas and types of evidence to get through to the vision of their wearer. But this simile implies, of course, that there is a further issue before us, Which of these two media gives the clearer view of the world of politics?

First of all, then, what does a naturalistic understanding of political life involve?

Moulded as it has been by the influence of religious feeling and thought, both classical and Christian, the system of scientific beliefs has itself been represented by two different yet unrelated notions: on the one hand, the idea of transcendence, of a self-contained and permanent order rising above the unstable plurality of the merely sensuous; on the other hand, the concept of the physical and temporal incarnation of the godhead. These categorizations have emerged in styles of naturalistic thinking which together mark the limiting moments of the scientific character. First science as deductive thought, as a stable world of ideas whose generalizations consist of an analysis of these structural concepts and of the relations between them. Secondly, science as a body of knowledge which rests on hypothesis, observation and experiment, on the empirical study of fact with a view to establishing, for example, regular causal patterns, classificatory systems or functional relationships. And it is clear that a science of politics, genuinely conceived, must assume a form compatible with this configuration of scientific beliefs.

Political knowledge as a deductive system of scientific ideas is a notion that can be traced back at least to the beginning of the modern world. Whatever may have been his real intention, Thomas Hobbes certainly—or usually—seems to be arguing that the only sound basis of political understanding is to establish an unassailable axiom about the propensities of human nature and then to elaborate deductively, and in the geometrical mode—the most exact form of reasoning that he knew—what followed, from this premiss, about political society. Somewhat later, both Jeremy Bentham, a typical Enlightenment rationalist whose ambition it was to be the Newton of the moral sciences, and his disciple James Mill adopted a similar form of logical demonstration from admitted principles, claiming to reduce the study of government to such a formal system of argument, and political and legal decision-making to matters of calculation. And, just as theoretical economists of a certain kind long proceeded in this fashion, beginning with a model of the rational, utilitarian individual and deducing therefrom theories about the behaviour of the market, so latterly, similar attempts have been made to establish pictures of political (rather than economic) man governed by a like spirit, as in the so-called 'theory of economic democracy' of Anthony Downs who posits a basic rule about the rational pursuit of power within the framework of a democratic polity and from this draws a series of deductive conclusions. In a similar way, William H. Riker has used axioms about rationality and assumptions drawn from games theory as the basis of logical inferences about the behaviour of parties and other human groups.

But I suppose that one of the most typical and elaborate present-day equivalents to this type of general theory in the field of politics is the systems analysis of writers such as David Easton. This kind of exercise is confessedly imitative of the natural sciences: Easton uses as the motto for his book on *The Political System* a citation from Charles A. Beard praising the great intellectual enterprise of subduing the phenomena of politics in the naturalistic fashion. And within the general framework of this approach, a similar intent is also indicated, for example, by the use of diagrammatic formulation, the building of theoretical models, the stress on the potential value for quantitative expression of the variables concerned, and by the vocabulary employed: equilibrium, steady state, inputs and outputs, feedback loops, and so on. And I regard this mode of analysis as, in the broad sense, deductive because (as it seems to me) the whole project is really an examination of what is involved in the axiomatic concept of a system, that is to say, the idea that societies of all kinds have a built-in tendency to equilibrium. Definitionally implicit in this notion are the other key ideas of structure, mechanism, process, function, role, self-regulation, developmental accommodation, and so on. It is necessarily in such terms, too, that the world of politics is seen: that is, as a complex system of interrelationships maintained in a steady state by certain structures and functions. And the whole constitutes a stable (if sometimes amorphous) order of ideas transcending the actual welter and contingency of political life and change as ordinarily experienced.

Knowledge derived from empirical inquiry into actual political behaviour is also a flourishing enterprise and has been from the time of Machiavelli, Bacon and all their followers from the seventeenth century on—the 'indolent inductives' as they have been so aptly called. And there is no doubt that, in this fashion, a vast amount of data has been acquired about the world of politics. Nowadays (as Professor W. J. M. Mackenzie has recently reminded us) a great deal of this sort of work is carried out in connexion, for instance, with community power studies, the analysis of administration and organization of various kinds, the psychology of small groups (raising matters such as leadership, participation, communication and so on), and also with the great number of societies that have political arrangements of a kind rather different from those with which we are familiar in the western or developed world. Moreover, the ease of handling effectively large quantities of material has been immeasurably increased by the advent of the 'big machines', computers, and by data banks and such like. Of course, all this is not merely, or necessarily, an exercise in 'hyperfactualism', that is to say, collecting facts for their own sake and in the hope that, later on, some ideas will emerge to explain them or give them meaning. Much of this type of work has been carried out under the inspiration and guidance of causal hypotheses of one sort or another, much as Marx, for example, tried to describe the basic factors at work in the development of human society and the necessary laws governing this process of change. On the other hand, most of the generalizations have, of course, been properly more modest than this, middle- or low-grade propositions of one sort or another. Often, it must be confessed, these are of a trivial or rather obvious order, such as Gosnell's famous generalization that non-partisan stimulation of voting will (in certain conditions) increase the number of people who vote. Alternatively the object has been to propound a typology of a whole range of political systems or of some aspect of them, it may be of a certain kind of institution, such as local governments or parties, or of a process such as legislating or decision-making.

Because, then, of the most impressive and profound achievements of modern science, both intellectual and practical, it has often been assumed that the world of man and society would be most suitably examined and made intelligible (and thereby perhaps most effectively controlled) by the use of naturalistic categories and methods. This attitude is, indeed, part of the cultural bias of our time, a symptom of the age. So, quite often, one reads without any surprise that a genuine knowledge of society comes into being only 'with the extension of the scientific method . . . to the social world of man himself'.[5] And many sociologists, in particular, claim that their subject is no more than 'the application of the scientific perspective to the study of society'.[6] And as we are all often urged to be sociologists now, a good many students of politics have (as I have indicated) not been slow to follow suit in this respect.[7]

Now, it would, of course, be ridiculous to suggest that this naturalistic approach to political studies is in any respect improper or wholly without value. There can be no question of putting up a notice outside the political estate saying 'Scientists keep out!' Further, it would be absolutely absurd to urge a point of view that might seem to cast some sort of aspersion on scientific method as such. Certainly, I do not want to do this. But what I do wish to stress is that this scientific perspective is not the only one available and may be misleading, may not be the most fruitful, at least so far as the study of the political world is concerned.

My reasons for suggesting this do not rest at all on the incidental practical difficulties which arise in the application of these methods to a political or social subject-matter: for example, that it is difficult to conduct experiments in sufficiently stringent conditions, that the observer's values are likely to intrude easily, that the existence of free-will is an awkward obstacle in the way of generalization, that there are such problems as those of the self-denying and self-fulfilling prophecies, and so on. These are real difficulties but they are by no means insuperable; nor are they special to the social sciences. No, the real perplexity rests on different and (as I see them) more fundamental grounds; and it centres on various forms of what might be called abstraction, a feature of scientific beliefs that makes them, in fact, akin to the process of reductionist designation I criticized earlier in this lecture.

The first form of abstraction is involved in the attempt of general theories to transcend or encompass the variable and complex features of practical life and to arrive at a stable view of this experience which, unlike the original, is completely uniform and ordered, and free of all contingency. Consider, for example, the functional type of axiomatic theory to which I referred a little while ago. This has many virtues: it can be rigorous and stimulating in analysis; prolific of new terminology and questions; and it is capable of fascinating internal adaptation and development. Yet there is an air of unreality about it all, even of superficiality. It is almost as though the sophisticated management and elaboration of the theory becomes an end in itself and proceeds on its abstract, or tautological, way of having little regard for or relevance to an understanding of particular political realities. It becomes detached from the specific and concrete events, processes and decisions it is supposed to explain, and it is sometimes difficult to see how its notions can be cashed. This

> is an abstraction
Remaining a perpetual possibility
Only in a world of speculation.

And this is altogether apart from other, internal, difficulties that this type of theory involves, such as the question whether too little stress is placed on change and on the role of dysfunctional factors; or, more importantly, whether a pattern of behaviour can be said to be explained (in any real sense) by showing its bearing on the whole structure of society.

The second type of abstraction involves the selection and hiving off of certain aspects of the given experience for special emphasis and consideration. And, since the beginning of modern physical science, something of this sort has always been acknowledged as a crucial aspect of scientific analysis. This recognition was reflected, for instance, in the old distinction made between the primary and secondary qualities inhering in an object or process, the former being those which could be grasped in scientific terms (such as mass or velocity, in fact anything quantifiable) while the latter were attributes which could not be so conceived and which were, therefore, scientifically irrelevant or merely subjective. It was this same contrast which underlay the so-called 'dissociation of sensibility', the great abyss which appeared to have opened up between the scientific understanding of an objective mechanical world on the one hand, and the world of moral, aesthetic and religious values on the other. The root of the matter was really the process of analysis which seemed to be involved in scientific investigation. An object, for instance, was regarded as a collection of various attributes or qualities which could be notionally distinguished. These particulars could then be classified and compared and become the basis of an elaborate taxonomy; or certain of them could be set apart, associated with others of a like kind, and these relationships be regarded as instances of a general law. The important thing is the process of dissection involved, and the destruction thereby of the concrete individual object originally in view in favour of a concentration of attention on certain aspects. In this fashion, the scientific understanding can be seen as stepping aside from experience as a whole into a stable shadow-land of its own making. Not illegitimate of course; and this is an immensely powerful mode of enquiry. But it is necessary to recognize what is assumed and what may follow if we view all objects unremittingly in this way in a sort of dead and spiritless disconnexion. Something is lost. However, exponents of a science of society often recognize quite frankly that abstraction of this sort is a crucial aspect of the kind of analysis they enjoin and seem to suggest even that in this lies the strength of their position.[8] Yet this must mean that the procedure they favour does, whatever its power, impose definite limitations on, and involve a sort of one-sidedness in, the view of politics achieved.

For example, there is the matter of the relevance of some of the naturalistic techniques of inquiry. Thus, quantitative methods may be very useful and open up an inviting range of possibilities of obtaining more information about, say, voting behaviour and movements of opinion. But there is also much about which they may be able directly to tell us very little, for instance, how and why a decision on a particular issue was taken by government. And these areas that the methods cannot illuminate are often the more important ones politically. So to overstress the undoubtedly interesting results of quantitative inquiry in limited matters is rather like the behaviour of the drunken man who has lost a coin in a dark street and who keeps looking for it under a lamp-post because that is the only place that is well lit!

What is involved here is particularly well illustrated by the comparative method. This method is of considerable significance in the social sciences generally where it is often a substitute for the direct experimentation which is not possible. As variables cannot be controlled in a laboratory, a great number of different yet supposedly similar sets of conditions are looked at at the same time. What is done is, in effect, to isolate (that is to say, abstract) certain significant features or functions which seem to resemble one another and to use these as a basis of classification and comparison often on an international basis. So, it is suggested that 'the French National Assembly, the British House of Commons, the German Bundestag and .the Italian Chamber of Deputies can be compared. These institutions have identical general characteristics'. In the same way it is thought possible to compare the office of Prime Minister (or its apparent equivalent) in all the great countries of the contemporary world; or believed that the general structures of, say, the decision-making process are analogous wherever this process occurs.[9] Well, of course, these things *can* be compared; and such an exercise is, I suspect, a usual part of university courses on political institutions. But I doubt very much whether it serves any useful purpose beyond giving its practitioners a feeling of cross-national omniscience. Certainly, the task is (so far as it appears valuable) corrupting and the conclusions are necessarily thin and superficial as well as misleading.

I say this because there are many problems some of which seem quite intractable. There is the difficulty of knowing that the elements compared are really alike. And if they occur within the same cultural context then their autonomy may be very hard to establish; while, if they are not so situated, then it is very likely that the differences will be more important than the similarities. Again, if generalizations (or 'syndromes' as I believe they are sometimes called) are to be based on genuine comparison then the evidence for each element concerned must vary neither in quality nor amount; and negative instances (to which all too often little attention is paid) assume a vital significance. Moreover, the whole process is based on abstraction of the kind I am here concerned with. What are compared are not two or more whole, organic entities but selected aspects of them only. Not the House of Commons and the U.S. House of Representatives but rather chosen features of the activities of these institutions which are removed from the total context of their operation, in which alone they have meaning, and held apart as specimens for investigation and, possibly, as instances of a general classification or principle. And there is the further problem that even such abstracted elements as these may nevertheless be of very complex make-up.

Some odd things are done in the name of this comparative exercise. To take an extreme case, the American ethnologist Murdoch compared the two party system in Great Britain and the U.S.A. with the dualist lineage organization of some Indian villages in the American south-east. I must confess I doubt very much indeed whether such a comparison can contribute much to an understanding of the world of politics. In a very different context, and to give another example, some very dubious generalizations about the nature of militarism have been put forward by Alfred Vagts and others on the basis of a comparative study of military castes, observations which rest on data of very variable sorts and quality, and which can be quite misleading; as they are, for instance, about the British military tradition and the political and social role of senior officers within that tradition. The error is to suppose that there is some sort of common denominator in all forms of military organization. And, in fact, what is said to be comparative in this sort of project is often merely illustrative; that is, instances are chosen (usually on a limited and rather unsystematic basis) to exemplify a theme independently arrived at. The conclusions based on these so-called congruities are often oversimplified and may, to use Professor Evans-Pritchard's phrase, be little more than 'crude qualitative approximations'.

And this view is confirmed when one considers the other major form of abstraction involved in the scientific view of politics and which may be called the distortion of externality. That is to say, political phenomena tend to be seen only as events to be observed, measured, classified, compared, regarded as instances of general laws, and so forth, much as A. F. Bentley wanted in some such fashion to examine group activity from the outside, or as a functionalist is concerned not so much with the actual motives or ideas of actors in a socio-political situation, but rather with the objective role of their activity as it serves to maintain societal equilibrium (as it must in accordance with the demands of his general theory). Events alone are analysed; and ideas may be ignored.

Yet this surely omits a crucial dimension of understanding? For human behaviour is only fully comprehensible when seen, not as a series of events, but as activity, that is, in terms of the conscious ends that guide the people concerned in terms of the thought implicit in what they do. This is particularly true of such a world as politics which is so infused with ideological and moral considerations. In this sense, a naturalistic view of politics is empty and defective so far as this element is put to one side. And what is necessary, on the contrary, is to eliminate the contrast between external events and internal ideas that seems implicit in the naturalistic approach, and to deal instead with the concrete activity as a whole, the thought expressing itself in action. Consider, for instance, a political institution of any kind. This is not a thing or object which can satisfactorily be observed and analysed as if it were a specimen or an experiment in a laboratory. It is a group of people behaving in a certain way and in accordance with given rules; it is an activity, part of a form of life. And as such it can only fully be comprehended in terms of the ideas and purposes immanent in it which give it meaning and make the rules acceptable.

It follows that we need a less abstracting, less mutilating process of understanding than that provided by naturalism. And this is where recourse may usefully be had to history.

Now, the nature of historical inquiry is, in its turn, variously conceived. And one of the limiting moments of its character is indeed determined by naturalism itself. For there is a great and continuing tendency to see history as a part of science or as ancillary to it. Yet if history is thus regarded, historical fact necessarily assumes one of the forms of scientific abstraction I have described. For example, it may help to sustain a set of assumptions, say about human nature, which form the basis for a system of deductive inference; or which by providing material about, perhaps, the process of economic or cultural development, helps to demonstrate a general principle of change. Or, again, as a sort of reservoir of data, history can supplement researches into the contemporary world and, in this way, contribute to a cumulative body of knowledge useful in solving the problems of human relations. But, in any of these roles, a fact is something separated from the full flow of historical experience and subordinated to organizing generalities derived from outside history itself. It is true that this is one way to make history seem more than the doubtful story of successive events: but it is the naturalistic way. And, of course, this history which masquerades as science can offer no more than the appearance of escape from the toils of abstraction whilst binding its shackles still tighter. It is merely naive to suppose that science and history must deal with 'individual cases' in the same way; and that it is unnecessary to make any further distinction.

The turn must be, instead, to the contrasting aspect of the historical character which is concerned not with the establishment of generality but with the fullest possible study of the occasion and development of the historical 'individual'. What is studied is not examined as an instance of a law or theory or principle but for its own sake as a unique entity. Of course, I use the term 'individual' in a special sense here. I do not simply mean a human person alone, but any person or group of persons, institution, activity, idea, process, or whatever seems to the historian to constitute a unity. This individual may be, therefore, of varying scope. It might be a specific politician like Lord Attlee, or a group of politicians such as a party or faction, it might be a given office such as that of Prime Minister, an idea like the Divine Right of Kings, or an event such as the passing of the great Reform Bill, and so on. Whatever is thus chosen by the historian, and whatever its scope, is then recounted as a complete story in all necessary detail and in the most coherent manner possible. And the identity sought is one in which all the differences and tensions are present and comprehensively encompassed in the overall meaningful picture. So, it is clear that the historical approach, understood in this way, may be aligned with the appropriate manner of determining the character of the world of politics which was discussed earlier.

Certainly it is to be contrasted with the abstracting forms of naturalism. Such a study of the historical individual can never be unrealistic in the way that general theory can be, for it never departs from concrete reality and is always concerned with this in all its detail.

Similarly, and for the same reason, it does not break down the objects of its attention into sets of separated particulars. And, in a very important respect, it can never be accused of ignoring the realm of ideas. For there is a sense in which this realm is its real home (notwithstanding the fact that some recent and influential schools of history have tended to ignore this dimension). In the introduction to his *Lectures on the History of Philosophy*, Hegel is reported as having said that everything that has ever happened is the struggle of mind to know itself.[10] So, whereas naturalism sees things (as I have called it) externally, history, in its independent guise, is concerned with the 'inside' in a very special way. This is what (following Hegel) Croce and Collingwood meant when they said that all history is the history of thought. So the world of fact studied in history is really the knowing mind as such. And, if this is so, it follows that human activity (including politics) is only meaningful, not as seen externally, but as the story of the thought implicit in that activity. It is essential, therefore, to lose the distinction between purposes and events, thought and reality, ideas and institutions, and to deal with the concrete activity as a whole: the thought or indwelling life expressing itself in action. And politics, like any other endeavour, is thus seen as an aspect of the attempt, by the human spirit, to build itself a world which is compatible with how it wishes to live. And it is, of course, in this sense, that the study of politics is especially concerned with the examination of political thought—in its relation to the context from which it emerges, to the activities and institutions in which it finds expression, to its various levels of articulation and coherence.

III

When we come to consider how these two systems of belief— naturalism and history—stand in relation to one another, it is obvious that a number of situations is possible. They might be seen as separate but equally legitimate views of experience as a whole. Or as pertaining to two quite contrasting regions of thought and activity. Again, it is possible to view them as distinct moments in a scale of forms of knowledge. Then, perhaps, as involving two different but nevertheless complementary methods. At least this range of options is open to us; and the names of exponents of each possibility come readily to mind. Of course, these prospects all seem to imply an antithesis between the two ways of thinking involved. Scientific understanding is concerned with what is universal and proceeds by way of abstraction and generalization. While, in contrast, the concrete reason of history deals with the individual in its own right and not as an instance of a general law or classification; and it shows, too, how it is possible to have knowledge of things that are constantly altering without invoking either an unchanging realm or substrate or law to provide stability.

Yet these two styles of thought need not go entirely unreconciled. And I do not mean simply that the processes of scientific thinking must rest on historical experience or that they seem in some respects to reflect historical notions of change. I do not refer to connexions of this kind. I mean rather that it is possible to see them both as necessary, to see that, different as they are, they are nevertheless aspects of a single identity which is composed indeed of this very contradiction. And such a unity may be found in a philosophical point of view.

Consider the way in which we have been examining the world of politics. This inquiry has not itself been a naturalistic or historical one. Rather it has been a discussion, at another level or in a different perspective, of how naturalism or history view that world. And from these second-order speculations comes the conclusion that the character of the political world is itself indicated or determined by these two modes of understanding. These systems of belief open up a range of possibilities about the nature of that world and what we should think about it. They are (so to say) the moments of its configuration. And in this manner *both* of them are involved in a comprehension of its nature and differentia, of the limits within which the character of this world emerges.

The character of the world of politics may, then, be grasped in this way, and it may 'be called a philosophical way. True, the philosophical style employed in the analysis is, I admit quite unashamedly, unmodish and indeed downright old-fashioned. But it is, in my view, useful for all that. If nothing else, it has given some indication of what should be avoided and what, perhaps, can be achieved in the study of politics; also, it has implications about how this study should be organized.

For instance, it is appropriate always to recall the limitations inherent in naturalism. At the same time, it is manifestly necessary that something should be learned about this important approach to political studies; though those universities or students of politics who stress only this way of inquiry and who think that political studies is a profession which seeks to explain in terms not historical, are adopting a point of view that, whatever its strengths and virtues, is one-sided and inherently defective in important respects. Rather, we must (like the hero of Homer) gaze on all the pleasures of naturalistic fascination and yet not be seduced by them; and remember that the charms of history are, indeed, more enticing still.

Again, it is clearly implied that the study of institutions and ideas, into which the teaching of politics is traditionally divided, must not be completely separated, as is so often the case in practice. For they constitute an historical whole and should not be sundered. As I have said, a political institution is a form of activity which can only properly be comprehended if the ideas and purposes implicit in it and which give it meaning are also grasped. The aim in this respect should be not a formal or even a sociological study of institutions merely— let alone an indulgence in the superficialities of comparison—but rather an examination in depth of a political tradition as a whole, in all its aspects, to establish its full range of character. And to do this properly means dealing in a much wider compass of material than is usually invoked in courses on political institutions.

Implications of this sort are many and they have practical pedagogic consequences which it is fascinating to contemplate. Among them there is just one more that I must mention specifically, and this concerns the study of political thought. One of the notions I mentioned a little while ago was that all history is the history of thought and that politics was (in this sense) to be seen as world of ideas which, of course, has a history of its own. Now, political thought is of two, or perhaps three, kinds. First of all, there is political theory. And this is either political doctrine, that is, persuasion or recommendation of some kind cast in ideological form; or it is the analysis of the concepts and arguments used in political discussion. Obviously both these exercises (which may sometimes get mixed up) will be conducted in the style regarded at the time as being most convincing or rational. And then there is the history of political thinking, the history of both political doctrine and analysis at all levels of articulation and complexity. Within the framework of such a history, political theory of either kind is simply the latest entry in the account and is itself to be considered and explained in the context of this history as a whole. And I would like to draw one specific conclusion from all· this: that if the fullest (though not the only possible) account of the world of politics is provided by an historical inquiry into the detail of given political traditions; and if this involves the study of institutions and behaviour in terms of the ideas that give them meaning; if, further, all history is in this sense, basically the history of thought; then it follows that the palm must be awarded to that aspect of political study which is called the history of political thinking. But I hasten at once to confess two things. One is that I am *parti pris* in this matter having, both by interest and accident, come to specialize in this particular aspect of political studies. The other is that I would not at all wish to espouse the cause of what is often taught under the title, the history of political ideas. A mere catalogue or chronology of political opinions and doctrines, without any attempt to achieve proper contextual reference and thematic coherence, is a travesty of what the study of this history ought to be. Again, the detailed analysis of the concepts and arguments of a few, rather arbitrarily selected, 'great books', is not such a history at all but merely what I have called political theory in another guise; and the rationale of this pseudo-philosophical manner of inquiry itself is (as I have said) a matter for historical explanation. So when proponents of this analytical theory and the historian go out together for a ride then, as Collingwood says, the historian comes back with the philosopher inside.

But these are, I suppose controversial matters; and I must now conclude. Or rather, I have come to an end. For there is not really any conclusion in this kind of discussion. Only, at best, a widening understanding of the possibilities that lie ahead. We began with some problems about the world of politics as a whole; and now face some difficulties about the character of the university study of that world. One question succeeds another; and the new is in some respects the old in a fresh form. But the intervening exercise is not necessarily valueless if it has provided some alternative, and perhaps more suitable or convincing, perspectives to those with which we first started. So (if I may once again cite Mr. Eliot in his Bradleyan mood),

> the end of all our exploring
> Will be to arrive where we started
> And know the place for the first time.

NOTES

1. M. Duverger *Introduction to the Social Sciences* (tr. Anderson, London, 1964) p. 11.
2. *Philosophical Investigations*, I. 65-7; *Blue and Brown Books*, pp. 17-20, 117.
3. Cf. M. Oakeshott 'The Idea of "Character" in the Interpretation of Modern Politics' (an unpublished paper presented to a meeting of the Political Studies Association, 1954).
4. Sir G. O. Trevelyan *The Life and Letters of Lord Macaulay* (London, 1889), pp. 106-7.
5. D. Martindale *The Nature and Types of Sociological Theory* (London, 1961), p. 27.
6. S. Cotgrove *The Science of Society* (London, 1967), pp. 24, 25, 37.
7. W. J. M. Mackenzie *Politics and Social Science* (Harmondsworth, 1967), passim.
8. e.g. Cotgrove *op. cit.*, pp. 14, 31; Duverger *op. cit.*, p. 12; S. F. Nadel *The Theory of Social Structure* (London, 1957), pp. 153-4.
9. Duverger, *op. cit.*, p. 262.
10. (tr. Haldane and Simson, London, 1892), i. 23.

13

Professor M. M. Goldsmith
ALLEGIANCE

I think I can claim that political theory is a subject entirely appropriate to a university. Not only has this University deemed it so, but it has a long history: Plato's *Laws* (as well as his *Republic* and other dialogues) and Aristotle's *Politics* prove that political theory was one of the original 'academic' subjects.

It is, moreover, a subject especially appropriate to this University, for the West Country has a considerable connection with political thought in England: Richard Hooker was born in Heavitree; Thomas Hobbes was a Wiltshire man; John Locke came from Somerset; and Walter Moyle, a notable eighteenth-century commonwealthman, was a native of Cornwall.

The problem I intend to discuss bothered Hobbes, the Royalist who fled an imminent civil war and produced a theory that legitimized obeying Cromwell, Locke who to justify King William published the book he had written in support of a rebellion he may have plotted, and Hooker, who attempted to discern the extent of men's obligations to obey the civil magistrate in matters of religion. But problems of allegiance cannot be confined to the philosopher's study. In the seventeenth century these problems bothered practical West Country men like John Eliot, John Pym and Edward Seymour; and they plague us still.

Even the motto of this city, *Semper fidelis,* points to the subject of allegiance. But it does not tell us to whom or to what we should be loyal. The questions that it raises centre around the relations between human beings and the societies that they inhabit. When are they obligated to obey the governments of those societies? What so obligates them? When and why and how are men not so obligated? And when is disobedience, resistance or rebellion justifiable or even obligatory?

These questions, formulations of the problem of allegiance or political obligation, remain live issues. Examples of situations involving the obligations, duties and rights of men in relations with their societies come readily to mind. The problem of allegiance is raised in its most acute form when men rebel or advocate rebellion against an existing government, perhaps even a duly constituted one. In 1940, Charles de Gaulle asked his countrymen to withdraw their allegiance from what seemed the lawful government and follow him. Were Algerians wrong in adhering to the nationalist rebellion? What of those who chose France? Similar questions might be asked about Vietnam, or Nigeria or Ireland or many other places.

While the rebels claim to be fighting for freedom and justice against a repressive and tyrannical regime, the authorities deny them any political legitimacy. They are, what M. Pierre Trudeau, Prime Minister of Canada, called the Front for the Liberation of Quebec, criminals and bandits. To the state such groups as the F.L.Q. or the Tupamaros are terrorists and their political actions are nothing but kidnapping and murder. Should such an organization become powerful enough to impose its own taxes and punishments, these are called extortion and coercion.[1]

Other situations involve questions about when men may or must obey or rebel, the extent to which they are obligated. Did the Germans owe allegiance to Hitler's state? Did they rightly obey its laws and the directions issued under those laws, not merely in waging war but also in setting up and operating extermination camps? Could they have rightfully disobeyed, resisted or rebelled? Were they perhaps obligated to do so?

Similar issues have been raised in the United States. The legality of the actions authorized by the government in South-East Asia has been challenged not only by individuals, but even by the Commonwealth of Massachusetts. Problems about the duty to serve in the armed forces have been raised: previously, conscientious objectors had to show that they objected to all use of force, usually by establishing that they belonged to one of the religious groups that traditionally did so. In this war, men eligible to be drafted have conscientiously objected on the basis of their adherence to a humanitarianism that excludes killing; others have urged conscientious objections to this particular war although they did not deny that some wars might be legitimate and admitted that they might validly be drafted in such a case. Has the state any right to demand that men risk their lives to preserve it and to carry out its policies? (That men have risked and lost their lives in its service need hardly be mentioned.) Is there an obligation to serve the state?

The problem of allegiance or of political obligation involves the questions of whether and to what extent men are obligated to obey the laws of the societies in which they live. Such questions are raised when individuals or groups claim that a society is maintaining a law, a policy, a practice, an institution or a system of institutions that is unjust. Racial segregation in the United States, apartheid in South Africa, discrimination against Catholics in Northern Ireland, persecution of Jews and other religious and ethnic groups in the Soviet Union are only a few of the situations denounced. Under what conditions (if any) are men justified in refusing obedience to specific laws or compliance in specific practices? When is collective civil disobedience right? And what of violent disobedience? Are there circumstances in which men would be right to withdraw their allegiance entirely or even rebel?

Perhaps as an American living in England I am unusually sensitive to allegiance problems, but it seems to me that questions about the right relations between states and the individuals and groups that live in them or under their authority are continually with us. Take the case of the *Gastarbeiter* in Germany.[2] Proceedings against public houses posting notices banning these foreigners had to be dropped. Since they are permitted only temporary residence they do not have the same legal protection as those who are 'part of the population.' But the point is less this particular anomaly, easily remedied, than the general status of such groups of people. Needless to say that the *Gastarbeiter* pay taxes but have no share in government. Problems exist too for the numerous immigrant communities in Britain: Indians, Pakistanis, West Indians and even Irish. Although some members of these communities are citizens, many are not. Curiously, new immigration laws rarely give members of immigrant groups who are not citizens any new political rights, such as the right to participate in local government requested by the Italians in Peterborough.[3] The existence of those subject to a political society who are not citizens, full participating members of it, raises two sets of problems. The first I have indicated above: What rights ought such persons to have? What are their duties and obligations? The second is, what conditions may a society set for membership?

But if people denied citizenship raise problems so too do those who possess it but wish to divest themselves of it. Here I would point both to those who wish physically to leave and to those who wish to 'drop out' into small communities, utopias or communes. Is there a right to opt out? Is there a right to emigrate?

Problems about allegiance, about rights, duties and obligations are thus raised in a number of contemporary situations. Some of these problems have received recent attention from political philosophers.[4] Indeed, the subject of political obligation is a traditional one in political philosophy.[5]

I am quite aware that there are other ways of treating this kind of problem. Aristotle and his modern successors have pointed out that human beings are naturally social animals. Each individual's social inheritance is acquired in contact with other humans. Each child is born into a society, taught to speak that society's language, wears that society's clothes, acts in its ways, believe its creeds, values what it prizes, follows its norms. It would be possible to examine how successful a society is in inculcating its values and norms. It would be possible to investigate loyalty as a matter of fact; under what conditions do men actually tend to rebel or disobey? How loyal are Lilliputians? Are they thoroughly imbued with the values of Lilliput? How many Brobdingnagians refuse to fight its wars, obey its laws, pay its taxes? Are there social or psychological factors more common among those who are loyal or those who rebel? Such questions I shall leave untouched. Avoiding the facts about allegiance or loyalty, the conditions that foster it, maintain it or destroy it, I shall confine myself to what can make it right.[6]

Political obligation or allegiance is a central problem for but one type of political philosophy. Its assumptions are inherently individualistic, it seeks to explain the legal and moral authority of society by deriving it from some form of individual commitment: an act, a promise, a performative utterance, a contract. In its most extreme and most explicit versions—those of Hobbes, Pufendorf and Rousseau—a number of individuals voluntarily contract together to form a society. Other versions are less explicit: Locke merely says that men incorporate themselves into a society and Hooker seems to have a similar view.[7] Although Hume regarded the social contract as a philosophical fiction and denied that allegiance needed to be grounded in promises, he nevertheless gave a conventionalist account: two men rowing a boat make no promises and the silent, informal but no less voluntary acceptance of the rules of justice is similar.[8] Among more recent examples of this tradition are R. M. Hare, H. L. A. Hart and John Rawls.[9]

In examining the principles of allegiance I shall sketch what I believe is the limiting case—that situation in which men are most clearly and most strongly obligated to their society. Such a situation exists when they are voluntarily members of a just society, a society that conforms to the principles of justice.

According to Rawls, the principles of justice and the framing of a just society may be best understood as a series of hypothetical social contracts. These contracts are to be thought of as occurring in a carefully defined original position, and subject to the assumption that there exists a set of conditions that make it possible and sensible for the contracting persons to accept moral constraint in their mutual dealings.[10] Thus they are not self-sufficient; they may have different interests and even different conceptions of what is good; they are not incapable of communicating; the resources at their disposal are limited; co-operation is not futile; and they are roughly equal—or at least not so unequal as to divide automatically into superiors and inferiors. Finally, these persons are rational in at least a limited sense: they can be conscious of their needs and interests; they are not inherently envious, i.e., the mere perception that someone else is better off does not discontent them; they can plan a course of action and foresee to some extent the consequences of adopting various social institutions; they can adhere to a course of action, resisting immediate temptations to achieve longer term ends.

Any set of persons characterized by these conditions could be the participants in the original contract. Although we usually imagine them as individual human beings, they might be families or other groups. But it is not difficult to imagine species whose characteristics and conditions were very different, for example, a race of telepathic molluscs incapable of aiding each other or one of intelligent tortoises, less susceptible to harm and less capable of inflicting it than men. David Hume pointed out that the jealous virtue of justice could have no place were humans as solicitous for others as for themselves, or were they capable of no benevolence to others, or were they placed in a condition of unlimited abundance, or in one of desperate scarcity.[11]

To arrive at the principles of justice we must imagine that persons subject to the circumstances described are adopting principles by which all their complaints, claims, practices and institutions will in future be judged. Placed in an 'analytic analogue' of the state of nature, they are deemed to be ignorant of any facts about themselves which could prejudice their choice of principles. They do not know their natural talents or their positions in society, or even what social institutions exist; they do not know their interests or their systems of ends—they do not know their ambitions, preferences and values. We must imagine our participants having a draught of the waters of Lethe, or some other suitable potion, that deprives them of knowledge of their own abilities and circumstances without depriving them of knowledge of human characteristics and social circumstances.

Persons so circumstanced placed in this original position and constrained to adopt principles of appraisal would, Rawls contends, adopt two principles of justice. First, each person participating in a practice or an institution, or affected by it, has an equal right to the most extensive liberty compatible with a like liberty for all. Second, inequalities defined by institutions, or fostered by them, are to be so arranged that they will work out to everyone's advantage and attached to positions and offices open to all.[12]

In the absence of information about his own abilities, the position he holds in society and the actual conditions that he will live under, no person can discover principles that will further his own interests. Each will propose or accept only principles which would least disadvantage him under any foreseeable circumstances; each must consider how the principles proposed would affect him were he placed in typical positions or roles in various social institutions. Rawls's principles of justice thus involve a solution to the game of discovering moral principles that could be mutually agreed between independent, self-seeking persons. The solution involves an agreement to share the benefits of natural talents used in social collaboration; and it subordinates utility to liberty and equality. Indeed, it might be regarded as an attempt to discover the precise amount of Kantian cement needed to bind utilitarian atoms.

Having agreed upon these principles of justice by which all their institutions are to be appraised, let us suppose with Rawls that our participants now proceed to complete their social contract. Thus, they move to a constitutional convention, choosing a constitution consistent with the principles of justice. Finally, the legislative body chosen under the constitutional procedures, operating according to them and guided by the principles of justice, enacts laws. At each of these stages the participants have whatever additional knowledge they require in order to make their decisions rational.

Given the normal conditions of the modern state, it is at least arguable that out of the possible just constitutions, they would choose one of the variants of constitutional democracy. Maximum and equal civil liberty and political rights are required by the first principle of justice. Deviations from equality are required not only to benefit the least well-off representative man participating in or affected by the institution but also the positions must be open to all. That social regulation should be carried out according to promulgated rules arrived at by known and public procedures and administered impartially would seem to be required. In addition to the requirements of the rule of law, a constitutional order limits the powers of its various agencies—no man and no institution being permitted to determine and maintain its own rights and powers. A constitutional regime in which offices are variously open to competition on the basis of ability, electoral success or lot, in which officials are responsible for their actions and in which legal and political redress is available seems required by the principles of justice.

A constitution consistent with the principles of justice does not solve every problem; indeed it cannot guarantee that only just laws would be enacted. Although he supposed that the people could never be corrupted, even Rousseau admitted that they could be mistaken. No political institutions can guarantee that no inefficient, unjust or harmful policies will ever be enacted or that no unjust actions will ever be undertaken. A just constitution merely provides 'imperfect procedural justice' by its procedures devised to exclude unjust results and promote just ones.[13]

I have now completed my sketch of the situation in which men would owe allegiance most clearly and most strongly, for the strongest case of political obligation I can imagine would occur where the procedures outlined above were followed. Where a number of equal and independent persons acknowledged the principles of justice, agreed upon a constitution satisfying those principles and followed these constitutional procedures in operating their institutions, they would then not only have a duty to support just institutions but also would have voluntarily undertaken an obligation to support these particular institutions.

But surely this has never in fact been done, for no societies have as yet been founded by well-informed amnesiacs. Nor am I suggesting that we must all·go through such a procedure before we owe allegiance. The procedures sketched above are not presented to be imitated, but rather as a criterion: social arrangements are just if they accord with what would be adopted by persons situated in the original position, and persons living under those arrangements are obligated to the extent that they voluntarily accept them. Explicit agreement is one form of voluntary acceptance, but it is not necessary for a person to have contracted in order to be obligated. Those who are members of a just society (or even of one which is for the most part just) are obligated by participating in its practices and planning to continue to do so. By accepting the benefits of the institutions, they implicitly accept the obligation to share the burdens when their turns come. They have obligated themselves (*prima facie*) to support the institutions.

Although there can be no guarantee that unjust laws or policies will never be adopted, a constitutional system will provide both institutional safeguards against injustice and procedures by which citizens may appeal for redress. For example, in constitutional regimes subjects are protected from arbitrary, irregular or illegal actions by the institutions we describe as the rule of law. A constitutional regime must also provide legal means by which an aggrieved subject can test the validity of actions he regards as unjust.

But it is not sufficient that legal redress be available. Surely no political society can be regarded as just, as providing the maximum liberty for each compatible with the like liberty for others, unless it allows its members political redress as well. To intervene effectively in the political process, citizens will require the usual political rights: freedom to hold and propagate opinions, to meet, to associate, to petition officials. And I would include the right to demonstrate which seems to me a mode of petitioning the public as well as governmental officials, a way of bringing one's case before one's fellow citizens. The right to petition originally provided a way of bringing one's case directly to the notice of the sovereign; surely the demonstration noticed by newspapers, radio and television is the current analogue.

The limits of obligation are reached in the situation of civil disobedience. Civil disobedience is a public, open act of disobedience of a valid law, or a valid legal or administrative act. By acting openly in violation of a law, the disobeyer renders himself liable to punishment; he submits to arrest and to trial as an earnest of the force and sincerity of his convictions. Furthermore, the disobeyer must eschew harming persons or property. Civil disobedience is an act of political protest. It involves an appeal by an individual or a group which has exhausted the constitutional and legal procedures available, or which finds those procedures blocked, to the sense of justice of the other members of the society. (The sense of justice might be described as the general willingness of the members of the society to accept, however imprecisely defined, the principles of justice as binding in their dealings with each other).[14]

Acts of civil disobedience, being highly conscientious appeals to the common moral commitments of a society, are most likely to be effective when the issue involves fundamental political and civil rights. Although such acts violate a law, they recognize the validity of the system. And as a consequence, they should count as acts of allegiance. (I do not suggest that acts of civil disobedience are justified by the sincerity and sacrifice of the disobeyers. In some cases the political society rightly or wrongly will recognize the justice of the cause and in others deny it. When this happens the disobeying group will face both prudential and moral questions: does it still believe itself justified? What tactics should it now adopt?)

So far I have argued that a person is obligated to a just or mainly just political society where he has explicitly agreed to the principles of justice and the institutions of the society or where he has participated in such a society, accepting its benefits and planning to continue to do so. The limiting case of participation is civil disobedience where such a serious violation of the principles of justice is alleged that in the view of the civilly disobedient they are justified in setting aside or overriding their obligation to obey even the unjust laws of the society in order to appeal for the rectification of the alleged injustice. And there may be other duties and obligations—for example, some may share E. M. Forster's preference: 'if I had to choose between betraying my country and betraying my friend, I hope I should have the guts to betray my country.'[15]

My contention then is that the social contract serves as the limiting case of the voluntary assumption of political obligation, the criterion of the greatest possible obligation to a political society, from which the less explicit cases deviate. Moreover contractarian notions about allegiance are not mere fantasies of political philosophers' feverish brains, for they are embodied in many political institutions and political rituals. Explicitly we declare our obligation by pledging allegiance, by toasting the Queen, by standing for the national anthem.[16] Implicitly we acknowledge it when we vote or otherwise fulfil our obligations as citizens, and even when we treat the laws (on the absence of probable sanctions) as binding us to certain kinds of conduct we would not otherwise regard as wrong.[17]

What counts as giving allegiance or denying it is determined by the conventions of each particular society. Standing to attention, saluting the flag, pledging allegiance, toasting the Queen, singing the anthem are modes of conduct which declare loyalty; they are performative acts and utterances rather than mere expressions of feeling. And the meaning with which these acts are charged, just as what words or acts constitute a contract or a promise, depends upon the current conventions of a particular society. Because the flag has been a symbol of national unity for the United States and saluting it and venerating it inculcated, flag desecration could be charged with a special meaning. In some circumstances, voting for a particular political party, spoiling one's ballot or even refusing to vote could acquire the same meaning—although the French anarchists never succeeded in establishing that every abstention was an anarchist vote.

Public officials are regularly inducted into their offices by ceremonies in which they swear allegiance or affirm their political obligations. Many associations, from the Boy Scouts to the Mau Mau, use oaths. All such rituals might be regarded as nothing but forms of socialization; the ceremony, the pledge, the oath, the anthem, the salute, all intended to induce adherence, their frequent repetition nothing but a training device. However efficacious such techniques might be in inculcating loyalty, a purely behavioural explanation cannot save the moral phenomena. The techniques could scarcely be effective did not men believe that they were undertaking binding obligations, committing themselves to act in certain ways.

All these practices emphasize that men believe and act on the belief that allegiance is voluntarily undertaken.

So far I have described those situations in which political obligation is strongest and defended the notion that it is voluntarily undertaken. But there are many situations in which men are not full and voluntary members of just societies.

At least one of the duties of members of imperfectly just and unjust societies would be to endeavour to make their societies more just. No doubt this leads to great moral dilemmas—gratitude for benefits received may be owed to that society and its members and this obligation as well as others may conflict with the duty to make the society more just. There is furthermore the practical problem of the choice of means. Organization and agitation may be illegal, and therefore a form of rebellion. A citizen must then consider whether legal or illegal means are likely to lead to the best consequences, for even rebellion is an activity requiring a prudent choice of means and intelligent timing.

If men owe allegiance because they have voluntarily given it by word or deed, then they must have a right not to give allegiance, a right to rebel. Ultimately, men choose to ascribe validity to a government or refuse it. What I am suggesting is that they have a right to do so.

This right is an option right, or a right of action rather than one of recipience; such a right always involves a liberty to do or to forbear, a kind of limited sovereignty. Unlike welfare rights, option rights do not have as their correlatives specific duties or obligations on the part of some other person or persons. Let me illustrate the difference. When one has a right by contract to receive a sum of money or the performance of some action, specific persons (legal or natural) have correlative obligations. The same is true if one is entitled by law to a pension or a salary. Here too some legal or natural person (or persons) will have a duty to dispense the funds. These are welfare rights, rights of recipience or rights to specific performances, but option rights are liberties over one's own choices, actions and property—to do or not to do, to use or not to use, to give or deny permission. Within a legal system, option rights are usually limited in various ways and they have as their correlatives only the absence of a right on the part of others to interfere. Thus, within the law, if I have a right to speak, you have no right to stop me. On the other hand, not only are you under no obligation to listen, but you are not obligated to help me be heard. Again, you may use your car to go on the highways in whatever direction you choose, subject to the restrictions imposed in the highway code, and normally no one has a right (they have no-right) to hinder you. But option rights may be exercised in ways that make their enjoyment difficult. If we all choose to speak simultaneously none of us will be heard. If we all choose to drive through the West Country on a summer weekend, the result will be the usual traffic jam on the Exeter bypass. Other privileges and liberties are easy to discover: anyone is at liberty to pick up the apparently ownerless pound note, but only one person can do so.

In short, the correlative of an option right or liberty is a no-right rather than an obligation or a duty. And such a right is the opposite of an obligation: many legal option rights over our persons, our services and our possessions exist only until we obligate ourselves to use them in a certain way or transfer them to another. The most extensive option right imaginable is Hobbes's right of nature: 'Nature hath given to every one a right to all. That is, it was lawfull for every man in the bare state of nature, or before such time as men had engag'd themselves by any Covenants, or Bonds, to doe what hee would, and against whom he thought fit, and to possesse, use and enjoy all what he would or could get.' But even if Hobbes was extravagant in describing it, there must (if allegiance be voluntary) be a liberty, a 'natural' option right to give or refuse it. [18]

Most social contract theorists have severely restricted the right to withdraw allegiance. Only when Hobbes's sovereign threatens a man's life or exiles him does his obligation end; only when he is in the power of another state is a man free to submit anew—and a population is freed only when Leviathan is destroyed. Locke is more generous; he recognizes that a government acting tyrannously forfeits its right to be obeyed.

One frequently recognized mode by which allegiance might be withdrawn has been emigration. Physically moving from one society to another usually terminates the first's effective control over the emigrant and it has sometimes been deemed to terminate both its jurisdiction over him and his membership in it as well. The case for recognizing emigration as withdrawing allegiance is even stronger when the emigrant voluntarily acquires full membership, citizenship, in his new society.

But if political theorists have restricted the right to withdraw allegiance, they have been even more chary of a right to refuse it, denying it to all but those who rejected the original contract. Few have attempted to meet the stock criticism that an original contract could hardly bind subsequent generations. [19] Thus arises the social contract theorist's dilemma: the more precise he becomes about the state of nature, the clauses of the original agreement and the obligations undertaken, the more he exposes himself to the objection that it never occurred; the greater the verisimilitude of his fiction the more readily is its truth denied. Part of the difficulty has been that social contract theories have often served rhetorical purposes as well as a philosophical one. They have seemed to explain not merely how men could be legitimately obligated, but also served to persuade men either that they did in fact owe allegiance to their existing government, or that they could not possibly do so. In contemporary discussions of political obligation, this double purpose has been curiously transformed into the fallacious assumption that a theory of political obligation would prove that all those subject to a political system were obligated.[20] Clearly if allegiance is voluntary, then it cannot follow that anyone is obligated except voluntarily.

So far I have argued that there must be a right to withhold or withdraw allegiance. I do not mean a right to be exercised only by emigration, but rather one that could be exercised without physically departing. It would be a right limited by the condition that it could not be used simply to avoid doing one's share in a just practice, to shirk the burdens imposed by participating in just institutions. One cannot rightly accept the benefits and then refuse to fulfil the obligations incurred by accepting them. Nor need recognizing that all humans receive some benefits from the societies they live in make that right a nullity. Participating in a political society and its practices, and accepting the benefits of them can create a *prima facie* obligation only when those practices are just. Since the various offices must be equally open to all, only those who are full members, citizens, can have accepted benefits that bind them so stringently. (Others who have accepted benefits under different circumstances will not have obligated themselves so strongly; they may at most have created a presumptive obligation).[21]

But why should even those who have bound themselves most strongly by acts and words be incapable of ever changing their allegiance? Why should the acts and words that bind citizens to political societies be irrevocable and irreversible? Do we not need a ceremony, more solemn than resigning from a club, let us say a political equivalent of divorce, by which citizens could dissolve the bonds of allegiance, undo their political obligations?

Such an act, even rightly performed, would not dissolve all obligations to the society one lived in. No political equivalent of alimony would be necessary for the former citizen would still be subject to taxes, the obligation to pay them being based upon the benefits received from living in that society.

Moreover resigning membership would leave the former citizen a status that has existed in many societies and still actually exists. This status has however received little theoretical attention. Non-citizens inhabiting a society might be distinguished into three types: visitors, sojourners and denizens. Visitors come for a limited stay; after a brief period they intend to depart. And although they undertake to obey the laws of the country they visit, they should not be required to participate in practices they regard as unjust. Normally they are protected by the laws of the society they are visiting. While they are usually allowed the ordinary civil rights prevalent in that society, they are not allowed the political rights of full citizens. Frequently some allowances are made for such people. Permitted when in Rome to do as the Romans do, they are usually also permitted to remain aloof from some of the strange and alien institutions they encounter. The second type of non-citizen is the sojourner. Since they intend to stay for a longer period, sojourners differ from visitors. But they do not regard themselves as permanent residents. They retain an ultimate allegiance elsewhere, to a homeland to which they will return. Denizens, the third type of non-citizen, differ from sojourners in having no ultimate intentions of leaving. Like the resident aliens in Athens or the *perioikoi* in Sparta they are subjects but not citizens.

So far four types of people subject to the jurisdiction of a political society have been discovered: citizens (full members), denizens, sojourners and visitors. But in addition there are people who claim to owe an ultimate allegiance to a group, an ideal or someone or something other than the political society. Sometimes they are willing to be citizens, but only on a limited basis. St. Augustine's *peregrini* might be put in this category along with such groups as Quakers and conscientious objectors. Fully withdrawn religious sects and other communities, who live within the jurisdiction of a political society while refusing to recognize its authority, must be classified as denizens.

If men may give or withhold their ultimate allegiance as they choose, then they need not vest it in the state. Fixing their ultimate loyalty elsewhere, such men or groups would only owe limited obligations to the political society. They might view their obedience to its laws as entirely prudential—thinking themselves morally bound to obey the laws only in so far as that obedience could be derived from their other duties and obligations.[22] One might imagine a variety of possible limits or restrictions on the allegiance such men or groups were willing to give: some might avow an ultimate allegiance to God which would be unlikely to conflict with their obligations to a political society; others might be unwilling to participate in any institution that took human life or used force against human beings; still others might be so pledged to an alternative society that they could acknowledge no obligation whatever to the existing political society.

Full and limited withdrawals of allegiance are exercises of an option right to give and withhold allegiance. But one is rarely fully at liberty: man may be born free but he is everywhere in chains. Men are generally obligated in some degree to the societies they live in. There may be some dispute about to what extent and when they may justly exercise their right. Furthermore, the members of a just society have a right (and a duty) to preserve and maintain their just institutions.

Surely this right may conflict with the right to withhold or withdraw allegiance fully or partly. Against the claim to withdraw allegiance, society may counterclaim some degree of support. The stronger the society and the more loyal its members, the greater will be its ability to tolerate within its territorial boundaries groups which deny it some or all of their loyalty. The generosity of the liberal society may be repaid by the support of groups which could not give more allegiance than such a society demands. Denizens and limited citizens who are tolerated are excused from the services which may be demanded of full members, but some other form of service may be substituted. Such exceptions may be legally recognized.

The willingness to tolerate those who are prepared to commit themselves only partly to a political society is defensible. One of the characteristics of being human is the capacity to recognize and to undertake moral commitments. The explicit promulgation by the partial citizen of the limits he puts to his allegiance demonstrates that he understands being obligated. His very conscientiousness makes him a better risk to keep his word. After all, if there is a right to withdraw allegiance even to a just society, then no one owes absolute and unqualified loyalty to the state. But toleration of those who acknowledge no obligation to a society especially if they claim allegiance to some counter-society, for example a revolutionary group, may be a different matter. Where their numbers are small they may be regarded as harmless eccentrics, or they may be dramatizing their dissent. But the right to withdraw allegiance and vest it elsewhere is a natural right; it cannot be claimed as a political or social right. Presumably the political society will continue to claim jurisdiction over such individuals, ignoring their rejection of it and treating them as subject to its laws and procedures. It is, of course, bound to treat them justly.

The natural right to give or withhold allegiance may be exercised in a number of different ways, only one of which is by becoming a full member or citizen of a political society. It may also be possible to become a citizen while accepting only limited obligations. The right to withdraw allegiance may be exercised by emigration; the *Universal Declaration of Human Rights* in articles 13(2), 14 and 15 seems to recognize this right. It may also be exercised by rejecting the status of citizen, withdrawing allegiance from the state and perhaps vesting it elsewhere thereby becoming a denizen. Perhaps there should be a legal right to do so. Finally, there are those who have placed their allegiance in some rival to what claims to be the lawful authority such as one or the other side in a civil war or a revolutionary group. Here alone there can be no question of transforming the natural right into a social one.

Asserting that there is a right to give, renounce or withhold allegiance inevitably raises further questions. To be human means being capable or recognizing, acknowledging and undertaking moral commitments. In other words, all who have this capacity, along with the peculiarly human genetic make-up, are members of humanity, the human community. To be a member of some particular society within that community is to subscribe to and to participate in the institutions of that society. Unless otherwise bound, men have a liberty to bind themselves into a society or to join an existing society. Thus all men have a natural (option) right or liberty to belong to some society. But has any man a right or liberty to join any society he chooses, or do societies have the right to exclude whom they please? To what extent may a society define the terms and conditions of being a member of it?

Here I wish to put aside the duties of aiding other human beings in distress. Charity and humanity are not at issue and I do not wish to discuss all the duties men have as members of the human community.

Although each human being has a right to give his allegiance as he chooses, that right is an option right. It therefore implies no correlative obligation or duty on the part of any society to admit an applicant to full membership. However not all applicants need apply from the same initial status. If a society is to be just, it may not indefinitely exclude denizens who live under its jurisdiction from citizenship. I think that a society could set conditions which evidenced a denizen's desire and ability to commit himself to the society and his familiarity with its institutions. But permanently to exclude those participating in the institutions of a society from full participation is to doom them to an institutional status of permanent inferiority. This seems a clear violation of the first principle of justice. It would be possible for a society to set cultural, educational or linguistic criteria for membership provided it did not operate institutions that prevented inhabitants from acquiring these competences. Even though a society would not be wrong to require all prospective citizens to pass these tests, it might admit children of citizens to full membership without them, arguing that they were not privileged but merely presumed capable as a result of their education. Thus there may be some sense in the widespread rule conferring citizenship on all those born within a society's jurisdiction.

But if a society need not accept applicants for membership except from denizens may it close itself entirely? May it exclude all immigrants, thereby preventing anyone from qualifying for membership? Here we must call to mind not only the problems of immigration from the poorer parts of the world to the industrial countries but also the situation of small, tribal societies. Does the

African or Indian have a right not to be excluded from taking up residence in Britain, or the United States or Canada or Australia or France, should he wish, and then becoming a citizen? And conversely do I have the right to apply to become a Masai or a Sikh?

Perhaps for a large society some just restriction on entry is possible. I can imagine an argument that relied on showing that more than a certain number of immigrants at various points in the economic development of a society had disastrous effects on the society and its future. In other words, there may be such a thing as a just immigration policy, similar in conception to Rawls's just savings policy.[23] I do not think, however, that it can be a policy based on pigmentation of skin. (Incidentally I am not supposing that immigration is the only or the best or even any solution to the problems posed by the existence of large discrepancies in wealth among nations; nor am I suggesting that no moral principles other than the principles of justice apply).

If large political societies, states, may not rightly close themselves entirely, is the same true for smaller political societies, tribes? Must we say that all such closed groups are wrong or grant them a privilege denied to states? It seems to me that such societies need not violate the principles of justice if they remain small as well as exclusive. They must not acquire territorial dominion which gives them jurisdiction over others. Presumably some mode of living in proximity to other groups would have to be worked out; but the minimum price a society would have to pay for maintaining itself as an exclusive club would be to eschew *libido dominandi:* to give up ruling others.

Thus, although no society is obligated to admit applicants without restriction, the right to refuse applicants is not absolute. It is a right limited by the conditions which prevail within a society and by the way that the society has organized itself.

In this discussion of allegiance or political obligation I have adopted a contractarian theory. I have not maintained that the social contract describes how men acquired obligations but rather that by describing the situation in which obligation is maximized, it provides a criterion by which existing obligations can be measured. I have also emphasized the chief consequence of this view; if allegiance is voluntarily undertaken then there must be a right to refuse and even to withdraw it as well as to give it. I have tried to indicate some of the restrictions upon the right to withdraw allegiance, which includes the right to emigrate and the right to rebel, and I have tried to show the extent and the limits of a society's right to deny membership to those who wish to join it. In all this I have not tried to describe how human beings and societies actually behave; I have not attempted to discuss the conventions and practices of various societies or when and why men do give and withdraw allegiance, I have only tried to show what can make these actions right.

NOTES

1   However stridently both contending parties claim legitimacy are these claims valid? Or do they merely bolster the morale of each side? For the view that the difference between such contenders, in this case kingdoms and robber bands, was not that one was just and the other unjust but simply that one was too powerful to be punished, see St. Augustine *De civitate dei*, Book IV, Chap. 4.
2   See *The Times*, 4 November 1970, p. 12a.
3   *Ibid.*, 18 March 1970, p. 3b (6*).
4   See for examples: Sidney Hook (ed.), *Law and Philosophy* (New York, 1964); Thomas McPherson, *Political Obligation* (London, 1967); Roland Pennock and John W. Chapman (eds.), *Nomos XII: Political and Legal Obligation* (New York, 1970); Claude Ake, 'Political Obligation and Political Dissent', *Canadian Journal of Political Science*, 2 (1969), 245-255; see also the symposium on political obligation and civil disobedience in the *Journal of Philosophy:* Richard A. Wasserstrom, 'Disobeying the Law', Hugo A. Bedau, 'On Civil Disobedience', Stuart M. Brown, Jr., 'Civil Disobedience' in *Journal of Philosophy* 58 (1961), 641-681.
5   Professor A. J. Ayer in his Eleanor Rathbone Memorial Lecture, 'Philosophy and Politics' (Liverpool, 1967), seems to regard the ground of political obligation as the sole question of political philosophy—he says political philosophy is mainly concerned with a single question (p. 9). Professor Ayer identifies thirteen answers but finds none worthy of serious consideration. It turns out that political philosophers were not answering that question at all; they were persuasively advocating various forms of social organization (p.21). (I must confess that I cannot tell whether Professor Ayer means to castigate the academic study of the history of political ideas for wrongly forcing all its philosophers into this mould or whether he believes that the philosophers themselves mistakenly thought they were discussing obligation.)
6   *Cf.*, Jean-Jacques Rousseau, *Contrat social*, Book I, Chap. 1.
7   See Richard Hooker, *Of the Lawes of Ecclesiasticall Politie*, Book I, Chap. 10: 'Two foundations there are which beare up publike Societies; the one, a naturall inclination, whereby all men desire sociable life & fellowship; the other, an order expressly or secretly agreed upon, touching the manner of their living together.'
8   David Hume, *A Treatise of Human Nature*, Book III, Part II, Sects. 2, 8.
9   See R. M. Hare, 'The Lawful Government', in P. Laslett and W. G. Runciman (eds.), *Philosophy, Politics and Society,* Third Series (Oxford, 1967); H. L. A. Hart, *The Concept of Law* (Oxford, 1961), esp. pp. 55-60, and 'Are there any Natural Rights?', *Philosophical Review,* 64 (1955), 175-191; John Rawls, 'Justice as Fairness' in Laslett and Runciman (eds.), *Philosophy, Politics and Society,* II (Oxford, 1962), 'The Justification of Civil Disobedience' in Hugo Adam Bedau (ed.), *Civil Disobedience* (New York, 1969), and 'Legal Obligation and the Duty of Fair Play' in Hook (ed.), *Law and Philosophy.*
10 For a discussion of the significant conditions of discourse about rights, see M. P. Golding, 'Towards a Theory of Human Rights' in *The Monist,* 52 (1968), 521-549.
11 Hume, *Treatise,* Book III, Part II, Sect. 2.
12 John Rawls, 'Justice as Fairness', p. 133.

13   See John Rawls, 'Distributive Justice', in Laslett and Runciman (eds.), *Philosophy, Politics and Society*, III, esp. pp. 76-79 where he distinguishes among perfect, imperfect and pure procedural justice. Perfect procedural justice is exemplified by a situation originally vividly described by James Harrington: when two girls share a cake fairly, one divides, the other chooses (see *Oceana*, Preliminaries, Part I). In pure procedural justice there is no criterion for a proper outcome apart from the correct application of the procedure, e.g., gambling. In many cases there are no procedures that will purely or perfectly ensure a just outcome: no procedure for criminal trials could guarantee that the guilty would never be acquitted and the innocent never convicted.

14   John Rawls, 'The Justification of Civil Disobedience', pp. 246-247, and 'The Sense of Justice', *Philosophical Review*, 72 (1963), 281-305. For a review of the literature, see Paul F. Power, 'On Civil Disobedience in Recent American Democratic Thought', *American Political Science Review*, 64 (1970), 35-47.

15   E. M. Forster, 'What I Believe' in *Two Cheers for Democracy* (London, 1951), p. 78.

16   When applying for a passport an American citizen must declare: 'I have not (and no other person included in the application has), since acquiring United States citizenship, been naturalized as a citizen of a foreign state; taken an oath or made an affirmation or other formal declaration of allegiance to a foreign state; entered or served in the armed forces of a foreign state; accepted or performed the duties of any office, post, or employment under the government of a foreign state or political subdivision thereof; made a formal renunciation of nationality either in the United States or before a diplomatic or consular officer of the United States in a foreign state; ever sought or claimed the benefits of the nationality of any foreign state; or been convicted by a court or court martial of competent jurisdiction of committing any act of treason against, or attempting by force to overthrow, or bearing arms against, the United States, or conspiring to overthrow, put down or to destroy by force, the Government of the United States'; the applicant then takes an oath of allegiance: 'Further, I do solemnly swear (or affirm) that I will support and defend the Constitution of the United States against all enemies, foreign and domestic; that I will bear true faith and allegiance to the same; and that I take this obligation freely, without any mental reservations, or purpose of evasion: So help me God.'

17   To vote rationally in the sense of maximizing his utilities, a citizen must calculate the benefits he could expect from various results (his party differential) and the probability that his vote will produce that result (his vote value). Thus he will not only abstain when he can expect no greater benefit from one result than from another but also when he believes his vote has little probability of affecting the result, a condition almost always true in a large electorate. Moreover, if voting is not assumed to be costless, then anyone abstains for whom the costs exceed the benefits. Thus we arrive at a situation in which no-one votes unless he expects either that few others will vote or that his vote will decide the election. Each voter must therefore estimate how close the election will be and what other voters will do. See Anthony Downs, *An Economic Theory of Democracy* (New York, 1957), pp. 36-50, 240-247, 260-267.

     Downs overcomes this problem (1) by supposing that 'Rational men in a democracy are motivated by a sense of social responsibility relatively independent of their short-run gains and losses' and (2) by introducing as a benefit the value to the citizen of maintaining democracy. But since this benefit will accrue to abstainers as long as the system is preserved by other citizens, the sense of social responsibility is crucial. It turns out to be a commitment to the system— participation is a rule of the game (pp. 267-270).

Rational voting thus requires a prior obligation to do one's share in maintaining a system of practices. For an illuminating discussion, see Brian Barry, *Sociologists, Economists and Democracy* (London, 1970), pp. 13-46.

18   Thomas Hobbes, *Philosophical Rudiments concerning Government and Society* (i.e., *De Cive*) Chap. I, Sect. 10. See also H. L. A. Hart, 'Are there any Natural Rights', pp. 179, 187-188.

For clarification of the relations among rights, liberties, no-rights obligations, *etc.*, see Wesley N. Hohfeld, *Fundamental Legal Conceptions* (New Haven, 1934), pp. 36-50.

19   Rousseau requires initial unanimity (*Contrat social,* Book I, Chap. 5). Although Hobbes usually does so too, at one point he deems meeting with the intention to form a society sufficient to create a democracy (*Philosophical Rudiments,* Chap. VII, Sect. 5); at another he apparently allows the majority to bind all into a society (*Leviathan,* Chap. 18). At least Locke grappled with the problem of subsequent generations (*Second Treatise,* Chap. VIII, Sects. 116-122).

20   John Ladd triumphantly parades this as a reason why there can be no such thing as political obligation; see 'Legal and Political Obligation' in *Nomos XII*, p. 26. See also Kurt Baier 'Obligation: Practical and Moral', *ibid.,* pp. 128-129 for a similar criticism of contract theory.

Since delivering this talk, I have benefitted from an unpublished paper by John Rees, 'On Justifying Political Obligation', read at Gregynog, 12 March 1971.

21   *Prima facie* obligations can be overridden only by moral obligations of greater weight, but presumptions are rebuttable. See Richard C. Brandt, 'Utility and the Obligation to Obey the Law', in *Law and Philosophy,* pp. 43-55.

22   For the argument that a man's ultimate loyalty may be owed to a small group of which he is a voluntary member, see Michael Walzer, 'The Obligation to Disobey', in David Spitz (ed.), *Political Theory and Social Change* (New York, 1967), pp. 185-202.

23   John Rawls, 'Distributive Justice', in *Philosophy, Politics and Society,* III, pp. 73-76.

14

Professor A. H. Birch

THE NATURE AND FUNCTIONS OF REPRESENTATION

Before I turn to my subject I should like to pay a brief word of tribute to my predecessor, whose sudden death eighteen months ago must have been a great shock to the University. Victor Wiseman had a distinguished career in teaching, in scholarship and in public service. His involvement in all these activities was characterised by energy, enthusiasm and good humour, and in his years at Exeter he built up a Department which is well regarded in other universities and which I am very pleased to have joined.

One of the characteristics of my subject is that political scientists talk about issues that other people fight about. Representation is one such issue. It has led to riots, revolutions and civil wars; it has divided the English-speaking world; and a few months ago it even threatened to divide the Exeter Guild of Students from the University Senate. In these circumstances I feel that it may be appropriate for me to use this occasion to illustrate the way—perhaps a rather dull way—in which a political scientist approaches such a contentious topic. I will refer first to the nature of representation and then to its functions.

Any inquiry into the nature of a concept must rest upon philosophical assumptions of one kind or another, and I am sufficiently a child of my time to think Wittgenstein a better guide in these matters than Plato. Words have usages rather than essential meanings, and the relationship between these usages is well captured, I think, by Wittgenstein's analogy with the relations between members of a family: they have a common origin and they may have a recognisable family character, but the student would be missing the distinctive nature of each member if he were to concentrate all his attention on what they had in common. In the case of representation I believe there are four main usages, each of which is logically distinct from the other. Three of these have both political and non-political connotations, while the fourth is purely political.

265

The first and perhaps the most common usage is found when the term 'representative' is employed to describe a person who has the acknowledged duty of defending or advancing certain interests specified by his principal. A sales representative is a representative in this sense of the term; so is a man sent by a dualist to arrange the location and weapons of the duel with his opponent's representative; so is an ambassador, and so is a lawyer appointed to defend the interests of his client in a court hearing. The representative does not necessarily act exactly as his principal would; in some situations the representative may drive a harder bargain than his principal would feel able to do, while in others the representative may be restrained by professional etiquette and conventions. But in all cases the function of this kind of representative is to achieve certain goals set by his principal, and the extent to which these goals are achieved is a criterion of successful representation. As a form of shorthand, I will henceforth describe this kind of representation as 'delegated representation'. In a modern political system the most conspicuous form of delegated representation is of course that by spokesmen for pressure groups.

One question which commonly arises in connection with delegated representation is the extent to which the representative is, or should be, bound by the instructions of his principal. This question has been discussed in scores of books, hundreds of articles, thousands of speeches. No agreement has been reached on the answer, for the simple reason that no meaningful answer is possible when the question is phrased in general terms. It is a question to which the answer depends almost entirely on the exact circumstances of the representative relationship under discussion. For example, a lawyer cannot be so closely bound by his client's instructions as a sales representative can be bound by his firm's instructions, because the lawyer is governed by a strict code of professional behaviour and has duties to the court as well as to his client. How closely the lawyer will follow instructions also depends on the nature of the case: a lawyer in a divorce case might expect to receive fairly detailed instructions about the kind of evidence to call and the kind of settlement to work for, whereas a lawyer defending a man charged with murder would expect a fairly free hand in reaching decisions about the best line of defence.

Another question which often arises is the extent to which a representative of this kind can bind his principal. It is sometimes assumed that if a representative of this kind agrees to a proposal this can be taken to imply the consent of the principal. In fact this is only sometimes the case. The relationship between representation and consent varies, and depends upon all sorts of contingent factors. Thus modern ambassadors hardly ever have power to commit their governments, but when international communications were slower ambassadors were sometimes given such powers. The relationship between representation and commitment or consent is therefore (like the question of instructions) a matter for historical enquiry, depending as it does on the exact circumstances of each situation.

The statement that a man is a representative in the sense of being an agent therefore conveys only a limited amount of information. It does not tell us how the man was appointed, what kind of man he is, whether he acts under close or loose instructions, or whether his agreement to a proposal binds his principal. However, it tells us something about his functions and probable behaviour, and is therefore to be sharply distinguished from the second general usage of the term, which refers not to the functions but to the descriptive characteristics of the representative.

This second usage is well exemplified in the term 'representative sample', which indicates a sample of the relevant population chosen by statistical methods so that the main characteristics of the population will be mirrored in the sample. The term is used in the same sense, but more loosely, to denote a person who is in some respects typical of a larger class of persons to which he belongs. This usage occurs in such statements as 'the varied membership of the club is represented fairly well in the composition of the executive committee' or 'a State Assembly full of lawyers is hardly representative of the farmers whose produce is the basis of the State's prosperity.' Since a representative body would be ideally constituted, in this sense of the term, if it were a microcosm of the larger society, I shall describe this kind of representation as 'microcosmic representation.'

The statement that a man is a representative in this sense does not tell us anything about his functions or intentions or even about his behaviour. It simply tells us something about his personal characteristics. However, many writers have of course asserted that a man's characteristics, particularly social and economic characteristics, have a strong influence on his behaviour, so the fact that ruling groups rarely represent the population in a microcosmic sense has sometimes been adduced as an explanation for their evident failure to govern properly. As is well known, Jeremy Bentham's conversion to the cause of parliamentary reform occurred when he became convinced that a House of Commons dominated by the upper classes was unlikely to do more than advance upper-class interests. Many of the arguments of the early Utilitarians were based on the belief that the country needed a parliament which would be representative in this microcosmic sense, so that its members, while pursuing their own interests, would automatically further the interests of the whole population.

Of course, this highly influential school of thought was based upon a whole set of fallacious arguments. Quite apart from the philosophical limitations of Utilitarianism, which hardly need repetition, their political programme was beset by practical difficulties. One cannot get a representative sample by calling for volunteers, particularly when the job in question requires special talents and rewards them with a high degree of insecurity. The world has never seen a representative assembly which is representative in a microcosmic sense, but for this very reason the concept of microcosmic representation has proved a particularly useful tool for critics. It has been applied not only to elected assemblies but also to other centres of power, and we have been told that the administrative class of the Civil Service contains too many graduates from Oxford and Cambridge, that the Royal Ulster Constabulary contains too many Protestants, and that University Senates contain too many professors. All this is quite natural and criticisms of this kind may be expected to be a permanent feature of the political scene in free societies.

Occasionally the concept is used in a slightly different way. A few years ago that splendidly forthright character Lord Boothby said: 'Ideally, the House of Commons should be a social microcosm of the nation. The nation includes a great many people who are rather stupid, and so should the house.'[1] This was evidently a defence of the status quo, and a *Times* leader writer invoked the concept for the same purpose when he said, in relation to a proposal to increase Member's salaries, that 'the House of Commons should be a microcosm of the nation and this it can never be if the great bulk of its members are professional politicians.'[2] This last argument, which has been frequently used during debates on M.P.'s pay, is a remarkable combination of two erroneous factual assumptions with a value judgement of which the sincerity may be questioned.

The third main usage is found when someone is described as representing a number of persons in a symbolic way. The term 'symbol' is normally applied to an emblem or physical object which calls to mind some larger and usually more abstract entity, as the hammer and sickle symbolizes the Soviet Union and the scales of justice symbolize the essential character of the law. In similar fashion a symbolic representative calls to mind, or serves as a concrete embodiment of, a whole group or category of persons.

This usage is neither so common nor so important as the other kinds of usages, but it must not be ignored because symbolic representation—and the demand for symbolic representation—plays a significant part in political activity. It is often the case that the appointment of a member of a minority group to a position of prestige is valued not so much for any influence that he may have as for the fact that the appointment symbolizes the acceptance of the group as full members of the community.

Until the eighteenth century I believe that all representatives fell into one or other of these three categories, for elected members of parliamentary assemblies were essentially delegated representatives whose function was to defend or advance the interests of various propertied classes within the community. But in that century a new and purely political concept of representation was developed. The group who took the lead in this were the English Whigs, who believed that Parliament should be the centre of political power rather than acting merely as a check on the power of the King and his Ministers. If Parliament were to be a deliberative and decision-making body, it was clearly necessary that the Member of Parliament should be free to do what he thought best in the national interest rather than act as a spokesman for the interests of his constituents. It was this belief that led Burke to make his famous speech to the electors of Bristol, in which he was not saying anything new but merely repeating sentiments that had been previously expressed by a score of Whig politicians, beginning (so far as I can trace it) with Algernon Sydney.

A similar position was adopted by the Abbé Sièyes and his fellow revolutionaries, who included in the first revolutionary constitution of France the clear statement that members of the National Assembly could not be given any mandate. The French position was that the assembly embodied the will of the nation, not that it reflected the will of the people, and during the nineteenth century this doctrine, with its associated prohibition of instructions, was incorporated in the constitution of nearly every country in Western Europe.

From the theoretical point of view this doctrine poses a certain problem. Before the French Revolution elected representatives had been viewed on the Continent as delegates, so that there were three parties in the representative process: the principal, the representative, and the party or authority to whom representations were to be made. But according to the new theory of the revolutionaries, political representatives were no longer to be thought of as intermediaries of this kind but were to contrive, in their collective capacity, to act as the voice of the nation. This has led Giovanni Sartori to comment that as soon as French representatives were given the name of 'deputies' they ceased to deputize for anyone.[3]

Now, one must never begrudge the tendency of Latin writers to produce paradoxes, but an Englishman like myself may perhaps be forgiven for thinking that the clue to this apparent problem was provided by Thomas Hobbes, who had long previously developed the view that representation was essentially a process of authorization. I do not believe this to be true of all forms of representation, but I think it is clearly applicable to elective representation. To say that a man is an elected representative in a national assembly is to say that he has been authorized by those who took part in the election to exercise certain powers. This concept of elective representation is in my understanding purely political and quite independent of the other concepts I have mentioned.

Of course, it is sometimes said that elected representatives will do their job better if they are also representatives in one of the other three senses of the term, but this is an independent argument which does not follow from the nature of elective representation and is in my view of very doubtful validity.

My argument about the nature of representation may therefore be summarized as follows. First, I believe that all forms of representation fall into one or other of the four categories I have mentioned. Secondly, I believe that these four concepts of representation are logically independent of one another, that none of them can be reduced to a sub-division of any other, and that there is no valid intellectual process by which they can be put together, like the four quadrants of a circle, to form something called the 'true nature of representation.' They are different concepts, related etymologically but not forming parts of a whole.

I turn now from the nature of representation to its functions in the political process and I have to report that virtually all discussions on this matter have been heavily influenced by the political values of the writers. Most of the literature about representation has been produced by democrats who saw the extension of representative processes as a means of increasing popular control of governments, and as most political scientists see themselves as democrats I suppose it is natural that they should commonly have fallen into the assumption that this is the only function that representative institutions serve. But clearly this is inadequate, for democracy is a recent and perhaps temporary form of government confined to only a minority of political systems, whereas representative processes of one kind or another are almost universal.

The only scholar who has attempted to produce a value-free definition of the functions of representation is David Apter of Yale University. I propose to quote his definition in full, not so much for its intrinsic interest but because I wish to comment on the language in which it is couched.

In Apter's formulation, the functions of political representation are defined as follows:

1. *Central Control:* the ordered maintenance of discipline in a political system on a day-to-day basis.
2. *Goal specification:* the identification and priority ranking of policies; hence, a sharing in policy formulation on the basis of a longer term.
3. *Institutional coherence:* the continuous review, reformulation, and adaptation of the fit between boundaries of sub-systems, including the regulation of overlapping jurisdictions, and including as well, ideological adjustment.'[4]

The question which this poses in my mind is why such a distinguished scholar should produce such an ambiguous and unhelpful statement. My belief is that here Apter has fallen victim to the jargon in which he writes, and as this kind of jargon is becoming more popular (and it would not be difficult to find examples far worse than this) I must digress for a moment to say that I regard it as wholly undesirable. I do not question the value of sociological analyses of political behaviour, but I believe that there is everything to be gained (and very little to be lost) from expressing the results of these analyses in plain English. Of course, there are some academic subjects, particularly in the Science Faculty, which have a distinctive mode of explanation and a distinctive language also, so that a necessary part of an education in the discipline is to learn the language. But politics is not this kind of subject, and when political scientists adopt a specialised terminology which they have invented for themselves or borrowed from other disciplines the consequence, all too often, is that they surrender the advantages of using the English language in a clear and precise way for the dubious benefit of increasing their prestige in the eyes of those other political scientists who have fallen into the same trap.

The way I would approach the problem of explaining the functions of political representation is to outline all the main functions that it can serve—which I take to be eight in number—without making the assumption that every representative system necessarily serves all these functions. The student who wishes to compare systems can then assess their performance along each of these eight dimensions and construct a profile for each system.

These eight functions can be grouped under three general headings and one of these is certainly the provision of channels through which the public can exercise influence over those who govern them. This can best be called the function of popular control and there are three ways in which it can be exercised. In the first place, citizens in a country possessing a system of competitive elections can choose between rival teams of politicians. Some thirty years ago, Joseph Schumpeter argued in a most brilliant book that this is the essence of democracy and that one ventured into doubtful territory if one pretended that representative institutions necessarily gave citizens an appreciable degree of influence over the actions of government. He maintained that representative systems can clearly be distinguished from other systems in terms of their institutional arrangements but he did not know what evidence could be found for the proposition that representative systems promoted the will of the people more effectively than other systems.[5]

Notwithstanding the logic of this view, most commentators have regarded the choice of leaders as a means rather than an end, the end being the exercise of influence over the policies to be pursued. If exercised before the event this influence leads to responsiveness; if exercised after the event, it comes under the heading of accountability.

Different types of representative serve the function of responsiveness to varying extents. Delegated representatives are invariably responsive to the wishes of their principals, for this is the reason for their appointment and they are apt to be discharged if they ignore it. Elected representatives are not in this position and, although it has often been argued that they ought to be bound by some kind of electoral mandate, it is evident that this argument rests upon an unrealistic view of their position. It is of course quite reasonable to say that the winning party in a British general election has a mandate to govern, a statement which indicates that the constitutional authority which Ministers derive from their appointment by the monarch is buttressed by the sense of legitimacy that they enjoy as a consequence of their electoral victory. But to say that the party has a mandate to implement certain policies is fallacious both as description and as prescription. Of course, this is not to say that there are no issues on which politicians respond to public opinion, for we can all think of examples like race relations and the location of airports which would disprove such a proposition. But it is in the nature of government, here or anywhere else, that responsiveness to specific pressures by specialized and well-informed groups is much more common than responsiveness to the sentiments of an amorphous mass electorate.

If we turn to accountability, we turn to a function of representation that is performed somewhat more effectively by systems of competitive elections. There can be no doubt that in this country the most plausible way of interpreting the result of a normal general election— there are of course always exceptions—is to describe it as a verdict on the competence of the previous government.

Perhaps at this point I may refer to a piece of research I did a few years ago. At the time of the 1964 general election I conducted a survey, with the help of three colleagues, in which we re-interviewed some four hundred electors, in two Yorkshire constituencies, who had previously been interviewed at the time of the 1959 election. We used a somewhat similar questionnaire and with the assistance of a computer we made a fairly exhaustive analysis of the responses in an attempt to trace the nature of the swing of opinion. It proved quite impossible either to explain the results in terms of any issue or set of issues or to explain them in terms of the personalities involved. But in 1959 the respondents had been asked a battery of questions to test their opinions on the competence and leadership of the two main parties, and their judgements were graded on a nineteen-point scale. When we compared the 1959 gradings with ones derived from similar questions which were put in 1964, we found that all groups showed a loss of confidence in the Conservative Party and an increase of confidence in the Labour Party. This was just as true of consistent Conservatives and of consistent Labour supporters as it was of the fairly small proportion of people who had actually changed their vote, so that in their movement of opinion over this period the floating voters were typical of the electorate as a whole. I think this and other findings of this survey suggest that the British electoral system fulfils the function of accountability reasonably well, at least in regard to the Government and Opposition. However, it does not render individual M.P.'s accountable save in quite exceptional instances like that of the unfortunate Mr. Gordon-Walker.

If the broad function of providing for popular influence over decisions can be sub-divided into the specific functions of competitive choice, responsiveness and accountability, there are other functions—in my view five other functions—which have nothing to do with popular influence or control. Two of these which may be grouped together are the function of recruiting leaders and the function of enabling leaders to govern in a responsible fashion. I suppose it is a commonplace to observe that one of the ways in which political activity differs most sharply from economic or social activity is that political life involves a pretty clear distinction between leaders and led. Only a tiny minority of people become full-time politicians, and in most modern societies representative institutions constitute the main agencies of recruitment for the political élite. Naturally this is not the case in military dictatorships or in those traditional systems of government where leaders are drawn from a ruling family or caste. But in virtually all other types of government, democratic or dictatorial, politicians are normally recruited and political leaders selected through the party system. It is as true in the USSR as it is in the USA that the party is the agency which interests people in politics, persuades them to accept minor offices, chooses between candidates for election, grooms potential leaders for stardom, and mobilizes support for them when they are successful.

A related function of a representative system is that of giving political leaders sufficient support and scope for them to be able to balance conflicting pressures and formulate long-term plans for government. Politicians have frequently to take unpopular decisions and sometimes to carry through a reversal of previous policies, both of which require room for manoeuvre.

It follows that the function of providing for responsibility has certain institutional implications. If responsiveness were the main function of a representative system it would be appropriate to have frequent elections and probably a rapid turnover of politicians, as was urged by some of the more radical founders of the American constitution. The function of public accountability implies that the turnover should not be too rapid, for unless representatives believe that they have a fairly good chance of re-election the prospect is unlikely to influence their behaviour. The function of responsibility implies that elections should not be too frequent either and in practice all electoral systems embody a compromise between these three requirements.

Consideration of the need for responsibility also emphasizes the value of there being several levels of representation. One of the conditions of achieving both responsiveness and responsibility in government is that the raw demands made by spokesmen for particular interests and localities should be transmuted by discussions within the representative system into more moderate demands which are more consonant with each other and with the interests of the society as a whole. In this way a representative system can act not only as a set of information channels but also as a filter.

The last three functions to which I want to draw your attention may be grouped under the general heading of 'the maintenance of the system', and they may appropriately be described as legitimation, the mobilization of consent, and the relief of pressure.

That most insightful of all political theorists, Jean-Jacques Rousseau, opened the third chapter of *The Social Contract* with the following observation:

> The strongest is never strong enough to be always the master unless he transforms strength into right and obedience into duty.

He added that force itself does not create right and that 'we are obliged to obey only legitimate powers.' The wisdom of these remarks has been confirmed time and time again, and history reveals only a limited number of ways in which rulers have been able to acquire an aura of legitimacy. Heredity is one way; membership of a particular caste is another; while in military dictatorships a military training is said to confer certain political virtues that are lacking among civilians. In the present era, however, election by popular vote is the source of legitimacy that commands the most widespread respect. The legitimizing effect of a large turn-out at the polls extends from countries where there is a genuine choice between candidates to those in which there is none, the difference being that in the former fifty-one per cent is enough to do the trick whereas in the latter anything less than ninety-seven per cent would be thought rather worrying. And this points to the other side of the coin, which is that a mass boycott of elections constitutes a public refusal to re-authorize the regime which is almost certain to endanger it. A good example is the partial boycott of the Nigerian federal elections in 1964: this was successful in only seventy constituencies out of three hundred and twelve, but it nevertheless caused a major constitutional crisis and signalled the beginning of the end of Nigeria's experiment with representative government.

The legitimizing function of representation can also be seen where representatives are appointed rather than elected. A commission of inquiry into industrial relations would lack legitimacy in the eyes of workers unless it included at least one trade unionist among its members. The microcosmic representation of the various sections of Canada in the Cabinet and Supreme Court helps to bolster the legitimacy of the Canadian federal government, while the customary inclusion of a Roman Catholic and a Jewish judge among the nine members of the United States Supreme Court does the same for that institution.

A related function of representation is the mobilization of consent. This was the chief original purpose of the older European parliaments, and it has been well described by historians. Stubbs tells us that in 1261 Henry III summoned the Knights of the shires so that 'they might see and understand for themselves that he was only aiming for the welfare of the whole community.'[6] Edward I's motives have been described in the following way by Helen Cam.

In 1275 Edward I summoned knights to his first parliament, not to take an active part in drawing up the Great Statute of Westminster, but rather to hear and understand the reforms in local government which it contained and to carry back . . . the explanation of the new provisions for restraining the corruptions of sheriffs. In 1283 and again in 1295 and 1307 Edward I was undoubtedly, like his contemporary Philippe de Bel, making use of the representative system for propaganda purposes; demonstrating to the communities of shire and borough, on whose material assistance he was bound to rely, the justice of his own cause against the villainy of his enemy.[7]

Things have not changed a great deal over the past seven centuries, except that Members of Parliament now sometimes play a smaller part in the mobilization of consent than the delegated representatives who act on behalf of interest groups. In so far as the latter are successful in their negotiations with the administration they are inevitably drawn into the position of agreeing (explicitly or implicitly) to persuade their members that the compromises they have arrived at are satisfactory.

The general rule here is that all channels of political communication tend to become two-way channels, as can be seen very clearly in the operation of advisory and consultative committees. Thus, several nationalized industries in this country have consultative committees which were set up with the explicit purpose of representing consumers and bringing their complaints to the attention of the public corporation concerned. In practice, close contact between the committees and the corporation officials has generally had the effect of persuading the committees that most public complaints are unjustified, and these numerous consumers' committees have on the whole been more successful in bringing the excuses and policies of the authorities to the attention of the public than in bringing public pressure to bear on the corporations. In 1970 public criticisms of the quality of British radio and television services led to the suggestion that a new Broadcasting Council should be established to oversee all the broadcasting media and deal with complaints from aggrieved members of the public. The *Daily Telegraph* made the following comment:

> Alas, this suggestion will not begin to solve the problem. It is our experience generally that boards which are set up to regulate and supervise some activity, whether on behalf of the government or the consumer, are soon captured by the industry in question and fashioned into its apologists.[1]

It is highly unlikely that this tendency is confined to Britain. The generalisation that all channels of political communication become two-way channels can be supplemented by the generalisation that, unless political passions are aroused, the party with most expert knowledge will tend to get the better of the argument. All representative institutions, if skilfully handled, can serve to mobilise consent to the policies of those actually running the industry, agency or government involved.

A closely related function of representation is that of relieving pressure on a regime from critics and dissenters. Representative institutions can do this partly by offering opportunities for grievances to be aired and partly by diverting the activities of potential revolutionaries into constitutional channels.

The ventilation of grievances is a familiar topic and we all know of the proliferation of committees and commissions and councils which wise authorities create in order to provide an outlet for anger and to protect the leadership from direct attack. The disarming of potential revolutionaries is a more difficult matter to assess. It is easy enough to say that the American political system would be more secure if the Black Panthers spent their time canvassing for municipal elections, but can one say with any confidence that France and Italy have contained the threat posed by their large Communist parties more successfully by permitting Communists to compete in elections than they would have done if they had banned the parties? Historical generalizations on this scale are probably better avoided, but it is certainly possible to find examples in which the creation or modification of representative institutions has helped to protect a regime from threats to its stability.

Of course, if this sort of move is to succeed, the timing of the operation is crucial. After the Easter Rebellion of 1916, the British authorities decided to create a new body called the Irish Convention to act as a forum for discussion between representatives of all groups. This move was too late, the Convention failing because it was boycotted by the extremist groups whose presence was most essential. On the other hand, the Conservative Party's promise before the 1970 election to create a Scottish National Assembly was clearly too early, because the Scottish Nationalists do not pose a serious threat and the establishment of such an assembly would provide them with a new platform from which to propagate their demands. It is also possible to find examples in the academic world, since some universities have suffered from the refusal of their authorities to meet student demands for representation until it was too late to avoid trouble while, at the other extreme, it is noticeable that the two most liberal and progressive institutions of university education in Britain have experienced more disruption than any of the others.

If I may now recapitulate the argument in outline, I have suggested that there are four types of representation, each logically distinct from the others, and that in political life these forms of representation can serve eight functions. Three of these functions, which can be designated as competition for power, responsiveness and accountability, can be grouped under the general heading of popular control; two of the functions are to provide for leadership and responsibility; and the other three are concerned with the maintenance of the regime. I have described these last three as the function of legitimation, the function of mobilizing consent and the function of relieving pressure. Those of you with a practical interest in politics may feel that I should now go on to rank these functions in order of importance, but I do not see this as part of my task. There are situations in which we should all want to say that some functions are more important than others, but judgements of this kind depend partly on the historical circumstances of each case and partly on the political values of the person making the assessment.

The role of the political scientist is not to evaluate so much as to classify, and one use of this kind of analysis to the student of comparative government is that (as I suggested earlier) it gives him a systematic way of comparing representative systems. By using these categories the student can construct a profile for each of the systems with which he is concerned, in which the Fifth Republic, for instance, would score more highly than the Fourth Republic on leadership and responsibility but less highly on responsiveness, and the representative system in the Soviet Union would get better marks for the mobilization of consent than it would for accountability.

But, much more important than this kind of comparison, the value of conceptual and functional analysis, in my understanding, is simply to facilitate rational discussion of political questions. Of course, the task of bringing rationality into political discussion is rather like the task of cutting a path through a jungle where the thickets grow almost as quickly as they can be chopped down, but if one lives in a jungle it is nevertheless a necessary activity—and some of us find it positively enjoyable.

NOTES

1. In a talk broadcast by the BBC on 1 September 1960.
2. *The Times*, 17 January 1958.
3. See Giovanni Sartori, 'Representational Systems', in *International Encyclopaedia of the Social Sciences* (The Macmillan Co. and the Free Press, New York, 1968) p. 466.
4. David E. Apter, *Some Conceptual Approaches to the Study of Modernisation* (Prentice-Hall, Englewood Cliffs, N.J., 1968) p. 311.
5. J. A. Schumpeter, *Capitalism, Socialism and Democracy* (Harper Bros., New York, 1942).
6. William Stubbs, *Select Charters and other Illustrations of English Constitutional History* (9th edn., The Clarendon Press, Oxford, 1929) p. 395.
7. Helen M. Cam, *Liberties and Communities in Medieval England* (Merlin Press, London, 1963) pp. 226–7.
8. *Daily Telegraph*, 4 January, 1971.

15

Professor M. Cranston

POLITICS AND ETHICS

An inaugural lecture has one, if only one, agreeable traditional feature. Like a newly elected Member making his first speech in the Academie Française, a new professor pays tribute to his immediate predecessor in the chair. In the Academie Française newcomers do not always think well of their predecessors, and they make an art of being rude about them in a studiously polite way. I do not know if this situation ever arises in English universities; but I, at any rate, am in the fortunate position of wholeheartedly admiring the previous incumbent of this chair, Professor Michael Oakeshott, a true philosopher. I need hardly say at the London School of Economics what an outstanding scholar and teacher he is, or what a congenial and patient man he is to work with, but I do think it worth remembering, now that political philosophy is becoming rather a fashionable subject, that Professor Oakeshott did more than anyone else in England to keep it alive at a time when other people were saying that political philosophy was dead.

There was a time when anyone who gave a lecture on politics and ethics would be expected to begin by saying what he meant by 'politics' and 'ethics'. But if this expectation still exists, I fear I shall disappoint it. I will go so far as to say that by ethics I mean the theory of morals. As for politics, most of us know what we mean by that already, although we may well get worried if we look up the definitions provided in books by academic theorists: in such places, we read, for example, that 'politics is the authoritative allocation of values in a community' (David Easton)[1], 'politics is the struggle for power' (Max Weber)[2], 'politics is a systematic effort to move other men in the pursuit of some design' (Bertrand de Jouvenel)[3], or 'politics is who gets what, when, how' (Harold Lasswell)[4]. None of these sounds right: for the reason, I believe, that none of them *is* right. They do not correspond to what we find when we look at that complex

279

activity known as politics. For what is it that people who take up politics actually do?

First of all, they talk. It has always surprised me that Professor Oakeshott, in making the point that politics is a practice, compared it to the art of cookery.[5] For surely if politics is an art, it is one of the performing arts, and not one of the creative ones. Plato noticed this when he compared the politician to the flute-player.

But the flute-player isn't right either. As a performer, the politician is theatrical, not musical. The world of politics is undoubtedly a stage, and every politician is an actor on it. I might well be asked: is not an academic lecture, including an inaugural lecture, as much a 'theatrical' event as a political speech? I have no wish to deny it. I would only add that in speaking of the politician as an actor I mean no disrespect. It seems to me a pity that the word 'theatrical' should have become a pejorative one; as it undoubtedly has. And it might be worth pausing to consider why. The most thoroughgoing attack on the theatre that I know of is one that Rousseau makes in his lecture *Lettre à Monsieur D'Alembert.* In this letter, Rousseau depicts the theatre as an evil institution with no saving grace or merit, and the métier of the actor as a totally corrupt one. A word that recurs often in this letter is the word 'representation'. Rousseau attacks the theatre because fictions and falsehoods are represented on the stage as realities. In his *Social Contract*[6], he translates this hatred of representation in dramatic art into a hatred of representation in parliamentary government. Readers will remember his argument that representatives or deputies do not, and cannot represent the people who elect them. As soon as they are elected, Rousseau says, the representatives become the rulers. And the people, instead of ruling themselves, are enslaved by the deputies they have voted for. This is the basis of Rousseau's belief that representative government is fraudulent. Dramatic art he considers an evil for other, but equally striking reasons.

About half way through his *Lettre à Monsieur D'Alembert,* Rousseau asks: "What is the talent of an actor?" He answers: 'The art of counterfeit: the art of assuming a personality other than his own, of appearing different from what he is, simulating passion while his feelings are cold, of saying something he does not believe just as naturally as if he really believed it . . .'[7]

Conscious, perhaps, that these words might put the reader in mind at once of politicians, Rousseau hastens to add that there should be no confusing the actor and the orator.

'The difference between the two is very great,' he writes, 'When the orator presents himself to the public it is to make a speech, and not to put on an act; he represents no one but himself; he fulfils only his own rôle; he speaks only in his own name; he does not say, nor should he say, anything other than what he thinks; the man and the *persona* are identical; he is where he should be, and he discharges the same duty which any other citizen in his place would discharge.'[8]

I don't think one needs to make any detailed comparison between Rousseau's uncharitable description of the actor and his flattering description of the orator to see that neither his criticism of the one nor his praise of the other is altogether fair. For if a man offers, as an actor does, what is plainly declared to be an imitation, it is illogical to complain that what he offers is an imitation. And, correspondingly, it is no praise of actual orators to protest that *the* orator, namely the ideal image of an orator, is a man who is wholly and patently sincere. And, indeed, if Rousseau had based his conception of the orator on a consideration of the orator's rôle in the real world, he might have given us a different picture.

The political speaker is simply not a citizen who stands up artlessly and tells you what he has in mind. The orator is a man whose function is to persuade his hearers to accept, or agree or approve of a certain policy. And this is an intricate art, which requires both natural talent and some professional formation. The calling of the politician is one that deserves a great deal of respect. And I think Rousseau does no service to him by praising him for qualities that he does not possess. He is unfair to the actor in attributing to him faults which cannot logically be considered faults: and he is unfair to the orator, in ascribing to him virtues which it would be foolish to expect him to have.

The life of politics is an arduous one. A man who chooses it is continuously put to the test. He has to satisfy other people time and time again. He has no security of tenure, as a civil servant, or a professor has. A politician can never be sure how popular he is, although he soon knows when he is not wanted. Even the humblest member of a legislative body like the House of Commons has to satisfy his party leadership, his constituency committee and the voters. Any one of these bodies has the power to dismiss him. So he cannot simply speak spontaneously; his speeches have to measure the demands and the expectations of all these very different people. Like an actor, he must know how to please and persuade and engage the sympathies of others. If he is to succeed he must be dedicated to his calling: and no matter how great his native gift he must master the techniques of public debate and public relations; he must even look after his looks.

If politicians talk, they also, of course, decide, legislate, vote, pass resolutions and settle the rules that we ordinary people have to observe. But politicians do not do all these things in public. There are many text books about 'decision-making' and decision-theory', but this is really one of the least known parts of political life. We know who votes where in Parliament in response to that very theatrical device, the division bell. But we do not know how Ministers speak and vote in the cabinet, or what discussions go on between leading members of the opposition party. In the theatre of politics, the curtain is firmly rung from time to time, and a large and extremely important part of the drama is enacted in secret.

It is frustrating for political science that political life is so sensitive to observation. For either a politician is exceedingly conscious of an audience, and addresses himself to it whenever he speaks; or he makes sure that all observers are excluded. In the one case he is thinking all the time of the effect his words are having; in the other, he takes care that his words shall be heard only by his colleagues and their confidential staff. For this reason, the political scientist whose modest desire is to observe what we like to call the political process has the choice of joining the audience and being talked at, or putting his ear to a hole in the curtain, and finding it firmly blocked. Of course there are records from the past, but that only means that the political scientist becomes a kind of contemporary historian. And, perhaps, that is what political science, for the most part, is: a felicitous union of history and philosophy, for us as it was for Aristotle.

Politicians, in a sense, do more important work than actors: but why does Rousseau insist so much on the moral distinction between the two? I think perhaps the explanation is that Rousseau had such strong feelings about the disjunction between appearance and reality. He regarded appearance as the domain of deception and therefore as bad; and reality as the province of truth, and therefore as good. The theatre was bad because it was an admitted temple of illusions. The political forum, on the other hand, was good, for it was there that men assumed the full reality of citizens. Appearance and reality he conceived to be antithetical; so he could never fully understand the life of politics, where appearance is almost as important as reality: is even indeed a part of it.

Rousseau demanded sincerity, rather as existentialists of more recent times demand authenticity. And this is something far in excess of what we can fairly demand of any political speaker. We expect our orator to be consistent in what he says, to sound as if he believed it, both to be and to appear at least moderately honest. But we do not expect him always to speak as if he were on oath. Franklin Roosevelt was a very worthy statesman, but no one who reads his letters, with their assurances of affection to any Tom, Dick or Harry who might help to get him nominated and elected President, can believe that Roosevelt was literally sincere in what he wrote. Perhaps a man who wrote letters like this in private life might incur our criticism, but politics is *not* private life, and we must introduce different considerations when we judge it.

The options that are available to a man in politics are often very limited, and the risks attached to each of the several courses open to him may be almost equally great. It is easy for the critic, and especially for the scholar, to condemn his failings. I once heard Lord Attlee say to an academic person who was telling him how to run his government, 'If a politician makes an ass of himself, he loses his seat; but a professor who makes an ass of himself is never going to lose his chair.'

It is not at all easy for the politician to be wise—or even to be sure what is right and wrong. A private person who is constantly straight, frank, open, scrupulous, and morally transparent is a man we wholeheartedly admire. Or shall I say, we should wholeheartedly admire, for such men are not altogether common. But what if a statesman exhibits similar qualities?

One of the things that helped to make a Machiavelli or Machiavellian was the experience of watching Piero Soderini enact the role of *ganfaloniere* of Florence. Soderini was a man of intense, unyielding and high moral principles. The result of his behaving with scrupulous and impeccable justice towards the Spaniards was that the Spanish army invaded the Florentine town of Prato and committed hideous atrocities. Machiavelli drew from this the lesson that the statesman should not allow his dealings with other states always to be governed by the same moral scruples that governed the dealings of private persons.

I do not share the view of those who say that Machiavelli introduced the idea of a politics without morality. His argument, on the contrary, seems to me to be that there is only one true morality: but that the ruler must sometimes disregard it. Machiavelli's words are that the ruler: 'should not depart from what is morally right if he can observe it, but should know how to adopt what is bad when he is obliged to.'[9]

It is worth noting that Machiavelli makes no pretence that the bad is anything other than bad. He says that bad things must be done by rulers, but only very sparingly, and then in a manner which is as much concealed as possible. Like Rousseau, Machiavelli dwells on the distinction between appearance and reality. But unlike Rousseau, Machiavelli attaches value to the appearance of virtue as well as to the practice of it. He tells his *principe*; that he 'should know how to appear compassionate, trustworthy, humane, honest and religious, and actually *be* so, yet he should have his mind so trained that when it is necessary he can become the contrary.'[10]

This suggestion opens the door to the alarming and to my mind wrongful doctrine of the *raison d'état*, but before we join together in deploring it, we must surely admit that Machiavelli has made an important point here. Since a ruler has to deal with other rulers who are sometimes rapacious and unscrupulous, he cannot easily always observe the same moral law which should govern the conduct of individuals within a civilised community. But at the same time, it is his duty as the head of one such civilised community to uphold the moral law. So even if he has sometimes to contravene the principles of that morality, he cannot let his willingness be known. It is not only that a reputation for deceit makes it hard for a man to deceive successfully. There is another consideration. A *principe* is a prominent person. If he bears visible witness to the notion that deceit is sometimes permissible, other people are only too likely to follow his example in their private lives. And this is something that Machiavelli is most anxious to avoid. No one should be given any excuse or encouragement to be bad, just because the *principe,* in the cause of duty, is sometimes obliged to be bad.

The world judges by appearances, if only because appearance is all the world has got to judge by. If we think of the men who have been banished from British public life for moral turpitude in the past hundred years or so—of Sir Charles Dilke, for example, or Parnell and the others, the reason for their fall was plainly the open scandal rather than their sinful deeds, for the same kind of sinful deeds, we have since learned from the biographies, were being done by men more prominent in the kingdom than Dilke or Parnell. The difficulty is that once the sinful deed has been exposed, others in authority dare not allow themselves to appear to condone it, so they are swift to punish a man for doing things they themselves have done, but effectively concealed. One of the reasons for the enduring hostility of rulers, and politicians generally, towards Machiavelli is that he advises them to do consciously and deliberately what many of them already do naturally, and prefer not to think about. The important difference is that Machiavelli never authorised the use of deception for the protection of politicians' careers; he authorised the use of deception only for the concealment of those necessary acts of state which violate morality.

The curious thing is that even Rousseau himself, when he thinks most earnestly about the possibilities that politics affords, himself not only excuses insincerity, but positively recommends it. When he writes in *The Social Contract* about the most important *orateur* of all, the law-giver, the founder of the republic, he says that the orator must not speak in his own words to the public, because the vulgar do not understand the language of the learned. He urges the law-giver to have recourse to dissimulation, and to suggest to the crowd that the proposals he himself has devised have been laid down by the deity: 'Thus,' as Rousseau put it, 'compelling by divine authority persons who cannot be moved by human prudence.'[11]

Readers of Rousseau's *Emile* may remember rather similar deceits and strategems being employed by Emile's tutor to bring up the boy in the path of virtue. So I do not think Rousseau can be said to have consistently believed that sincerity, authenticity, transparency is always imperative in either private or public life. Indeed if frankness is to be the virtue that we are going to set such store by, Rousseau is plainly inferior to Machiavelli. For what Rousseau has done is to insinuate by the back door the principle of dissimulation he has rejected at the front. Whereas what Machiavelli has done, paradoxically, is to strip from the ruler the very veils that he is telling the ruler to wear.

Of the two Machiavelli is in many ways the more sympathetic moralist. And if it seems perverse to apply the word 'moralist' to a man who plainly says that the ruler cannot always be moral, let me suggest that readers should consult the vast literature which exists in the Christian Church on the subject of casuistry. Or if that is too daunting an undertaking, let me simply cite the late Dean of Lichfield's biography of Archbishop William Temple where Dr. Iremonger judges Dr. Temple to have been too kind, loving and chaste a man to be an effective headmaster of an English public school.[12] If the clergy thus considers purity of soul a handicap in the field of Christian education, can we reproach Machiavelli for considering rigidity of moral scruples a handicap in government and diplomacy?

To assert that there are certain exceptions in the application of the moral law, is by no means to deny—but rather to affirm, that the moral law has a general application: and a general application so compelling that any exceptions to it need careful justification and very delicate concealment. It was certainly no part of Machiavelli's scheme to separate politics from morals, or to contemplate politics in the light of a science from which all normative factors were removed. That was to be the enterprise of a much later generation.

Politicians talk. But has politics a language of its own? It has certainly not a distinctively technical language as most trades and professions have. In phonetics, for example, there are technical terms like 'fricative', 'sonorant' and 'vocalic' which are used in a specific way and which apprentices in the subject have to learn. Of course there are also words that 'belong', so to speak, to politics: words like 'democratic', 'free', 'just', 'legitimate' and so on, but far from the application of these words being settled by convention, it is just these things that are argued over. In phonetics there is general agreement as to which speech sounds shall be classified, for example, as fricative; but there is no agreement in politics as to which states shall be classified as democratic. An even more important difference is that the word 'fricative' in phonetics implies no evaluation of good or bad. It is simply a neutral technical term. The word 'democratic', by contrast, is loaded with evaluative content. In the 1930's and earlier many people detested democracy, and they spoke the word with a voice of disapprobation; on the other hand, many people esteemed democracy, and they invested the word with their sense of approval. It was a highly controversial word. More recently this has changed, and 'democracy' has become a word of commendation, virtually throughout the world, although it is certainly not the case that what was most commonly thought of as democracy before the war has been universally adopted.

And yet the dictionary definition of the word has not changed. The latest editions give the same report on usage as the old editions: democracy is a 'system of government by the people.' But where are these systems to be found? Some theorists say that democracy is the kind of government that is practised in America, so that all you have to do, to learn about democracy, is to study American government at work. Others direct our attention to the people's democracies, such as the German Democratic Republic or the Democratic Republic of North Korea. There are those who say that the only vestiges of democracy left in the modern world are to be found in Switzerland. Then, by way of contrast, there is Professor C. B. Macpherson who has argued that we can find democracy alike in capitalist and communist and under-developed countries, although it assumes in those places a variety of forms.[13] Professor Macpherson has thus succeeded where Woodrow Wilson failed: he has made the world safe for democracy by the adroit device of proposing that almost all known forms of government may be classified as democratic.

Of course they all want to be, and we ought not to be surprised that once a word has become a universal prestige word, as 'democracy' has become, that everyone should claim it. The problem that falls to political philosophy is to ask whether any criteria can be invoked to judge the claim of a given system to be a democratic one.

If 'democratic' is a word which has become more prestigious with the passage of time, there are other words we hear in political talk which have become increasingly pejorative. Think of the word 'bourgeois'. The dictionary meaning of this has never changed: to be bourgeois is to belong to the town-dwelling middle-class as distinct from the nobility, the peasantry and the working-class. It is the class to which most of us belong. So naturally it has no glamour for us. And yet in its earlier use, the word 'bourgeois' was spoken with esteem, even by people like Voltaire. The nobility seems habitually to have used it with scorn—as we might expect—and we could well understand the peasantry and the working class doing so too. But the peculiar thing is that the bourgeois class has itself taken to using the word 'bourgeois' with as much implied hostility as the other classes. So everyone has turned out to agree that 'bourgeois' is bad. So if you have to stand for election in a very bourgeois constituency such as Bournemouth or Kensington or Cheltenham, and you said 'Protect the *Bourgeoisie*' you would not earn a single vote, but you might do quite well if you said 'Protect the middle classes.'

Yet, from a certain point of view, you would be saying the same thing. But not from the point of view of politics. In the one case you would be employing a word so loaded with miscellaneous disapprobation that it is political folly to use it. In the other case you would be using a word which the majority of voters would hear with kindly recognition. From the point of view of politics, the most important feature of the word *'bourgeois'* is that it has become contaminated. With the passage of time, some of the words we use become degraded and some become elevated. And a political speaker has to be alert to these changes, if he is to make use of words persuasively.

Some changes happen quickly. Take, for example, the word 'sovereignty'. When I was an undergraduate this was a word in low repute in England. Harold Laski was only one of several who suggested that sovereignty was a concept we ought to get rid of altogether.[14] Even as short a time ago as 1969, Professor Stankiewicz published a book called *In Defense of Sovereignty*[15] because he felt that the concept needed rehabilitation. But in the past year or two we have heard the word 'sovereignty' used without hesitation as the name of a cherished principle. Even some of Laski's own political disciples objected to the idea of Great Britain joining the Common Market because, they said, it would 'infringe our sovereignty'. I shall spare you my own views on both the Common Market and the subject of sovereignty itself: I am concerned here only with the fortunes of the word 'sovereignty'; it seemed only twenty-five years ago to give off an unpleasing odour of nationalistic narrowness, but today it is invested with the proud spirit of British independence.

Or consider the word 'violence'. Until a few years ago, this word was invoked only as a word of condemnation. Its use implied the presence of excessive or unjustified force. Both in moral theory and ordinary conversation, the distinction between force and violence was plainly understood. Force was something always regrettable but in certain circumstances permissible. The word 'force' had no judgement of condemnation built into it as the word 'violence' had. We might say: 'He used force and was wrong to do so.' But we did not need to say 'He used violence and was wrong to do so,' because that would be to utter a pleonasm. 'Violence' was wrong by definition.

Recently this seems to be changing. We even find the word 'violence' used as a word of praise. And what used to be called force, is now called violence. Sometimes this is done deliberately, by Sartre, for example, who argues that violence is what lies behind all civil society: and who would like to see violence used to institute a revolution. And whereas there is permissible force and wrongful force in traditional thinking, for Sartre there is bad violence or good violence. Although I don't think many people subscribe to Sartre's political theory, or even perhaps understand it, many people nowadays have taken to using the word 'violence' as he does.

Admittedly, the word 'violence' is given a laudatory sense in the writings of several minor political theorists who flourished before the war: but such theorists used to be thought of as fascistic, and indeed it was long regarded as the badge of a fascist to speak in praise of violence. Even as ruthless a tyrant as Stalin never admitted to use of anything other than force.

Now it is becoming increasingly accepted that the word 'violence' may be used either as a neutral or a laudatory word.[16] This may well mean, and I suspect it does, that the fascist *ethos* is coming to life again among us: but it also means that words—and especially the words we use in politics—can gain prestige as well as lose it, and that the normative implications of a word are never fixed and precise.

If we examine the to-and-fro of political debate we notice how words, and even phrases are picked up from one speaker by another, picked up even from an antagonist in the debate, and used by a speaker to his own advantage. Some phrase maker, for example, introduces a fanciful expression, such as 'equality of opportunity' as something he wants to recommend. It sounds good. It is taken up by speakers of all parties. And before long everyone is declaring that equality of opportunity is what we all want—a great national ideal.

This is the kind of euphoria which political philosophy tends to spoil. For it asks such questions as: what sense can we make of this so-called principle? The two words concerned contradict one another: for the concept of opportunity is logically connected with competitive disparity of advantage, whereas the concept of equality is logically connected with parity of advantage, so it is far from clear what their union could possibly signify. Of course the word 'equality' is keenly appreciated on the left, and the word 'opportunity' is much cherished on the right: and a phrase which exploits the prestige of both may well appeal to a large public, but only at the expense of both sides accepting a loss of definition, allowing the concepts to become blurred and soft and nebulous. This may not be an undesired result. In politics there is a tendency for speakers to adopt a yielding, feminine attitude to words, an attitude which favours the use of them in a slack and unexacting way. Journalism does nothing to halt the process. Indeed the phrase-maker is a creature who flourishes more on the margin of politics than in politics itself. A man I once knew, Sir Norman Angell, had written a book called *The Great Illusion*. It was about war, and it had been immensely popular. A short while after it was published the 1914 war broke out, and Norman Angell's great illusion became the great and terrible truth. But that didn't hinder the success of the book. Norman Angell was venerated as a sage, knighted and awarded the Nobel Prize. We may perhaps remark a parallel case in Professor Kenneth Galbraith's *The Affluent Society:* a year or two after it is published. Wall Street flops, the dollar is devalued, Washington is broke and no one in America admits to having any cash. But never mind, *The Affluent Society,* like *The Great Illusion,* is already a classic. In the realm of pamphleteering the title is everything, and the reassuring unforgettable titles keep rolling off the press: *The Lonely Crowd, The Divided Self, The Naked Ape, The Female Eunuch, The One-Dimensional Man*—glittering phrases that win for their authors a place in the immortality of folklore.

But politics is not the same as pamphleteering. The pamphleteer is never called upon to answer for his words. But if a politician makes a phrase that proves strikingly inept, it will be hurled against him, again and again. Think of Neville Chamberlain and his 'peace for our time', or President Johnson and his 'great society', or Mr. Harold Wilson's 'The pound in your pocket is not worth a penny less' not to mention Mr. Heath's election words about keeping down the prices of the contents of the shopping bàsket. A memorable phrase can be disastrous, for the simple reason that it is remembered. A politician has good reason to be nervous of words, and want to soften all those sharp edges, in case they cut him. But it is part of the task of political philosophy to try to recover clarity.

The twentieth century, among its many other disagreeable characteristics, has been an age of dogma. The eighteenth century doubted, the nineteenth century believed, but the twentieth century knows—or rather it thinks it knows. And among the dogmas which have informed the thinking of our century there are two that have a particular importance. The first asserts that statements of fact are so totally distinct from judgements of value that there can be no question of deriving one from the other.

The thought behind the dogma is not new. It was suggested, with a particular intention, by David Hume in the eighteenth century. It was repeated in different contexts in the nineteenth century. And there is no denying, that in its limited formulation, it is true: statements of fact *are* logically distinct from judgements of value, and for purposes of analysis we must take them apart. But what the twentieth century has elevated into a dogma is the further assertion that there can be no rational fusion of fact and value or any logical derivation of judgements of value from statements of fact.

In the past few years, this dogma has lost much of its hold on people's minds. Recent work in ethics has done a good deal to discredit it. Several methods have been demonstrated by which judgements of value can be logically derived from statements of fact.[17] The analysis of language has shown that the function of certain words is to be at the same time both descriptive and evaluative.

The other dogma which has informed so much theorising in the twentieth century is the dogma of the identity of determinism and human freedom. This derives from the suggestion put forward by Hobbes and Locke that there is no such problem as the free will problem, on the grounds that there is no antithesis between determinism and freedom, men's actions being at the same time both determined and free. On the basis of this dogma, twentieth century investigators have directed their research into the explanation of human behaviour as a search for determining causes, and the study of man has become no different in kind from the study of rats.

This second dogma, too, has lost a good deal of its hold in the past year or two. The case against determinism has been put from so many different points of view in philosophy that hardly anything remains to be said in support of it. It has even been accepted by the more sophisticated champions of Marxism, and what was once presented as a form of scientific historicism is now put forward as a form of libertarian metaphysics.

However, these two dogmas—the divorce of fact and value, and the marriage of freedom and determinism—have both been incorporated into positivism, the doctrine which has shaped so much of the thought and even the culture of our time. This is a doctrine which has taken various forms, and each with its own bearing on theorising about politics. An early and influential type was legal positivism. This, of course, is the doctrine that law is the system of rules and penalties which is actually enforced in any state. Law, as one theorist put it, is fact. Law is the code which is actually imposed by the courts and the authorities, as distinct from any ideal code, which ought, or should be upheld. Legal positivists, therefore, dispute the traditional conception of natural law as being the supreme law. For them natural law is no part of law at all. It is either philosophy or nonsense, which, from the point of view of positivism are not very different.

Legal positivism rest squarely on the dogma of the mutual impenetrability of fact and value. In asserting that law is fact, the legal positivist assumes that he is denying that law is value. What his dogma forbids him to see, is what anyone must see who reflects on law as a system: that justice is an integral part of the system which constitutes law. Justice is part of the meaning of the word 'law'. Law is both normative and factual. And in this respect it is very like politics.

Another form of positivism which has had a great vogue in the twentieth century is historical positivism by which I mean the belief that history is a science, a science dedicated to the search for facts and the discovery of the causes of past events and movements through the observation of regularities in what is called historical phenomena. In the positivist dream, the historian is a man who records facts without judging them, and then, as a scientist, goes on to discover the cause of things. Since human choices and decisions are seen as part of a succession of cause and effect, positivist historians think it is just as sensible to look for the cause of the French Revolution as it is for an engineer to look for the cause of an explosion in the cellar.

This enterprise in historical scholarship coincided with another, more extensive one, that of positivistic social science. Again the divorce of fact and value was duly proclaimed. Social science was to stay in the realm of fact: in the elegant German word of Max Weber, it was to be *wertfrei*. It was also going to discover the causes of things—the causes, not so much of past events, as the positivistic historians did, but of movements and changes in society generally. It was going to do for society what the natural scientists had done for nature. It was going to discover laws.

Some of the laws they produced have to do with politics. For instance, there was Robert Michels' 'iron law of oligarchy', the law that a minority will always prevail over the majority. Some of us may not think this law any great improvement on Rousseau's observation that the ministers of a state will always tend to turn themselves from the servants into the masters of the people, but at least we must admit that Robert Michels adds something to the iron law of oligarchy: he adds the iron.

But we mustn't be frivolous: because the formulations of theorists like Michels had a great influence on the development of political science. It inspired after the first world war an attempt to reform, or revolutionize, political science on the same positivistic lines, something which was spoken of at the time as the endeavour to transform political science into a 'genuine science'.[18] Once more the two dogmas were repeated. Political science must stick to facts and banish values. And it must look for the causes of things, the causes, that is, of political behaviour, through the collection of data, the observation of regularities and the formulation of general laws.

This now seems a rather old-fashioned, as well as a defective account of what a science is: but at the time it found a response. And positivistic political science took root and thrived in America, taking over more and more political science departments in the ever-expanding North American universities. The tradition of Aristotle was discarded. The history of political ideas, political theory and history, even the study of institutions and laws was pushed aside by this new aggressive science, whose aim according to one of its most noted exponents, Professor Robert Dahl, was to state 'all the phenomena of government in terms of observed and observable behaviour of men.'[19] It was then that we first heard talk of eliminating political philosophy.

But if positivist political science flourished in America, it soon changed its nature in the process. It began to claim a different identity from that with which it started out. In the writings of its exponents which date from the 1920's and the 1930's, the gospel of the *wertfrei,* empirical and objective social science is reiterated. But in the 1940's, American political science assumes the guise of a policy science in the service of democracy. One of the best and liveliest of the American political scientists, Professor Harold Lasswell, suggested that political science was as much directed to the defence of democracy as was military science itself.[20] Plainly such a science is not value-free, whatever else it may be.

There is a well-known article on Lasswell by Professor David Easton,[21] which suggests that Lasswell's work was never really value-free. Easton argues that Lasswell's early work rests on a veiled acceptance of the élitist values of Pareto and Robert Michels and that the real difference between Lasswell's earlier and later work is that he renounced this unavowed acceptance of élitism in favour of an avowed acceptance of the value of democracy. But there seems to me to be another characteristic of Harold Lasswell's early work, which is more important than any veiled adhesion to élitism, and that is the kind of science which Lasswell had in mind when he spoke of science: for this is something he shared with other practitioners of behavioural political science. The kind of science which served as their model was not physics, but psycho-pathology, a science which is itself deeply permeated by conceptions of value. So 'science' in Aristotle's sense had been abandoned only to make way for 'science' in Freud's sense. Psycho-pathology is a therapeutic science, not only interested in facts, but equally, and indeed primarily, concerned with such conceptions as cure, normality, health, satisfaction, adjustment and so forth. There is nothing *wertfrei* here.

A very large part of positivist political science in America was based from the beginning on this therapeutic model, so that when American political science proclaimed itself in the 1940's to be a 'policy science' it was not so much changing its nature, as becoming aware of its real nature.

Of course, not every social science postitivist has followed this pattern of transforming their subject into a therapeutic enterprise. The leading behavioural psychologist, Professor Skinner of Harvard, has attacked what he calls 'the medical analogy' and the prevailing tendency of social science to think of the problems of men in society as the problems of patients needing cure. But Skinner can hardly be said to have remained true to the ideal of a *wertfrei* social science. In his latest writings he has come out in favour of measures more far-reaching than anything that has ever been proposed by Harold Lasswell and his colleagues. Skinner says that the only way to build a better life for men is to undertake a wholesale reconstruction of the environment, since it is, he believes, the environment which determines everybody's state of mind. Skinner, in other words, has come out frankly in favour of what Sir Karl Popper used to call 'utopian social engineering.' Some of you may agree with Skinner, and you are entitled to do so. But what nobody could possibly argue is that a behaviourism which is directed towards the improvement of men through the reconstruction of the environment is a science concerned with the realm of fact alone. When Skinner speaks of 'improvement' and 'better cultures' and a 'better way of life' he betrays himself as someone who is talking of norms.[22] If his positivism is not therapeutic, that is only because it is more radically programmatic. The dogma of the divorce between fact and value has never been repudiated. But the writings of those who subscribe to it serve themselves to refute it.

There is no politics in heaven because everybody is perfectly good and perfectly wise. There is politics on earth because men have a partial but not a perfect moral insight and a partial but not a perfect understanding.[23] Politics is in part an argument about values between men who agree about some values but disagree about others. If they did not agree about some—about the desirability of truth and justice, for example—they could not engage in a dialogue at all; there could be no politics. But the dialogue is unending because there is no perfect knowledge of justice, and every man has to subscribe to his own order of axiological preferences.

Politics is secondly an argument about the future, or more narrowly, about the future consequences of proposed lines of action. Again, no man knows the future. We must each make our own conjecture or surmise, and justify that surmise as best we can. A politician must argue: if we do this, then so and so will come about: and then go on to make a value judgment once again and say, that this so-and-so which would come about would be good or bad.

In talking politics we cannot avoid making value judgments. They are part of the very words in use. Besides, the most serious form of political speech is an argument, and an argument entails an appeal to norms of more than one kind.

The most absorbing political arguments are those which embody both disagreements about the moral aspects of a projected policy and disagreements about the probable future consequences of adopting it.

I speak of 'moral aspects', but it is worth noticing that there are at least three types of value judgment which rest on a concept of right or good.

First, there are considerations of duty in the strict sense of the word. If there is any universal moral law at all, it is the rule that contracts must be kept. Locke once said that the keeping of promises was a duty that belonged to man as man and not only as a member of civil society. If men are bound to keep promises, then it seems not unreasonable to argue that institutions, including states, are similarly bound.

Secondly, there are considerations of prudence, by which I mean the use of intelligent foresight to avert future harm. Again, it is commonly held that a government ought to protect its people from injury.

Thirdly, there is a further type of value judgment which is made in political arguments: and this of the good conceived in terms of public advantage or gain. Prudence is negative: it is matter of avoiding evil, or preventing things getting worse than they are. Gain, or what is often called utility, is a matter of promoting what is expected to be an improvement.

Other values, such as liberty and compassion, are invoked in the course of political arguments, but these three kinds occupy a central place; and indeed even liberty is often expressed as a right, one of the historic rights of man. The notion of right is logically connected with that of duty and each is a different aspect of the concept of justice. It would hardly be an exaggeration to say that almost all political arguments, by their very nature, turn on considerations of justice or prudence or public gain. Some politicians are often suspected of being the spokesmen of private or sectional interests. And conceivably some of them are. But they must hide that fact. The important thing is that nobody in a political argument can stand up and say 'My friends or clients *want* this or that'.

Admittedly in business negotiations, and the like, the representative of one party can say: 'Our price is *so* and we won't take less.' His strength in the negotiation will depend entirely on his power to enforce his demands, and has nothing to do with the justice of the claim. But negotiation is not politics, and politics is not negotiation. In politics you must appeal to justice or the public interest.

A politician who pleads for better pensions for wounded soldiers cannot simply say: 'These men want more, and won't take less'. He must argue that they are entitled to more: that it is just for them to have it. In other words, he must translate the claim into a right.

In another case, a political speaker will appeal to prudence. We hear a lot of this in debates about defence and finance. If someone in Parliament wants to recommend a rather mean policy, such as withdrawing the subsidy on the fees of overseas students or taking away the free milk from schoolchildren, he cannot simply stand up and say: foreign students and schoolchildren have no vote so let's make them suffer first; he has to get up and say: these measures are extravagant; and prudence compels us to cut down on luxuries. Then, of course, the argument becomes, what is and what is not a luxury, a waste to be eliminated in the interests of economy.

In addition to such appeals to prudence, there is the appeal to public gain or utility. A politician advocating the building of an airport would be a fool to say: 'The shareholders in the aviation industry desire this innovation.' He will have to argue that increased facilities for travel and trade would be to the public advantage. He must depict the proposed innovation as an improvement from the point of view of all.

You cannot just give voice to mere demands in politics: you must express claims as just entitlements: you must recommend policies as prudential or advantageous to the public as a whole. You may equally, of course, appeal to the public interest or to some other universal norm. Sometimes such appeals are bogus, or fraudulent; but like all forms of counterfeit, these are entirely dependent on the secure existence of the genuine.

However, it one thing to say that norms are inseparable from politics, and quite another to decide what order of priority should be given to such values in judging a question of public policy. In the case of a private person, we might well agree that duty should come first, prudence second, and considerations of gain last. But we are unlikely to agree that the same hierarchy obtains in people's judgments of proposed political policies. And those who say that Machiavelli was

Satan on earth are usually the first to say that, in practical politics, considerations of duty must come second or third to considerations of prudence or gain.

And assuredly the situation of the private person, thinking of his own duties and desires *is* different from the situation of the statesman thinking of what to do on behalf of his country. It is by no means clear what is meant by an institutional obligation, for although it is explained by analogy with a private person's obligation, it is clearly different. For the man who is obliged is the same man who promises. But in the case of a state, one ruler or government may give the promise, and another be called upon to keep it. Then again it is one thing for a private person to risk his own neck in the course of duty; but another thing for a statesman to put the lives of all his people in danger. The one might well be heroic: the other could easily be unpardonable folly. Again we should admire the man who decides to forgo all thought of gain for himself. But we might think ill of the statesman who threw away the possibility of gain for his whole people.

So the situation of the statesman is more awkward than that of the private man. Moral dilemmas are fairly rare in private life: but in politics the path of duty is often opposed to what looks like the path of gain, and not infrequently different from the way of prudence. Saint-Simon, I think, once said: *'la politique et la morale ne font jamais bon ménage.'* I don't think it is true, but can understand why it is said.

Prudence is unlike duty. We derive our knowledge of our duty from our past promises and our present situation or from our conscience, but prudence entails an estimate of future possibilities. The prudential course of action is one dictated by what a reasonable mind must expect to happen. It is not always easy to be prudent, but it does not demand any superhuman skill.

The pursuit of positive gain or improvement is much more difficult. How are we to know that things will turn out one way rather than another, and judge that the long term results will be good rather than bad? Here in England we live in a country where nature has been ravaged by people who thought that what they were doing was improving life for themselves and their posterity.

To sense future danger and avoid it is sometimes more or less instinctive, but to envisage the unfolding of a future good calls for a more uncommon wisdom. In politics men need, as Machiavelli tells us, a very profound worldliness: an experience of life and affairs, and a culture of the mind which teaches men what they may expect other men to do. They can never *know;* but they can learn to measure probabilities. Measure them, of course, only to a limited extent, for in politics, as Machiavelli again reminds us, a prominent part is always played by *fortuna* or luck.

In recent times, we have had the promise of a more comprehensive and systematic futurology. Part of the programme of positivist social science was to discover laws which would apply to the future as well as to the past and present. There is an idea going back as far as Francis Bacon that science will save us, and the behavioural sciences have been infected with the same conception of their mission. They promise to save us by enabling the statesman to contemplate future problems in the light of calculated projections from accumulated facts and solve such problems with the aid of carefully formulated laws of human behaviour. And how often do we see our behaviouralists, waiting in the wings of the theatre of politics, a large stack of data in one hand and a begging bowl in the other: 'Give us the money for research', they say, 'and we will give you the solutions.'

This is what is promised. But what the politician gets is information. Rivers of it. There is indeed so much information pouring forth today that politicians and public servants are flooded with it. Information has become a real threat to knowledge.

The more information you have the more you need an interpreter, an expert. But such can experts be trusted? If behavioural science could really be value-free, its practitioners might readily seem to be, almost by definition, impartial. But when behavioural science turns out to be impregnated with admitted or unadmitted value judgments, suspicions are aroused. Politicians have indeed become increasingly suspicious. The tendency nowadays is for the statesman to look for expert advice only to experts whose political, or ideological persuasions are akin to his own: we read in recent memoirs that Mr. Crosland, as Minister of Education, set up his own informal 'brains trust' on educational reform composed of Labour Party intellectuals. And on a larger scale, when President Kennedy and President Nixon each called in professors from Harvard to advise him in Washington, Mr. Kennedy took care to choose progressives and Mr. Nixon took equal care to choose conservatives.

I think this is an unfortunate development. It is also reactionary: a reaction, notably, against faith in a *wertfrei* social science and towards ideological social theory, towards the attitude which says: 'everybody is ideologically biased, so let me have someone who is biased in my way'

This reactionary argument rests on the assumption, which I believe to be manifestly false, that you have either got to make no value judgments at all, or make ideologically slanted ones, that there is no middle way between being *wertfrei* and being biased. The truth of the matter, I think, is much simpler. And that is, that we must each make our own preferences but that we ought to be able to justify our preferences. Reasonable grounds can be given for some evaluations that cannot be given for others. There is a very great difference between a measured and critical recognition of values, and the rigid adhesion to a doctrine or a prejudice. 'Criticism' is a crucial word. For in the theatre of politics, the political philosopher is a kind of dramatic critic. He may grow fretful in the stalls and yearn to mount the stage himself, but just as critics are notoriously bad actors, so philosophers make wretched politicians. Think of Gentile becoming Mussolini's minister of education, or Heidegger joining the Nazi party, of Lukacs going to Moscow to support Stalin. Or perhaps we had better not think of them.

Then again there is a temptation for the philosopher to see himself as a dramatist, writing the plays which the politicians enact. Lenin sometimes fancied himself enacting a drama which had been composed by Marx, but, if he did, he altered the script so much, that Marx would not have recognised it. And in truth, of course, Lenin was both playwright and player. Rightly so. For in the theatre of politics there is no place for any other kind of dramatist. The politician is an actor who must furnish his own script, even if he does not actually write it. That is why we judge him by his words. Rousseau was right when he said that the orator is no one but himself. And in politics the orator can never rid himself of responsibility for what he says.

The critic is there to remind him of it. He is there also to analyse and explain the drama, and to appraise the performances. Without dramatic criticism, dramatic art would probably decline. Without political philosophy politics might well go on as merrily as ever. But the trouble is that it would not be understood, it would be a practice without consciousness of the norms which inform its activity, ignorant even of its own identity or nature. If the day ever comes when political philosophy is really dead, the triumph of information over knowledge will be complete.

NOTES

1. David Easton, *The Political System*, New York, 1953, p. 129.
2. Max Weber, *Politik als Beruf* (Quoted by G. E. G. Catlin in Gould and Thursby, *Contemporary Political Thought*, New York, 1969, p. 27.)
3. Bertrand de Jouvenel, *The Pure Theory of Politics*, Cambridge, 1963, p. 30.
4. Harold D. Lasswell, *Politics: Who gets what, when, how*, New York, 1936.
5. *Rationalism in Politics*, London, 1962, p. 119.
6. J.-J. Rousseau, *The Social Contract*, Trans. Cranston (London, 1968) Book III, Chapters 10 and 15.
7. *J.-J. Rousseau, Citoyen de Genève, à Monsieur D'Alembert*, Amsterdam, 1758, p. 143.

8. *op. cit.*, p. 146.
9. *Il Principe,* Ed. L. A. Burch, Oxford, 1891, Chapter 18, p. 305.
10. *idem.*
11. J.-J. Rousseau *The Social Contract* (ed. cit.), p. 87. It is interesting to note that Rousseau fortifies this recommendation in his text with a quotation in the footnotes, from Machiavelli's *Discorsi,* ◥, xi; 'The truth is that there has never been in any country an extraordinary legislator who has not invoked the deity, for otherwise his laws would not have been accepted.'
12 F. A. Iremonger, *William Temple,* London, 1948, pp. 144-6.
13. C. B. Macpherson, *The Real World of Democracy,* Oxford, 1966.
14. Harold J. Laski, *The Grammar of Politics,* London, 1967, pp. 64-65.
15. W. J. Stankiewicz, *In Defense of Sovereignty,* New York, 1969.
16. And not only in pamphleteering or journalism. The word 'violence' is used in this manner in several papers presented at the conference of the Institut International de Philosophie Politique at Colmar, July 1971, on the general theme of *La Violence.* These papers will be published by the Presses Universitaires de France, Paris, in an edition prepared by Robert Derathé.
17. See, for example, Alasdair MacIntyre, *Against the Self-Images of the Age,* London, 1971; W. D. Hudson (ed.), *The Is-Ought Question,* London, 1969; Charles Taylor, *The Explanation of Behaviour,* London, 1964.
18. See, among the many publications on this subject: G. E. G. Catlin, *The Science and Method of Politics,* New York, 1926; B. R. Crick, *The American Science of Politics,* Berkeley, 1959; H. Eulau, *The Behavioural Persuasion,* New York, 1963; A. F. Bentley, *The Process of Government,* Evanston, 1935; S. Rice, *Quantitative Methods in Politics,* New York, 1928.
19. Robert Dahl, 'The behavioural approach', *American Political Science Review,* Vol. LV, No. 4, December 1961, p. 763.
20. Harold Lasswell, *Democracy Through Public Opinion,* Menasha, Wisc., 1941. 'The emergency affords a remarkable opportunity for the moral defense of America.' (p. 175).
21. David Easton, 'Harold Lasswell', *Journal of Politics,* Vol. 12, No. 3, August 1950, p. 450.
22. In *The Listener,* September 30, 1971, Skinner writes: 'Governments still hold the individual responsible and are said to be best if they govern least because the individual is then free to behave well because of inner virtues. All this continues to direct attention from the task of building a social environment in which people behave well . . . and lead enjoyable lives. It obscures the fact that the problem is to design better cultures—not better people.' Listener, Vol. 82, No. 2218, p. 431.
23. For an enlargement on this point see J. R. Lucas, *The Principles of Politics,* Oxford 1966. Sections 1 and 2.

16

Professor Bernard Crick

FREEDOM AS POLITICS

Need a student of politics apologize for a tedious obsession with the matter of freedom, particularly when so many people, both philosophers and the man at the back of the bus, appear to believe that freedom is keeping at arm's length?

My point will be that there is a reciprocity between freedom and politics, properly understood, not an animosity. Certainly freedom and government or freedom and order live always in tension and often in animosity; but in so far as any government responds to some political factors, this is then a sign of some freedom; and those comparatively few governments who govern in a manner systematically political are then properly called 'free governments'— which otherwise might seem empty rhetoric and a contradiction in terms.

Indeed, I am persuaded of the value, both moral and scientific, of an old and unfashionable way of looking at things which would link politics and freedom together, not merely in civil wedlock, but in permanent progenitive embrace. Politics is the collective need to bargain, to compromise and to conciliate between differing interests, whether conceived as material or ideal, whose existence is accepted, at least for a time, as natural. Freedom is the act of an individual making choices among all such relationships and activities; it cannot simply be regarded, as even some liberal philosophers and many artists have thought, as freedom from politics and publicity. Put in its most abstract way, the very possibility of privacy depends upon some public action; and conversely public life is indeed all just 'telegrams and anger' if it does not accommodate private happinesses.

This is not a very fashionable point I want to make. It may sound more like rhetoric than analysis. Certainly I am more inclined to stand on my chair than to sit on it. So I must insert some argument that freedom is *both* a value and an institutional precondition for any scientific study of society. Freedom, indeed, I will seek to show, need not be either just rhetoric or analysis; for being both a concept and an institution, it has a history. If it has no end, it has a fairly clear beginning; that is why students of politics have to go back to the *polis* of Athens. If the Greeks were not the first to experience it, they were the first to give lectures about it. To say that history is the unfolding of freedom, as would Hegel and Marx, may be meaningless or at times simply false; but it is far from meaningless to say that the most important task for history and political studies, both intellectually and morally, is to write an account of the origins and conditions of freedom. The task is difficult but conceivable: Lord Acton was to be pitied for failing to complete his history of liberty, not blamed for the brave attempt.

That we in the West, where freedom grew, are sometimes simply too embarrassed to state the obvious can be seen by the clarity with which a masterly Japanese contemporary, Professor Masao Maruyama, has argued that freedom is both a fact and a value for political science (and is indeed in its origins as distinctively Western as science). 'It is unreasonable to expect any genuine social science to thrive', he says, 'where there is no undergirding of civil liberty.' He suggests that all forms of autocracy depend on the truth not being known about how they are actually governed. But equally, the other side of the coin, he says: 'The extent to which politics can become the object of free scientific inquiry is a most accurate barometer by which to measure the degree of academic freedom in a country.'[1] It is interesting that much the same answer to the same problem has recently been reached independently by someone else who has also lived under both autocracy and freedom. Professor Giovanni Sartori, in discussing Max Weber's famous demand that the social sciences should be *wertfrei,* value free,[2] points out that this is a very fine ideal which could only possibly be applied in a free society: modern totalitarianism persecutes both neutrality and objectivity and old-fashioned autocracy allows it only subject to censorship. And I think our instinct to go further is not wrong. The laboriousness of marshalling the evidence should inhibit us more than any embarrassment about the claim: that scientific advance itself is closely related to the political history of liberty (though we then need to distinguish between science and technology).

So the matter is still important. So important indeed is the concept of liberty that we are all reluctant to define it too closely, wanting to apply it to everything we value. Other people's states of freedom, after all, commonly appear as either wilful self-deception or as anarchy— however gentle. Thomas Hobbes had quite a lot to say about liberty and anarchy; even 'conscience' to him was but 'a worm within the entrails of the body Commonwealth'. And then there are some who while they do appreciate what freedom is, better than some of its democratic champions, yet reject it either as an intolerable burden, too capricious, demanding and uncertain a companion, or else despise it as an unwanted brake, hindrance or obstacle to economic betterment and intensified nationalism. Erich Fromm wrote a psychoanalytic account of the origins of Nazism entitled *The Fear of Freedom*; and numerous authors have added wine to old hash by quoting Dostoyevsky's sardonic words on those whose supreme need it is 'to surrender as quickly as possible the gift of freedom . . . with which they, unfortunate creatures, were born'. Thus freedom may always be rescued from platitude by observing the refugees from it and by mixing with its opponents. Acton once wrote to Mary Gladstone *à propos* the Jesuits:

> It is this combination of an eager sense of duty, zeal for sacrifice and love of virtue, with the deadly taint of a conscience perverted by authority, that makes them so odious to touch and so curious to study.[3]

In not claiming too much, we must beware of not claiming too little. This, I think, Isaiah Berlin has done in his otherwise admirable, influential, bewitching and powerful *Two Concepts of Liberty*.[4] I want to argue with deep and genuine respect that, while he has shown a great skill in defending the nymph of Liberty from abuse, he has been unnecessarily modest in denying her exercise and is at fault in letting her languish with so little to do.

Berlin has argued, using 'liberty' and 'freedom' virtually as synonyms, that there are two fairly clear and distinct traditions of the use of the word and concept: 'negative liberty', which is freedom *from* constraint; and 'positive liberty', which is freedom *to* achieve some one good thing. 'Positive liberty' men thus commonly say of 'negative liberty' men that they are being 'just negative': liberty to them must consist in fulfilling the proper object of the good life. Berlin shows that 'negative liberty' is what is often called 'the liberal view'; and he argues that attempts to go beyond that, to assign a positive object to free actions, prove philosophically paradoxical and politically autocratic.

He makes no bones about 'negative liberty' being just 'negative liberty': that it is inadequate as an account of political activity, certainly of the alleged 'ends of political activity' or of 'justice'. He quotes Bentham: 'Every law is an infraction of liberty.' Laws are plainly needed; but to be under the constraint of laws is not to be—as some positive liberty men would say—free or more free. He even quotes Bentham again, with evident approval, as saying: 'Is not liberty to do evil, liberty? Do we not say that it is necessary to take liberty from idiots and bad men, because they abuse it?'

'Positive liberty' is characterized as the valuing of freedom only as a means towards some end, identifying it with some good extrinsic object, even if just 'freedom from error'. Berlin quotes a dictum of the Jacobin Club: 'No man is free in doing evil. To prevent him is to set him free.' Here one agrees with Berlin wholeheartedly: agrees that there is such a theory of freedom and that its consequences are both linguistically self-contradictory and often morally obnoxious. Indeed, I would make so free as to slightly extend Berlin's analysis here to identify three common sub-groups of theories of positive liberty: there is a *moral* theory of positive liberty—as in the degrading confusion of either 'Oh God . . . whose service is perfect freedom' or 'the truth shall set you free'. There is a *material* or *economic* theory of positive liberty—as in Harold Laski's 'liberty is the existence of those conditions in society which enable me to become myself at my best'[5] (to which the answer is quite simply that not being unemployed etc., is not the same thing as being free). There is finally a *psychological* theory of positive liberty—as in Rousseau's argument that one must only will generally, that one must sink one's selfish self utterly in the general welfare and that he who does not see this 'must be forced to be free', for he is really denying his own chance of self-realization.

Plainly, whatever freedom is, it is not being forced. But even if not being forced, freedom surely also appears pragmatically paradoxical, at least, if of one's own free will one puts oneself in a situation in which one's freedom of choice is radically diminished. Does it really tell us anything to say that a man is free to put himself under a discipline of silence, continence and abstinence from all worldly things? Or that those Germans who mistakenly voted for Hitler were still free at the moment of voting? If freedom simply means absence of constraint, then actions that destroy the possibility of exercising freedom are free actions. In a logical sense so they are; but in the same sense, so is everything else. Here I begin to get slightly restive and to feel that the subject is unnaturally restrained by Berlin's too purely linguistic analysis (or too purely contemporary?). Isn't it, in fact, more *informative* and *explanatory* to say that such people are rejecting freedom—often very consciously— rather than exhibiting it?

Berlin argues that we should realize that we cannot always be free and that there are always some things we think so valuable that we gladly sacrifice some liberty in order to achieve them: full employment and a decent standard of living, for instance. But let us not call this sacrifice, he says, freedom. In times of emergency, let us admit, he suggests that we *are* being repressive, otherwise the distinction is lost for ever between free and necessary actions (or actions deemed to be necessary); and we then end up by saying that 'freedom consists in the recognition of necessity'[6] or some such blinding nonsense. One agrees. Basically all advocates of 'positive liberty' are, at the very best, confusing the conditions of freedom with the thing itself. 'There cannot be freedom until X and Y' is very different from 'X and Y, here they are. So you're free—damn you.'

But in avoiding one error, Berlin walks too cautiously. He virtually separates the word from any possible social or political context. Can one really just 'be careful', as distinct from being careful about and for something? Is liberty simply an absence of constraint? I don't find this very precise or convincing even just as a matter of verbal usage. I would call such a condition simply 'isolation' or more often 'loneliness'—put more sympathetically, 'splendid isolation' or 'the self-reliant individual' (who is not human, but an anatomical abstraction, and put sociologically, impossible). The strange gap in such defensive battles as Berlin's against the arrogance of 'positive liberty' is any systematic recognition that freedom is, firstly, a peculiar type of relationship between people and, secondly, an *activity* by people.

Berlin can only tell us in the end that we are free to do what we are not stopped from doing: freedom consists of the infinite range of opportunities to act, not in a limited range of actual actions. Things move until they are checked. This is an analogy from physics and mechanics under the influence, remote, refined but precise, of Thomas Hobbes. But why draw one's analogies from mechanics? If one presses linguistic analysis into philology, both 'freedom' and 'liberty', both the German and the Latin roots, indeed the Greek equivalents, had little to do with natural science but were primarily 'status' words—words that described certain legal and social rights. But back to this point later. What is missing in Berlin's analysis, odd though it may sound to say so, is any analysis of the link between freedom and political action—a typically liberal lack, if a socialist may say so (though a Tory could say so equally well). Freedom is being left alone from politics—is it?

He cannot indeed entirely avoid this impasse of triviality. He has to cover it, as we all do, by exhortation. And as readers of Hume will know, no one can exhort more forcefully than a prince of sceptics on a negative tack:

> The 'negative' liberty that they strive to realize seems to me a truer and more humane ideal than the goals of those who seek in the great, disciplined authoritarian structures the ideal of 'positive' self-mastery, by classes, by peoples or the whole of mankind.[7]

Now, as much as one agrees with much of this, it seems to me not very helpful to speak of 'negative liberty' as an 'ideal' which people can 'strive to realize'. How can one strive to realize a state of affairs in which one is constrained as little as possible when everyone recognizes that social and moral constraints are always present and, in fact, these restraints more often form the object against which men strive in order to get them taken off themselves and put on others? Some content is needed somewhere. While it seems dangerous and paradoxical to attach freedom to particular objectives, yet it seems trivial and hopelessly incomplete to leave it purely negative.

I think certain positive things can be said. There is, for instance, fairly general agreement about the formal condition in which it is held to be justifiable to constrain people. Other things are sometimes tacked on, like 'public decency', 'good taste', libel and slander, but the essential condition is commonly held to be that even established and habitual liberties may be justifiably constrained if their exercise threatens public order—the fact of government at all. Governments govern and even in a well-nigh perfect liberal state, presumably, things will be stopped when they threaten the survival of the State. Abraham Lincoln put the matter nicely:

> It has long been a grave question whether any government not too strong for the liberties of its people, can be strong enough to maintain its liberties in great emergencies.

Disputes flourish, of course, about what constitutes an emergency: Élie Halévy once suggested that it was the distinctiveness of modern tyranny to preserve artificially a 'state of emergency' from wartime on into what could well have been peace.[8] But this formal recognition that liberty depends upon order is neither trivial nor unimpressive. When we wonder whether Weimar Germany and Republican Spain did not cut their own throats by appearing to apply a liberal American 'clear and present danger' test to restricting the liberties of enemies of republican government, rather than using the harsher (though admittedly more speculative) Roman *'principiis obstat'*, we are shifting the argument, quite properly, from 'what does one mean by liberty?' to 'what does one mean by public order?'

Friends of 'negative liberty' do in fact tend rather hopefully to say, as it were, 'Locke until Hobbes', even if they can no longer quite believe in 'Locke after Hobbes': they recognize the difficulty, but seem unwilling to stop and talk to it. If there is this positive limitation of 'public order' on even such 'negative liberty', may we not be able to put a little flesh of historical and sociological circumstance on to the otherwise rather dry linguistic bones of liberty? Berlin himself says that 'to demand more than this [negative liberty] is perhaps a deep and incurable metaphysical need'.[9]

Indeed it is. Some synthesis is needed which will avoid the extreme of tyranny latent in 'positive liberty' and the anarchy or quietism of 'negative liberty'—if we take them to be political concepts at all. I am not criticizing Berlin's distinction as far as it goes. Down with positive liberty and two cheers for negative liberty! But the distinction is a dangerously incomplete account of what freedom has been and is.

At one point he himself comes near to the view I am about to suggest. At the end of a passage in which he points out that all ideas of 'natural rights' imply absolute values—which are never, in fact, clear, enforceable or universally agreed upon, he says:

> Perhaps the chief value for liberals of political—'positive'—rights, of participating in the government, is as a means for protecting what they hold to be an ultimate value, namely individual—'negative'—liberty.[10]

Berlin has to admit that 'negative liberty' at least needs positively asserting if it is to be political at all. He is at least close to the view that true freedom is something neither positive nor negative in his senses, but a relationship and an activity: an individual acting voluntarily in public or for a public—whether in art or politics.

Free actions, surely, are *actions* of individuals; but they arise from and affect the actions of others. Free actions are unpredictable, otherwise we would say that they are determined and necessary; a free action is an action of which it cannot be said that it must have happened. All public communication and actions are subject in some degree to constraints, both necessary ones which arise from the other people and the materials involved, and contingent ones of social circumstance; but it can never be said that there are no alternative actions possible, unless the person simply chooses—in Berlin's pure negative sense—not to act and then, presumably, to hope for the best.

In Thomas Mann's short story, or parable of Fascism, *Mario and the Magician*, he portrays the 'gentleman from Rome' as initially resisting the hypnosis of the charlatan in the seaside village, but eventually he succumbs and is publicly degraded. Mann's educated observer notes:

> As I understood what happened, the gentleman was beaten because he took up a posture for the struggle which was too negative. It would seem that the mind cannot live by not wanting to do something. It is not sufficient in the long run not to want to do something. Indeed there is, perhaps, such an uncomfortable closeness between the ideas of not wanting to do something and of not wanting to be bothered to make any longer the effort of wanting not to do it, i.e. being prepared to do what one is told, that between the two the idea of freedom is gravely endangered.

Berlin really commits what logicians call a 'category mistake'. Freedom is not an attribute of all possible actions, it is one type of action; it is *political* action. Even Acton saw this in his famous definition—if I am correct in putting emphasis where I think it should be: 'By liberty I mean the assurance that every man shall be protected *in doing* what he believes his duty against the influence of authority and majorities, custom and opinion. . . .'[11] The Whig cart of consent is here put before the Tory horse of government, but at least they are together: participation and action are part of freedom, neither conditions nor consequences, but the thing itself.

Freedom, then, needs rescuing from the philosophers—or from a type of philosopher who construes usage too narrowly—and needs placing in its historical and sociological setting. The earliest words we have for freedom have little relation to words for 'absence of constraint' or 'unimpeded movement' of matter. They were social status words: one suspects that the mechanical words were in fact analogies from these— not *vice versa* as is usually supposed. After all it is a bold metaphor to say that the wheel is free, rather than the man who chooses to make it come unstuck.

The Greek *eleutheros* means free in the sense of not a slave. Someone was *eleutheros* if his status was such and if he displayed the qualities which the Greeks associated with this status: disinterestedness and generosity—also a certain outgoing forcefulness.[12] A freeman would possess *arete,* like Homer's Achilles,[13] would be 'a doer of deeds and a speaker of words'—what the Romans called *virtus,* or, in a debased and revived form, Tom Brown's 'manliness'; or better what both Robespierre and Jefferson, liking it, or Dr. Johnson, disliking it, meant by 'patriotism'—before that word became debased too: the active citizen moving freely from private to public in the common interest. The Latin *liber* and *liberalis* correspond almost exactly to the Greek. In time the social meanings of the Roman word grew less: from the constant contrast between the freeman and the slave and between the freeman and the barbarian (who did not know freedom), the ethical meanings came to dominate it: a man's character would become *liberalis*—as we still call people 'liberal-minded' and once called people 'liberal-handed'. The English word 'free', from the Anglo-Saxon *freora manna,* kept, in a feudal world, its social significance longer and its ethical significance appears more vague and empty, as in Chaucer's knight who had 'Trouthe and honour, freedom and courtesye'. Am I alone in fancying that the word 'freedom' even today carries a slightly more positive connotation, a status enjoyed or a status to be achieved, than does the gentler 'liberty'? At any rate, Berlin chose the word 'liberty' where I have chosen 'freedom'.

If we treat freedom, then, as a social-status word and thus susceptible to historical and sociological study, we can sensibly study the relationship between freedom and order—even though the result will be different in every circumstance. But I am naive enough to see no general philosophical difficulty. It is not enough, though it may be occasionally necessary, to polemicize against 'determinism' or 'historicism' as does Karl Popper. I take 'freedom of the will' for granted—what else can one do? The problem remains of relating freedom of the will to action and to order. Indeed I can see two types of order in which constraints are not merely justified, in the nature of the activities, but may be sensibly felt positively to enhance liberty: politics and love. I simply limit my remarks to politics.

Politics, like freedom, very like freedom, is ubiquitous in some minimal and thin sense, but in thicker and richer senses is something highly specific and by no means universal. Politics cannot exist without government any more than freedom can exist without order: freedom is always freedom within a context. Some governments harry freedom and others nurture it. Government is the general ability to make decisions between different groups which can collectively be regarded as society for most purposes. Politics as an institution is the conflict of differing interests (whether ideal or material) in an acknowledged mutual context. Politics as an activity is the conciliation of these differing interests in the public context created by a state or maintained by a government. Politics as a moral activity is the creative conciliation of these interests.

Now perhaps some politics exists everywhere—even in the court of the Grand Mogul, the Kremlin or the Brown House. And by the same token *some* freedom must then exist—though the barber, the court jester or the second gravedigger may appear far more free than even the Grand Vizier, the Chief of Police or old Polonius. In a palace or a court they will dislike it, but will try to ignore it; but in the party headquarters of a modern one-party state they will commonly hunt it down: differences of opinion are a sign of insufficient dedication or of unpurged Jewish, bourgeois or colonialist decadence.

Politics as a *system,* however, only exists in relatively few states: those states which actually make their decisions in a political manner and encourage politics, which then becomes (the most vital distinction of all) public politics. These states, which I pedantically call 'political regimes', are commonly and misleadingly called democracies (which they all became during the First World War as casualties mounted); but *all* industrial and industrializing states are democracies, whether they allow free politics or not: they all depend on the consent of the majority, as peasant cultures never did, and most of them need the actual enthusiasm of the new class of skilled manual workers.[14] These states are perhaps better known by their more proud and ancient—and once more precise—name of 'republic'.

In such political regimes or republics, freedom varies in its scope and content, but always it exists as a positive activity.[15] As both Montesquieu and Rousseau said, quite correctly, the stability of republics depends on the virtue of their citizens.

This was once seen more plainly than now; before the rhetoric of 'democracy' obscured the precise and limited sense of the word 'politics' which I find so useful; and before there began a kind of liberal panic at modern power which, fortified by literary aestheticism, turned freedom from participation in communal affairs into a conscious attempt to be left alone—which one never is. Just one example: Chief Justice Fortescue could write sometime in the 1470s in his *De Laudibus Legum Angliae*:

> A king of England cannot at his pleasure make any alterations in the laws of the land, for the nature of his government is not only regal, but political. Had it been merely regal, he would have a power to make what alterations and innovations he pleased in the laws of the kingdom, impose tallages and other hardships upon the people whether they would or no, without their consent, which sort of government the civil laws point out, when they declare 'Quod principii placuit legis habet vigorem'. But it is much otherwise with a king whose government is political, because he can neither make any alteration or change in the laws of the realm without the consent of the subjects, nor burden them against their wills with strange impositions, so that a people governed by such laws as are made by their own consent and approbation enjoy their properties securely, and without the hazard of being deprived of them, either by the king or any other.[16]

We may know that in such a passage the signification of 'a people' and 'subjects' who give their consent is narrower, very much narrower, than the words might suggest. But this does not alter the fact that, however small the aristocracy or elite concerned, the relationship was political, and that in so far as there was politics there was an experience of freedom—even if only within a governing class. That by itself is something. In history we must talk, like Edmund Burke, of 'liberties' rather than of liberty. Historically, indeed, liberty as we know it arose within aristocracies or the merchant oligarchies of the medieval free cities. It was practised in Parliament long before it was widely sought after or tolerated in the country. When men came to talk of a proletariat they were talking of a community shaped by oppression and dedicated to achieving justice by means of intense discipline and solidarity; individual freedom has seldom been even a working-class value, let alone something consciously proletarian. But this need only embarrass that kind of conservative who confuses the value of things with their origins. As a socialist, I can quite happily say that freedom was in England—and in most other countries—an aristocratic invention, but that it can, should and must be made popular.

Hannah Arendt has written, with only slight exaggeration, that 'the *raison d'être* of politics is freedom and . . . this freedom is primarily experienced in action'.[17] As she herself comments, any attempt to derive freedom from the political must sound strange and startling because of two peculiarly modern fallacies. The first derives from the complete separation in many people's minds between the concepts of private and public—so that the very point of freedom is often thought to be an escape from the public realm (as if even lyric poetry did not need to be heard); the second arises because from at least the time of Rousseau we have thought that freedom is an activity of the will and of thought rather than of action. Sartre is one of the few moderns, besides Hannah Arendt and Simone Weil, who has seen this distinction clearly. In a review of François Mauriac's *La Fin de la Nuit* he wrote:

> We must understand that for M. Mauriac, freedom cannot construct. A man, using his freedom, cannot create himself or forge his own history. Free will is merely a discontinuous force which allows for brief escapes, but which produces nothing, except a few short-lived events.[18]

Or as he said in his essay on Descartes, the 'experience of autonomy does not coincide with that of productivity'. Put in plainer terms, to mark the end of my criticism of Berlin, freedom is doing something with it, not just sitting pretty on it. Put in more complex terms, to show the importance of insisting that freedom is an activity, I would quote Arendt again:

> Political institutions . . . depend for continued existence upon acting men; their conservation is achieved by the same means as brought them into being. Independent existence marks the work of art as a product of making [she means, once made it is always there]; utter dependence on further acts to keep it in existence marks the State as a product of action.[19]

Where there is politics there is freedom. There is some freedom, even if limited to contesting aristocratic clans, wherever government recognizes by institutional means the need to consult with conflicting interests—whether (as I have argued elsewhere) through prudence (being unable to predict the outcome of coercion) or through principle (when, in some sense, the moral equality of individuals is part of the culture—whether in the manner of Jesus Christ or of Immanuel Kant).

'Freedom' can hardly be treated as a condition for a political system because, in a minimal sense, it is almost a pleonasm for politics; and because, in more elaborate senses, it is a derivative of an already existing political system or culture. A political system is a free system—though the order is thus: freedom depends on politics as politics depends on government.

It is notorious that political regimes will often consciously run risks with their very stability rather than curtail particular freedoms. Only anti-political regimes are for ever preparing the individual to sacrifice his freedom of action for the collectivity, or try to persuade him that freedom is not choosing between *and* making possible alternatives, but is the euphoria or transfiguration that comes from making the right choice in good company.

Some freedom in a negative sense may exist in the autocracies, between the gaps of the laws, the indifference of the ruler, and the inefficiency or corruption of the bureacracy. But in totalitarian and ideological societies not merely are fields of free activity hunted down, even in spheres irrelevant to the mechanisms of control of traditional autocracies, like art and music, but free actions are, as part of the ideology, deemed to be impossible. Everything, in theory, is sociologically determined—whether by economic or by racial factors, the only real competitors in this league. But political societies neither enshrine such fabulous theories, nor do they even imagine the need to claim that all human actions should submit to the test of public policy.

Freedom depends on some distinction and *interplay* between private and public actions, for it is neither isolation from politics (as the liberal often wants to believe), nor is it loneliness (as following the concept of being an 'intellectual' has often involved). Freedom and privacy both thrive when government is conducted publicly in the manner called political. Freedom, then, is neither isolation nor loneliness: it is the activity of private men who help to maintain, even if not personally participating in, public politics. Privacy is itself a social relationship. Men who cease either to identify or to value politics usually lose and at the best weaken freedom. Politics is the public actions of free men; free men are those who do, not merely can, live both publicly and privately. Men who have lost the capacity for public action, who fear it or despise it, are not free, they are simply isolated and ineffectual. As Aristotle said, the man who seeks to dwell outside the *polis,* or the political relationship, is either a beast or a god.

'Political freedom'—as we may now call it, to distinguish it firmly from 'negative liberty'—is simply the habit and possibility of men as citizens acting freely. An absolutely unique and a reasonably private man says or does something unpredictable and uncommanded in public—or for a public—which has some effect, however slight, on others: that is a free action—whether in art or politics. Freedom depends upon people continuing to act freely in actual public affairs, and in being willing to run risks by speaking bluntly in public, not in constantly taking one's own temperature, according to some abstract standard laid down by god, don or judge, or according to the foundation myths of one's country, to see if one is still left free or not. Eventually the answer will then be—not. Freedom does not consist in being able to choose between pushpin and poetry, but in actually choosing. Although both choices are possible, neither is necessary or entailed.

By such purely negative conceptions of freedom, such people then discover, not surprisingly, that they are cut off utterly from society, are 'alienated', and then 'the whole system', nothing less will do, is blamed. This whole system must then be changed and freedom becomes the concrete service of some one single abstract idea. It is both sad and instructive to see how readily 'great individualists' fall victim to systems of thought and allegiance in which *nothing but* public values and social purposes are allowed. Such exciting extremes of unnecessary despair and unguarded hope come from a failure to accept freedom for what it is: a creative relationship between the private and the public, the assertion of both as complementary, not rival.

There is *fortuna* as well as *necessitá* in politics—as the greatest of all republican apologists, Machiavelli, reminds us. We have been simply fortunate in England that the habit of acting freely in public affairs came so early, so that tolerance of the free actions of others became accepted as a condition of one's own. Tolerance is always relative, of course, but so it must be; for there are always some things, quite simply, which we should not tolerate.[20] We should not tolerate, for instance, threats to toleration: we should not allow freedom to destroy freedom. And nor should we tolerate tyrants: tyrannicide is praiseworthy and is an essential part of the tradition of political thought.[21]

I find these questions easy in principle—not worth an examination question even; the difficulties are entirely practical. Yet toleration was far stronger when it was accepted as one of the facts of political life than when it was finally and pompously espoused by the Victorians as a matter of principle—so as to remove it from the low company of compromising politicians. For tolerance became important and secure in England not because most men just believed,

out of indifference or out of the exhaustion of ecclesiastical
animosities, that many different things were not worth the
discomforts and risks of public life, but because many of them
believed that many different things were worth the risk. Tolerance
arose from the clash of moralities, not from their absence. The means
of conflict became more civilized, literally politicized, but the causes
did not vanish. We tolerate opinions because opinions do matter: if
not, it would be simpler not to tolerate them (the manner in which
most governments of most countries do, in fact, act). Tolerance
comes not through caring for nothing, but through caring for many
things—just as freedom comes from *acting* freely, not from just being
left alone or having some narrow 'everything' done for one.

Freedom and toleration supplement each other in one very
important respect: they make it easier both to find out and to tell
truths about human behaviour. Freedom implies, as in the scientist's
use of hypothesis, creative speculation on goals and an exploration of
alternatives. Tolerance implies, as in Coleridge's 'willing suspension
of disbelief' for the literary critic, greater understanding. Valéry's
maxim seems to me as good for the practice of politics as for
scholarship: 'The first task of anyone who would refute an opinion is
to master it a little more surely than its ablest defenders.' Now it is an
evident peculiarity of 'political regimes' or republics that they are the
only type of government whose system of authority is not destroyed
by allowing significant truths to be discovered and told about who
actually rules and how. All governments try to hide things, both for
lazy convenience and for *raison d'état*. But general censorship is only
a necessary device in autocracies; political regimes can cheerfully
admit that things are done as they are done, and for political reasons.

If consultation and compromise are to be effective, if it is possible
at all to govern politically amid freedom, then it is necessary for
government to find out reasonably accurately what various interests
want or are likely to put up with, and what is their relative strength.
There must then be found people representative of these groups who
are free to speak the truth. Representative institutions are
fundamentally a matter of communication and not of rights.
Aristotle remarked on how difficult it is for a tyrant to find people
who will tell him the truth about what is going on. If this is to be
done—and it surely contributes to the stability of any government—
then the penalties of mistaken or unwelcome advice must not be too
drastic. Particularly in complex matters of modern economic
planning, it is helpful to any government for there to be some spheres
of independent thought and action. The weakest of all justifications
of autocracy in some developing countries, for instance, is that
economic shortages (including those of manpower) do not allow the

'luxury of public debate' on economic policy. One wonders how they can afford not to, since the consequences of mistakes must be so much more drastic. Of course, they do get independent advice—but in the only possible way that does not extend internal liberties and knowledge: from outside experts. This is related to an ancient device of autocracy, the recruitment of key advisers from abroad who are given a life of isolated luxury in the palace compound or the Grand Hotel.

The plea of 'necessity' is, indeed, the great enemy of freedom and knowledge. Professor Ernest Gellner has recently suggested that there are in fact only two conditions needed in our times for a social order to make valid and rightful claims on members of the society— that: '(1) It is bringing about, or successfully maintaining, an industrially affluent society. (2) Those in authority are co-cultural with the rest of the society' (he is referring to nationalism).[22] This is a commendably short way, at least, to treat the problems of political obligation and justice. 'The question of how to retain or acquire liberty', he says, is only meaningful after 'the hump' of wealth is passed.[23] One ventures to suggest that in societies which do have such a simple view of government, the recognition of 'over the hump' will always be delayed. It is a view of government which arises naturally from, but which then can fatten unnecessarily upon, emergency. As Machiavelli argued, this is a view appropriate to state-founding or state-saving (in an emergency), but one not likely to preserve a state through time. In order to create or save a state, he implies in *The Prince*, 'concentrate power'; in order to preserve a state through time, 'spread it' (*The Discourses*). If Gellner's categories of industrial affluence and nationalism were indeed crystal clear, then freedom and politics might in practice be willingly squeezed out. But the ambiguities of these categories will lead to dispute, over means if not of ends; and it may again be dramatically discovered that some degree of freedom is a functional necessity for economic and social advance. To my mind this has nothing to do with capitalism or free enterprise; state planning will inevitably arise in circumstances of war and emergency, of acute shortages or of acute aspirations. But effective planning must depend on the most public and honest gathering of information, discussions of how to evaluate it, criticism of plans and preparation of those likely to be affected by them. Planning is in no sense the necessary enemy of freedom; in many practical circumstances, it is a necessary precondition for its exercise.

That conscious control of an environment increases, not diminishes, the range of choices to be made was the theme of Malinowski's posthumous bood, *Freedom and Civilization* (1947)— overshadowed by Popper's *Open Society and Its Enemies* but, I think, a greater work. He argued that freedom was to be seen as a cultural phenomenon before ever philosophers tried to say that this or that was private or public. Certain cultures had been able to make deliberate choices of what purpose to achieve, or what policies to adopt. These had in fact been the successful cultures, both economically and intellectually. Freedom was the capacity for adaptation, and so a clue to survival as well as to increased knowledge. So Malinowski, in terms less ponderous than Arendt, argued that freedom was not to be identified with any particular object, but with a type of process or activity which was self-critical, self-perpetuating and inventive, concerned with both means and ends. Since it is seldom read—and embarrasses most anthropologists for having gone somewhat beyond the evidences of field-work— let me quote two passages at some length:

> Those who attempt any definition of freedom in terms of negative categories are chasing an intellectual will-o'-the-wisp. Real freedom is neither absolute nor omnipresent and it certainly is not negative. It is always an increase in control, efficiency, and in the power to dominate one's own organism and the environment, as well as artifacts and the supply of natural resources. Hence freedom as a quality of human action, freedom as increase of efficiency and control, means the breaking down of certain obstacles and a compensation for certain deficiencies; it also implies the acceptance of rules of nature, that is scientific laws of knowledge, and of those norms and laws of human behaviour which are indispensable to efficient cooperation.[24]

He concludes a chapter on 'The Semantics of Freedom'

> . . . our conception of freedom is positive and objective; it is essentially pragmatic, and implies a social and technical context. It implies always the benefit from action and responsibility by individuals and groups alike. The instrumentalities of freedom we find in the political constitution of community, its laws, its moral norms, the distribution of its wealth, and the access to such benefits as health, recreation, justice and religious or artistic gifts of culture. To scour the universe for possibilities of freedom other than those given by the organization of human groups for the carrying out of specific purposes, and the production of desirable results, is an idle philosophic pastime.[25]

All this has been very abstract. I have said little or nothing about the actual history of freedom, about its conditions in the modern world, nor about its relation to politics in Britain at the moment. All these things need to be done and, in bits and pieces of gold, silver and lead, are being done. But important and laborious enterprises usually go wrong at the beginning; not at the end. If one asks the wrong question, one will never get an answer. Thus 'negative liberty' is the wrong end of the right stick; it only defines what we seek to avoid harming in others while we act more positively ourselves. Without action, there is no liberty of any kind. Even Lincoln was too negative in saying that 'the price of liberty is eternal vigilance'. Better to have said that liberty is eternal vigilance—if by vigilance is implied 'observer-participation'.

I have really returned to a view of 'freedom as citizenship' which was current in the late seventeenth century and throughout the eighteenth, but which hardly survived the mid-nineteenth century. It was swallowed either by worship of the state—as in nationalism—or by alienation from the state and a belief among many liberals, that all power is inherently evil.[26] This viewpoint did not centre so much on individual rights against the state, but on those conditions which were necessary to operate successfully the kind of state characterized as republican. The viewpoint was often called 'Roman', or writers spoke of 'the liberties of the ancients' (as in the title of Benjamin Constant's famous essay).[27] But its genius was Machiavelli in his *Discourses,* where republican power is shown to be stronger and more stable and lasting than that of a *Principate*—given citizens who have not lost their *virtu:* the qualities of endeavour, involvement and audacity which hold states together—'the native hue of resolution'.[28]

A recent author writing on Tocqueville, while using Berlin's categories of 'positive' and 'negative' liberty, points out that Tocqueville is not easy to understand in these terms: for there is an element of both positive and negative liberty in him, of social responsibility and of personal freedom. 'Both require, in his eyes,' writes Mr Lively, 'the defence of politics against socially determined activity.' Tocqueville, he concludes, posed the 'essentially classical' idea of the free man as an active participant in communal affairs.[29]

Tocqueville was important not so much because he was the sayer of wise and quotable saws, but because he was among the first to appreciate the distinction between cause and condition in the writing of history. History does not determine the outcome of events, it narrows the range of alternatives. History presents us with alternatives: we are not just 'free to choose', we are not truly free unless we do choose. Freedom is thus moral freedom: it involves choosing and acting in such a way that the area of free choices for others is not impaired—which it always will be if we do not act at all. Men may not always act that way, but Tocqueville is saying that if they choose to recognize each other as men, then, very simply, they should.

There are no protective devices which can be minutely and precisely copied from one country to another; but to Tocqueville the

American example (for him it was only an example) was sufficient to
show that a conscious and rational allegiance to some laws and
customs could restrain even the majority against itself. No laws work
without the will; but good will is useless if it does not become an
institution. So to Tocqueville it was plain that understanding and
action must go hand in hand. The individual is only truly an
individual when acting a part with other men. The central state is
strong when its roots are local and when allegiance is conditional.
American Federalism was not the antithesis of power; it was
potentially among the strongest forms of power. Freedom is not the
antithesis of authority; it is the only form of authority—except,
again, love—which can be accepted without force or deception. All
this was once embraced in the classical concept of 'republican
liberties'.

I am happy to take such a classical—even pagan—stand on the
matter of freedom. Progress is not always in the same direction in
everything. We need to recover this lost relationship between
common citizenship and freedom. More precisely, we need to extend
it to the people before other forces in our society succeed in treating
them entirely as masses. But to characterize the view as 'classical' is
perhaps better to identify its origins than to characterize its present
mode— which is, quite simply, social, or even socialist. It is socialist
at least in the sense that it is both an inadequate account of freedom
to think of it as being left alone, as the liberal implies, or as simply
preserving the fruits of experience, as the conservative implies, for it
does involve the constant need to do new things in a premeditated
manner—the adaptation of man to circumstance and environment in
such a way that his capacity for future adaptation is not impaired.

Schiller wrote in his *Aesthetic Letters:* '. . . a political
administration will always be imperfect when it is able to bring about
unity only by suppressing variety. The state ought to respect not only
the objective and the generic, but also the subjective and specific in
individuals.'

But, in the end, nothing can be done if people do not wish to help in
doing it themselves; the conditions can be provided, but it takes
individual human action, since man is free, to bring about a result.
Beaumarchais, good bourgeois though he was, still saw the dark side
of this when he wrote in his *Notes and Reflections:*

> Slaves are as guilty as tyrants. It is hard to say if freedom can more justly
> reproach those who attack her than those who do not defend her.

We live in a world in which so many merely fail to defend freedom out
of ignorance, indifference, laziness or cowardice, but can either scorn
her, from the loftiest of mistaken motives, or else underestimate her
by usage too narrow and pedantic.

Appendix

'FREEDOM AS POLITICS': POPULAR SUMMARY

Pick a big one when, with academic sagacity,
One attacks to hide one's own inadequacy;
So, like Peachum to Lockitt, I abuse another
Who is my craft-master and elder brother,
No less than Professor Sir Isaiah Berlin
Picked not for any irredeemable sin
But for being, like a Liberal in love,
Reluctant to go far enough,
Sensing an impropriety in every call
On freedom made by rough political.
I pick no quarrel, just a bone over tea
With one of the *Two Concepts of Liberty*.
In his inaugural lecture, Sir Isaiah,
Oxford but modest, said that he'd require
Positive and negative liberty well kept apart;
If we choose: the virgin, not the tart.
Positive is wanting some one thing so bad
That it drives German and Russian sages mad;
This view of things has come to such a pass
That zealot sees his leader in the looking glass,
And if I look in and still see reflected stubborn me
Then I must be freed from error, forced to be free.
Freedom as choosing rightly opens the college door
To everybody else's nineteen-eighty-four.
Negative at least preserves me as myself
Sitting down Don-like to a well-stocked shelf,
Choosing wines, teas and coffees not quite at random
But knowing *de gustibus non est disputandum*.
Now this is all quite so and very very well,
It saves me thinking heaven hell
But leaves me with no clear end in view
When restless Liberty demands 'What's there to do?'
Makes walking *Frau Welt* and *Femme Libre* home
Almost an object on its own.
Berlin treads so judicious, nicely and precise
That he trips up, old lady-like on ice;
Liberty is surely not just taking care
But taking care at least to get somewhere.
Sartre and Hannah Arendt complexly say
That freedom is living through the day
And acting out in public view
Some play purporting to be new;
Is shaping, through some mutual pact,
Some hand-made thing which once we lacked.

Freedom is not just avoidance of the State,
Like some computerized blind date.
Nor just an angry affirmation of 'my will'
It's more like doing something meant to fill
The social gap between the loneliness of I
And groups of demonstrators in full cry;
Something between lying naked in my sheets
And donning uniform to dominate the streets.
Freedom is painting it, but not quite knowing what
Will follow from each original job-lot;
But it is painting it, not just thinking around
Projects which never quite get off the ground.
Freedom is how she always mistreats me,
But neither enduring masochistically
Nor is it just how I can kick her back,
But simply how we interact.
Berlin has little answer for the rude
Who call our freedom just 'a breakfast food'—
And so it is, but Dr Bircher-Benner's Swiss Müesli
Which can sustain most needs of life quite nicely.
But don't measure politics by the aesthete,
I've no complaint at politicians cooking good red meat,
Just let's protect ourselves from those who want it raw
And fed our heart's blood, clamour then for more.

*   *   *

Freedom was Cicero and Pericles.
Not T. D. Weldon on his knees
Picking hairs off Oxford fleas.
Freedom was Lincoln, Lilburne and William Tell,
Not Goethe's doubting gentleman from hell
With the Don-like negative soft sell.

The modern sceptic's version of the Fall
Does not involve a tempter's stirring call
But simply not doing anything at all.

So ends my anti-Berlin for this day
In which—ungrateful wretch—I roundly say
That half truths are just a kind of play.

Does cricket mean we always field?
And get the buttoned foil to wield
Till left like Peer Gynt's onion peeled?

Life is real and life is free
To choose and make creatively,
Is wakeful coffee and not sleeping tea.

Life is you and life is me
Conceiving the community
Interindependently.

NOTES

1. M. Maruyama, *Thought and Behaviour in Modern Japanese Politics* (Oxford University Press, 1963), pp. 227-8 and 229.
2. G. Sartori, *Democratic Theory* (Praeger, 1965), chapter 3. See also W. G. Runciman's brilliant discussion of this problem in his *Social Science and Political Theory* (Cambridge University Press, 1963).
3. *Letters to Mary Gladstone* (1st edn), p. 251, quoted by Gertrude Himmelfarb in her edition of Acton, *Essays on Freedom and Power* (Free Press of Glencoe, 1948), p. 1.
4. Berlin, *Two Concepts of Liberty*, Chapter 8, pp. 119ff.
5. But compare several such formulations in chapter 4 of his *Grammar of Politics*, Allen & Unwin (5th edn, 1948), with an explicitly negative formulation throughout his *Liberty in the Modern State* (Pelican, 1937), p. 49, for instance. Laski appeared to adopt whichever best suited his mood of the moment or 'the felt needs of the time'.
6. Engels, *Anti-Dühring* (Martin Lawrence, 1934), p. 128. But there is, admittedly, a certain melodrama in his use of 'necessity' where the argument of the whole passage plainly implies 'circumstance', 'conditions' or 'limitations'—something not, as it were, 'necessarily necessary'. Some criticism is purely verbal. How rarely do people mean 'necessity' when taken contextually.
7. See above, p. 157.
8. *L'Ere des Tyrannies* (Paris, 1938), pp. 213ff.
9. See above, p. 158.
10. See above, p. 152.
11. Acton, *The History of Freedom and Other Essays* (London, 1907), p. 3.
12. See the section on 'Free' in C. S. Lewis, *Studies in Words* (Cambridge University Press, 1960).
13. See Werner Jaeger's discussion of *arete* in vol. 1 of his *Paideia* (Blackwell, 1947).
14. It seems to me quite unjustifiable (*vide* nearly all American political scientists) to deny the equal propriety and to miss the theoretical significance of the Napoleonic usage of 'democracy' rather than the Jeffersonian. Democracy can be an element in many different kinds of government, but no government can be democratic. See chapter 3 of my *In Defence of Politics,* and also C. B. Macpherson, *The Real World of Democracy* (Clarendon Press, 1966).
15. I do not see that this sense of 'positive' offends Berlin's logical objections to 'positive liberty'. He objects to identifying liberty with any one goal or good; my objection is to identifying it with one particular goal or good. Freedom as human activity must always be attached to some object; what is objectionable is when it is held that there is only one true object for everyone. Freedom is choice-amid-clash of alternatives, not the absence of conviction. And it is a different matter, even, for individuals to hold 'positive liberty' views in our shared objectionable sense, than for the state power. The threat they then represent will be relative both to their influence and to the character of the ideal. Some of Professor Sir Karl Popper's objections, for instance, to 'essentialism' (the great killer) are fairly silly when one considers the character of most such folk and the context in which they react. Both Berlin and Popper seem to me profoundly unhistorical and unsociological in their imagery of, as it were, 'what would happen if things were taken to their logical conclusion'. When things were, it was not because of a mistake in logic.

16. Quoted by T. F. T. Plucknett in his eleventh edition of *Taswell-Langmead's English Constitutional History* (Sweet & Maxwell, 1960), p. 218.
17. In her essay 'What is Freedom?' in *Between Past and Future* (Faber, 1961), p. 151—to which I am in debt. Exaggeration, for surely politics is the institutionalizing of freedom, possibly its justification, not literally a *raison d'être*.
18. J.-P. Sartre, *Literary and Philosophical Essays* (Rider, 1955), p. 17.
19. Arendt, *Between Past and Future*, p. 153.
20. As recently argued with great brilliance in Robert Paul Woolf, Barrington Moore and Herbert Marcuse, *A Critique of Pure Tolerance* (Beacon Press, 1969).
21. See Irene Coltman, *Private Men and Public Causes* (Faber, 1962). And Hobbes warned against reading the 'books of policy' of the Greeks and the Romans: 'From the reading, I say, of such books men have undertaken to kill their kings.'
22. E. Gellner, *Thought and Change* (Weidenfeld & Nicolson, 1964), p. 33.
23. *ibid.*, p. 38.
24. B. Malinowski, *Freedom and Civilization* (Allen & Unwin, 1947), p. 59.
25. *ibid.*, p. 95.
26. See Preston King, *Fear of Power* (Frank Cass, 1967).
27. 'The Liberty of the Ancients Compared to that of the Moderns'; see the discussion of this in Bertrand de Jouvenel, ed., *Futuribles* (Droz, Geneva, 1963), pp. 99–102.
28. Oddly Berlin comes close to this view, but then shies away. He refers (above, p. 148) to: '. . . what Mill called "pagan self-assertion". . . . Indeed, much of what he says about his own reasons for desiring liberty—the value he puts on boldness and non-conformity, on the assertion of the individual's own values in the face of the prevailing opinion, on strong and self-reliant personalities free from the leading strings of the official law-givers and instructors of society—has little enough to do with his conception of freedom as non-interference, but a great deal with the desire of men not to have their personalities set at too low a value, assumed to be incapable of autonomous, original, "authentic" behaviour. . . .'

   Now I am not saying that Mill was ever wholly consistent, but 'little enough to do with' indeed! Mill plainly meant what he said: such behaviour was freedom. 'Non-interference' is a necessary but not a sufficient condition for what Mill meant by freedom. 'Pagan self-assertion' was equally important. (Here is my whole difference with Berlin—perhaps in some circumstances a slight one: between being able to choose and actually choosing.)
29. J. Lively, *The Social and Political Thought of Alexis de Tocqueville* (Oxford University Press, 1962).